Translating Buddhism

Translating Buddhism

HISTORICAL AND CONTEXTUAL PERSPECTIVES

Edited by

ALICE COLLETT

SUNY PRESS

Cover: Palm-leaf manuscripts, Sarasvati Mahal Library, Thanjavur, Tamil Nadu, India.

Published by State University of New York Press, Albany

Printed in the United States of America

For information, contact State University of New York Press, Albany, NY
www.sunypress.edu

Library of Congress Cataloging-in-Publication Data

Name: Collett, Alice, editor.
Title: Translating Buddhism : historical and contextual perspectives / Alice Collett.
Description: Albany : State University of New York, 2021. | Includes bibliographical references and index.
Identifiers: LCCN 2020048633 (print) | LCCN 2020048634 (ebook) | ISBN 9781438482934 (hardcover : alk. paper) | ISBN 9781438482941 (pbk. : alk. paper) | ISBN 9781438482958 (ebook)
Subjects: LCSH: Buddhist Literature—South Asia—History and criticism. | Buddhist Literature—South Asia—Translations into English. | Translators. | Translating and interpreting—Religious aspects—Buddhism.
Classification: LCC BQ1029.S64 T73 2021 (print) | LCC BQ1029.S64 (ebook) | DDC 418/.03294382—dc23
LC record available at https://lccn.loc.gov/2020048633
LC ebook record available at https://lccn.loc.gov/2020048634

10 9 8 7 6 5 4 3 2 1

Contents

Abbreviations vii

Introduction 1

PART I. TEXTS

Chapter 1
Translation in Search of a Text: The Craving for Stability 19
Collett Cox

Chapter 2
Translating the Buddha's Body 49
Natalie Gummer

Chapter 3
On Reading *Vinaya*: Feminist History, Hermeneutics, and Translating the Female Body 69
Amy Paris Langenberg

PART II. TRANSLATORS

Chapter 4
Translating the Theravāda Commentaries: Why, How, for Whom? 109
Oskar von Hinüber

Chapter 5
The Impact of Nineteenth-Century Missionary Translations of Theravada Buddhist Texts 127
Elizabeth Harris

Chapter 6
Words or Terms? Models of Terminology and the Translation of Buddhist Sanskrit Vocabulary 149
Ligeia Lugli

PART III. WORDS

Chapter 7
Translation and Historical Context: Interpretations of *Antevāsinī* 175
Alice Collett

Chapter 8
Translating the *Tīrthika*: Enduring "Heresy" in Buddhist Studies 195
C. V. Jones

Chapter 9
Translating *Paṭicca-samuppāda* in Early Buddhism 227
Dhivan Thomas Jones

Chapter 10
Why Is Literal Meaning Insufficient? A Study of *Desanāsīsa* Explanations in the Pāli Commentaries 259
Aruna Gamage

Contributors 283

Index 287

Abbreviations

AKB	*Abhidharmakośabhāṣyam*
AN	*Aṅguttaranikāya*
AN-a.	*Aṅguttaranikāya-aṭṭhakathā* (*Manorathapūraṇī*)
BGVNS	*Bodhisattvagocaropāyaviṣayavikurvāṇanirdeśasūtra*
BL	British Library Collection, Early Buddhist Gāndhārī Manuscripts
DN	*Dīghanikāya*
DN-a.	*Dīghanikāya-aṭṭhakathā* (*Sumaṅgalavilāsinī*)
DN-aṭ.	*Dīghanikāya-aṭṭhakathā-ṭīkā* (*Līnatthavaṇṇanā*)
Dhp.	*Dhammapada*
Dhp-a.	*Dhammapada-aṭṭhakathā*
Dhs.	*Dhammasaṅgaṇī*
Dhs-a.	*Dhammasaṅgaṇī-aṭṭhakathā* (*Atthasālinī*)
Dhs-anṭ.	*Dhammasaṅgaṇī-anu-ṭīkā*
Dhs-mṭ.	*Dhammasaṅgaṇī-mūla-ṭīkā*
Dīp.	*Dīpavaṃsa*
G.	Gāndhārī
HPL	*Handbook of Pāli Literature*

Itv.	*Itivuttaka*
Itv-a.	*Itivuttaka-aṭṭhakathā* (*Paramatthadīpanī*)
J.	*Jātaka*
J-a.	*Jātaka-aṭṭhakathā*
Kv.	*Kathāvatthu*
Kv-a.	*Kathāvatthu-aṭṭhakathā* (*Paramatthadīpanī*)
MĀ	*Madhyama-āgama*
Mhv.	*Mahāvaṃsa*
MN	*Majjhimanikāya*
MN-a.	*Majjhimanikāya-aṭṭhakathā* (*Papañcasūdanī*)
MN-aṭ.	*Majjhimanikāya-aṭṭhakathā-ṭīkā* (*Līnatthavaṇṇanā*)
Mil.	*Milindapañha*
Nett.	*Nettippakaraṇa*
Nett-ṭ.	*Nettippakaraṇa-ṭīkā*
Nidd. I	*Mahāniddesa*
Nidd. II	*Cullaniddesa*
P.	Pāli
Ppk-anṭ.	*Pañcappakaraṇa-anu-ṭīkā*
Ps.	*Papañcasūdanī*
PTS	Pali Text Society
Pṭsm.	*Paṭisambhidāmagga*
Pṭsm-a.	*Paṭisambhidāmagga-aṭṭhakathā* (*Saddhammappakāsinī*)
RGVV	*Ratnagotravibhāgavyākhyā*
Skt.	Sanskrit
Sp.	*Samantapāsādikā*
Sp-ṭ.	*Samantapāsādikā-ṭika*

Spk	*Sāratthappakāsinī*
SN	*Saṃyuttanikāya*
SN-a.	*Saṃyuttanikāya-aṭṭhakathā* (*Sāratthappakāsinī*)
SN-aṭ.	*Saṃyuttanikāya-aṭṭhakathā-ṭīkā* (*Līnatthavaṇṇanā*)
Sd-ṭ.	*Sāratthadīpanī-ṭīkā*
Sv.	*Sumaṅgalavilāsinī*
T.	*Taishō Shinshū Daizōkyō* 大正新脩大藏經
Th.	*Theragāthā*
Th-a.	*Theragāthā-aṭṭhakathā* (*Paramatthadīpanī*)
Tib.	Tibetan
Thi.	*Therīgāthā*
Ud.	*Udāna*
Ud-a.	*Udāna-aṭṭhakathā* (*Paramatthadīpanī*)
V-a.	*Vinaya-aṭṭhakathā* (*Samantapāsādikā*)
Vibh.	*Vibhaṅga*
Vin.	*Vinaya-piṭaka*
Vism.	*Visuddhimagga*
Vism-ṭ.	*Visuddhimagga-ṭīkā* (*Paramatthamañjūsā*)
Vjb.	*Vajirabuddhi-ṭīkā*
Ymk.	*Yamaka*

All references to Pāli texts in this volume are to the Pali Text Society editions, unless otherwise stated.

Dictionaries

Apte	Apte, Vaman Shivaram. 1890. *The Practical Sanskrit-English Dictionary*. Poona: Shiralkar.

BHSD Edgerton, Franklin. 1953. *Buddhist Hybrid Sanskrit Grammar and Dictionary*. 2 vols. New Haven: Yale University Press.

CPD Trenckner, V., et al. 1924–2011. *A Critical Pāli Dictionary*. Vol. 1, fasc.1-III, fasc. 8. Copenhagen: Royal Danish Academy of Science and Letters; Bristol: Pali Text Society.

DLP Crystal, David. 2008. *A Dictionary of Linguistics and Phonetics*. Malden, MA: Blackwell.

DOP Cone, Margaret. 2001–2020. *Dictionary of Pāli*. 3 vols. Oxford: Pali Text Society.

MW Monier-Williams, Monier. 1899. *A Sanskrit-English Dictionary*. Oxford: Oxford University Press.

PED Rhys Davids, T. W., and William Stede. 1921–1925. *Pāli-English Dictionary*. London: Pali Text Society.

WCD *Webster's Seventh New Collegiate Dictionary*. 1963. Springfield, MA: G. & C. Merriam Company.

Introduction

Although many Buddhologists spend a great deal of their time involved in acts of translation, there has not been, to date, much research published that explores the key questions, problems, and difficulties faced by translators of Buddhist texts and epigraphs on an (often) daily basis. This volume focuses on South Asian Buddhism, and on translations of Old and Middle Indo-Aryan languages into English. The essays in this volume, which all began as papers for the UK Translating Buddhism Conference, York St. John University, in the summer of 2016, address some of the many questions that can arise for anyone engaged in translation processes in relation to historical sources. In my Welcome Address at the conference, I cited a rare article by K. R. Norman, published in the 1980s, that tackles translation issues in Buddhist studies, particularly, in this case, of Pāli texts. Paraphrasing Norman, I listed a set of questions he formulated in his short article, questions that remain relevant today, and that formed both the backdrop for the conference and this volume: How important is historical context in helping us determine meaning? What aids are available to a translator? How does the translator give the translation meaning in a readable way? Can we understand words/passages from understanding their religious context? How important is a literal translation? How interpretive can we be? How do we find direct parallels between languages? Do commentaries and subcommentaries help or hinder? These and related questions are addressed by the essays presented here, as initial attempts to assess our translation practices.

Translation studies has been a subdiscipline in "Western" academia since the 1980s, but translation theory and practice itself is, to quote a biblical idiom, as old as the hills. Initially, translation studies, as it emerged as a discipline, was Eurocentric/Western in its purview, but by the beginning of the twenty-first century scholarship had begun to broaden out. Leo Tak-hung Chen's excellent work on translation theory in relation to China was published in 2004, then other works began to appear that expand scholarship on translation studies and include discussion of India and other parts of Asia. Works that stand out in this regard are *In Translation: Reflections, Refraction, Transformations*, edited by Paul St. Pierre and Prafulla C. Kar (2007), and *Decentering Translation Studies: India and Beyond*, edited by Judy Wakabayashi and Rita Kothari (2009). In their introduction, Wakabayashi and Kothari observe: "The recent signs of interest in non-Western translation are driven by a desire to push back the largely Eurocentric boundaries of the discipline and to remap the field . . ." (2009, 4). Wakabayashi and Kothari's praiseworthy volume "foregrounds some local moments of translation" that present challenges to overarching theories, in the hope that "they will contribute to a more stratified and nuanced analysis, to new questions and perhaps new answers" (2009, 5). In recent years, a few Buddhologists have begun to ask similar questions, and a few publications have begun to appear that treat these issues. The first book devoted to the topic, which focused on Tibetan Buddhism, appeared in 1995, and the second was published just last year, after a twenty-year gap, in 2016.[1] This volume—*Cross-Cultural Transmission of Buddhist Texts: Theories and Practices of Translation*, edited by Dorji Wangchuk—is a collection of essays from a Hamburg conference of the same name that took place in 2012. The essays are presented clinically, that is, as a collection arranged alphabetically, by author, with no introduction included in the volume. This presentation betrays the state-of-play of the subdiscipline of translation studies within the field of Buddhist studies. It is, as yet, undefined. This is perhaps not surprising, given that the vital work of scholars in the field to produce translations is not always given due credit. In 1996 Haberman and Nattier published a short piece in *Religious Studies News* on the way in which translations of important Asian texts were not recognized by "Western" academia for the achievements they are. The creation of an edition in the source language and the task of translation require commitment, time, energy, hard-earned skill and dedication, and remains invaluable for an understanding of social and religious history. However, its value has not always been appreciated

1. The first book was Doboom Tulku's edited collection, *Buddhist Translations: Problems and Perspectives* (1995).

within academia, as Haberman and Nattier argue. Publications that are wholly translations, and not discursive volumes, have not always curried favor in some academic circles, the worst instance of which they recount: "One anecdote even tells of a search committee meeting in which a senior professor waved a candidate's book—a sophisticated translation and explication of a medieval Asian text—in the air and shouted, 'This isn't a book! It's a translation!'" (1996, 1).

When we work within a discipline or subdiscipline, we know the parameters that govern how we work: these are the sources to engage with, this is how to evaluate the evidence, these are the types of theories to engage with. And indeed, if a scholar ventures too far outside of the expected parameters, it often has negative consequences for the reception of his or her work.[2] But when such parameters are yet to be defined, the nature of academic work pertaining to that area is naturally heterogeneous. In this volume, scholars raise and address similar questions; however, we each arrive at the questions via analogous but inimitable routes. For example, Collett Cox has spent many years working on early Buddhist manuscripts, so a translation question that engages her, in this context, is the question of how a text comes into being, how it comes to be constituted. Natalie Gummer, on the other hand, has been working with Mahāyāna *sūtras* since the time of her PhD studies at Harvard. Her fresh framework for how we interpret Mahāyāna *sūtras* has far-reaching implications, including implications for translation theory and practice. How, she asks in her chapter, do we take aspects of the medium into account in translation? If the text has a performative function, how does that affect our translation? Thus, both scholars raise questions about the nature of the Indian / South Asian Buddhist textual tradition—questions that pertain to translation—but arrive at their questions via consonant experiences as researchers that are nuanced at the intersection with translation issues. Hence, they situate their discussions differently, and the prism of their unique experiences as translators impacts the contours of their investigations. Similarly, Ligeia Lugli has been part of the Mangalam Research Center's Buddhist Translators Workbench project for some years, and as part of her work needed to conduct interviews. In so doing, she became aware of how interviewees possessed notions of a technical terminology

2. The other side of the coin is, of course, that new innovations can come from transcending such boundaries.

in Buddhist texts that were different from her own and those of others engaged in the project. This engendered interest to consider the extent to which words in Buddhist texts are indeed functioning as technical terms. In my own contribution to the volume, I also challenge overarching assumptions that certain words can invariably be understood as technical terminology, but the route via which I arrive at my conclusions could hardly be more different; I situate my own considerations within what are for me comfortable parameters—as part of my decades-long scholarship on the social history of women in ancient India.

Each scholar in the volume brings something different to the table, and although each scholar has a background in Buddhist studies, the volume comprises contributions from linguists, religious studies specialists, and historians. Bringing these contributions together into one volume that may, at times, appear piecemeal, all I present here to you are questions. The beating heart of the volume is, I hope, question after question about what the subdiscipline is, about how we define it, how we shape it, and how we want it to be constituted. As such, the volume is more similar to heterogeneous edited collections of past decades than the more intensely thematic ones of recent years. The similarity comes in this, the very nature of the volume; edited collections in the past have been volumes that do what this volume is attempting to do, make tentative steps into an unexplored field. Defining a field or subfield is an exciting but onerous task, and formation takes time. I present this volume as one step in what will be, I am sure, a long process.

The volume is grouped into three sections. Part 1 focuses on the nature of the text that is to undergo translation, and on theory. The three contributors in this part address such questions as: How does a text become constituted? How do we translate more than literal meaning? How does our perception of genre affect translation practices? Part 2 is concerned with translators. The authors in this section assess the motives of early Buddhist translators, examine colonial agendas that impact translation, and theorize about modern translators' perceptions of technical terminology in Buddhist texts. Part 3 consists of four chapters of applied examples, each tackling one key word or phrase and examining issues relating to translation of the item. In this section, some of the broader theoretical concerns raised in parts 1 and 2 are applied to these specific examples. First, the word *antevāsinī* is examined, contrasting its appearance in texts and epigraphs and considering the extent to which it can be understood as a technical term. Next, translations of *tīrthika* are surveyed, and the Christian basis for its translation as "heretic" dissected. In the penultimate chapter of the volume, the foundational doctrine of *paṭicca-samuppāda* is discussed, translation of it surveyed, and its function as a conceptual metaphor examined. Finally, chapter 10 looks at an exegetical word often employed by Buddhist commentators in the Pāli tradition—*desanāsīsa*—and its own multivalent explanatory function is explored, as part of a broader remit to investigate the problems with a literal translation of the term itself.

Detailed Chapter Summaries

CHAPTER 1

To begin the volume—as she began the conference with her keynote—Collett Cox raises several questions that underscore many of the topics discussed by the other contributors to the volume. After a brief biographical preface, she sets out her initial questions: What exactly is translation? How do source and target languages influence our translation? What roles should prevailing views about translation play in our translation choices? Is the translator always herself a "visible" part of the process? Is our goal linguistic equivalence? How does our theoretical stance shape our translation practice? Cox acknowledges these are not new questions, looking back to early and medieval Chinese translators of Indian Buddhist texts, some of whom commented on translation practice. Here we find a familiar problem being debated: how closely should the translation mirror the source language?

Next, Cox assesses what exactly it is we understand a "text" to be. Do we consider there to be an original or ideal version of the text, which all other versions aspire to emulate, or do we see the text as process, as "multiple forms as historical instances fashioned by all of its authors, transmitters, commentators, translators, and audiences"? Cox notes that different responses to these questions have led to tensions in scholastic communities, including our own, the vicissitudes of which she details.

Looking, finally, at concrete factors that might influence the exact ways we understand a text to be constituted, Cox discusses the context and medium of composition and transmission, and the nature of extra-textual evidence. Here, as elsewhere, she has recourse to the Gāndhārī material she is familiar with, which she uses to demonstrate that factors affecting composition and transmission may not be consistent, noting that different Gāndhārī manuscripts can suggest either a ritualistic or archival purpose underlying internment. She also makes use of the manuscripts to demonstrate that there can be multiple or single textual witnesses. Cox concludes that, in Buddhist studies, given that text-as-process seems the most realistic perspective to adopt, therefore, the best approach to translation is the "historically sensitive" approach, that "takes into account the historical context of a particular text or textual genre" including "the material context within which the text functions and the interpretive perspective of its stakeholders, whether they be traditional or contemporary, religious or political."

Chapter 2

Natalie Gummer's contribution is concerned with Mahāyāna *sūtras*. In her forthcoming monograph—*The Language of the Sūtras*—set to be a seminal work, she rigorously and diligently argues for a new way to read Mahāyāna *sūtras*, as much more than a simple exposition of Buddhist doctrine. In her chapter in this volume, in which she concentrates on the *Suvarṇa(pra)bhāsottama*, she relates the themes of her broader project to the issue of translation. If the Mahāyāna *sūtras* are performative, and engaging with them "makes the Buddha present and transmits his essence to listeners," how can this function of Mahāyāna *sūtras* become integral to a translator's objectives and what are the implications for translation if it does? Gummer assesses how statements about the Buddha's embodiment are embedded in the language of the Mahāyāna *sūtras* and provides us with some examples as to how an awareness of that might affect and shape translation. She focuses on three examples. First, a long series of parallel clauses in one passage of the *Suvarṇa(pra)bhāsottama*, all beginning with the word *sarva* (all), that mark out "the rhythm conveying the all-pervasive power of the *sūtra*." Gummer argues that a translation that is sympathetic to and functions to support the performative arch of the texts would attempt to maintain the rhythm of the Sanskrit syntax, so that the English words of the translation act to communicate the performative function of the texts in the same way the Sanskrit does. The second example she uses is again a repetition, this time of *adya* "today" with a first-person pronoun, which combine to iterate the present moment of preaching and hearing of the *sūtra* and the doctrine. Gummer translates this combination with the emphatic "This very day, I . . . ," asking us to bear in mind the power of such statements at the moment (i.e., the present day) on which the *sūtra* is preached and heard. Her third example is the repeated vocative phrase *tvaṃ satpuruṣa* alongside a string of verbs in the future tense, which describe the impact of the preaching of the *sūtra* on the *dharmabhāṇaka*, and again functions at an intersection "between form and content." Ultimately, Gummer concludes that some aspects of the performative nature of the text are untranslatable in any attempt at verbatim English prose and verse that make up translation practice; however, efforts to attempt to capture elements of this do enable a more thoroughgoing communication of the nature of the texts that enables the modern (silent) reader to comprehend them more completely.

CHAPTER 3

In Amy Langenberg's chapter, the third in part 1 of the volume, on texts, she addresses questions relating to genre and hermeneutics. Taking a step further on from Cox's survey of how a text becomes constituted, and from Gummer's argument for the nature and character of the text to be taken into consideration when translating, Langenberg challenges us to consider ways in which reading texts through various optics affects translation practice. She begins her chapter with a survey of past scholarship on *vinaya* that tends to "assume that *vinaya* texts can be mined for historical information." She also notes critics of such an approach, such as Finnegan and Hallisey, who expose the limitations of such readings. She critiques ways in which *realia* have been read into *vinaya* literature. These include the strategy relating to "irrelevance," whereby it is understood that material not relevant to the main thrust of the narrative must be revealing *realia*, and "counterargument," a proposal that tenders that the rules were made in order to address behaviors that were actually happening, and she also mentions, in opposition, the perspective of "presentations," an understanding that *vinaya* are more about the views of the compliers than social reality.

Next, Langenberg discusses how, despite their canonical status, *vinaya* texts have not always been "enduring blueprints for monastic life from the time of redaction forward." She summarizes arguments that illustrate how *vinaya* texts have not always been fully known or utilized by Buddhist communities, with sometimes only a digest being on offer, and ways in which they are used not as compendiums of religious rules governing behavior, but more ritualistically, or as part of civil or state law.

Langenberg's own suggestion for how to read *vinaya* is that they should be read alongside other contemporaneous sources—much as I do in my chapter in this volume (chapter 7)—and it is only through such endeavors that we are able to fully comprehend the import of the texts. She illuminates her point through comparison of a monastic rule for nuns relating to bowing with dharmaśāstric prescriptions on salutation rituals and expectations. Here she notes not only the complementarity of language used in both sources but also the complementarity of ideation. She concludes that the monastic rule in question that governs the behavior of nuns "seems to be participating in the social logic and gestural traditions also described in these various *dharmaśāstra* contexts." She concludes by returning to the question of translation, with an assessment of how interpretive practices relating to ascription of genre affect translation.

Chapter 4

In his chapter, the first in part 2 of the volume, on translators, Oskar von Hinüber addresses the question of why the Pāli commentaries were translated into Pāli in the first place, and considers who the intended audience might have been. With regard to the extant *aṭṭhakathā*s, he raises the question in relation to their translation from—what has come to be understood as—their original Sinhala form, although von Hinüber questions that. Sources that provide some insight into possible motivations of these early translators are the well-known twelfth-century story of Buddhaghosa, in which it is requested that he translate the Sinhala commentaries into Pāli so they could be of great benefit to the world. This story, although late, concurs with the introductory and concluding verses of the *aṭṭhakathā*s of the *vinaya-*, *sutta-*, and *abhidhammapiṭaka*s that show that the commentaries are translations. The anonymous author of the *Vinaya* commentary specifically states it is their desire that the translation into Pāli will be of benefit internationally, that is, outside of Sri Lanka. Buddhaghosa and the anonymous author of the *abhidhamma* commentary do not state such grand ambitions, declaring, instead, their aim "to raise the commentaries to the same linguistic status as the canonical texts by the use of Pāli as an appropriate language." Von Hinüber then details some subsidiary evidence that supports this notion that the commentaries were originally in the Sinhala language. Taking one step further, he then questions whether there was in fact a stage prior to that—an original Indic form of the commentaries that was taken to Sri Lanka and translated into Sinhala. As is the case with many of the questions he discusses, the evidence for this is slim. Here, von Hinüber considers uses of a rare central Indian word for brick (*giñjaka*), etymologies, and the possible trace of an old eastern Middle Indic form of *kicchi* in the *Vinaya* commentary to make his case. This, he posits, is evidence enough for us to consider Indian originals behind the Sinhala versions as a possibility.

Up to this point, von Hinüber has been looking back on the commentaries as they may have existed prior to the time of Buddhaghosa. Looking forward from that point, he then explores who might have been the intended audience of the newly restructured, modernized, and freshly translated Pāli *aṭṭhakathā*s. He poses the question, how do we "find those monks, who were supposed to use the commentaries outside the Mahāvihāra, even outside Ceylon in India and perhaps beyond in *dīpantare* [other countries]?" Attempting to answer this, he surveys evidence for Theravāda, or Theriya, presence in South India, which is predominantly material and epigraphic. The most revealing of which are inscriptions from Nāgārjunakoṇḍa, dating to the third century CE, that even suggest proselytizing activity on the part of the Theriyas.

Von Hinüber concludes by surmising that the commentaries were translated "to modernize the texts in old Sinhala Prakrit linguistically by giving them, at the same time, a new and better structure." The ambitions of certain commentators were to internationalize the Mahāvihāra agenda, while other commentaries appear to have been translated into Pāli to reassure Mahāvihāra monks "of the orthodoxy of their views."

CHAPTER 5

When considering issues in relation to translation of South Asian texts into Western languages, the questions of colonialism and orientalism often arise. These issues are addressed in Elizabeth Harris's chapter. Here, Harris seeks to foreground nineteenth-century missionary translators working in Sri Lanka on Sinhala and Pāli language and Buddhist texts. Harris argues that the life and work of such missionaries have not been given due consideration in debates about orientalism and colonialism and this is an imbalance she seeks to address. Her argument for revalorizing their importance is threefold. First, she highlights that they were chronologically prior to many other noted orientalists, such as T. W. Rhys Davids. Second, that the type of orientalism evinced by them enables a nuancing of the vicissitudes of orientalist discourses, in which she demonstrates that an uncritical Saidian perspective can flatten the narrative. Finally, Harris asserts that their work had significant impact on other orientalists who followed them and, indeed, on the complexion of Buddhist modernism.

These observations are made through a study of the translation practices of three Sri Lankan missionaries: Benjamin Clough (1791–1853), Daniel J. Gogerly (1792–1862), and Robert Spence Hardy (1803–1868). In each case, Harris chooses one noted work by the translator, or one dimension of their work, through which she elucidates each of their contributions—both progressive and delimiting aspects—and begins to explore some of their motivations behind their translation tasks. For Clough, Harris concentrates on volume 2 of his Sinhala-English dictionary; for Gogerly, his translation of the *Cūḷakammavibhaṅgasutta*; and with Spence Hardy, his work on Buddhist cosmology and the biography of the Buddha. Harris skillfully demonstrates how the views and preoccupations of a translator interpose in translation choices—a resounding lesson for any context. In this case, she highlights how the translators' own adherence to a religiosity distinct from the one that underpins the texts (and languages) being translated is impactful. She notes how, with a proselytizing agenda in mind, translation choices are shaded in particular ways.

Chapter 6

Ligeia Lugli's chapter engages with modern translators of Buddhist texts. As a result of a project she worked on for the Mangalam Research Center, Lugli became interested in the notion of terminology and the role it plays in translations of Buddhist literature. Her chapter explores the question of whether many common words used in Buddhist texts—especially those that espouse aspects of doctrine and practice—are in fact words or terms. She begins her chapter with a concise survey of classical and more recent theories of the use of terminology in language and concludes with a focus on the Sanskrit word *saṃjñā*, by way of example.

According to the classical model of terminology, a "term" is quite different from a "word." Lugli identifies the core of the theory as positing that "a lexical item qualifies as a term only if it stands in biunivocal relation with its referent and is unambiguously defined." That is, to qualify as a term, the same word must always be used for the phenomenon in question, in the same way. However, new theories have emerged over the last few decades that challenge this definition and argue instead that "terms are dynamic and stand on a continuum with general language words." The new theorists assert that the concepts behind terms can be multifaceted and vague, terms can behave more like ordinary words than the classical model allows, words and terms are on a semantic continuum, and the need for contextualization is not obviated by the designation of a word as a term. The impact this has on translation is that translators need to take care when assessing each instance of appearances of common words (that denote doctrine and practice) in relation to terminological value, that is, the extent to which they are functioning as a technical term in that instance. Failure to correctly assess this can create problems. While aware of the many complexities that vex translators of ancient Buddhist texts—temporal distance, hermeneutical questions, and language issues—Lugli argues that in Buddhist studies there has been, historically, an overemphasis on rendering words as technical terms. This stems from opaque adherence to the classical model of terminology. To illustrate her point, Lugli then presents a case study of *saṃjñā*, an instrumental word in early Buddhist discourse that has, historically, proven difficult to translate. Lugli surveys the many attempts by modern scholars to render correct translations of this word (or term) and highlights some of the consternation caused by adherence to the classical model whereby scholars attempt to find a singular English word or phrase applicable in all instances. She concludes her discussion with her own suggestion that, rather than trying to find one suitable English word or phrase that is applicable in all instances, instead, the best way to understand *saṃjñā* is to see it as corresponding to a "lexical gap" in the English language. That is, there is no one corresponding English word that comfortably fits all occurrences of it in Sanskrit Buddhist texts; no word in English covers the semantic spectrum of *saṃjñā* nor is able to express the concept in a way that replicates the specialized parameters of its usage in Buddhist texts.

CHAPTER 7

Chapter 7 is my own chapter, the first in part 3 of the volume, the section that focuses on applied examples. Taking up themes already discussed in parts 1 and 2 of the volume, I examine the question of the extent to which *antevāsinī* can be considered a technical *vinaya* term. This investigation blends with questions already posed by Collett Cox, on the stability of texts; by Amy Langenberg, on how we read *vinaya* texts; and by Ligeia Lugli, on the nature of technical terminology on Buddhist literature.

According to Buddhist *vinayas*, *antevāsinī*—and its male counterpart *antevāsin*—is a term used to denote pupilage within the tradition. It is part of a fourfold classification of defined roles that relate to ordination and become delineated through formal monastic procedures. The ordination system is formulated around a novice period that involves training. An individual wishing to join the order has a *pabbajjā* ordination and becomes a novice (*sāmanera/ī*) and a pupil (*antevāsin/ī* or *saddhivihārika/ā*) with both a preceptor (*upajjhāya/ā*) and a teacher (*ācariya/ā*). After a period of two years, the novice takes full or higher ordination (*upasampadā*) and becomes a monk or nun (*bhikkhu/nī*). According to the *vinayas*, this formal process happens in gender-segregated communities; that is, male novices have male preceptors and teachers and female novices have female preceptors and teachers. The epigraphic evidence, however, challenges our perception of *antevāsinī* as a technical *vinaya* term repetitively denoting a role with clear parameters that is enacted within a community segregated along gender lines. In inscriptions we find records of women who consider themselves direct pupils (*antevāsinī*) of male monastic teachers, a situation that, according to *vinaya* norms, should not happen. Given this seeming discrepancy between the textual and epigraphic evidence, doubts are raised about the exact meaning of the term. The question is not one of literal translation, which is invariably "pupil" in each case, but rather with semantics and terminology configuration, that is, the extent to which *antevāsinī* can be understood as a standardized technical *vinaya* term, with the same semantic range, always specifying a particular collection of behaviors.

CHAPTER 8

In the second chapter of applied examples, C. V. Jones challenges translations of *tīrthika* as "heretic." Initially, Jones takes us on a short tour of the origins of the term "heretic" in Abrahamic and Western contexts. Here, he skillfully reveals that a heretic came to be understood as the "enemy within" a religious tradition, one who adheres to "a heterodox, potentially divisive position within the parameters of one's own tradition." Next, in a survey of writers of modern dictionaries of Old and Middle Indic languages relevant to purpose, Jones highlights the consistency with which the primary translation of *tīrthika* from Buddhist texts was "heretic." Although, recently, there have been a few other options suggested, "heretic" has remained the option of choice. Jones then turns to Buddhist texts themselves. First, he groups together systematizers and commentators on Buddhist thought who understood the *tīrthika* as some sort of opponent of a rival school. Such opponents might have, for instance, contrasting views about the nature of the self, or the nature of liberation, but were most often not—in contrast to the semantics underpinning "heretic" in Christian usages—inside the Buddhist community, espousing false views as the truth. This Jones especially demonstrates in his exegesis of a *Ratnagotravibhāgaśāstra* passage.

Jones next surveys texts that present a *tīrthika* as an obstacle to practitioners as they seek to advance on the Buddhist path. Interestingly, certain of the Mahāyāna texts that present this possibility also allude to a Śāntideva-type notion of the obstacle as an aid on the path. Finally, in his reverse trajectory, Jones returns back to the beginning and surveys the initial uses of *tīrthika* in the earliest Buddhist sources. Demarcated by an awareness of historical milieu, he identifies the shared religious metaphor of the cycle of transmigration understood as a flood, which needs to be traversed by the religious adept, and which may be the origin of the notion of a *tīrthika* as a ford-maker who is so enabled and able to galvanize others. He also notes the early Buddhist nuancing of this metaphor to allude to states of mind. Acknowledging Buddhism's move away from these shared *śramaṇa* metaphors, he concludes that while a *tīrthika* is one of a distinct religious view, doctrine, practice or sect to one's own, nowhere in Buddhist literature is the term used in a sense that warrants translation of it as "heretic," a translation choice which he implores we abandon.

Chapter 9

In the penultimate chapter of applied examples, Dhivan Thomas Jones considers the doctrine *paṭicca-samuppāda*. Noting, initially, its significance as a fundamental doctrine of early Buddhism, Jones begins his assessment of the term with a twofold goal in mind—to argue in favor of one of the usual English translations of the term over others and to reconsider the extent to which the concept needs to be considered as a theory of causation or, indeed, an articulation of human experience in the world.

He begins, picking up on points already made in the volume, by designating *paṭicca-samuppāda* as a specialist term that "refers unambiguously to a particular concept." He then takes in turn the two individual components of the compound and surveys the semantic range of each. Putting the conclusions of these subsections together with an analysis of the nature of the term as a syntactic compound, he concludes that "dependent arising" is the neatest expression of the full literal meaning of "(a phenomenon's) arising dependent on (a causal basis)."

Having established his basis translation point, Jones then proceeds to a more existential discussion of the nature of causation in early Buddhist thought, and a reflection on whether the notion of causation here is not theoretical but experiential. That is, rather than the concept expressed by *paṭicca-samuppāda* being simply a doctrinal statement on the nature of the world, does it instead attempt to communicate some fundamental aspect of human experience that a practitioner needs to become aware of to proceed on the path? Jones's essential point here is that there is more of a metaphorical slant than is often considered to be the case. He argues that *paṭicca-samuppāda* needs to be understood as a conceptual metaphor, that is, an item of language that enables "transfer of meaning from one conceptual domain to another." Closing with a discussion of agricultural metaphors relating to organic growth that accompany expositions of the doctrine, Jones concludes that if textual expressions of *paṭicca-samuppāda* were constructed out of familiar metaphors of life and growth in the ancient Indian milieu, then our own translation of it into English ought likewise to be as comfortable a fit as possible.

CHAPTER 10

The chapter that completes the volume is a study of the word *desanāsīsa* as it appears in Pāli commentarial literature attributed to Buddhaghosa. The word is often translated as "a headword for a discourse," or variations on that theme. However, in this chapter, Gamage questions such translations and explores the extent to which they are unerringly applicable and function to communicate the breadth of meaning of *desanāsīsa* in the various contexts in which Buddhaghosa employs it. Gamage argues that *desanāsīsa* has a broad application and is in fact similar to the grammatical *ekaśeṣadvandva* in that it is often used in a similarly reductive way. He identifies three discrete ways in which *desanāsīsa* is employed in Buddhaghosa's commentarial expositions of the canon. First, he argues, *desanāsīsa* is used to highlight synecdoche, that is, to indicate instances in which a word operates as a part signaling a whole, or two or more parts. One example he gives for this is the use of the word "mother" to infer both parents. Second, he notes its usage to highlight merismus. In this function, *desanāsīsa* is employed to indicate a situation when two (often opposing) things are used to represent more. Third, Gamage argues that *desanāsīsa* also indicates metonymy. Given the range of applications for the rubric *desanāsīsa*, any literal—or even dynamic or interpretive—translation may fall short of being able to convey a meaning that does justice to the multifarious exegetical purposes that underpin Buddhaghosa's use of the word.

Essentially, the bare components of the subdiscipline of translation studies (in Buddhist studies) are texts, translators, and words. The volume so constituted, each part raises and attempts to address some questions in relation to each of these factors. Relating to texts, contributors discuss the nature of Buddhist texts, how it is we came to have an understanding of what constitutes a text, how we might engage in translation practices that communicate something more than literal words, upholding other aspects of the function of the text for its intended audiences and explorations of hermeneutics, genre, and intertextuality. Motivations of translators old and new are explored and questions raised about how ambitions, perceptions, and prejudices of a translator might impact translation. Finally, through some applied examples, so-called technical terms, religious titles, doctrine, and exegetical strategies have been explored.

Conclusions that can be drawn from the contributions that make up this volume are admittedly piecemeal but nonetheless considerable: that a "historically sensitive" approach to translation is the most fitting for Buddhist studies; that it is possible to translate taking into consideration more than a literal rendition of the words in the source language; that hermeneutics and genre impact translation choices; that Buddhist translators themselves did not always possess the same motivations; that colonial attitudes have influenced translations and production of dictionaries in a variety of ways; that the classical model of terminology has been impacting translation choices Buddhist studies scholars have made; that what comes to be understood as technical terminology went through developmental processes; that Christian presuppositions impacted translation choices; that loose translations of core doctrine need to be challenged; and that Buddhist exegetes used words in multivalent ways that are not always possible to convey via literal translation.

References

Chen, Leo Tak-hung. 2004. *Twentieth-Century Chinese Translation Theory: Modes, Issues and Debates.* Amsterdam: John Benjamins.

Doboom, Tulku, ed. 1995. *Buddhist Translations: Problems and Perspectives.* New Delhi: Manohar.

Haberman, David J., and Jan Nattier. 1996. "Whatever Became of Translation?" *Religious Studies News* 11, no. 4 (November): 13.

Norman, K. R. 1984. "On Translating from Pali." *One Vehicle: Journal of the National University of Singapore Buddhist Society* 1: 77–87.

St. Pierre, Paul, and Prafulla C. Kar, eds. 2007. *In Translation: Reflections, Refraction, Transformations.* Vol. 71. Amsterdam: John Benjamins.

Wakabayashi, Judy, and Rita Kothari, eds. 2009. *Decentering Translation Studies: India and Beyond.* Amsterdam: John Benjamins.

Wangchuk, Dorji, ed. 2016. *Cross-Cultural Transmission of Buddhist Texts: Theories and Practice of Translation.* Indian and Tibetan Studies 5. Hamburg: Department of Indian and Tibetan Studies, Universität Hamburg.

Part I

Texts

Chapter 1

Translation in Search of a Text

The Craving for Stability

Collett Cox

As translators, we find ourselves in a dilemma. On the one hand, we live on the level of textual minutia, making isolated grammatical and semantic decisions, but on the other hand, each specific decision requires consideration of larger contextual and methodological issues. As novice translators, we are consumed by the perspective of every word, and the immediacy of every decision demands our total attention. As we become more experienced, the perspective of the text as a whole begins to surface, and broader issues that lie embedded within each passage emerge. We begin to see alternative translations and the implications of our translation choices within a larger textual context. Over time, these broader issues become second nature, and we may proceed almost as passive agents, unaware of our translation practices, whether on the specific or the broader level. However, at some point this broader level, the meta-level of what the process of translation involves and the methodological decisions that it entails, begins to reveal itself more clearly. Here we have two options: we can ignore such broader considerations as a distraction from our immediate task, or we can engage them and reflect on the activity in which we have been immersed. I have chosen the second option, which is the topic of this chapter.[1]

First, a bit of biographical context. I have been engaged in translation in one sense or another for my entire scholarly life, first as a student, then as a teacher, and always as a scholar, and yet I had never given much thought to the act of translation per se. My work took an unexpected turn when I became part of the Early Buddhist Manuscripts Project at the University of Washington and began to work on manuscripts dating from the first century CE, which are written in the Gāndhārī language and the Kharoṣṭhī script. Initially, I thought that this would be an intense but familiar experience since it too involved the translation of texts, but I discovered that working from manuscripts exposed problems that lie hidden within all translation work, problems that I had previously been able to ignore. By working with these very damaged manuscripts, often of texts without a parallel in any other Buddhist collection, I was placed in a "primary role" as the editor who establishes the text. I had to make decisions about paleographic and linguistic problems requiring that I take into account both codicological issues of manuscript production and contextual issues of textual composition, transmission, and history. As a result, I could no longer pretend that I was a mere "passive translator" but had to give active consideration to my own activities vis-à-vis the text. For many translators, work with seemingly "established" editions leads to

1. This chapter gave me the opportunity to explore what was, at least for me, a new field of "translation studies." See, for example, Chesterman and Arrojo 2000; Bassnett 2002 [1988]; Kuhiwczak and Littau 2007; Munday 2008; Bermann and Porter 2014. This diverse field includes both pragmatic or "prescriptive" recommendations for oral interpreters and a second area more relevant for the work of translating Buddhist texts, namely, methodological and theoretical analyses of all acts of translation including written textual translation. I have observed within this scholarship a certain degree of resistance to the idea of "translation studies," paradoxically, on the part of those involved in translation work themselves. See, for example, accounts in Chesterman and Wagner 2016. This resistance and its attendant antipathy to "theoretical" studies underlie comments familiar to many of us working with texts: for example, "Yes, translation entails issues that one should consider, but I simply don't have time to think about them," or more forcefully, "We just translate, that's all!!" I would argue that, for all of us, whether we empathize with these comments or not, methodological and theoretical issues have a significant impact on our work, and we must attend to them.

the unthinking assumption that one is translating "objective" texts, but as my title suggests, translators are like the characters in Pirandello's play, *Six Characters in Search of an Author*, who, in searching for the definitive text, realize that they are in fact its actual creators (Pirandello 1954).[2] Hence our problem: what precisely is the text that we are translating, and what is our role in this translation process? Indeed, we too may discover that there is no stable text to be found.

The Translation of Written Texts: Initial Questions

I will begin from the issue of "translation" in perhaps the most straightforward sense, that is, the translation of written texts from one language to another, but all translators recognize that the practice of translation is by no means straightforward. Within the discipline of Buddhist studies, issues of textual translation become doubly important since we are often engaged in a recursive exercise, translating the translations of others and uncovering meaning on at least three levels, namely, the text and its author(s), the traditional translators, and ourselves.

A consideration of the translation of written texts presumes certain general questions, the first being, "What exactly is a translation?" In the case of Buddhist materials, we find examples that render problematic the assumption that textual translation, as its etymology would suggest, is a thoroughgoing "transference" from a source to a target language (Pym 2007, 156; Munday 2008, 36ff., 197ff.). For example, the "transference" of early Indian Buddhist texts among the closely related Middle Indo-Aryan Prakrits and then to Sanskrit might seem to represent a much simpler case of "transposition" rather than "translation," even though there were of course important interpretive decisions made in the process. In the case of the Kokuyaku Issaikyō Japanese translations of Buddhist texts from Chinese, despite the two very different languages involved, "translation" consisted primarily of placing syntactic markers among the Chinese characters of the original text. Further, we might consider whether "translation" should also include the "transference" of a text from one context to another. As

2. For Pirandello's reflections on his own perspective as an author, see Pirandello 1925.

examples, we might point to quotations, entire discussions, or arguments from one text that appear recontextualized in another. Should these also be considered translations?

As a second question, how do the source and the target influence our translations? Here, the source refers to the text including both its language and context, and the target, to the audience and its language and expectations. Further, what role should the prevailing views about translation in both the source and target cultures play in our translation choices? Here, we should take note of the early Indian Buddhist flexibility with regard to the presentation of the Buddha's teaching, which contributed to a liberal attitude toward translation that continued throughout Buddhist history.

Third, is it possible for the translator to adopt a position of "discursive invisibility," or is the translator always in fact an active participant in the (re)creation of the text?

Fourth, what are our objectives, and how do we judge a translation? Is our goal "equivalence" of the translation and the source text, or is such equivalence desirable or even possible? Specifically, should we adopt a free and "naturalizing" method of translation, which presents the text in terms familiar to the reader, as found in the translations of Martin Luther or John Dryden? Or should we adopt a more literal, "alienating" method, which uses unfamiliar or even foreign terms that force the reader to adopt the perspective of the text, as in the case of the translations of Friedrich Schleiermacher (Munday 2008, 26, 34)?

Finally, how does our theoretical stance shape our translation practice and affect decisions about format, style, and level of discourse, about additional material such as the apparatus, introduction, and notes, and finally about the translation medium as print or electronic? In the end, these general questions might elude categorical answers, but they will, inevitably, guide our ongoing process of translation.

Reflection on Translation: Chinese Buddhist Translations

Now, within the long tradition of the Chinese translation of Buddhist materials, we are fortunate to find explicit discussions of translation-related issues preserved in the various prefaces or epilogues that accompanied the translations themselves.[3] Although certain important translators like Kumārajīva in the fourth and fifth centuries or Xuanzang in the seventh wrote virtually nothing explicitly about their translation practices, many others from the second to the eleventh centuries did, and they conceptualized problems in terms that fit well with the questions that I have just raised.

First, two general points. We must keep in mind the methods by which Buddhist texts were translated into Chinese, that is, often by committee, or later by bureaucratic projects, and involving both oral and written media. Second, we should note that Chinese "translations" did not necessarily correspond to their source texts in length or format. Indeed, abridgements and composite texts were common. Kumārajīva, for example, was known for his practice of heavy excision, and there are many examples of "composite" or combined editions made from previous, separate translations, for example, Zhi Qian in the case of the *Dharmapada* (T. 214, 3rd c.), Zhi Mindu (4th c.) in his composite translation of the *Vimalakīrtinirdeśa*, among others (Cheung and Lin 2006, 62, 67–68, 74).

Throughout these Chinese discussions of translation, we encounter a familiar issue, namely, whether a translation should be faithful to the source text or free and therefore more easily comprehensible and immediately appealing. Over the long course of this debate, the distinction was usually presented in terms of the qualities of "unhewn" (*zhi* 質), that is, literal, straightforward, and conveying the meaning directly, as opposed to "refined" (*wen* 文), that is, involving embellishment, beauty, and elegance in both style and language (Cheung and Lin 2006, 60–61, 90, 74). Among "unhewn" translators might be included, for example, Dharmarakṣa (3rd c.) and Dao'an (4th c.), and among "refined" translators, Zhi Qian (3rd c.) and Kumārajīva (4–5th c.) (Cheung and Lin 2006, 76, 79–80, 102). Despite their very different approaches, representatives from both groups used similar metaphors to express dissatisfaction with their own translation efforts. For example, Dao'an considered translations to be "wine diluted with water," and Kumārajīva, "rice that has been chewed by someone else" (Cheung and Lin 2006, 90).

A compromise position between these options of "unhewn" and "refined" is presented by Sengrui (4–5th c.), who suggests that translators

3. For translations of these materials from the earliest period through the Song dynasty, see Cheung and Lin 2006. For Xuanzang in particular, see Lung 2016.

should "follow the source" (*anben* 案本) and not be concerned about whether a translation is either word-for-word or aesthetically appealing (Cheung and Lin 2006, 105). This view is echoed by Bianji (7th c.), a member of Xuanzang's translation team, who attributes to Xuanzang the view that a translator should not use affected language and should neither add nor subtract from the text or its message (Cheung and Lin 2006, 154; Lung 2016, 105). However, even a brief comparison of Xuanzang's translation of the *Abhidharmakośabhāṣya* (T. 1558) with the Sanskrit text and with Paramārtha's earlier Chinese translation (T. 1559) indicates that Xuanzang routinely added material, including introductory and concluding comments for discussions of doctrinal topics or points as well as transitions from argument to argument (Cox 1995, 62–63 n36; Lung 2016, 108).

This same issue of literal versus free can also be observed in disagreements concerning the method to be used in translating particular terms. The method of "matching the meaning" (*geyi* 格義) common in the earliest period of the translation of Buddhist texts into Chinese entailed translating foreign Buddhist concepts in familiar, often Daoist terms. By contrast, Kumārajīva and later translators worked to develop a body of standardized and specifically Buddhist translations (Cheung and Lin 2006, 62, 95ff.).

Approaches to Translation: The Problem of History

All of these questions concerning translation presume the problem with which I began, namely, "What precisely is the text that we are translating?" or in short, "What is a text?" While my work on the Gāndhārī manuscripts raised this question in an acute form, it is in fact fundamental and unavoidable for everyone translating texts. Indeed, our preconception of what the "text" is has a determining effect upon our working assumptions and our approach to both text editing and translation. Specifically, do we presume an "essential" text, to which the later editors and translators aspire by removing the accretions, accidents, and errors of history? Or do we in fact only find the text as "process," existing in and through history? In the former view, there are two possibilities: either an "original text" that represents the author's intention or an "ideal work" that exists as an abstraction intended by its different versions. In the latter view, the text exists in multiple forms as historical instances fashioned by all of its authors, transmitters, commentators, translators, and audiences, that is, by the collective of interpretive communities that reach up to and include the editor and translator in the present moment.

Thus, these various questions raise the issue of history, which forms the very crux of our problem in working with texts. In short, do we accept that a text, like any cultural product, has a history and that both the text and its possible meanings change over time? If so, then how do we engage seriously with that history? Within the history of any given text, we might provisionally distinguish three stages—composition, transmission, and reception—each of which embodies the interests and influence of the different agents that create the text: namely, authors, scribes, exegetes, editors, translators, and readers (Bushell 2005, 59; Zeller 1975, 257). Further, in our own activities with texts, such as transcribing, editing, translating, interpreting, and so forth, we in turn interact with these different agents and their respective concerns.

This sediment of multiple activities in working with texts has led to tensions among the scholarly textual disciplines, in particular, between those engaged in the initial stage of editing, or "textual criticism," and those engaged in the later stages of uncovering the meaning, or what in current parlance might be referred to as "literary criticism." This contrast is reminiscent of the terms "lower criticism" and "higher criticism" as used in biblical scholarship, where "higher criticism" specifically referred to "historical criticism," or clarifying the "world beyond the text."[4] Both "lower" and "higher criticism" were subsumed within the traditional field of "philology," but philology has since become a problematic and contentious term. At present, many engaged in "textual criticism" adopt the philological label as a badge of honor signifying that they are involved in solid textual work as contrasted with what they consider to be ungrounded theory. By contrast, those engaged in "literary criticism" bristle at the characterization of their own work as philology, which they associate with a mechanical sorting of textual minutia, a task considered to be merely preparatory and devoid of interpretive complexities.

Unfortunately, heated arguments between the so-called "lower" and "higher criticisms" have divided our field for at least the last fifty years, even

4. For biblical criticism, see part 1, "Traditional Methods of Biblical Criticism," in Haynes and McKenzie 1993; see also Greetham 1989, 16; McGann 2013, 274.

though activities in these two areas are actually coincident and inseparable. In response to this tension, we find at present certain textual scholars who advocate a unitary "New Philology."[5] These "New Philologists" of course find antecedents within the many theoretical approaches of the nineteenth and twentieth centuries, which, despite their variety and often intense disagreements, can be distinguished according to certain basic perspectives concerning the relationship among the author, the text, the reader, and the meaning, which are applicable to both textual criticism and literary criticism. In tracing these theoretical approaches in very general terms, we might begin with nineteenth-century Romanticism and then philology, both of which focus on the author.[6] For Romanticism, the text is the pure emanation of the individual genius of the author. Philology also privileges the author's intention as the source of textual meaning, but this can be uncovered only through the reconstruction of the material and historical conditions of both the author and the text. With twentieth-century "New Criticism," the emphasis shifts from authors and their historical context to the text itself, including both its formal characteristics and its own inherent meaning. Even though the author does have some influence, the text is understood to exist independently, and its meaning can be grasped through "close reading" alone, apart from reconstituting the text's historical context. This meaning is considered to be objective and independent of both the author's intention (the intentional fallacy) and any affective influence of the text upon readers (the affective fallacy).

New Criticism's ahistorical perspective stimulated methodological challenges that viewed the text in temporal rather than in static or spatial terms and emphasized variation in meaning dependent upon historical

5. For example, in the field of Sanskrit literature, Sheldon Pollock proposes a "critical philology" whose objective he claims is simply "to make sense of texts." It should incorporate both close textual work and theoretical interpretation, which are coupled with an appreciation for the historical conditions of the text and the biases of one's own position as a "philologist" interpreter (Pollock 2009, 934). Pollock suggests establishing "critical philology" as an independent academic discipline that brings together a variety of scholarly approaches, thereby allowing the cultural evidence of texts to reveal their significance from a number of different perspectives. For "new philology" in the context of medieval manuscript studies, see Nichols 1990 introducing the special issue of *Speculum* (vol. 65, 1990) on the topic "The New Philology."

6. For overviews of the history of methods of textual criticism, see Greetham 1989, 1996, 1999, and 2013; Cohen and Jackson 1991; McGann 2013; Sargent 2013, 228–235; Snell-Hornby 2006.

context. Although these challenges differ in their particular emphases, they all share the view of "text as process" constituted by certain conditions. For example, the "New Historicists" emphasize the dependence of texts upon both historical and sociocultural context.[7] Those associated with "Genetic Criticism"[8] or with the German "Historical-Critical"[9] school engage in "compositional criticism" that gives importance to the materiality and the stages of the text over time, including both preparatory stages, or "pre-text," and later stages, or "versions."

By contrast, "Reader-Response" theorists shift the focus from either the author or text as such to the reader and audience.[10] In other words, a text is considered to be repeatedly reconstituted in different historical contexts by its readers, and its meaning varies accordingly. This shift in focus is based upon a fundamental change in perspective concerning the production of meaning. Reader-Response theorists suggest that meaning does not arise from one position within the reified triad of the author, text, and reader but rather is a "transactive" or an "intersubjective" event. However, complete relativism is avoided since this intersubjective meaning is shaped by each of the three positions, that is, the author, text, and reader, and in turn by the sociohistorical and institutional contexts in which they are embedded.

Finally, we return to the New Philologists, who argue for an approach that acknowledges and even celebrates the contextual determination and instability, or as they put it, the "unfixedness" and historical "situatedness" of texts.[11] This is expressed through such notions as Zumthor's textual "mouvance" or Cerquiglini's textual "variance," as well as McGann's "socialized concept of authorship and textual authority." These New Philologists also explicitly distinguish among the "text," the "work," and the "document," or "artifact." Whereas nineteenth-century philology would focus

7. For the "New Historicist" approach, see Foucault 1971; Geertz 1973; McGann 1983 and 1991. See also Veeser 1989; Levinson 1989; Gallagher and Greenblatt 2000.

8. For "Genetic Criticism," see Falconer 1993; De Biasi 2004, De Biasi and Wassenaar 1996. See also Deppman, Ferrer, and Groden 2004; Lernout 2002; Davis 2002; Bushell 2005.

9. For the "Historical-Critical" approach, see Gabler 1981; Gabler, Bornstein, and Pierce 1995; Zeller 1975.

10. For "Reader-Response" theory, see Jauss 1970; Fish 1980; Mailloux 1982 and 1990.

11. For the "New Philologist" approach, see Driscoll 2010; Zumthor 1972; Cerquiglini 1999; McGann 1983.

on establishing one "text," and New Criticism on the abstract "work," the New Philologists take a radically historical approach. Obviously influenced by the New Historicists, Genetic Critics, and Reader-Response theorists, they focus on the documentary or artifactual side, that is, on the material and cultural conditions for each instance of textual production.

Approaches to the Text: Concrete Factors

The approach that we adopt in our work with texts will be determined by our own assumptions and objectives in relation to the text, the author, and the meaning, specifically, whether we see the text as stable or variable, and the author and textual meaning as singular or multiple. However, our editing and translation practices will also be influenced by certain concrete factors. The first such factor is the context and medium of textual composition and transmission, that is, the context as ritual, pedagogical, archival, and so forth, and the medium as oral, written, or "hybrid" oral and written. The second factor is the nature of our textual evidence, specifically, the number of textual witnesses as multiple or single, as well as "secondary transmission" materials including quotations, commentaries, translations, and so forth. A third concrete factor influencing our editing and translation practices, which I will merely mention here, is extra-textual evidence, for example, documentary evidence as found in the prefaces, biographies, catalogs, and histories in the case of Chinese translations of Buddhist texts and in India, at least in the early period, inscriptions and other archaeological remains, and, very rarely, textual colophons.

Concerning the first concrete factor, we can readily acknowledge that both the context and medium influence not only text format but also the type and degree of textual variation over time. For example, if we turn to the early Buddhist Gāndhārī manuscripts, we find certain clues for the context and medium of their composition and use. While the various Gāndhārī manuscripts taken as a whole are quite diverse in genre (Salomon 2014), the Senior collection contains only *sūtra* texts and, according to its accompanying inscription and colophon, was apparently commissioned as a whole at one time (Salomon 2003; Allon 2014). These manuscripts are in excellent condition and were probably placed into the clay pot in which they were found immediately after being written, possibly as part of a merit-making, ritual act. The British Library collection by contrast includes texts of a number of genres, and the damaged condition of the manuscripts may indicate that they were well used before being placed in the clay pot.[12] Certain manuscripts are marked with the interlinear notation "it is written" (G. *likhidago*; see Salomon 1999, 71–76; Lenz 2003, 105), suggesting that they were recopied from another manuscript archetype, but we do not have sufficient evidence to conclude that these manuscripts came from a monastery archive or library. In fact, for most scrolls that can be definitively identified as belonging to a longer, multi-scroll text, the extant manuscripts contain only the beginning portion of the text in question (Salomon 2011, 182–183). It is of course possible that only the first scroll survived, but it is also possible that these particular texts were never actually written out in full. In this latter scenario, only the first scroll would have been written down to serve, *pars pro toto*, as an efficacious symbol of the entire text, and this might once again point to texts that were written down primarily for ritual and not archival purposes.

Other Gāndhārī manuscripts suggest an intermixture of oral and written media. The narrative *pūrvayoga*, or *avadāna* texts, which contain stories of the effects of past action, are written in a laconic almost abbreviated style with frequent use of formulaic phrases marking textual ellipsis such as "expansion should be according to the model" (G. *vistare yaṣayupamano siyadi*; see Lenz 2003, 85–91). These texts make little sense as written records of complete texts but would be useful as mnemonic aids that were intended to be filled out with additional material when recited orally. Rather than having an archival or ritual purpose, they might have served a pedagogical function, that is, as more casual notes to be used in the process of studying or teaching. Finally, the comparatively later Gāndhārī manuscripts from Bamiyan would support the existence of archival collections of written texts.[13] For example, certain fragments within the Schøyen collection are identified as belonging to the *Mahāparinirvāṇasūtra* and come from sections one-third and two-thirds of the way through the text, suggesting that the original manuscript was very possibly a complete written copy (Allon and Salomon 2000, 244). Other as yet unidentified Schøyen Gāndhārī fragments are marked with high folio numbers, again indicating long written texts (Jantrasrisalai et al. 2016, 4, 6).

12. For the view that the British Library manuscripts were well used and damaged when initially placed into the clay pot, see Salomon 1999, 82–84. For a contrasting interpretation, see Lenz 2003, 108–110.

13. For these Bamiyan manuscripts, which are divided among the Schøyen, Hirayama, and Hayashidera collections, see Salomon 2014, 6–8.

In this way, the cumulative evidence from the Gāndhārī manuscript discoveries argues for a view of texts as passing through different stages in both medium and context of use. While some of the older manuscripts point to a hybrid oral and written medium that served primarily a ritual or pedagogical function, certain more recent manuscripts appear to represent complete texts written down presumably for archival purposes. This complex hybrid model continues to characterize Buddhist textual transmission in India, as suggested by David Drewes in his work on Mahāyāna texts (Drewes 2015).

If we turn then to the second concrete factor, that is, the nature of our textual evidence, we find that the number of textual witnesses and the availability of secondary transmission materials affect both our editing and translation practices. Most traditional methods of textual criticism are based upon multiple textual witnesses and presume an original text by a single author. Textual variants are then viewed as accidents to be removed or errors to be corrected in a quest to restore this original text as closely as possible. Methods such as stemmatics have been developed to guide the establishment of critical editions as simulacra of the original by determining lineages of related manuscripts on the basis of similar variants.[14] Unfortunately, this method can be confounded by contamination or borrowing among different text versions, and it is not useful for oral or hybrid traditions since it assumes only one original text. Also, it is impractical for a text with hundreds or even thousands of extant manuscripts, as is the case for certain South Asian, Sanskrit texts.[15]

14. For stemmatics, see "The First Phase of Lachmann's Activity as a Textual Critic," in Timpanaro and Most 2005, 75–83; Tarrant 2016, 50–64; Greetham 2013, 29–31. For potential difficulties with the stemmatic approach, see "Bipartite Stemmas and Disturbances of the Manuscript Tradition," in Timpanaro and Most 2005, 157–187.

15. For the application of stemmatics to Sanskrit texts, see Witzel 2014. Several recent publications have focused on criticism and translation especially of South Asian texts: for example, the special issue of *Wiener Zeitschrift für die Kunde Südasiens* (vol. 52/53, 2009–2010) on the topic "Text Genealogy, Textual Criticism and Editorial Technique"; the special issue of the *Journal of the International Association of Buddhist Studies* (vol. 36/37, 2013–2014 [2015]) on the topic "Authors and Editors in the Literary Traditions of Asian Buddhism," which contains a particularly relevant article by Silk 2013–2014 [2015]; and the volume *Cross-Cultural Transmission of Buddhist Texts: Theories and Practice of Translation*, edited by Dorji Wangchuk (2016b), which contains, in particular, De Semini and Sferra 2016; Lung 2016; Seyfort Ruegg 2016; Silk 2016; and Wangchuk 2016a.

Two other methods of textual criticism, and the dominant approaches to text editing within the twentieth century, are the so-called "copy-text," or "best-text," method and the "eclectic" method, both of which abandon the strict mechanics of stemmatics.[16] In the "copy-text" method, the editor adopts the single textual witness, often without regard to its age, that is considered to represent most closely the final text as intended by the author, often the text or manuscript that contains the fewest "accidental" errors such as spelling, punctuation, word division, and so forth. However, since this method also assumes a single original text, it too is not useful for oral and hybrid texts. Further, since it ignores text history and offers no method of assessing different versions, ultimately all decisions involving substantive emendations are left almost entirely to the editor's own individual judgment. The so-called "eclectic" method gives even greater power to the editor, who combines readings from many different textual witnesses to create an "ideal" text that is assumed to represent the author's intention better than any individual witness alone. This method is especially problematic since it relies exclusively on the experience and judgment of the editor and, in the end, creates a text that never actually existed.

Now in the case of Indian Buddhist materials, it is not uncommon that only a single textual witness survives. In this case, the editor must rely upon a so-called "diplomatic" or "documentary" method, which entails a transcription of the single manuscript but also inevitably includes some editorial emendations, more readily in the case of "accidentals," and more cautiously, if at all, in the case of substantive problems.[17] For such emendations, an editor consults any available secondary transmission, namely, quotations, commentaries, translations, and so forth, but, with only a single textual witness, there are no other textual criteria by which to weigh the significance and value of the various secondary transmission sources. In the absence of such secondary transmission sources, textual emendations depend only on the editor's experience and judgment and thus, as in the case of the eclectic method, run the danger of resulting in an "ideal" but never historically existent text.

16. For the "copy-text" and "eclectic" methods, see Greg 1950; Bowers 1964; Tanselle 1989. See also Cohen and Jackson 1991; Tanselle 1995; Greetham 2013; Zeller 1975.

17. For a "diplomatic" or "documentary" approach to text editing, see Iversen et al., 2016, 403. For specific applications, see Crostini 2016; Gejrot 2016; Jensen 2016.

While some form of this last diplomatic or documentary method is the only option in the case of a single textual witness, it can also be used for texts that have a more complex history, for example, texts whose composition and transmission are obscure, or multiple versions of one text connected with a given author, or oral or hybrid texts without single authorship. In the case of such texts, documentary editing methods can be supplemented by recent methods that eschew the model of an original or stable text and accord greater consideration to text history and variety of context. Specifically, the New Philologists, mentioned previously, attempt a "historically sensitive" approach that seeks meaning neither in authorial intention nor in an implicit or "ideal" text but in the varying contexts of textual reception. Such a view begins from the radical historical character of textual composition and transmission and assumes that each textual witness stands within a matrix of complex diachronic and synchronic historical connections with other texts, all of which are key to understanding both its format and contents. A historically sensitive view also takes into account the historical context of a particular text or textual genre, that is, the material context within which the text functions and the interpretive perspective of its stakeholders, whether they be traditional or contemporary, religious or political. Thus, the resulting historically sensitive translation will be, at least ideally, a translation that constitutes a totalizing effort and encompasses variation rather than critical selection.

For example, Jerome McGann adopts a "socialized concept of authorship and textual authority," which includes not only the author but also editors, publishers, and so forth (McGann 1983, 8). "Authorial intention" is not singular but becomes just one point in a sequence of social negotiations among multiple individuals and institutions, and textual authority is constituted anew in each social or institutional context. John Bryant, in his research on literary works that were revised by an original author, proposes the model of a "fluid text" to encompass textual versions that flow from one to another, a model that he contends more accurately characterizes the process of textual composition and precludes any assumption of a single, sanctioned text or version (Bryant 2002; Bryant 2007).[18] A text edited with regard to its nature as fluid is not presented as a single "authoritative text" with selected readings but takes the form of a series of

18. For a similar view of "fluid texts," specifically in relation to the early Buddhist commentarial and *abhidhamma* traditions, see Cousins 2013–2014 [2015], 419.

versions representing the author or authors in different interpretive contexts. To this, the editor offers critical editing observations and adds a historical "revision narrative" that provides the historical and social conditions for each stage. Hans Zeller proposes a thoroughgoing historical approach in which the various versions of a text are all potentially of equal value (Zeller 1975). The intention of the original author is important only as one stage in a text's history, and, like all stages, it is the product of its own particular context. In describing textual history, Zeller proposes the metaphor of a cylinder, whereby different versions constitute horizontal planes perpendicular to the axis, which represents the "text" as it might be conceived in the abstract. The natural influence of one version upon another, or what some approaches describe pejoratively as "contamination," is here represented as the projection of one plane upon another (Zeller 1975, 244). The purpose of a historical critical edition is then to create a reproduction of this cylinder, which represents the complete history of the text. Thus, the editor becomes a historian whose primary job is to clarify the contextual influences and manner of reception by different audiences at the various stages that constitute this textual history. Finally, the inevitable instability of texts viewed historically is captured perhaps most evocatively through the term "variance" coined by Bernard Cerquiglini (1999). In his work on medieval French narrative manuscripts, Cerquiglini noticed that these texts had been constantly rewritten and reappropriated in different contexts without any apparent self-consciousness that some "objective" text had been recast or undermined. From the perspective of textual stability, these "rewritings" become variants, or aberrations that depart from the assumed authoritative text. However, Cerquiglini insists that this quality of "variance" is the primary characteristic of all texts, and textual editions must give it priority.

Such historically sensitive methods of textual criticism are also the most suitable for oral and hybrid texts (Niles 2013) and are therefore of particular interest for early Indian Buddhist materials, for early Chinese translations, and for ritually performed Buddhist texts in all cultural contexts and periods. At any particular point in time, such orally composed and transmitted texts can exist in various forms, and, over time, each of these forms will inevitably change. Responding to such conditions of oral composition and transmission, Albert Lord, in his study of Serbo-Croatian oral literature, proposed the model of a "multiform" text, that is, a text that exists in multiple, alternative, and equally "correct" forms, and within this model of "multiformity," there is no assumption of a stable text, which would be implied by such terms as "version" or "variant" (Lord 1971 [1960]; Lord 1991). Now, those of us working with classical Indian materials, whether religious or literary, might object that not all types of oral composition are the same and that methods of transmission, even within a single tradition, change over time. As a result, after a certain point in time, a stage of pure, oral "multiformity" can give way to a hybrid oral and written textual environment. This perspective also underlies Gregory Nagy's suggestion that, for any "text" at any given moment as well as over time, the degree of its multiformity varies in accordance with a number of conditions. In his work on Greek epic literature, Nagy distinguishes five periods of greater fluidity or rigidity in dependence upon a text's medium as primarily oral or written, the emergence of established performance or interpretive traditions, and editorial work (Nagy 2001, 110–111).

Such "oral-derived" texts, that is, written versions of texts that were composed orally, are in fact complex, "hybrid" objects that also present special editing problems. Any aspect of the written text, especially what appear to be variants or errors, might actually result from different oral performances or recitations, or even from scribal errors or interpretive decisions. This last point reminds us that, in the case of the written transmission of all texts, scribes play an active role, and textual variation should not be assumed to reflect a simple "error" but might instead indicate a conscious attempt by the scribe to revise or "correct" the text. Thus, in editing oral texts, hybrid texts, and even written texts that have a long history of manuscript transmission regardless of their origin, if we followed the pattern of many past editors and worked to establish or restore "correct" texts, we would mask their complex origins and history.

One practical problem remains: namely, how is it possible to present editions or translations that incorporate this sensitivity to historical context and textual variance? Several of the theorists mentioned previously appeal to the hypertext capability of digital or electronic media, which creates a more flexible, multidimensional environment and does not require that an edition be presented in the form of a single textual version.[19] In the case of the Gāndhārī manuscripts, a new text presentation and database

19. For discussions of the potential and problems of digital and electronic editions and translations, see Tarrant 2016, 151–156; Apollon, Belisle, and Régnier 2014; Driscoll 2010; Eggert 2013; Sargent 2013.

program has been developed called READ (Research Environment for Ancient Documents), which incorporates linkages between transcriptions and manuscript images, the sequential versioning of text editions, hypertext capabilities for both editions and annotations, as well as a complete dictionary database of all manuscripts.[20] Regardless of the specific method adopted, we are clearly at the point of a major transition in medium, such as that between scribal and printed texts, and we must allow this new electronic medium and its capabilities to influence our editing and translating practices.

A Historically Sensitive Approach: Examples in Buddhist Studies

Just as in the case of these theorists, scholars in Buddhist studies should adopt methods of editing and translating that accord with the materials with which they work, and I would suggest that these "historically sensitive" approaches are the most appropriate for Buddhist texts. In the case of early Indian Buddhist materials, we must recognize their oral origins and take into account the hybrid nature of their transmission even after the regular use of writing. In fact, certain texts, for example, the *Aṅguttaranikāya* among the *sūtra*s or the *Dhammasaṅgaṇī* within the Pali *abhidhamma* collection, are considered incomplete presentations of what are understood to be greatly expanded, "complete" texts. In addition, since so little of the Indian Buddhist textual record remains, we must view any particular textual witness with proper caveats that highlight the historical circumstances of its preservation. All such preserved texts then represent at most only one stage in a long textual history whose details are perhaps forever lost.

A historically sensitive approach is also appropriate for textual materials that emerge over time within a religious tradition as the products of shifting ideological concerns. We should not decide among various textual materials and their different interpretations from some later privileged position, whether tradition-grounded or tradition-external, but must instead

20. For READ (Research Environment for Ancient Documents), see Stefan Baums and Andrew Glass, "Gāndhārī Language and Literature: Research Environment for Ancient Documents," https://gandhari.org/blog/?p=251.

attempt to understand each interpretation by taking into account the historical dynamic of change in both group identity and in the content of the texts themselves. We must remember the apologetic perspective of the religious tradition, whose particular forms of expression shifted with differing sociohistorical conditions but whose changing interests always dictated the sanctioning of only certain specific texts, authors, and interpretations. This apologetic perspective was expressed through "secondary transmission" materials that subsume and thereby preserve only selected versions of a given text specifically through commentarial exegesis and intertextual citation, which mold previous texts through interpretation and extract sections that are thereafter transmitted as authoritative.

One example of this exegetical practice is the use in early *abhidharma* texts of certain *sūtra* passages as proof-texts for a position or contested issue, which then become the standard *sūtra* passages referred to in all later discussions of the same issue (Cox 1995, 14, 57, and 2020, 48–49). For example, we find that many of the proof-texts and arguments used in Vasubandhu's *Abhidharmakośabhāṣya* can be traced to the Vibhāṣā compendia extant in Chinese translation and were undoubtedly taken from an exegetical tradition or compendium of the same type (Cox 1995, 81–85, 136–137). In addition, the structure of Vasubandhu's text follows closely that of the *Abhidharmahṛdaya* texts within the *abhidharma* lineage of Gandhāra (Willemen, Dessein, and Cox 1998, 269–275). Although Vasubandhu does exercise judgment in the selection of materials from his sources and often weaves them together according to his own polemical structure, this dependence of a text with a generally acknowledged single author upon prior collective materials should call into question any naïve views we might have about authorial intention and the assumption of a stable textual creation.

Still later Indian Buddhist materials offer another example of convoluted textual history and authorship in the figure of Śāntideva, whose *Śikṣāsamuccaya* has been viewed as a straightforward anthology of textual selections on important topics. Accordingly, Śāntideva becomes a compiler and not a creative or "original" author of this text. However, through a careful study of verses appearing in both the *Śikṣāsamuccaya* and Śāntideva's independent work, the *Bodhicaryāvatāra*, Paul Harrison draws two related conclusions (Harrison 2007). First, the *Śikṣāsamuccaya* contains much more "original" material composed by Śāntideva himself than conventionally thought. Second, and perhaps more important for our purposes here, a second recension of the *Bodhicaryāvatāra*, entitled *Bodhisattvacaryāvatāra*, suggests that Śāntideva returned to this work throughout his life, revising and expanding it through at least two versions. Harrison concludes that the *Bodhicaryāvatāra* "in the form we now have it was finalised after the [*Śikṣāsamuccaya*]" (*Bodhisattvacaryāvatāra* → *Śikṣāsamuccaya* → *Bodhicaryāvatāra*) (Harrison 2007, 226; Saitō 2001). This conclusion is consistent with Bryant's notion of a "fluid text," that is, as Harrison notes, "a work continually 'in progress,' with multiple drafts being released into the communication networks of the Indian Buddhist community" (2007, 226).

The Gāndhārī manuscripts also provide evidence of the advantages of a historically sensitive approach. Several examples can be found in Gāndhārī manuscript BL 28, which contains an exegetical or scholastic text (Cox forthcoming). Now, most early *abhidharma* texts are structured as commentaries either on one *sūtra* or collected passages from *sūtras*, or as topical matrices, or as outright catechesis. In contrast, BL 28 has a thoroughly polemical structure, presenting arguments between the text proponent and at least two opponents. The extant portion of the text preserves their disputation over the topic of existence, specifically, first in relation to the efficacy of past action, and second in relation to the proposition "everything exists" (G./Skt. *sarvam asti*, P. *sabbam atthi*).

No parallel has as yet been identified for the text recorded in BL 28. Nevertheless, strong affinities exist between it and other *abhidharma* works: in particular, the Pāli *Kathāvatthu*; the **Āryavasumitrabodhisattvasaṅgītiśāstra* (T. 1549), which is extant only in Chinese translation; and the later Sanskrit *Abhidharmakośabhāṣya*. Specifically, both the format and contents of arguments presented in BL 28 resemble those in the first two early texts, the *Kathāvatthu* and **Āryavasumitrabodhisattvasaṅgītiśāstra*. At times, the resemblance to the *Kathāvatthu* is so strong, spanning geographical and later sectarian boundaries, that it seems justified to assume a shared corpus of early, pan-Indian arguments and exegesis. However, their differences are as important as their similarities. Whereas BL 28 is relatively simple and open-ended in both format and syntax, the *Kathāvatthu* is highly structured and rigidly formulaic and thus betrays the effect of later formalizing and standardizing. As a result, we are justified in seeing within BL 28 evidence for the historical transformation that must have occurred in the *Kathāvatthu* and, we might assume, in all early Indian Buddhist texts.

The connection between BL 28 and the *Abhidharmakośabhāṣya* also suggests a body of shared contexts within which certain doctrinal points were developed. Both the initial and final, fragmentary portions of BL 28 contain references to religious practice, specifically, to the arising of contaminants (G./Skt. *anuśaya*) on the basis of past and future objects. This specific point and the controversy to which it led may well have been the stimulus for the examination of the existence of past and future factors in the intervening text. If this is the case, the structure of the larger text that contained BL 28 resembles that of the fifth chapter of the *Abhidharmakośabhāṣya*, in which the examination of the existence of past and future factors is also placed within a discussion of the conditions for the arising of contaminants.[21]

If, in interpreting these apparent connections between BL 28 and either the *Kathāvatthu* or the *Abhidharmakośabhāṣya*, we assumed a model of textual stability, we would attempt to determine the "original" text and the direction of borrowing or contamination. However, if we adopt a historically sensitive approach, we would think instead in terms of multiple texts or recensions that represent different accounts or "versions" of the same argument topos. Such intertextuality viewed from a historically sensitive perspective allows us to contextualize BL 28, but, just as important, the evidence of BL 28 allows us to clarify the historical context of these other texts and understand the process through which they developed.[22]

BL 28 provides another example that illustrates the broader interpretive consequences of a historically sensitive approach. In his criticism of the proposition "everything exists," the text proponent in BL 28 refers to his opponent with the appellation Mahāsarvāstivāda (G. *mahasarvastivaḏa*). However, since this particular appellation is not attested in other *abhidharma* texts, the function of the adjective *maha-* within the compound *maha-sarvastivaḏa* is not certain, nor is it clear what the text proponent has in mind in using this term. We might assume that he is referring simply to a Sarvāstivādin, whether in an honorific or a pejorative sense, as we might understand the term in the context of Sarvāstivāda canonical texts, other scholastic texts, or later doxographies. However, it is here that we encounter a problem. The positions attributed to this Mahāsarvāstivāda

21. *Abhidharmakośabhāṣya* 5 vss. 25–28 (Pradhan 1975, 295.2–301.18).

22. For intertextuality in various genres of Buddhist literature, see the special issue of *Buddhist Studies Review* (vol. 33, nos. 1–2, 2016) guest edited by Cathy Cantwell, Elisa Freschi, and Jowita Kramer on the topic "Reuse and Intertextuality in the Context of Buddhist Texts."

opponent in BL 28 are in some cases inconsistent with those associated with the Sarvāstivādins in contemporaneous or later sources. In fact, certain views attributed to the Mahāsarvāstivāda in BL 28 are associated in other texts with groups such as the Dārṣṭāntikas or Vibhajyavādins. How should we interpret this? It is of course possible that the text proponent misunderstood or intentionally misrepresented the Sarvāstivāda position. However, it is equally likely that actual Sarvāstivāda groups at that time were more diverse and varied in their views. Indeed, analogous discussions in the **Āryavasumitrabodhisattvasaṅgītiśāstra* support this conclusion of greater variety in Sarvāstivāda positions. Thus, even in the case of a school as seemingly well defined as the Sarvāstivāda, we should not assume a monolithic group that remained essentially stable but must instead conclude that it was multibranched and underwent significant changes over time. Hence, BL 28 allows us to see that, as in the case of the texts themselves, the labels used by various groups and the identities to which they refer are also cultural products firmly rooted in historical conditions.

As a final example, the Gāndhārī manuscripts demonstrate the advantages of a historically sensitive approach in the case of perhaps a more familiar text, namely, a fragment that can be correlated with the first and fifth sections of the *Aṣṭasāhasrikā Prajñāpāramitā*. Since the fragment has been dated through radiocarbon analysis to the first through second centuries CE, it is our earliest attested witness for this text, which is extant in a Sanskrit version as well as seven Chinese translations and a Tibetan translation. Among these various versions, the Gāndhārī manuscript and Lokakṣema's Chinese translation are the earliest, and the Sanskrit and the Tibetan translation are the latest (Karashima 2011; Falk and Karashima 2012; Falk and Karashima 2013). This varied secondary transmission offers excellent material for a study of the Aṣṭa's history, and indeed the early Chinese translation by Lokakṣema in particular provides invaluable evidence for the reconstruction of the Gāndhārī fragment. However, if we approach these various witnesses with the assumption that they represent different versions of a single, underlying text, we encounter a problem. From the earliest to the latest witnesses for this text, we find substantive textual accretions, so much so in fact that even the term "version" might be misleading. Perhaps more importantly, comparison reveals not just accretion but complex textual interrelationships that cannot be adequately represented even through a multibranched textual lineage. Instead, these various textual witnesses, if allowed to speak for themselves, attest to a historical reality of convoluted patterns of transmission and preservation and indeed multiple textual lineages, a situation that was undoubtedly typical of most early Indian Buddhist texts. However, this historical reality has become obscured through the process of the sanctioning, culling, and revising of texts by the tradition, and as an inevitable consequence of manuscript loss.

Such a historically sensitive approach entails a fundamental but quite simple shift in perspective: rather than assuming and looking for constancy, we expect and highlight difference. In the case of text editing and translation, rather than seeking a stable text that is "authoritative" as the product of a single author, we see all versions, interpreters, and contexts as of potentially equal heuristic value, depending of course upon our initial questions. The various Buddhist interpreters, including reciters, scribes, commentators, and translators, at each stage will present themselves as faithful transmitters of the text, and the tradition will invest particular figures with authority. However, these self-presentations and assessments should not be accepted as objective fact. Instead, they also become historical data of significance for our understanding of individuals and institutions at specific points in time. A historically sensitive approach would allow us to clarify their particular sociohistorical conditions and detect both their interpretive contributions and the distinctive nature of their textual products. Thus, as historians our purpose is to clarify this succession of reinterpretation, and this then becomes the "meaning" of the text. For Buddhist materials in particular, this approach is necessary and indeed therapeutic since it undermines our "craving for stability" and negates the seductive appeal of an "essential" text, which the tradition teaches us cannot be found.

References

Allon, Mark. 2014. "The Senior Kharoṣṭhī Manuscripts." In *From Birch Bark to Digital Data: Recent Advances in Buddhist Manuscript Research—Papers Presented at the Conference Indic Buddhist Manuscripts: The State of the Field, Stanford, June 15–19 2009*, edited by Paul Harrison and Jens-Uwe Hartmann, 19–33. Österreichische Akademie der Wissenschaften, philosophisch-historische Klasse, Denkschriften 460. Bd. / Beiträge zur Kultur- und Geistesgeschichte Asiens 80. Vienna: Verlag der Österreichischen Akademie der Wissenschaften.

Allon, Mark, and Richard Salomon. 2000. "Kharoṣṭhī Fragments of a Gāndhārī Version of the Mahāparinirvāṇasūtra." In *Buddhist Manuscripts, Volume I*, edited by Jens Braarvig, 243–273. Manuscripts in the Schøyen Collection. Oslo: Hermes Academic.

Apollon, Daniel, Claire Belisle, and Philippe Régnier. 2014. *Digital Critical Editions*. Topics in the Digital Humanities. Urbana: University of Illinois Press.

Bassnett, Susan. 2002 [1988]. *Translation Studies*. 3rd ed. London: Routledge.

Bermann, Sandra, and Catherine Porter, eds. 2014. *A Companion to Translation Studies*. Blackwell Companions to Literature and Culture. Chichester, UK: Wiley Blackwell.

Bowers, Fredson. 1964. "Some Principles for Scholarly Editions of Nineteenth-Century American Authors." *Studies in Bibliography* 17: 223–228.

Bryant, John. 2002. *The Fluid Text: A Theory of Revision and Editing for Book and Screen*. Editorial Theory and Literary Criticism. Ann Arbor: University of Michigan Press.

———. 2007. "Witness and Access: The Uses of the Fluid Text." *Textual Cultures: Texts, Contexts, Interpretation* 2, no. 1: 16–42.

Bushell, Sally. 2005. "Intention Revisited: Towards an Anglo-American 'Genetic Criticism.'" *Text* 17: 55–91.

Cerquiglini, Bernard. 1999. *In Praise of the Variant: A Critical History of Philology*. [1989 *Éloge de la variante*]. Baltimore: Johns Hopkins University Press.

Chesterman, Andrew, and Emma Wagner. 2016. *Can Theory Help Translators? A Dialogue between the Ivory Tower and the Wordface*. London: Routledge.

Chesterman, Andrew, and Rosemary Arrojo. 2000. "Shared Ground in Translation Studies." *Target* 12, no. 1: 151–160.

Cheung, Martha, and Wusun Lin. 2006. *An Anthology of Chinese Discourse on Translation. Volume One. From the Earliest Times to the Buddhist Project*. Manchester: St. Jerome; Kinderhook, NY: InTrans.

Cohen, Philip G., and David H. Jackson. 1991. "Notes on Emerging Paradigms in Editorial Theory." In *Devils and Angels: Textual Editing and Literary Theory*, edited by Philip G. Cohen, 103–123. Charlottesville: University Press of Virginia.

Cousins, L. S. 2013–2014 [2015]. "The Case of the Abhidhamma Commentary." *Journal of the International Association of Buddhist Studies* 36/37: 389–422.

Cox, Collett. 1995. *Disputed Dharmas: Early Buddhist Theories on Existence—An Annotated Translation of the Section on Factors Dissociated from Thought from Saṅghabhadra's Nyāyānusāra*. Studia Philologica Buddhica: Monograph Series 11. Tokyo: International Institute for Buddhist Studies.

———. 2020. "Exegesis, Abhidharma, and Scholasticism: Evidence from Early Buddhist Gāndhārī Manuscripts." In *Les scolastiques indiennes: genèses, développements, interactions*, edited by Gérard Colas and Émilie Aussant, 39–56. Études thématiques 32. Paris: École française d'Extrême-Orient.

———. Forthcoming. *A Gāndhārī Abhidharma Text: British Library Kharoṣṭhī Fragment* 28. Gandhāran Buddhist Texts. Seattle: University of Washington Press.

Crostini, Barbara. 2016. "Editing a Greek Catena to the Psalter from a Single Illuminated Manuscript: Vaticanus graecus 752." In *The Arts of Editing Medieval Greek and Latin: A Casebook*, edited by Gunilla Iversen et al., 54–71. Studies and Texts, Pontifical Institute of Mediaeval Studies 203. Toronto: Pontifical Institute of Mediaeval Studies.

Davis, Oliver. 2002. "The Author at Work in Genetic Criticism." *Paragraph* 25, no. 1: 92–106.

De Biasi, Pierre-Marc. 2004. "Toward a Science of Literature: Manuscript Analysis and the Genesis of the Work." In *Genetic Criticism: Texts and Avant-Textes*, edited by Jed Deppman, Daniel Ferrer, and Michael Groden, 36–68. Philadelphia: University of Pennsylvania Press.

De Biasi, Pierre-Marc, and Ingrid Wassenaar. 1996. "What Is a Literary Draft? Toward a Functional Typology of Genetic Documentation." *Yale French Studies* 89: 26–58.

De Semini, Florinda, and Francesco Sferra. 2016. "On the Fence between Two Wor(l)ds: Theory and Practice in Translating Indian and Indo-Tibetan Texts." In *Cross-Cultural Transmission of Buddhist Texts: Theories and Practice of Translation*, edited by Dorji Wangchuk, 159–192. Indian and Tibetan Studies 5. Hamburg: Department of Indian and Tibetan Studies, Universität Hamburg.

Deppman, Jed, Daniel Ferrer, and Michael Groden, eds. 2004. *Genetic Criticism: Texts and Avant-Textes*. Philadelphia: University of Pennsylvania Press.

Drewes, David. 2015. "Oral Texts in Indian Mahāyāna." *Indo-Iranian Journal* 58: 117–141.

Driscoll, Matthew J. 2010. "The Words on the Page: Thoughts on Philology, Old and New." In *Creating the Medieval Saga: Versions, Variability and Editorial Interpretations of Old Norse Saga Literature*, edited by Judy Quinn and Emily Lethbridge, 85–102. Viking Collection 18. Odense: University Press of Southern Denmark.

Eggert, Paul. 2013. "Apparatus, Text, Interface." In *The Cambridge Companion to Textual Scholarship*, edited by Neil Fraistat and Julia Flanders, 97–118. New York: Cambridge University Press.

Falconer, Graham. 1993. "Genetic Criticism." *Comparative Literature* 45, no. 1: 1–21.

Falk, Harry, and Seishi Karashima. 2012. "A First-Century *Prajñāpāramitā* Manuscript from Gandhāra—*parivarta* 1." Texts from the Split Collection 1. *Annual Report of the International Research Institute for Advanced Buddhology* 15: 19–61.

———. 2013. "A First-Century *Prajñāpāramitā* Manuscript from Gandhāra—*parivarta* 5." Texts from the Split Collection 2. *Annual Report of the International Research Institute for Advanced Buddhology* 16: 97–169.

Fish, Stanley Eugene. 1980. *Is There a Text in This Class? The Authority of Interpretive Communities*. Cambridge, MA: Harvard University Press.

Foucault, Michel. 1971. "Orders of Discourse." *Social Science Information* 10, no. 2: 7–30.

Gabler, Hans Walter. 1981. "The Synchrony and Diachrony of Texts: Practice and Theory of the Critical Edition of James Joyce's Ulysses." *Text* 1: 305–326.

Gabler, Hans Walter, George Bornstein, and Gillian Borland Pierce. 1995. *Contemporary German Editorial Theory*. Editorial Theory and Literary Criticism. Ann Arbor: University of Michigan Press.

Gallagher, Catherine, and Stephen Greenblatt. 2000. *Practicing New Historicism*. Chicago: University of Chicago Press.

Geertz, Clifford. 1973. *The Interpretation of Cultures: Selected Essays*. New York: Basic Books.

Gejrot, Claes. 2016. "Original Value: On Diplomatics and Editorial Work." In *The Arts of Editing Medieval Greek and Latin: A Casebook*, edited by Gunilla Iversen et al., 122–137. Studies and Texts, Pontifical Institute of Mediaeval Studies 203. Toronto: Pontifical Institute of Mediaeval Studies.

Greetham, D. C. 1989. "Textual and Literary Theory: Redrawing the Matrix." *Studies in Bibliography* 42: 1–24.

———. 1996. "Textual Forensics." *PMLA (Publications of the Modern Language Association)* 111, no. 1: 32–51.

———. 1999. *Theories of the Text*. New York: Oxford University Press.

———. 2013. "A History of Textual Scholarship." In *The Cambridge Companion to Textual Scholarship*, edited by Neil Fraistat and Julia Flanders, 16–41. New York: Cambridge University Press.

Greg, W. W. 1950. "The Rationale of the Copy-Text." *Studies in Bibliography* 3: 20–37.

Harrison, Paul. 2007. "The Case of the Vanishing Poet: New Light on Śāntideva and the *Śikṣā-samuccaya*." In *Indica et Tibetica: Festschrift für Michael Hahn, Zum 65. Geburtstag von Freunden und Schülern überreicht*, edited by Konrad Klaus and Jens-Uwe Hartmann, 215–248. Vienna: Arbeitskreis für tibetische und buddhistische Studien Universität Wien.

Haynes, Stephen R., and Steven L. McKenzie, eds. 1993. *To Each Its Own Meaning: An Introduction to Biblical Criticisms and Their Application*. 1st ed. Louisville, KY: Westminster / John Knox Press.

Iversen, Gunilla, et al., eds. 2016. *The Arts of Editing Medieval Greek and Latin: A Casebook*. Studies and Texts, Pontifical Institute of Mediaeval Studies 203. Toronto: Pontifical Institute of Mediaeval Studies.

Jantrasrisalai, Chanida, Timothy Lenz, Lin Qian, and Richard Salomon. 2016. "Fragments of an Ekottarikāgama Manuscript in Gāndhārī." In *Buddhist Manuscripts, Volume IV*, edited by Jens Braarvig, 1–121. Manuscripts in the Schøyen Collection. Oslo: Hermes Academic.

Jauss, Hans Robert. 1970. "Literary History as a Challenge to Literary Theory." A Symposium on Literary History. *New Literary History* 2, no. 1: 7–37.

Jensen, Brian M. 2016. "A Modified Diplomatic Edition of *Lectionarium Placentinum*." In *The Arts of Editing Medieval Greek and Latin: A Casebook*, edited by Gunilla Iversen et al., 198–217. Studies and Texts, Pontifical Institute of Mediaeval Studies 203. Toronto: Pontifical Institute of Mediaeval Studies.

Karashima, Seishi. 2011. *A Critical Edition of Lokakṣema's Translation of the Aṣṭasāhasrikā Prajñāpāramitā*. Bibliotheca Philologica et Philosophica Buddhica XII, The International Research Institute for Advanced Buddhology. Tokyo: Soka University.

Kokuyaku Issaikyō. 1958–1970. Tokyo: Daitō Shuppansha.

Kuhiwczak, Piotr, and Karen Littau, eds. 2007. *A Companion to Translation Studies*. Clevedon: Multilingual Matters.

Lenz, Timothy. 2003. *A New Version of the Gāndhārī Dharmapada and a Collection of Previous-Birth Stories: British Library Kharoṣṭhī Fragments 16 + 25*. Gandhāran Buddhist Texts 3. Seattle: University of Washington Press.

Lernout, Geert. 2002. "Genetic Criticism and Philology." *Text: An Interdisciplinary Annual of Textual Studies* 14: 53–75.

Levinson, Marjorie. 1989. *Rethinking Historicism: Critical Readings in Romantic History*. Oxford, UK: Blackwell.

Lord, Albert B. 1971 [1960]. *The Singer of Tales*. Cambridge, MA: Harvard University Press; rpt. New York: Atheneum.

———. 1991. *Epic Singers and Oral Tradition*. Ithaca, NY: Cornell University Press.

Lung, Rachel. 2016. "A Cultural Approach to the Study of Xuanzang." In *Cross-Cultural Transmission of Buddhist Texts: Theories and Practice of Translation*, edited by Dorji Wangchuk, 99–117. Indian and Tibetan Studies 5. Hamburg: Department of Indian and Tibetan Studies, Universität Hamburg.

Mailloux, Steven. 1982. "Textual Scholarship and Author's Final Intention." In *Interpretive Conventions: The Reader in the Study of American Fiction*, 93–125. Ithaca, NY: Cornell University Press.

———. 1990. "The Turns of Reader-Response Criticism." In *Conversations: Contemporary Critical Theory and the Teaching of Literature*, edited by Charles Moran and Elizabeth F. Penfield, 38–54. Urbana, IL: National Council of Teachers of English.

McGann, Jerome J. 1983. *A Critique of Modern Textual Criticism*. Chicago: University of Chicago Press.
———. 1991. *The Textual Condition*. Princeton: Princeton University Press.
———. 2013. "Coda Why Digital Textual Scholarship Matters; Or, Philology in a New Key." In *The Cambridge Companion to Textual Scholarship*, edited by Neil Fraistat and Julia Flanders, 274–288. New York: Cambridge University Press.
Munday, Jeremy. 2008. *Introducing Translation Studies: Theories and Applications*. London: Routledge.
Nagy, Gregory. 2001. "Homeric Poetry and Problems of Multiformity: The 'Panathenaic Bottleneck.'" *Classical Philology* 96: 109–119.
Nichols, Stephen G. 1990. "Introduction: Philology in a Manuscript Culture." The New Philology. *Speculum* 65, no. 1: 1–10.
Niles, John. 2013. "Orality." In *The Cambridge Companion to Textual Scholarship*, edited by Neil Fraistat and Julia Flanders, 205–223. New York: Cambridge University Press.
Pirandello, Luigi. 1925. "Pirandello Confesses . . . : Why and How He Wrote 'Six Characters in Search of an Author.'" *Virginia Quarterly Review* 1, no. 1: http://www.vqronline.org/essay/pirandello-confesses.
———. 1954. *Six Characters in Search of an Author*. Translated by Frederick May. Drama Library. London: Heinemann.
Pollock, Sheldon. 2009. "Future Philology? The Fate of a Soft Science in a Hard World." *Critical Inquiry* 35, no. 4: 931–961.
Pradhan, Prahlad, ed. 1975. *Abhidharmakośabhāṣyam of Vasubandhu*. Rev. 2nd ed. with introduction and indices by Aruna Haldar. Tibetan Sanskrit Works Series 8. Patna, India: K. P. Jayaswal Research Institute.
Pym, Anthony. 2007. "On History in Formal Conceptualizations of Translation." *Across Languages and Cultures* 8, no. 2: 153–166.
Saitō, Akira. 2001. "*Bodhi(sattva)caryāvatāra* to *Śikṣāsamuccaya* (*Bodhi(sattva) caryāvatāra* and *Śikṣāsamuccaya*)." *Indotetsugaku bukkyōgaku* (*Hokkaidō Journal of Indian and Buddhist Studies*) 16: 326–353 (1–28).
Salomon, Richard. 1999. *Ancient Buddhist Scrolls from Gandhāra: The British Library Kharoṣṭhī Fragments*. Seattle: University of Washington Press.
———. 2003. "The Senior Manuscripts: Another Collection of Gandhāran Buddhist Scrolls." *Journal of the American Oriental Society* 123: 73–92.
———. 2011. "An Unwieldy Canon: Observations on Some Distinctive Features of Canon Formation in Buddhism." In *Kanonisierung und Kanonbildung in der asiatischen Religionsgeschichte*, edited by Max Deeg, Oliver Freiberger and Christoph Kleine, 161–207. Österreichische Akademie der Wissenschaften, philosophisch-historische Klasse, Sitzungsberichte 820. Bd. / Beiträge zur Kultur- und Geistesgeschichte Asiens 72. Vienna: Verlag der Österreichischen Akademie der Wissenschaften.

———. 2014. "Gāndhārī Manuscripts in the British Library, Schøyen and Other Collections." In *From Birch Bark to Digital Data: Recent Advances in Buddhist Manuscript Research—Papers Presented at the Conference Indic Buddhist Manuscripts: The State of the Field, Stanford, June 15–19 2009*, edited by Paul Harrison and Jens-Uwe Hartmann, 1–17. Österreichische Akademie der Wissenschaften, philosophisch-historische Klasse, Denkschriften 460. Bd. / Beiträge zur Kultur- und Geistesgeschichte Asiens 80. Vienna: Verlag der Österreichischen Akademie der Wissenschaften.

Sargent, Michael G. 2013. "Manuscript Textuality." In *The Cambridge Companion to Textual Scholarship*, edited by Neil Fraistat and Julia Flanders, 224–235. New York: Cambridge University Press.

Seyfort Ruegg, David. 2016. "On Translating Buddhist Texts: A Survey and Some Reflections." In *Cross-Cultural Transmission of Buddhist Texts: Theories and Practice of Translation*, edited by Dorji Wangchuk, 193–266. Indian and Tibetan Studies 5. Hamburg: Department of Indian and Tibetan Studies, Universität Hamburg.

Silk, Jonathan. 2013–2014 [2015]. "Establishing/Interpreting/Translating: Is It Just That Easy?" *Journal of the International Association of Buddhist Studies* 36/37: 205–226.

———. 2016. "Peering Through a Funhouse Mirror: Trying to Read Indic Texts Through Tibetan and Chinese Translations." In *Cross-Cultural Transmission of Buddhist Texts: Theories and Practice of Translation*, edited by Dorji Wangchuk, 289–314. Indian and Tibetan Studies 5. Hamburg: Department of Indian and Tibetan Studies, Universität Hamburg.

Snell-Hornby, Mary. 2006. *Turns of Translation Studies: New Paradigms or Shifting Viewpoints?* Benjamins Translation Library 66. Philadelphia: John Benjamins.

Takakusu, Junjirō, Kaigyoku Watanabe, and Genmyō Ono, eds. 1924–1932. *Taishō Shinshū Daizōkyō*. Tokyo: Taishō Issaikyō Kankōkai.

Tanselle, G. Thomas. 1989. *A Rationale of Textual Criticism*. Publication of the A.S.W. Rosenbach Fellowship in Bibliography. Philadelphia: University of Pennsylvania Press.

———. 1995. "Critical Editions, Hypertexts, and Genetic Criticism." *Romanic Review* 86, no. 3: 581–593.

Tarrant, R. J. 2016. *Texts, Editors, and Readers: Methods and Problems in Latin Textual Criticism*. Roman Literature and Its Contexts. Cambridge, MA: Cambridge University Press.

Timpanaro, Sebastiano, and Glenn W. Most, 2005. *The Genesis of Lachmann's Method*. Chicago: University of Chicago Press.

Veeser, H. Aram. 1989. *The New Historicism*. New York: Routledge.

Wangchuk, Dorji. 2016a. "A Rationale for Buddhist Textual Scholarship." In *Cross-Cultural Transmission of Buddhist Texts: Theories and Practice of Trans-*

lation, edited by Dorji Wangchuk, 336–352. Indian and Tibetan Studies 5. Hamburg: Department of Indian and Tibetan Studies, Universität Hamburg.

———. 2016b. *Cross-Cultural Transmission of Buddhist Texts: Theories and Practice of Translation*. Indian and Tibetan Studies 5. Hamburg: Department of Indian and Tibetan Studies, Universität Hamburg.

Willemen, Charles, Bart Dessein, and Collett Cox. 1998. *Sarvāstivāda Buddhist Scholasticism*. Handbuch Der Orientalistik. Zweite Abteilung, Indien 11. Bd. Leiden: Brill.

Witzel, Michael. 2014. "Textual Criticism in Indology and in European Philology during the 19th and 20th Centuries." *EJVS (Electronic Journal of Vedic Studies)* 21, no. 3: 9–91.

Zeller, Hans. 1975. "A New Approach to the Critical Constitution of Literary Texts." *Studies in Bibliography* 28: 231–264.

Zumthor, Paul. 1972. *Essai De Poetique Médiévale*. Poétique Series. Paris: Éditions du Seuil.

Chapter 2

Translating the Buddha's Body

Natalie Gummer

By its own account, the *Suvarṇa(pra)bhāsottama* (*Sūtra of Utmost Golden Radiance*, hereafter referred to as *Suvarṇa*) is the real, eternal body of the Buddha. His body continues to act in the world whenever an eloquent preacher performs the *sūtra*. This ritual resuscitation of his speech-body enables essence-of-buddha to enter listeners and transform them, eventually, into buddhas. As I argue elsewhere (Gummer 2014), this verbal process of transformation substitutes consumption of the Buddha's body of dharma (the *sūtra* itself, that is) for the process of perfection through repeated self-sacrifice that constitutes the bodhisattva path. Consumption of the Buddha's speech, of his textually enshrined eternal *sūtra*-body of words, provides a nonviolent alternative to the (often quite bloody) bodily self-sacrifice through which he himself attained buddhahood, as narratives of the Buddha's previous lives describe in such graphic terms.

The translator of such a speech-body faces some particular challenges, for its ability to act depends upon crucial and complex relationships between the denotative content of the *sūtra* and its linguistic form, and between the past and the present. These relationships, about which the *sūtra* has much to say, are obviously central concerns in any translation project—let alone translating the Buddha's body. Translation lies at the point of articulation between these pairs—between linguistically and culturally specific form and content, and between textual and cultural production in the past and in the present. To use the metaphors of embodiment invoked in the *sūtras*, translation aims to make a past body, a foreign body that spoke to another time and place, present and relevant here and now, in our own very different time and place.

I begin by summarizing what the *sūtra* has to say about itself as a body that makes the Buddha present and transmits his essence to listeners; I then turn to consider how those statements are embodied, so to speak, in the language of the *sūtra* and assess the implications for scholarly translation practices by way of a few examples. I hope to show how attending to the performative strategies of the *sūtra* and the rhythmic and sonorous qualities of its language might better enable contemporary readers to encounter this verbal embodiment of the Buddha in the present.

The Buddha's Body of Words

The *Suvarṇa* and related Mahāyāna *sūtras* represent both their own verbal substance and the experience of taking in that substance through profoundly physical metaphors.[1] When the *Suvarṇa* is performed with appropriate eloquence by the *dharmabhāṇaka*, the preacher of the dharma, the substance that issues forth is designated by the *sūtra* itself as *dharmāṃṛtarasa*, the "liquid essence of the immortalizing nectar of the dharma."[2] This essence-of-buddha, at once nutritive, seminal, poetic, and consecratory, enters receptive auditors and initiates a multi-lifetime process of transformation from listener to speaker, culminating in the attainment of a buddha's perfect golden *dharmakāya*. And that body of dharma is the *sūtra* itself: fully embodying its words through textual practices like memorization,

1. The term "metaphor," while useful for capturing the representation of one substance (speech) in terms of others, as described below, obscures what I have become convinced is a much more "literal" (again, for lack of a better term) manner in which the Buddha is embodied and made present in the performance of the *sūtra*.

2. Skjærvø 2004, 5.22, 6.1.14, 6.2.12, 6.2.71, 6.5.8, 6.5.15, 6.5.43, 10.13, 10.41; Nobel 1937, 61.18–62.2, 65.8, 70.5, 75.13, 92.8, 93.1, 95.7, 122.1, 123.15. I rely on Skjærvø's edition, but I have also included citations from that of Nobel's because it is more widely available. In addition, the English translation of Emmerick (1990) includes page references to Nobel's edition, so citing Nobel allows interested readers to consult that translation.

recitation, and preaching transforms one into a buddha who dwells in his speech.[3] The words of the *sūtra* are thus both means and end—both the sacrificial body consumed through listening and internalization, and the body attained thereby. And the words that describe this process of bodily transformation constitute the body itself: bloodless *dehadāna* meets prediction to buddhahood in the self-referential strategies of the *sūtra.*

Understanding the nature of these innovations—by no means unique to the *Suvarṇa*—requires that we reexamine the long-recognized sacrificial context of the bodhisattva path, a context it shares with Brahmanical models for transformation.[4] Narratives of the bodily self-sacrifice of the bodhisattva advance an ethical critique of Vedic sacrificial ritual, in which the sacrificer, who is the real offering, offers an animal or vegetal substitute in his place and thereby obtains a perfect and eternal body in heaven. The bodhisattva refuses to substitute another for himself, instead sacrificing himself for others. By doing so, he generates the fiery internal *tapas* that supplants the sacrificial fire and eventually attains the beautiful golden body of a buddha. This reversal of sacrificial mechanisms informs not only the means of transformation, but also the end. Whereas in Vedic ritual and cosmology, fire is a life-giving force that, properly manipulated, serves to maintain cosmic order, early Buddhist thought identifies fire with the *kleśa*s, causes of suffering that are extinguished through the attainment of *nirvāṇa*—literally, the quelling of a flame (Collins 1982, 84; Collins 1998, 216–221). And yet attempts to reject or critique sacrificial paradigms inevitably also invoke and depend upon those same paradigms: the bodhisattva's repeated acts of self-sacrifice suggest that in order to put out the fire, he must first "completely cook" (*pari-√pac*[5]) himself into a perfect

3. These notions are by no means confined to the *Suvarṇa*. I examine them further in Gummer 2012, and in my monograph under preparation (*Performing the Buddha's Body*).

4. I treat in depth the topics summarized in the following three paragraphs in Gummer 2014. Reiko Ohnuma (2007, 249–256) discusses the relationship between sacrifice and the bodhisattva's gift of his body and helpfully summarizes previous scholarship on this topic.

5. On cooking as metaphor and ritual act in Brahmanical tradition, see Malamoud (1996, 23–53). Mrozik (2004, 2007) examines the application of the metaphor to processes of ethical cultivation in depictions of the bodhisattva path. I treat the use of this term in Buddhist *sūtra* literature in Gummer 2014 and in the aforementioned monograph under preparation.

buddha. The ethics of sacrifice may be called into question, but its ritual efficacy as a means of transformation remains at the center of narrative representations of the bodhisattva path.[6]

Significantly, sacrifice in the South Asian cosmos is achieved not only through violence (whether the other-inflicted violence of the Brahmanical sacrificer or the self-inflicted violence of the bodhisattva) but also through potent words. The structure and efficacy of Vedic sacrifice is profoundly poetic in its reliance on complex networks of association among the substances and images that inform sacrificial thought and action (Patton 2005; Proferes 2007). Conversely, the hymns and mantras uttered during the sacrifice are endowed with a striking materiality, such that "they are perceived as objects that shed light, as well as utterances that spread auspicious sounds" (Patton 2005, 94). Words have radiance, so they can cook; words have substance, so they can embody and be embodied. Indeed, the body that the sacrificer gains in heaven is explicitly identified with the verses of the Veda, which are termed *śilpa*, a work of art (Malamoud 2002, 23). And following the sacrificial logic of substitution to its logical conclusion, by the late Vedic period, the study and eloquent recitation of the Vedas was substituted for the violent ritual enactment of the sacrifice (Smith and Doniger 1989, 207–208; Carpenter 1992, 63; Patton 2005, 27; Freedman 2012). Ritual eloquence became a technology for transformative cooking—a technology requiring the memorization and internalization of ritual language (Patton 2005, 8, 173). And, while the eloquent ritual recitation (and embodiment) of the Vedas constitutes the paradigmatic result of this mnemonic ingestion, digestion, and gestation, comparable processes govern the memorization and oral performance of South Asian bodies of discourse much more broadly—including some Mahāyāna *sūtras*.

After all, it is one thing to glorify the often gory self-sacrifice in past-life stories of the bodhisattva—always in an important sense a *narrative* practice—but by opening up the bodhisattva path to a much wider group of present aspirants, Mahāyāna *sūtras* produce a significant problem: the potential emulation of these narratives by practitioners.[7] Bodily self-sacrifice

6. In the *Buddhavaṃsa*, for instance, the perfections are characterized repeatedly as a form of "cooking" (*pācana*); see Jayawickrama (1974, 2.120, 2.125, 2.130, 2.135, 2.140, 2.145, 2.150, 2.155, 2.160, 2.165).

7. The studies of early Mahāyāna literature by Nattier (2003, 144–145) and Boucher (2008, 33–39) make note of this concern, although neither author considers it in relation to sacrificial ritual.

is a powerful narrative ideal, but it is clearly untenable as a literalized and generalized religious practice. While *sūtras* like the *Suvarṇa* continue to laud the bodhisattva's "gift of the body," they also provide and promote an alternative, one that corresponds closely to the verbalization of Vedic ritual: they offer their own eloquent recitation as a dharmic substitute for flesh (*āmiṣa*) sacrifices—not only Brahmanical offerings but also the bodhisattva's body.[8] In place of the gift of the flesh body, they offer the dharma body. The *sūtra* is the Buddha's body, and as his body, the *sūtra* is food—a substitute for the food offering that the bodhisattva makes of his body. But the *sūtra* is not only means but also end: it is the eternal golden dharma body that, through practices of listening, study, memorization, and recitation, aspiring bodhisattvas can come to attain.

Can the *Dharmakāya* Speak in the Present?

Let me begin moving toward assessing the implications of this interpretation of the *sūtra* for translation by noting how self-referentiality functions in its textual strategies. The form makes the meaning manifest, while the meaningful content of the *sūtra* refers to its form, to its embodiment in language: it materializes in the moment of performance. This is most obviously the case in the oral performance of overtly self-referential passages, such as when a *dharmabhāṇaka* preaches that whenever a *dharmabhāṇaka* preaches, various deities will arrive in their invisible bodies—thus causing them to "appear" (albeit invisibly) before us. But the *sūtra* contains many more subtly self-referential passages, as well, in which the Buddha is made present through descriptions of his body—in terms, moreover, that highlight the material identity of Buddha and *sūtra* (especially the oral *sūtra*). Take, for instance, this verse from the fourth chapter, part of a praise of all buddhas in the *dodhaka* meter:[9]

---

8. On the contrast between dharma and *āmiṣa* in relation to the sacrificial gift of the body, see Ohnuma (1998, 325) and Gummer (2014, 1116–1119). In the latter, I make the case for reading the term in the *Vimalakīrtinirdeśa* as implying more than simply "material things"; the term is multivalent, and the *sūtra* plays deliberately with the different layers of meaning. I examine the dharma/*āmiṣa* contrast in greater depth, including its frequent occurrence in the Pāli canon, in my monograph (under preparation).

9. – ◡ ◡ – ◡ ◡ | – ◡ ◡ – –

śāntapraśāntaviśuddhamunīndraṃ varṇasuvarṇaprabhāsitagātraṃ |
sarvasvarāsvarasusvarabuddhaṃ brahmarutasvaragarjitaghoṣaṃ ||
(Skjærvø 2004, 4.2; Nobel 1937, 45.11–14).

The Lord among sages, calm, tranquil, and pure,
his radiant body the color of gold,
the Buddha sweet-sounding, surpassing all sounds,
resounding like thunder, with Brahmā's great voice.

In the Sanskrit, these intensely alliterative and rhythmic lines embed the name of the *sūtra* (*suvarṇaprabhāsa*) in a description of the Buddha, a frequent device for drawing attention to their bodily identity and for making that radiant golden body manifest in the mind of the listener. The third and fourth *pāda*s thoroughly conflate form and content in their sonorous description of the sound of *buddhavacana* (including, of course, this very verse). These strategies—making the Buddha's body appear through (and as) the words of the *sūtra*, and drawing attention to what we might call the materiality of speech—are pervasive in the *sūtra*, and to a significant extent constitute its performative efficacy. The *sūtra* feeds its audiences with the flavorful *rasa* of the mellifluous body of the Buddha.

Note the centrality of time in this complex interaction between form and content. The *sūtra* both asserts and enacts the inconceivable life span of the Buddha, making it possible for his *dharmakāya* to be present in the world here and now. He is not a relic of the past, the *sūtra* says, in its almost autocommentarial manner; he is not a dead teacher who belongs to history. He speaks whenever the *sūtra* is preached with *pratibhāna*, with the inspired eloquence that infuses the sound of the *sūtra* with the fiery *tejas* necessary for cooking beings into buddhas. And perhaps this dependence accounts in part for the deep concern in the text for its future preachers and listeners: the *sūtra* may be the eternal dharma body of the Buddha, but it only comes fully alive when it has orators and auditors.

I want to suggest that translators of Mahāyāna *sūtra*s face a similar challenge: how to take these infinitely complex texts composed and performed in another time and place and make them more than the dead relics of history. To be clear, I'm not making a theological argument: I don't mean to suggest that translators ought to take practitioners or "believers" as our primary audience (not that there's a thing wrong with doing so). I don't think the *Suvarṇa* requires "belief" to be effective any more than do the writings of Borges (to which I think the *sūtra* bears more than a passing resemblance).[10] I propose, rather, attempting to translate in such a way that we make it possible for contemporary audiences to be shocked and challenged and drawn in by the *sūtra*'s extraordinary vision of the power and vitality of its own words. Such a translation would also bring history alive, enabling readers to appreciate more fully the context of performance in which the sense and purpose of these *sūtra*s materialize.[11]

I am under no illusion that I could successfully produce such a translation. As anyone who translates knows, it's an exercise in recognizing limitations—both in one's language and in oneself. But I am guided by the ideal of a translation that makes it possible for the Buddha's body to speak, and to speak eloquently enough to generate the transformative moments of *saṃvega* ("aesthetic shock"[12]) that the *sūtra* itself envisions. The translator, like the *sūtra*'s preacher, must render the body constituted by the Buddha's speech in such a way that readers or listeners can experience the power of his sweet voice. And given the *Suvarṇa*'s strong interest in its own embodiment through performance, I want especially to privilege in my translation the complex relationship between form and content that becomes manifest in the present moment of oration. Doing so is particularly challenging, but also particularly important, because contemporary readers of English are accustomed to reading silently, and (arguably) most contemporary readers of Buddhist *sūtras* in translation—whether scholars, students, or practitioners—are accustomed to reading them as repositories of doctrine, not as performative embodiments of the Buddha. How do I translate *that*? And how do I translate it in such a way that it renders contemporary readers uncertain about their usual ways of approaching

10. On the numerous problems with assuming the centrality of "belief" as currently defined in those traditions we designate "religions," see Asad 2012; Latour 2014; Lopez 1998; Orsi 2012; Smith 1979.

11. On performance, performativity, and time in the *Suvarṇa* and the *Saddharmapuṇḍarīka*, see Gummer 2012; Gummer, 2020; Gummer, 2021.

12. The place of *saṃvega* in Buddhist literature and practice is examined in Brekke 2002; Brekke 1999; Coomaraswamy 1943; Heim 2003.

"religious" texts in general, and Buddhist *sūtras* in particular? I want my translation to make the process of reading sufficiently unfamiliar and uncomfortable to open up a space for developing new modes of engagement, without making it *so* uncomfortable that readers just close the book. A translation has the potential to challenge assumptions about what a *sūtra* is, and thereby to invite not only alternative interpretations of the *sūtra*'s content but also an alternative experience of reading.

Translating the Body of the Buddha

These goals may ultimately be unattainable, but they do provide a valuable touchstone as I translate. The notion of the text as the sonorous speech-body of the Buddha trains my attention on the complex relationship between form and content in the Sanskrit text. Some parts of the text are not so difficult to render in a way that I find reasonably satisfying, such as the verse I cited earlier. While capturing all the nuances of the Sanskrit is impossible (I am especially sorry to lose the sound play between the Buddha's golden color and his sweet voice—*varṇasuvarṇa/sarvasvarās-varasusvara*), I try to recreate some of the voiced, rhythmic, alliterative aspects of the language in English, and I translate verse as verse, with a meter that at least gestures toward the dactylic rhythms of the Sanskrit. I also try to preserve and draw attention to the repetition of phrases and images. For instance, since I translate the title of the *sūtra* (*Suvarṇa(pra) bhāsottama*) as "Utmost Golden Radiance," I maintain the same vocabulary for the related terms in the second line (*varṇa**suvarṇaprabhāsita**gātraṃ*), thus hinting, as the Sanskrit does so frequently, at the identification of the Buddha with the *sūtra*. And although the Buddha himself does not speak these lines, they are part of his speech-body, so I attempt to make them reflect, self-referentially, his rhythmic and resounding deep voice.

It stands to reason that verse would actually be easier to translate in a manner that conveys the oral, performative qualities of the text, since most contemporary readers of English are prepared to read verse differently than prose, and to notice and appreciate its formal and rhythmic qualities. But only about a third of the *sūtra* is in verse, and some of the prose passages are particularly challenging for contemporary readers. The longest chapter of the *sūtra*—and in Sanskrit, one of the most striking from the point of view of performative language—is the chapter on the Four Great Kings. It consists mainly of a protracted and intensely self-referential prose conversation between these deities and the Buddha about the power and efficacy of the *sūtra*. It lauds those who preach it and bear it in mind, and it catalogs the considerable benefits to be reaped by earthly kings who sponsor its performance. In other words, it self-referentially tells audiences how to perform and interpret the *sūtra* as a ritual of recitation, and offers strong incentives for doing so. When I teach this chapter using Emmerick's translation, my students' eyes glaze over before they hit the end of the first page. No insult meant to Emmerick—his is a straight rendering of the denotative content of the *sūtra* and doesn't pretend to be anything else. He doesn't differentiate prose and verse in any way, nor does he attempt to render the formal qualities of the language. These decisions have consequences, however: the very aspects of this long, intensely repetitive dialogue that could signal to readers its performative power—aspects that would be quite mesmerizing and potentially even shocking in a good oral recitation of the Sanskrit—are almost completely effaced.

Rhythmic repetition carries a significant portion of the meaning of this chapter, as the opening dialogue signals. The Four Great Kings wax eloquent regarding the virtues of the *sūtra* in a long series of parallel clauses all beginning with *sarva*. The passage ends with a pithy encapsulation of the *sūtra*'s agency.

> *ayaṃ bhadanta bhagavan suvarṇabhāsottama sūtrendrarājas* ***sarva****tathāgatabhāṣitaḥ* ***sarva****tathāgatāvalokitaḥ* ***sarva****tathāgatasamanvāhṛtaḥ* ***sarva****bodhisatvagaṇanamaskṛtaḥ* ***sarva****devagaṇapūjitaḥ* ***sarva****devendragaṇasaṃpraharṣakaḥ* ***sarva****lokapālastutaḥ stavito varṇitaḥ praśamsitaḥ* ***sarva****devabhavanābhāsitaḥ* ***sarva****satvānāṃ paramasukhapradātā* ***sarva****narakatiryagyoniyamalokaduḥkhasaṃśoṣakaḥ* ***sarva****bhayapratiprasrambhanaḥ* ***sarva****paracakrapratinivartanaḥ* ***sarva****durbhikṣakāntārapraśamanaḥ* ***sarva****vyādhikāntārapraṇāśanaḥ* ***sarva****grahapraṇāśanaḥ paramaśāntikaraḥ śokāyāsapraśamano vividhanānopadravapraśamayitā upadravaśatasahasrapraṇāśayitā* (Skjærvø 2004, 6.1.4–6.1.11; Nobel 1937, 64.6–65.6).

The *sarva* that begins each clause marks out a rhythm conveying the all-pervasive power of the *sūtra*. If a translator offers a literal rendering that privileges the English syntax (as Emmerick does[13]), this effect is erased. But retaining the emphasis on *sarva* that guides the Sanskrit syntax produces quite a different effect:

> O Illustrious Lord, this Utmost Golden Radiance, most sovereign of *sūtras*—
> all the *tathāgatas* utter it;
> all the *tathāgatas* watch over it;
> all the *tathāgatas* cherish it;
> all the assemblies of bodhisattvas revere it;
> all the assemblies of gods worship it;
> all the assemblies of lords of gods are elated by it;
> all the world protectors praise, laud, extol, and celebrate it;
> all the mansions of the gods are illumined by it;
> all beings are granted joy through it;
> all the sufferings of hell, the animal state, and Yama's realm are withered by it;
> all fears are allayed by it;
> all hostile armies are repelled by it;
> all the torment of famine is destroyed by it;
> all the torment of disease is expunged by it;
> all malevolent planetary influence is effaced by it.
> It is the creator of supreme peace,
> the destroyer of grief and adversity,
> the annihilator of various and sundry misfortunes,
> the demolisher of hundreds of thousands of misfortunes.[14]

13. Emmerick (1990, 25–26) translates thus: "Lord, this excellent Suvarṇabhāsa, king of sūtras, has been spoken by the Tathāgata, has been watched over by all the Tathāgatas, has been protected by all the Tathāgatas, has been taken care of by all the multitudes of Bodhisattvas, has been worshipped by all the multitudes of the gods, has been honoured by all the multitudes of the gods, has been praised by all the multitudes of the chief gods, has been honoured by all the world-protectors, has been praised, eulogised, extolled, shines in the dwellings of all the gods, bestows supreme blessing on all beings, dries up all the woes of the hells, the animals, the world of Yama, allays all fears, repels all foreign armies, removes all the oppression of hunger, removes all the oppression of illness, overthrows all the planets, creates supreme tranquility, removes grief and trouble, removes the various afflictions, destroys the hundreds of thousands of afflictions."

14. Note that I use visual emphasis as a translation technique, not merely as a way of facilitating comparison to the Sanskrit. This point is clarified further below.

Preserving and highlighting the parallel structure of these phrases allows them to accumulate in a tangible manner, building an edifice of rhythmic sound that supports the self-referential assertion in this passage of the *sūtra*'s pervasive power. I use visual structures to signal and highlight these audible effects: leading with the phrases that recur in the Sanskrit makes it much more difficult to miss their mounting intensity. Especially when uttered aloud, they produce a cumulative effect that strongly reinforces their content. In the Sanskrit, the same technique is employed throughout the chapter: in all the climactic moments of the dialogue, the prose shifts to a chantlike repetition that not only pleases the ear but also generates a heightened awareness of how the present moment of listening coincides with the content. This is the effect of the self-referentiality of such passages, especially in a context of oral performance. Someone listening to the preceding passage, for instance, would experience the coincidence of "all" the promised effects and their cause: the *sūtra* that is unfolding in the present moment. (This experience does not guarantee a specific response, obviously, but it does position the listener in relationship to the text in a way that encourages a response.)

In one such passage, the *sūtra* instructs the king of humankind as to how he should conceive of and make ritual preparations for the *dharmabhāṇaka*. The exalted status of the preacher and the radical "presencing" effect of the *sūtra* are established as much through the rhythmic beginning to each line of the passage—*adya*, plus the appropriate first-person pronoun—as through the specific content:

> *imāny evaṃrūpāṇi mahārājāna guṇānuśaṃsā saṃpaśyamānena tena rājñā dharmabhāṇako yojanāt pratyutthātavyaḥ | yojanaśatād yojanasahasrāt pratyutthātavyaḥ | tasya dharmabhāṇakasyāntike śāstṛsaṃjñotpādayitavyā | evaṃ cittam utpādayitavyaṃ*
>
> ***adya mama** śākyamunis tathāgato 'rhan samyaksaṃbuddha iha rājakule pravekṣyati | **adya mama** śākyamunis tathāgato 'rhan samyaksaṃbuddha iha rājakule bhojanam upabhokṣyati | **adyāhaṃ** śākyamunes tathāgatasyārhataḥ samyaksaṃbuddhasya sarvalokavipratyanīkaṃ dharmaṃ śroṣyāmi | **adyāham** anena dharmaśravaṇena avaivartiko bhaviṣyāmi anuttarāyāṃ samyaksaṃbodhau | **adya mayā**nekāni tathāgatakoṭiniyutaśatasahasrāṇy ārāgitāni bhaviṣyanti | **adya m'** atītānāgatapratyutpannānāṃ buddhānāṃ bhagavatām acintyā mahatī vipulā vistīrṇā*

> *pūjā kṛtā bhaviṣyati* | ***adya mama*** *sarvanarakatiryagyoniyamalokaduḥkhāny atyantena samucchheditā bhaviṣyanti* | ***adya mayā****nekānāṃ brahmendrarājatvakoṭiniyutaśatasahasrātmabhāvapratilaṃbhānāṃ kuśalamūlabījāny avaruptāni bhaviṣyanti* | ***adya mayā****nekānāṃ śakratvakoṭiniyutaśatasahasrātmabhāvapratilaṃbhānāṃ kuśalamūlabījāny avaruptāni bhaviṣyanti* | ***adya mayā****nekāni cakravartirājatvakoṭiniyutaśatasahasrātmabhāvapratilaṃbhānāṃ kuśalamūlabījāny avaruptāni bhaviṣyanti* | ***adya mayā****nekāni satvakoṭiniyutaśatasahasrāṇi saṃsārāt parimocitāni bhaviṣyanti* | ***adya mayā****cintyamahāvipulavistīrṇāparimitaḥ puṇyaskandhaḥ parigṛhīto bhaviṣyati* | ***adya mama*** *sarvāntaḥpuragaṇasya mahaty ārakṣā kṛtā bhaviṣyati* | ***adya mame****ha rājakula acintyā paramaviśiṣṭānuttarā mahatī śāntiḥ kṛtā bhaviṣyati* | *svastyayanaṃ ca* | ***adya mamā****yaṃ sarvaviṣaya ārakṣito bhaviṣyati* | *paripālitaś cānutpīḍitaś cākaṇṭakaś ca bhaviṣyati* | *sarvaparacakrānavamarditaś ca bhaviṣyati* | *anupasargaś cānupāyāsaś ca bhaviṣyati* | (Skjærvø 2004, 6.3.46–6.3.65; Nobel 1937, 80.18–82.9)

Keep in mind that the king (and any group of listeners) would, indeed, be hearing this passage *adya*, today, and from the *dharmabhāṇaka* himself, who is explicitly identified with the Buddha and destined to buddhahood. The form—the rhythmic repetition of *adya mama / adya mayā*—makes the content materialize *this very day*, as my translation attempts to emphasize:

> Great Kings, recognizing such virtues and benefits, the king should set out to greet the dharma preacher from the distance of a league; he should set out to greet the dharma preacher from one hundred leagues, from one thousand leagues. He must think of the dharma preacher as his teacher. He must think thus:
>
> "This very day, Śākyamuni, the *tathāgata*, the arhat, the perfectly awakened one, will enter my royal palace right here!
>
> This very day, Śākyamuni, the *tathāgata*, the arhat, the perfectly awakened one, will partake of a meal right here in my royal palace!

This very day, I will hear the dharma of Śākyamuni, the *tathāgata*, the arhat, the perfectly awakened one, which is spurned by the entire world!
This very day, through hearing the dharma, I will become one who will never turn back from unsurpassed, perfect awakening!
This very day, I will propitiate many hundreds of thousands of millions of *tathāgata*s!
This very day, I will perform inconceivable, vast, intense, lavish worship to the many hundreds of thousands of millions of past, present, and future *tathāgata*s!
This very day, I will be released from all the sufferings of hells, animal states, and Yama's realm!
This very day, I will plant the seeds of the roots of good merit so as to acquire many hundreds of thousands of millions of incarnations with the sovereignty of Lord Brahmā!
This very day, I will plant the seeds of the roots of good merit so as to acquire many hundreds of thousands of millions of incarnations with the status of Śakra!
This very day, I will plant the seeds of the roots of good merit so as to acquire many hundreds of thousands of millions of incarnations with the sovereignty of a wheel-turning king!
This very day, I will liberate hundreds of thousands of millions of beings from the cycle of rebirth!
This very day, I will gather an inconceivable, vast, immense, enormous, immeasurable mass of merit!
This very day, powerful protection will be provided for my entire retinue of courtesans!
This very day, inconceivable, wonderful, unsurpassed peace and success will be accomplished right here in my palace!
This very day, my entire realm will be protected, defended, and rid of oppression, obstruction, torment, misfortune, and devastation by hostile armies!"

This passage focuses attention on the present moment of preaching and hearing. It is followed by another, one of the most marvelous and convoluted in the chapter, where time completely collapses. The Four Great Kings and the Buddha discuss the amazing cosmological events that *will* take place when the *dharmabhāṇaka* preaches. This sequence culminates with the *dharmabhāṇaka*'s prediction to buddhahood by all the buddhas in the cosmos, who will throng to his side to hear him preach. And suddenly, the tense changes from the future to the perfect, and there they all are, present in the world narrated by the text—all the buddhas in the universe, offering him a prediction to buddhahood "in one voice." Here is the Sanskrit, beginning with the pronouncement of the Buddha to the Four Great Kings:

> *samanantaraprādurbhūtāni ca mahārājāna imāny evaṃrūpāṇi mahāprātihāryāṇi tāny anekāni gaṅgānadīvālukāsamāni tathāgatakoṭiniyutaśatasahasrāṇi taṃ ca dharmabhāṇakaṃ samanvāhariṣyanti | sādhukārāṇi ca pradāsyanti | sādhu sādhu* ***satpuruṣa*** *sādhu punas* ***tvaṃ satpuruṣa*** *yas tvam imam evaṃrūpam evaṃ gaṃbhīrārtham evaṃ gaṃbhīrāvabhāsam evam acintyaguṇadharmasamanvāgataṃ suvarṇabhāsottamaṃ sūtrendrarājanaṃ vistareṇa saṃprakāśayitukāmaḥ | na ca te satvā itvareṇa kuśalamūlena samanvāgatā bhaviṣyanti | ya imaṃ suvarṇabhāsottamaṃ sūtrendrarājānaṃ antaśaḥ śroṣyanti prāg eva udgṛhīṣyanti dhārayiṣyanti vācayiṣyanti deśayiṣyanti paryavāpsyanti vistareṇa ca parṣadi saṃprakāśayiṣyanti | tat kasya hetoḥ | sahaśravaṇena* ***satpuruṣa*** *'sya suvarṇabhāsottamasya sūtrendrarājasya anekāni bodhisatvakoṭiniyutaśatasahasrāṇy avaivartikāni bhaviṣyanty anuttarāyāṃ samyaksaṃbodhau |*
>
> *atha khalu tāni samantād daśasu dikṣv anekeṣu gaṅgānadīvālukāsameṣu buddhakṣetrakoṭiniyutaśatasahasreṣv anekāni tathāgatakoṭiniyutaśatasahasrāṇi svakasvakabuddhakṣetre pratiṣṭhitāni | tena kālena tena samayena ekapadenaikavācaikasvaranirghoṣeṇa tasya dharmabhāṇakasya bhikṣor dharmāsanagatasya etad ūcuḥ |*
>
> *upasaṃkram****iṣyasi tvaṃ satpuruṣā****nāgate 'dhvani bodhimaṇḍaṃ | pradarśay****iṣyasi tvaṃ satpuruṣa*** *bodhimaṇḍavarāgragato drumarājamūlopaviṣṭaḥ sarvatrailokyaprativiśiṣṭāni sarvasatvātikrāntāni*

> *vratatapaścaraṇabalādhānāny adhiṣṭhānāny adhiṣṭhitāny anekāni duṣkarakoṭiniyutaśatasahasrāṇi | samalaṃkar**iṣyasi tvaṃ satpuruṣa** bodhimaṇḍaṃ | paritrāy**iṣyasi tvaṃ satpuruṣa** sarvāṃs trisāhasramahāsāhasralokadhātūn | parāje**ṣyasi tvaṃ satpuruṣa** drumarājamūlopaviṣṭaḥ subhīmarūpaṃ paramabībhatsadarśanaṃ nānāvikṛtarūpam acintyamārasainyaṃ | abhisaṃbhot**syasi tvaṃ satpuruṣa** bodhimaṇḍavarāgragato 'nupamapraśāntavirajaskagaṃbhīrām anuttarāṃ samyaksaṃbodhiṃ | pravartay**iṣyasi tvaṃ satpuruṣā**ryasāradṛḍhavajrāsanopaviṣṭaḥ sarvajinābhisaṃstutaṃ paramagambhīraṃ dvādaśākāram anuttaradharmacakraṃ | parāhan**iṣyasi tvaṃ satpuruṣā**nuttarāṃ mahādharmabherīṃ | āpūray**iṣyasi tvaṃ satpuruṣā**nuttaraṃ mahādharmaśaṅkhaṃ | ucchre**ṣyasi tvaṃ satpuruṣa** mahādharmadhvajaṃ | prajvālay**iṣyasi tvaṃ satpuruṣā**nuttarāṃ dharmolkāṃ | pravarṣay**iṣyasi tvaṃ satpuruṣā**nuttaraṃ mahādharmavarṣaṃ | parāje**ṣyasi tvaṃ satpuruṣā**nekāni kleśaśatruśatasahasrāṇi | pratāray**iṣyasi tvaṃ satpuruṣā**nekāni satvakoṭiniyutaśatasahasrāṇi subhīmāt mahābhayasamudrāt | parimocay**iṣyasi tvaṃ satpuruṣā**nekāni satvakoṭiniyutaśatasahasrāṇi saṃsāracakrāt | ārāgay**iṣyasi tvaṃ satpuruṣā**nekāni buddhakoṭiniyutaśatasahasrāṇi ||* (Skjærvø 2004, 6.4.47–6.4.66; Nobel 1937, 89.10–91.4)

Once again, pronounced rhythmic repetition structures their prediction, through the key vocative phrase *tvaṃ satpuruṣa*, the steady string of future tense verbs, and the recapitulation of core images in the Buddha's description in verse of his own awakening in the preceding chapter, the "Chapter on Emptiness" (Skjærvø 2004, 5.23–5.24; Nobel 1937, 62.3–62.10). I attempt to evoke these syntactical and thematic echoes in my translation both in sound and in visual structure.

> "Great Kings, the moment that extraordinary marvels such as these appear, those many hundreds of thousands of millions of *tathāgatas*, equal in number to the sands of the river Ganga, will attend to the dharma preacher and bestow accolades upon him:
>
> " 'Wonderful, wonderful, honored sir! How very wonderful, honored sir, that you wish to fully elucidate this Utmost

Golden Radiance, most sovereign of *sūtras*, of such fine form, such profound meaning, such deep radiance, containing dharma of such inconceivable qualities! Those beings will not obtain just a trifling root of good merit who simply hear this Utmost Golden Radiance, most sovereign of *sūtras*—to say nothing of those who exalt it, uphold it, recite it, understand it, and fully elucidate it in an assembly! For what reason? Honored sir, just by hearing this Utmost Golden Radiance, most sovereign of *sūtras*, many hundreds of thousands of millions of bodhisattvas will become ones who will never turn back from unsurpassed, perfect awakening!' "

And then, everywhere in the ten directions, in many hundreds of thousands of millions of buddha fields, equal in number to the sands of the river Ganga, many hundreds of thousands of millions of *tathāgatas*, each ensconced in his own buddha field, at that very moment addressed the monk, the dharma preacher, on the dharma throne, with one speech, one voice, one sound:

"You will come, honored sir, in the future, to the seat of awakening!

You will display, honored sir, seated at the root of the king of trees on the glorious seat of awakening, powers attained through practicing vows and austerities, miraculous powers, hundreds of thousands of millions of arduous deeds—the most eminent in all the threefold world, surpassing those of all beings!

You will adorn, honored sir, the ground of awakening!

You will rescue, honored sir, all the three thousand world systems!

You will vanquish, honored sir, when you are seated at the root of the king of trees, the inconceivable army of Māra with its many hideous forms, that utterly terrifying vision, frightful in its appearance!

You will fully realize, honored sir, on the glorious seat of awakening, unsurpassed, perfect awakening, beyond compare, tranquil, pure, and profound!

You will turn, honored sir, when you are seated on the exalted, strong and solid, diamond throne, the

unsurpassed twelve-spoked wheel of the dharma, utterly profound, praised by all the victorious ones!
You will strike, honored sir, the unsurpassed, splendid drum of the dharma!
You will blow, honored sir, the unsurpassed, splendid conch of the dharma!
You will raise, honored sir, the unsurpassed, splendid banner of the dharma!
You will light, honored sir, the unsurpassed, splendid torch of the dharma!
You will rain down, honored sir, the unsurpassed, splendid rain of the dharma!
You will vanquish, honored sir, those many hundreds of thousands of enemies, the afflictions!
You will rescue, honored sir, many hundreds of thousands of millions of beings from the terrifying, vast ocean of fear!
You will liberate, honored sir, many hundreds of thousands of millions of beings from the cycle of rebirth!
You will propitiate, honored sir, many hundreds of thousands of millions of buddhas!"

These elements of repetition in the *sūtra*'s language, so central to its potency in the Sanskrit original, lie precisely at the intersection of its form and its content and contribute mightily to its affective power and to its presencing effect—in this case, the bizarre and wonderful effect of all the buddhas in the universe predicting the *dharmabhāṇaka* who stands before you to buddhahood—in one voice: *his* voice. As he embodies the speech of all buddhas, the prediction he speaks is realized. No wonder the Four Great Kings then burst out in verses praising the Buddha, who responds with verses praising the *sūtra*. No wonder that the Four are then shaken by intense *saṃvega* and exquisite bodily pleasure, burst into tears, and vow to protect the *dharmabhāṇaka* at all costs.

Aspects of this performative tour de force, especially the ritual cosmology from which its manipulations of language gain their power and coherence, are, in the end, untranslatable. How can one capture in an English translation the rich history of South Asian sacrifice that informs and enlivens this textual construction of the Buddha's body? I can gesture toward that history in an introduction, of course, but such nuances can only be subtly hinted at in translation. The formal aspects of the text, however, through which so much is conveyed when the *sūtra* is recited, are more amenable to translation. As these examples indicate, I aim to preserve aspects of the Sanskrit syntax that are crucial to its rhythmic cadence and to mark that cadence visually, so as to encourage readers to be aware of the sound qualities of the *sūtra* and make the crucial role of sound and rhythm in materializing the meaning and efficacy of the *sūtra* unmistakable. Through these strategies, I attempt to signal to contemporary silent readers of English the ways in which form and content might converge in the orated text, with the aim of at least opening up the possibility of reading the *sūtra* as the Buddha's speaking body.

Conclusion: Speaking in the Present

While I don't claim either that my interpretation of the *sūtra* is definitive or that the approach to translation I have begun to sketch out here is somehow superior to others, I do suggest that reading and translating the Sanskrit *sūtra* in light of the South Asian sacrificial cosmos illuminates heretofore underappreciated aspects of Mahāyāna literature and thereby opens up new potential approaches to translation. Indeed, the logic of substitution that lies at the heart of sacrifice—the logic that the bodhisattva refuses with his self-sacrifice, but that the Buddha embraces by offering his transformative speech-body for the consumption of listeners—offers provocative perspective on translation, a sacrificial process of substitution if ever there was one. And just as the Buddha's dharma-body, the *sūtra*, makes the Buddha present and accessible to new audiences when it is preached with eloquence, so too a translation offers the possibility of hearing the Buddha's voice speak in a new language, to new audiences. The translated *sūtra* is a substitute body, and whether that body is a dead relic of the past or a living voice that speaks in the present depends in part on the translation. Like the *dharmabhāṇaka*, the translator enables the Buddha's body to continue speaking—but only if she renders the text with sufficient eloquence.

The translator conveys more than the mere meaning of the words in the text: deliberately or no, she also conveys to the reader a set of implicit instructions on how to read the text. If the translator approaches the text as a dry doctrinal tome without any relevance to the present, it will become such a text in translation. But the *Suvarṇa* and related *sūtra*s are deeply concerned with enabling the bodily presence, and bodily gift, of the Buddha to continue on into the future. The performative, affective, and expedient aspects of the text, so often obscured in translations that approach *sūtras* as repositories of doctrine, bring it to life and help readers to interpret it in a very different way. And they offer scholars opportunities for rethinking and critiquing present practices—including, but not limited to, translation practices. That is the most exciting reason I know to read and translate Buddhist texts: to make what some take to be past and dead suddenly vital and challenging and provocative again—to translate the body of the Buddha.

References

Asad, Talal. 2012. "Thinking about Religion, Belief, and Politics." In *The Cambridge Companion to Religious Studies*, edited by Robert A. Orsi, 36–57. New York: Cambridge University Press.

Boucher, Daniel. 2008. *Bodhisattvas of the Forest and the Formation of the Mahāyāna: A Study and Translation of the Rāṣṭrapālaparipṛcchā-sūtra*. Honolulu: University of Hawai'i Press.

Brekke, Torkel. 1999. "The Religious Motivation of the Early Buddhists." *Journal of the American Academy of Religion* 67, no. 4: 849–866.

———. 2002. *Religious Motivation and the Origins of Buddhism: A Social-Psychological Exploration of the Origins of a World Religion*. Curzon: Routledge.

Carpenter, David. 1992. "Language, Ritual and Society: Reflections on the Authority of the Veda in India." *Journal of the American Academy of Religion* 60: 57–77.

Collins, Steven. 1982. *Selfless Persons: Imagery and Thought in Theravāda Buddhism*. New York: Cambridge University Press.

———. 1998. *Nirvana and Other Buddhist Felicities*. Cambridge: Cambridge University Press.

Coomaraswamy, Ananda K. 1943. "Samvega, 'Aesthetic Shock.'" *Harvard Journal of Asiatic Studies* 7: 174–179.

Emmerick, Ronald. E. 1990. *The Sūtra of Golden Light: Being a Translation of the Suvarṇabhāsottamasūtra*. 2nd ed. Oxford: Pali Text Society.

Freedman, Yitzhak. 2012. "Altar of Words: Text and Ritual in Taittirīya Upaniṣad 2." *Numen* 59: 322–343.

Gummer, Natalie. 2012. "Listening to the *Dharmabhāṇaka*: The Buddhist Preacher in and of the Sūtra of Utmost Golden Radiance." *Journal of the American Academy of Religion* 80: 137–160.

———. 2014. "Sacrificial Sūtras: Mahāyāna Literature and the South Asian Ritual Cosmos." *Journal of the American Academy of Religion* 82: 1091–1126.

———. 2020. "The Scandal of the Speaking Buddha: Performative Utterance and the Erotics of the Dharma." In *Buddhist Literature as Philosophy,*

Buddhist Philosophy as Literature, edited by Rafal K. Stepien. New York: SUNY Press.

———. 2021. "Sūtra Time." In *The Language of the Sūtras: Essays in Honor of Luius O. Gómez*, edited by Natalie Gummer. Berkeley: Mangalam Research Center.

Heim, Maria. 2003. "The Aesthetics of Excess." *Journal of the American Academy of Religion* 71: 531–554.

Jayawickrama, N. A., ed. 1974. *Buddhavaṃsa and Cariyāpiṭaka*. London: Pali Text Society.

Latour, B. 2014. *Rejoicing: Or the Torments of Religious Speech*. Cambridge, UK: Polity Press.

Lopez, D. S., Jr. 1998. "Belief." In *Critical Terms for Religious Studies*, edited by M. C. Taylor, 21–35. Chicago: University of Chicago Press.

Malamoud, C. 1996. *Cooking the World: Ritual and Thought in Ancient India*. New York: Oxford University Press.

———. 2002. "A Body Made of Words and Poetic Meters." In *Self and Self-Transformation in the History of Religions*, edited by D. D. Shulman and G. G. Stroumsa, 19–28. New York: Oxford University Press.

Mrozik, S. 2004. "Cooking Living Beings: The Transformative Effects of Encounters with Bodhisattva Bodies." *Journal of Religious Ethics* 32: 175–194.

———. 2007. *Virtuous Bodies: The Physical Dimensions of Morality in Buddhist Ethics*. New York: Oxford University Press.

Nattier, Jan. 2003. *A Few Good Men: The Bodhisattva Path According to The Inquiry of Ugra (Ugraparipṛcchā)*. Honolulu: University of Hawai'i Press.

Nobel, J. 1937. *Suvarṇabhāsottamasūtra—Das Goldglanz-Sūtra: ein Sanskrittext des Mahāyāna-Buddhismus*. Leipzig: O. Harrassowitz.

Ohnuma, Reiko. 1998. "The Gift of the Body and the Gift of Dharma." *History of Religions* 37: 323–359.

———. 2007. *Head, Eyes, Flesh, and Blood: Giving Away the Body in Indian Buddhist Literature*. New York: Columbia University Press.

Orsi, Robert A. 2012. "The Problem of the Holy." In *The Cambridge Companion to Religious Studies*, edited by Robert A. Orsi, 84–105. New York: Cambridge University Press.

Patton, L. L. 2005. *Bringing the Gods to Mind: Mantra and Ritual in Early Indian Sacrifice*. Berkeley: University of California Press.

Proferes, T.N. 2007. *Vedic Ideals of Sovereignty and the Poetics of Power*. New Haven, CT: American Oriental Society.

Skjærvø, P. O. 2004. *This Most Excellent Shine of Gold, King of Kings of Sūtras: The Khotanese Suvarṇabhāsottamasūtra*. Cambridge, MA: Department of Near Eastern Languages and Civilizations, Harvard University.

Smith, Brian K., and Wendy Doniger. 1989. "Sacrifice and Substitution: Ritual Mystification and Mythical Demystification." *Numen* 36: 189–224.

Smith, W. C. 1979. *Faith and Belief*. Princeton, NJ: Princeton University Press.

Chapter 3

On Reading *Vinaya*

Feminist History, Hermeneutics, and Translating the Female Body*

Amy Paris Langenberg

Introduction

The scene is Śrāvastī, North India, ostensibly during the lifetime of the Buddha. A monk is sitting on the ground, preparing to eat his midday meal. Another ascetic, a robed and shaven-headed woman known only as Gartodara's mother, stands by him, fanning his face and bowl to keep the flies away. She is also holding a pot of water, ready to fill his cup when he finishes his meal. Now gone forth into homelessness as followers of the Buddha, the pair had lived as husband and wife in their previous life as householders. As he eats, the monk makes conversation, bringing up some sore subject from long ago,[1] intuiting, perhaps, that it will irritate his wife.

*This volume had a long journey from conception to publication. Due to the extended timeframe, a revision of this essay has since been published in the *Journal of the American Academy of Religion* (Langenberg 2020). I wish to sincerely thank the editors of *JAAR* for allowing a version to be published here and State University of New York Press for including previously published work.

1. The Mahīśāsaka version of this text specifies that Gartodara's father had an affair while still a householder, which is the root cause of the tension between himself and his wife (Clarke 2014, 97).

She loses her temper, berates him, upends the water pot on his head, and proceeds to beat him about the head and shoulders with the fan handle. News of the disturbance reaches the Buddha, who issues a ruling that a nun shall not be permitted to stand by a monk with fan and pot (in the manner of a wife). If she does so, she has transgressed the discipline.[2]

This story from the prakritized Sanskrit *Mahāsāṅghika-lokottaravādin Bhikṣuṇī-vinaya* addresses the interleaving of marriage and monasticism and portrays the insubordinate figure[3] of Gartodara's mother. Shayne Clarke analyzes parallel versions of this story from the *Mahīśāsaka* and *Mahāsāṅghika vinayas* (in Chinese translation), the former of which, unlike our version, specifies the location of the interchange as being Gartodara's mother's dwelling place. He remarks upon the fact that the *vinaya* redactors "seem to assume that monks were able to enter nuns' residences freely, and to eat in the presence of their wives" (Clarke 2014, 97). For Clarke, *vinaya* stories like this one support his larger thesis that, despite its ideal of celibate homelessness, Indian Buddhist monasticism accommodated and legislated for various sorts of enduring family relationships. Although Clarke does not explicitly argue for it at length (and in fact argues against it at times), he is inclined to treat *vinaya* texts as our best evidence for "realia or social history," proffering *vinaya* literature as the antidote to a misleading overreliance on philosophically and doctrinally oriented *sūtra* texts in writing the history of early Buddhism (Clarke 2014, 17).[4]

2. *Pācattika-dharma* 79. Roth 1970, 216–217, §193.

3. According to Shayne Clarke, the Mahīśāsaka text describes her manner as "coquettish" or (as Clarke suggests in a footnote) possibly "diffident," depending on one's choice of translation (2015, 97n107).

4. In a signal article questioning the finality of *pārājika* 1, the monastic rule on expulsion from the order in cases of sexual behavior, Clarke remarks, "The picture that emerges suggests that, unlike other genres of Buddhist literature, the monastic codes provide us with glimpses of the values or concerns not necessarily of spiritual supermen or ascetic athletes, but of men who themselves may have been struggling to come to grips with what it meant to be a Buddhist monk in India around the turn of the Common Era" (2009, 4). After analyzing descriptions of pregnancy and briefly mentioning references to abortion, Clarke comments, "Although it is too early to tell how our vision of Indian Buddhist monasticisms might change if we take seriously the views both expressed and presumed by the authors and redactors of the extant canonical legal codes, it is beginning to appear that the Indian Buddhist *bhikṣuṇī*, for instance, may look very different from what we might assume and perhaps even from what some of us might want" (2014, 168).

Clarke, is, however, ambivalent. On the one hand, as his own work and that of his mentor, Gregory Schopen, richly attest to, *vinaya* texts are brimming with wonderfully gritty, real-feeling vignettes about life in the monastery. On the other, as Clarke himself argues, "the literary value of these narratives has yet to be fully appreciated, and the role of humour and comic sentiment in Buddhist texts—legal texts in particular—has yet to be fully recognized, much less studied" (Clarke 2009, 36). Returning to our entertaining narrative about Gartodara's parents, can this text or any other *vinaya* passage, or even *vinaya* in the conglomerate, be read as a keyhole text through which we may peer at the early community and learn how things "really were"? What are the limits of a historical approach that posits a strong relationship of mimesis between text and world? What, in general, are the problems and possibilities for making claims about the early female (or male) monastic community based on *vinaya* texts?

What follows is an attempt to answer these questions and, in doing so, reach for the baton proffered by Stephanie Jamison in her 2010 presidential address to the American Oriental Society. In her remarks, Jamison defended philology against its postmodern, feminist, and postcolonial detractors as a potentially powerful methodology for illuminating the lives of the ancient "subaltern," especially women. Though literary traditions of the ancient world are sometimes assumed to reflect the concerns of the elite male, and therefore to be useless for writing women's histories, Jamison insists that "texts are far more multi-valent, flexible, and multiply useful than they are given credit for." She also argues that "they can as easily subvert as assert the dominant paradigm." Moreover, if pressed at the right cleavages, disjunctures, and thin spots, "they can be made to reveal information about apparently invisible groups and topics" (Jamison 2011, 2–3). I concur.

A careful and savvy strategy for reading *vinaya* is particularly important for understanding the gendered history of Buddhist communities, not least because ancient Buddhist nuns have a tendency to continuously slip out of view. As I have argued elsewhere, ancient Buddhist nuns were social hybrids whose lives and ritual status were contested and poorly understood. As a result, their behaviors were often described and policed using norms associated with less contested social entities, such as married women, unmarried girls, or male ascetics (Langenberg 2013). A reading strategy for uncovering "the secret secret lives of texts," as Jamison has it, is all the more vital when the subaltern we desire to see and understand occupies such an unstable and distrusted social category.

The study of gender in early Buddhist texts has sometimes fallen prey to a tendency to generalize from isolated cases, or from one genre of literature, to conflate different types of "oppression" or "inequality" or, alternatively, to materialize instances of what looks like "equality" or "agency" or "autonomy" in order to produce a broad argument regarding nuns' status. Distortions and generalizations are perhaps inevitable features in a body of scholarship in its earlier stages of development, but, in the case of studies focused on the *vinaya*, they may also be the product of an impoverished engagement with broader hermeneutical and historiographic questions. In an attempt to confront head-on the issue of what the *vinaya* actually can tell us about the early nuns' community, this essay offers a survey of hermeneutical approaches in *vinaya* studies; articulates an approach based on accepted approaches within *vinaya* studies enhanced by innovations in the contiguous fields of religious studies, historical linguistics, comparative law, and *dharmaśāstra* studies; and makes some tentative observations about the possible relationship between nuns' *vinaya*s as texts and the realia of the early nuns' community based on this revised approached. These observations include the possibility that the ancient Buddhist nunnery was a place where monastic women exercised certain types of agency as practitioners, interpreters, and even authors of monastic discipline, despite their oft-mentioned subordination to the male community.

A Nuns' Monastic Code

For the purposes of this essay, I approach the hermeneutical and historiographical question of how to read a *vinaya* text in relationship to a unique example of the genre, the *Mahāsāṅghika-lokottaravādin Bhikṣuṇī-vinaya* (The Nuns' Monastic Code of the World-Transcending Great Assembly School), which contains multiple vivid tableaus of life in the ancient nuns' community. As Gustav Roth (who produced the 1970 critical edition of this text) and Ute Hüsken have noted, the *Mahāsāṅghika-Lokottaravādin Bhikṣuṇī-vinaya* exhibits unusual structural features that may relate to the intriguing questions of female autonomy and agency within the early community. Both draw attention to the fact that the story of the founding of a nuns' order and the promulgation of the eight *gurudharma*s are placed before the *bhikṣuṇī-vibhaṅga* (the commentary to the nuns' *prātimokṣa*), as an introduction (Hüsken 1997, 203–204; Roth 1970, xxix–xxx). Other *vinaya*s, including the closely related Chinese *Mahāsāṅghika-vinaya*, bury these passages later sections of the text, disconnected from the commentary on the *bhikṣuṇī-prātimokṣa* (Hirakawa 1982, 14–18). These topics, central to the self-understanding of nuns' communities, are, in other words, treated as miscellanea. Since the eight *gurudharma*s or rules to be respected are considered foundational and primary guidelines for the female community, placing them as an introduction to and in vital relationship to the *bhikṣuṇī-prātimokṣa* commentary makes for a far more coherent and accessible rulebook, from the perspective of the female community.[5] Moreover, whereas only those rules for *bhikṣu*s and *bhikṣuṇī*s not held in common are included in the *bhikkhunī-pāṭimokkha* of the *Pāli-vinaya*, the common rules are also listed in the *Mahāsāṅghika-Lokottaravādin Bhikṣuṇī-vinaya bhikṣuṇī-prātimokṣa* albeit in abbreviated form (Hüsken 1997, 202; Hüsken 1999).[6] In considering these unusual structural features, both Roth and Hüsken call attention to the "tendency . . . in regard to the arrangement and composition of our Bhi-Vin (Mā-L), the tendency being to supply a complete set of the Bhikṣuṇī-Vinaya as a whole which is consistent in itself" (Roth 1970, xxx; quoted at Hüsken 1997, 203).[7]

In his ponderings of the *Mūlasarvāstivāda-vinaya*'s vast bulk, and the processes that created it, Gregory Schopen comments on the increasing necessity for excerpted works through the middle period of Indian Bud-

---

5. Moreover, several *karmavācanā* or formal procedures are conveniently placed in the commentary of relevant eight *gurudharmas*. For instance, the ordination *karmavācanā* is placed after *gurudharma* 2, the "rule to be respected" that promulgates the *śikṣamāṇā* requirement.

6. Nolot writes, "Though its use presupposes the knowledge of and use of the corresponding code and related texts applying to monks. . . . it is meant as a complete manual for nuns" (1991, 525).

7. That the *Mahāsāṅghika-Lokottaravādin* redactors arranged their nuns' *vinaya* by their own lights is further suggested by the fact that some of the rules in the *prakirṇika* are *pācitiyya/prayaścittika* rules in other *vinaya*s. Another notable feature of this nun-centric text is that whereas the monks' community acts as an intermediary for the nuns' community in, for instance, the Pāli and Mūlasarvāstivāda traditions, whenever a situation arises requiring the Buddha's input, Mahāprajāpatī, credited with founding the Buddhist *bhikṣuṇī* community and a figure of great symbolic importance, is the messenger, communicating the nuns' concerns directly to the Buddha. It should be said, however, that it is not the only sectarian *vinaya* in which Mahāprajāpatī takes on this role as envoy.

dhism, "smaller, usable handbooks or collections" (Schopen 2000a, 96). Schopen's mention of "handbooks" resonates with the unusual structure of the *Mahāsāṅghika-Lokottaravādin Bhikṣuṇī-vinaya*, which is itself a sort of handbook, perhaps extracted from a larger "canon," and more portable and convenient for nuns to use. The unusually gendered nature of this particular "handbook" puts one in mind of Margaret Sanger's famous Little Blue Book for "working girls."[8] In its very structure, the *Mahāsāṅghika-Lokottaravādin Bhikṣuṇī-vinaya* invites us to engage in a feminist hermeneutic and historiography.

While this essay addresses hermeneutics, or the interpretation of texts, rather than translation in the most direct sense, the issues raised here are pertinent and parallel to issues of translation in at least three ways, all which Collett Cox addresses in her contribution to this volume. First, just as one's theoretical approach to a text, whether implicit or explicit, affects the hermeneutical keys one applies, in the same way, it inevitably affects translation practices, a point that Cox articulates in querying as follows, "How does our theoretical stance shape our translation practice and affect decisions about format, style, and level of discourse, about additional material such as the apparatus, introduction, and notes, and finally about the translation medium as print or electronic?" (00). Indeed, many of the issues raised here with respect to interpretation of *vinaya* within a feminist historiographic framework also apply to the project of translating *vinaya* from, for instance, Sanskrit into a European language. By way of illustration, this essay concludes with a specific example of a feminist reading drawing attention to the interpretation of particular Sanskrit words for female genitalia. Second, as Cox points out, what might be referred to as "higher criticism" or "literary criticism"—that is, practices of reading aimed at "uncovering meaning" (00)—cannot, in any case, be separated from so-called "lower criticism," that is, the detailed philological work of those engaged in the initial stages of editing or translating a text. The two

8. Published in 1920 and entitled *What Every Girl Should Know*, Sanger's book covers the basics of reproductive health and anatomy, sexuality, and venereal disease, and is dedicated "to the working girls of the world." The Little Blue Book series was itself a progressive publishing effort intended to make ideas, literature, and information more accessible to the working classes. It was certainly not the case, however, that copies of our text were similarly cheap or accessible, given the material culture surrounding written texts and the expense involved in their reproduction.

projects are, in Cox's words, "coincident and inseparable" (00). Hermeneutics, historiography, and translation practices are mutually dependent and intertwined. Finally, and most profoundly, just as translators must settle the question of just what kind of thing *is* the text they are attempting to translate, so must a particular text's interpreters. Translators and readers *both* must understand the genesis of any critical edition they create or utilize, make decisions about which redactions of the text they will rely on if there is more than one, decide whether to treat the text as stable and datable or subject to a continuous historical process, choose to interpret the text as if it is authored or set the notion of willed authorship to one side, and so forth. Thus, the issues that pertain in making historiographic and hermeneutical choices share a large area of overlap with questions related to translation, a point to which I will return.

Positivist Historiography and the *Vinaya*

The assumption that *vinaya* texts can be mined for historical information about the early community has been the implicit starting point of certain important works of Indology. For instance, in his 1956 monograph, *The Earliest Vinaya and the Beginnings of Buddhist Literature*, Erich Frauwallner compares the content of all extant *vinaya*s in the hopes of reverse-engineering an original text, which he refers to as the "old *Skandhaka*" and even describes as "the first great literary work of Buddhism" (Frauwallner 1956, 154). In this, he is motivated by the desire to uncover the beginnings of both Buddhist literature and "the Buddhist Church history" (Frauwallner 1956, 155). For Frauwallner, the "old *Skandhaka*," reached by discerning the common core of diverse *vinaya* traditions, can be presumed to represent more closely the situation of the early community than any sectarian text, a view that exists in some tension with his claims regarding its literary qualities. The underpinnings of Frauwallner's historiographical approach—that Buddhist *vinaya* texts provide access to the actual Buddhist world as it once existed—is shared by other Indologists of his and later generations, including critics such as Étienne Lamotte. Gregory Schopen's work, which seeks to illuminate the worldly, socially enmeshed early first-millennium monastic communities of Northern India, and which has dominated *vinaya* studies for several decades, employs a version of this inherited historiography, albeit replacing a quest for origins with a focus on the social history of a somewhat later period.[9] In the introduction to his translation from Chinese of the *bhikṣuṇī-vinaya* of the Mahāsāṅghikas, Akira Hirakawa also proposes this type of historiographically optimistic reading, remarking simply, "This volume is a translation of the precepts for *bhikṣuṇīs*. They provide much information about the daily life of the Order of *bhikṣuṇīs*" (1982, 1). Less concerned with origins than Frauwallner but still inclined toward a positivist historical reading of *vinaya* texts, Schopen and other scholars peer through the keyhole of the *vinaya* at the far-off world described therein.

Schopen, in particular, has examined narratives and rules about the business dealings of nuns as described in the *Mūlasarvāstivāda-vinaya*. More recently his analysis has focused on the ancient Buddhist nun as a legal person who may have engaged in business, called in promissory notes, or brought cases in court. In doing so, he states a wish to elucidate not "the religious subservience of the nun in Buddhist textual sources—about which we may have heard way too much" but "her legal status and her role there as an independent economic agent" (Schopen 2014, 114). Schopen's work has formed its own hub in a growing body of scholarship on the early nuns' community (Schopen 1997b; Schopen 2004; Schopen 2008; Schopen 2009; Schopen 2010; Schopen 2014a; Schopen 2014b). He is a master critical-historian, tracking terms and tropes through intertextual sleuthing and marshaling evidence from the material record to finesse his readings and question the text. He is also a sensitive reader of the Mūlasarvāstivāda tradition, knowledgeable about its idioms, attuned to variations of tone, and deeply aware (and appreciative) of its rich narratological features.[10] Schopen has essayed important interventions regarding the necessity of reading Indian Buddhist texts against material remains (especially inscrip-

9. He is apparently joined in this approach by Petra Kieffer-Pülz, who writes: "Unlike the primarily prescriptive Brahmanical law codes, the *Vinayas* contain narrative portions, commentaries, and casuistries, albeit to different degrees. These additional portions shed some light on the historical realities of the religious communities in which they were authored and subsequently redacted" (2014, 47).

10. For instance, Schopen has pursued the "stock character" of the *mahalla* or "silly, senile, and gullible old monk" across *vinaya* texts and comments on "un aspect burlesque" present in passages in which the *mahalla* appears (2010, 128–129). His seminal article arguing for the urbanity of early Indian nuns contains a long passage on the satiric dimensions of the character Sthūlanandā (2008, 253–255).

tions), written a seminal article on humor as a typical feature of *vinaya* texts, and drawn attention to a passage in the *Mūlasarvāstivāda-vinaya* that authorizes monks to supply standard place-names when the actual historical setting of a rule promulgation has been forgotten (Schopen 1991; Schopen 1997a; Schopen 2007). Despite these subtle readings of *vinaya* texts, which appear to express a sort of historiographical skepticism, Schopen has tended to sidestep the larger hermeneutical question of the relationship between text and world (Finnegan 2009, 35).

Narrativity and Representation

Diana Damchö Finnegan articulates a critique of this inherited Buddhological historiography in the first chapter of her 2009 dissertation, submitting that the nature of *vinaya* texts themselves compels the responsible reader to go beyond a hermeneutic that seeks to find "mimetic descriptions of actual historical practices" (2009, 41). Working from the Sanskrit *Mūla-sarvāstivāda-vinaya* texts found at Gilgit (abbreviated as MSV), Finnegan argues for a reading practice that foregrounds the highly rhetorical, literary nature of these materials. Her text, she notes, is rich with stories, and stories are not reportage. Furthermore, she suggests, certain even seemingly straightforward accounts of practices or happenings might be purely discursive constructs expressive of the concerns and preoccupations of the *vinaya* authors:

> When the MSV [*Mūlasarvāstivāda-vinaya*] recounts tales of unusual funeral or money-lending practices, or stories about the mischievous deeds of naughty monks, these might indicate such activity in the monastic communities when the MSV was finally redacted, or during one of its earlier layers of composition and agglutination. But then again, they might not. It might simply mean they were able to imagine such practices. . . . Alternatively, it might reflect the narrators' wish that their readers believe that the early sangha was rather badly behaved—perhaps so that the misdeeds of the narrator's contemporary monks might seem less egregious. . . . Or, quite possibly, the narrators feared that that monastics might one day engage in such activities . . . and fictitiously depicted such

> acts preemptively in order to prohibit them. Or perhaps what we see at any given moment arises from the obviously fertile imaginations of the consummate storytellers whose art dazzles us as we read the MSV. (Finnegan 2009, 28)[11]

As I interpret it, Finnegan's point is not that texts such as the *Mūlasarvāstivāda-vinaya* reveal nothing about ancient Buddhist social worlds, but that the hermeneutical strategy employed to illuminate those social worlds, the pathway from text to realia, must be explained and argued for, and that the literary and discursive qualities of the text must be taken very seriously. In this she stands close to the core position of Charles Hallisey who, also seeking to nuance Schopen's historiography, writes in reference to the *Pāli-vinaya*, "An important historical value of the canonical *Vinaya* lies in its being a coherent expression of a particular Buddhist *mentalité*. It will only be after we have learned how to combine our interest in 'what really happened' with a sensitivity to the changing thought-worlds of the Theravāda that we will begin to discern the historical reality behind the literary and archeological traces of ancient Buddhist monasticism" (Hallisey 1990, 208).[12]

Using *vinaya* as a window onto the world of the ancient Buddhist nun is an especially complicated project because, as Schopen himself observes, "we have to see her mostly through male, and often, disapproving, textual eyes" (2014a, 114). As several generations of feminist thinkers starting with Simone de Beauvoir have argued, representations of women are subject to gender norming, psychological projection, and mythos. Representational texts about women typically say more about the representer than the represented. Finnegan also makes this point when she writes: "Any reading that does not take into consideration the politics of representation is bound to be simply subjected to the authority of those

11. On the narrative exuberance of the *Mūlasarvāstivāda-vinaya*, which contains many stories not directly connected to any particular monastic rule, see also Yao 2015.

12. Related to Hallisey's interest in Buddhist texts as expressions of "a particular Buddhist *mentalité*" is Sheldon Pollock's call for a revitalized global philology that, understanding the historical-critical methodology to be a product of Western intellectual history and not a universal or hegemonic reading practice, takes indigenous exegetical practices seriously. An important example of scholarship that heeds Pollock's call is Maria Heim's excellent body of work on Buddhaghosa's commentaries (2014; 2018).

representations" (2009, 43). As an example of a *vinaya* passage subject to the processes of gender representation, consider the following from the *Mahāsāṅghika-Lokottaravādin Bhikṣuṇī-vinaya*:

> The Lord was staying at Śrāvastī. Sthūlanandā waylaid the nun Jetā who was on her way to Rājagṛha, saying, "You should stay here for the rains." She praised her to [local lay] families: "Āryā Jetā is excellent and full of good qualities, bound [by discipline], and restrained. Give her respect." [Jetā] approached those families, graceful when coming and going, observing, holding forth, wearing her monastic robes, and carrying her bowl. She was careful, upright,[13] steady, polite, and economical in speech. Gracious, she was pleasing to both gods and men. They honored her, greeted her, rose to meet her,[14] and offered her bowl, robes, and medicine for curing sickness. Sthūlanandā was not well turned out, did not practice good deportment, and had very dirty ripped robes [revealing] great breasts hanging down like gourds and large buttocks.[15] She was arrogant, unseemly, frivolous, fractious, and garrulous in her speech. [The families] did not respect her and did not host her. She threw [Jetā] out, gesticulating and saying things. The nuns related this incident to Mahāprajāpatī, who told the Lord. The Lord caused Sthūlanandā to be summoned and questioned her. The

13. The word I translate here as "upright," *unnaḍa*, is problematic. Nolot translates it as "without arrogance (*sans arrogance*)" (1991, 315). According to Bryan Geoffrey Levman's research on this term, Norman translates it as "unseemly" or "frivolous." Edgerton follows Kern in tracing it to Sanskrit *unnata* (raised, elevated). Norman traces the word to the Sanskrit word for "reed" (*naḷa*): that which is *unnaḍa* is like a raised reed—though prominent, it is, in fact, empty (Levman 2014, 293–297).

14. Sanskrit: *pratyutthihenti*. A parallel term appears in *dharmaśāstra* discussions of proper forms of greeting. See discussion under heading "Reading across and beyond Sectarian *Vinaya* Traditions."

15. The same or similar wording in parallel passages comparing Sthūlanandā or her breasts to gourds appears at Roth §139, §140, and §220. Sthūlanandā's large and unruly breasts also receive disciplinary attention at *prakīrṇaka* 24, after she is sighted performing walking meditation wearing no upper garment besides her breast-binding cloth (Roth 1970, 313, §277; Nolot 1991, 353–354).

> Lord said, "You have done badly, [Sthūlanandā]. Whichever nun says to another nun, 'You should stay here during the rainy season,' and then later throws her out or causes her to be thrown out, has committed an offense requiring expiation.[16]

As noted by several scholars, the nun Sthūlanandā (literally, "Fat and Happy") is a stereotyped recurring character in the *bhikṣuṇī-vinayas* whose function is to demonstrate uncouth, undisciplined behaviors so that they might be properly recognized and managed (Ohnuma 2013; Schopen 2008). Satirical stories of Sthūlanandā dramatize the female face of monastic undiscipline, including but not limited to problems with lay relations, disobedience, crassness, and sometimes, as here, the immoderate and aesthetically transgressive female body.[17] Sthūlanandā's characterization in our *vinaya* text as physically oversized and unattractive complies with aesthetic rules governing the representation of the disgusting or ugly woman. In fact, neither the rule nor the contextualizing story absolutely require any mention of Sthūlanandā's pendulous gourdlike breasts or large buttocks. The essential points could have been made with references to her behaviors alone; after all, nuns with more modestly sized breasts and buttocks are capable of poor hygiene, poor deportment, arrogance, crassness, garrulousness, and frivolity.[18] The argument that a nun called Sthūlanandā *really did* have pendulous breasts and large buttocks is, pardon the pun, a thin one. As stock images of uncouth femininity, these outsized and ungainly physical features serve the representational project of this passage from the *vinaya*.

16. *Pācattika-dharma* 136. Roth 1970, 285–286, §247. Nolot 1991, 314–316. My translation with reference to Nolot.

17. Sthūlanandā stories regularly reference her bodily functions. In one narrative, she enters the town to beg for alms with menstrual blood running down her legs (Langenberg 2016, 172). In another, she is described as eating and drinking so much that she is "full of shit and piss," leading to her need for a chamber pot, the contents of which she then deposits over the wall onto the head of a passing officer of the court (Schopen 2008, 242). See Handy (2016) for a similar reading of this passage.

18. Of relevance here is Susanne Mrozik's analysis of "virtuous bodies" in *sūtra*, narrative, and commentarial literature. Mrozik's work illuminates the physicality of virtue in the Indian Buddhist ethical worldview, the assumption that virtue is marked on the body (2006, 21–24; 2007). It could be argued that this Buddhist ethical principle may underlie the reference to Sthūlanandā's ungainly physique. The text itself, however, makes no such argument.

In short, stories about Sthūlanandā, and other nuns, must be read critically and suspiciously with due attention paid to "the politics of representation." Not only this, representational stories must be distinguished from and read comparatively with other texts from the *bhikṣuṇī-vinaya* literature that are not as subject to gendered representational interpolations. This ought to be done explicitly and systematically through the application of a stated exegetical strategy lest a representation be taken for a description and vice versa.[19]

Irrelevance, Counterargument, Imaginaire

Historical interpretations of *vinaya* involve a number of further complications and strategies specific to the genre, some of which have been at least partially theorized by *vinaya* scholars.[20] Though full of real-seeming

19. Furthermore, as Finnegan queries in her historiographic critique, how can one justify using a piece of evidence like the *Mūlasarvāstivāda-vinaya*, which belongs to no single period, as historical documentation (2009, 38)? If we in fact do think that, as Hirakawa claims, the *Mahāsāṅghika Bhikṣuṇī-vinaya* "provides much information on the daily life of the Order of *bhikṣuṇīs*," which nuns are we to assume it gives us information about? The conceit of the text is that it recounts interactions and activities of female ascetics that lived during the Buddha's time, but this literalist reading is impossible for serious historians. If we read it as describing the female community living at the time of the texts' redaction, we must then settle the date of the text, a task that is never straightforward in ancient South Asia. Prebish (1996) believes the Mahāsāṅghika *vinaya* tradition as a whole to be the most ancient of all. Tournier dates the rise of the *Lokottaravāda* as an autonomous school to the early centuries of the Common Era (2012, 94). According to B. P. Sinha, Roth dates the *Mahāsāṅghika-lokottaravāda Bhikṣuṇī-vinaya* to the second or third century BCE, so, sometime after the second council split (1970, front matter). Faxian carried the *Mahāsāṅghika-vinaya*, a text very close in content and sectarian affiliation to the *Mahāsāṅghika-lokottaravāda Bhikṣuṇī-vinaya*, from Pātaliputra to China in the early fifth century CE, perhaps providing a *terminus ante quem* for our text.

20. The most comprehensive methodological discussion in *vinaya* studies that I have found is Nicholas Witkowski's work on *pāṃśukūlika* (2017, 268–271). Witkowski addresses the possiblity of mining *vinaya* texts for what he calls "anthropological" information about the ancient community explicitly and at length. Like Clarke, his methodological approach to reading *vinaya* texts is beholden to Nattier's theorizations of history and normativity in her 2003 study of the *Ugraparipṛcchā*.

vignettes about life in the monastery and pragmatic assessments of human inadequacies, *vinaya* texts still fall into the category of the "normative." *Vinaya* hides its own complex textual history, attributing all monastic precepts to the Buddha, and is centrally concerned with legislating ideals rather than recording the realities of monastic life. In response to the problems of locating history in normativity, Jan Nattier borrows a hermeneutical principle from New Testament studies she terms "the principle of irrelevance." This principle says that "we may draw with some confidence on data found within a normative text . . . when incidental mention is made of items unrelated to the author's primary agenda" (Nattier 2003, 66; quoted at Clarke 2014, 16). The key to this principle is that certain conditions or behaviors are assumed to be standard by the *vinaya* compilers and are mentioned without comment on the way to making some other point. Thus, when Gartodara's mother's water pot and Gartodara's father's water cup are mentioned incidentally, we can confidently assume ancient monastics sometimes took water with their meals. The difficulty of applying this principle lies in deciding which details count as incidental, and in locating other hermeneutical principles for deciding upon the historical authenticity of other, less incidental details. Though he explicitly endorses this principle, for instance, Clarke does not always limit his historical inferences only to irrelevant or incidental items. For example, he takes the range of monastic rules focused on pregnancy and breastfeeding as evidence that renunciant Buddhist women in India "seem not to have seen the paths of 'reproduction or retreat' as necessarily mutually exclusive," even though reproduction is not incidental to those places in the text (2014, 149).[21]

Another commonly evoked rule of *vinaya* interpretation says that because certain precepts were promulgated and recorded doesn't necessitate that they were known or followed. In fact, it has been suggested that the presence of rules prohibiting a certain behavior implies that behavior

---

21. At other moments, however, Clarke strikes a note of caution. Citing a story in which the nun Sthūlanandā carries away an aborted fetus in her alms bowl, he asks: "Is the mention of a nun's disposal of an aborted fetus simply a narrative flourish? Or do we need to take this account seriously?" (2014, 168). From a perspective that centers issues related to unequal social position, this story about young women's efforts to conceal reproductive events that might threaten their status and safety in the family appears uniquely realistic.

was common within a community of monks and nuns.[22] This exegetical principle, which Nattier calls "the principle of counterargument" (2003, 67), is the basis for some of Schopen's best-known readings of *vinaya* texts about nuns. For example, he interprets a series of Mūlasarvāstivāda rules limiting the economic activities of nuns, including the selling of liquor and pimping of prostitutes, as indicative of the economic hardship of nuns and their consequent involvement in various female-accessible business enterprises (Schopen 2009; Schopen 2014b, 119).[23] Obviously, this reverse style of reading also needs to be selectively deployed. Rules forbidding monks to ordain *nāgas* or contort so as to insert their male organs in various of their own orifices should perhaps not be taken to reflect common practices. Again one is faced with the question raised by Finnegan: which rules directly reflect a real historical social landscape, and which belong to the realms of gender representation, literary flourish, normativity, or legal casuistry?

Nicholas Witkowski, whose methodological approach to *vinaya* materials is explicitly articulated and argued for in a recent article, and who owes much to both Nattier and Schopen, evokes a further reading practice, aimed at "utiliz[ing] *Vinaya* cases in order to articulate the views of the authors and the compilers" (Witkowski 2017, 270). This approach emphasizes the *attitudes* of *vinaya* compilers when they articulate certain rules. It discloses "anthropological" information relating not to visible shared behaviors but to the interior thought processes of ancient monastics, especially the *vinayadhāra*s, or monastic "lawyers." Witkowski's marking of this approach, which he characterizes, quoting Schopen, as "the presentation of . . . presentations," is helpful as it makes visible an important dimension of *vinaya* reading practice: the mapping of a cohesive and stable worldview informing monastic life (quoted in Witkowski 2017, 270). Schopen's "presentation of presentations" loosely resembles Hallisey's idea of "*mentalité*" and acknowledges the rhetorical nature of *vinaya* texts.

22. See Witkowski 2017, 269–270.

23. In the later article (originally published in 2012), Schopen briefly mentions that "both Guṇaprabha and other Indian sources indicate that, as in medieval Europe, distilling, brewing, and selling alcohol was preeminently women's work (*gṛhiṇīsilpa*)." In a note, he mentions the intention to treat these corroborating sources in greater detail in a future essay (Schopen 2014b, 119 and n5).

Working across genres of Pāli Buddhist literature (not primarily *vinaya*), Steven Collins references a similar idea with the term "imaginaire," which he glosses, following Jacques LeGoff, as the "imaginative world constituted by texts," and which he recognizes as existing in some relationship to the so-called real world. He writes, "Such worlds are, by definition, not the same as the material world, but insofar as the material world is thought and experienced in part through them, they are not imaginary in the sense of being false, entirely made up" (Collins 1998, 72–73).[24]

Practical Canons and Textual Communities

Vinaya scholars now mostly agree that their sources can't simply be read as faithful descriptions of ancient monastic communities at the time of redaction, if such can be identified, although, as we have seen, some are more historiographically optimistic than others. Steven Collins and Anne Blackburn provide an addendum to an optimistic historiography with their argument that *vinaya* texts also cannot simply be assumed to constitute enduring blueprints for monastic life from the time of redaction forward. The canonical status of *vinaya* texts in no way guarantees their use in particular monastic communities then or now. In examining the formation and significance of the Pāli canon, Steven Collins argues, "the actual importance of what we know as the Pali Canon has not lain in the specific texts collected in that list, but rather in the *idea* of such a collection." He further avers, "If we wish to delineate the actual canon or canons . . . in use at different times and places of the Theravāda world, we need empirical research into each individual case, not a simple deduction from the existence of the closed *tripiṭaka*" (Collins 1990, 104). Anne Blackburn's discussion of practical versus formal canons in Theravāda traditions (which she develops in conversation with Collins's work) is pertinent. On the subject of monastic discipline, Blackburn avers that, while the formal canon (*vinaya-piṭaka*) is symbolically important, it has

24. Witkowski himself, however, seemingly less caught up in the question of how "imaginary worlds" interpenetrate material worlds, regards the principles of irrelevance and counterargument to be more crucial to rendering the social facts of the ancient monastic landscape.

not been, in many cases, actually read or used for day-to-day discipline, at least not in a full and complete way. For instance, medieval communities in Sri Lanka seeking to train monastics and clarify disciplinary questions employed a "practical canon" consisting in certain ethically relevant *sutta* texts and a *vinaya* digest (Blackburn 1999).[25] Finnegan reminds us of a similar situation in Tibetan monasticism, where Mūlasarvāstivāda monks memorize and debate Guṇaprabha's *Vinayasūtra*, a *vinaya* digest, and leave the canonical *vinaya* on its shelf by the main altar, wrapped up in silk (2009, 25–26).[26] Since it appears to have been edited in such a way as to create a "usable handbook," the *Mahāsāṅghika-Lokottaravādin Bhikṣuṇī-vinaya* might have served as a practical and formal canon simultaneously.

Developments in the area of Buddhism and law (which I am distinguishing from *vinaya* studies proper) offer further perspectives on the complex issues at play in *vinaya* redaction and reception. Scholars, mostly working in later periods than the one to which the *Mahāsāṅghika-Lokottaravādin Bhikṣuṇī-vinaya* and the other sectarian *vinaya*s belong, are examining the historical relationships between civil or state law and Buddhist law. For instance Christian Lammerts's chapter in the edited volume by Cambridge University Press, *Buddhism and Law: An Introduction*, describes the intricacies of monastic inheritance in seventeenth-century Burma, showing that it did not fall under the exclusive jurisdiction of *vinaya*, and that at the same time, *vinaya* was appropriated for application to the lay community (Lammerts 2014). Lammerts's work in Burmese materials is one example of how the authority of *vinaya* texts has been mediated, its proscriptions subject to interpretation and enforced by politically important nonmonastics such as the king or by civil bodies like the court. Why

25. Arguing from the perspective of material culture and the production of palm leaf manuscripts, Stephen Berkwitz (2009) also comments on the inaccessibility of the canon and the variability of its physical written form in premodern Sri Lanka.

26. Hallisey echoes these observations: "Theravādins found the *Vinaya* both too little and too much. They found it too little in so far as the canonical text required elucidation and clarification, and, as a result, massive commentaries and glossaries were written on it. . . . they found it too much in so far as the size of the canonical *Vinaya* made it unwieldy and they consequently wrote diverse summaries and compendiums. . . . This associated literature makes relating the canonical *Vinaya* to actual practice in diverse contexts more complex than has generally been admitted by students of Buddhism" (1990, 206–207).

wouldn't similar processes of mediation and adaptation and interpretation have taken place within ancient Buddhist cultures?

In fact, the *Mahāsāṅghika-Lokottaravādin Bhikṣuṇī-vinaya* does contain narrative examples of monastic and nonmonastic law intersecting. For instance, in *Saṅghātiśeṣa* 4, Sthūlanandā clashes with a community of naked ascetics, her next-door neighbors, over a collapsed wall and attempts to resolve the dispute by consulting a council or tribunal (*āsana*) on behalf of her community.[27] Although the tribunal rules in the nuns' favor, the resulting bad feeling leads the Buddha to promulgate a rule forbidding nuns to enter into legal disputes with laypeople and renouncers alike. The rule further specifies that should a nun bring a complaint to the king's court (*rājakula*) or a tribunal, it will constitute a grave offense (*thūlaccayaṃ*).[28]

Work by Lammerts and others in the field of Buddhism and law documents a dynamic reception of canonical texts within lay and monastic communities. Lammerts's seventeenth-century Burma is arguably an example of what Blackburn calls "textual community," defined as "those who participate in shared practices of reading, writing, listening, interpretation, and performance, with reference to the same body of texts (perhaps, but not necessarily, a formal curriculum)" (Blackburn 2012, 164). According to Blackburn, thinking in terms of "textual community" corrects two major methodological mistakes: 1) textual reductionism, that is, assuming that a religion or a religious community is properly defined by an essence that is to be located in its major text or texts; and 2) "critical post-textualism," or rejecting texts completely in favor of practice. For Blackburn, a text is always also a practice.

Blackburn's idea of a "textual community" matches how certain contemporary monastic communities, existing in traditionally Buddhist cultures, appear to interact with *vinaya* texts. In an essay reporting and analyzing the proceedings of the 2007 Hamburg conference on reestablishing the *bhikṣuṇī* order in the Tibetan *saṅgha*, for instance, Ute Hüsken and Petra Kieffer-Pülz note divergent interpretations of monastic ordination among conference participants. While *bhikṣuṇī*s from the West (most of

27. Roth 1970, 106–107, §§139–140; Nolot 1991, 89–91.

28. Schopen has translated and discussed the significance of a parallel rule, albeit attached to a different narrative context, in the *Mūlasarvāstivāda-vinaya* and mentions that such a rule also exists in the *Pāli-vinaya* (2014a, 95–96; 2014b:,119).

whom would have received their *upasampadā* ordinations in Hong Kong, Taiwan, or Korea), and the academic scholars of the *vinaya* invited by the organizers, tended to regard the issue of higher ordination for women as a legal puzzle, a group of Himalayan nuns in attendance apparently held the view that ordination is a culturally rooted and ritually transformative event. They spoke of the importance of being ordained according to their own Mūlasarvāstivāda traditions as orally transmitted through their teachers, and in their own Tibetan language. This contextualized conception of *vinaya* discipline and procedure led the Himalayan nuns, who spoke only from the floor and were not given a place in the formal program, to adduce a greater skepticism than the Western nuns displayed (many of whom also belonged to Tibetan lineages) regarding the reestablishment of a *bhikṣuṇī saṅgha* within their tradition.[29] Hüsken and Kieffer-Pülz characterize the Himalayan nuns' reading of *vinaya* ordinances as "facilitating the performance of religion rather than as guiding legal acts" and argue that their reading is "a pointed reminder that rituals are grounded in day-to-day reality, and that they are subject to the same limitations as all other expressions of religious life." They further observe, "Although rules are the foundational framework, they can never cover all contextual issues, unless they are adapted when and as the need arises" (2012, 266). A strict legalistic reading of *vinaya* (which Blackburn would see as textually essentialist) obscures these necessary adaptions of canonical rules operating in local contexts.

On the face of it, Blackburn's hermeneutic may not appear to be fruitful for the study of a historical community such as the Mahāsāṅghika-Lokottaravādin nuns, who are evidenced mostly in a limited number of what might be called normative texts. How does one study a "textual community" without broad access to that community beyond its formal canon? I submit, however, that Blackburn's idea is potentially productive if, rather than regarding the *Mahāsāṅghika-Lokottaravādin Bhikṣuṇī-vinaya* as merely the text around which a textual community may have formed, we also view it as reflective of and the product of a textual community—that is, a group of nuns (and monks) who creatively interacted with and performed a shared body of disciplinary "texts," whether these were orally transmitted, transmitted through shared habitus, or by way of written documents.

29. See also Mrozik 2009.

Reading across and beyond Sectarian *Vinaya* Traditions

The notion of a universal and consistent translation of *vinaya* as text into *vinaya* as practice is made even more problematic by the fact that no two sectarian texts are identical. For this reason, it is now considered best practice for those interested in writing the history of Buddhist monasticism to read *vinaya* texts comparatively across the sectarian traditions.[30] Ingo Strauch's fascinating work on a *prātimokṣa* manuscript fragment from the Bajaur collection provides evidence that some Buddhist monastic communities were themselves engaging in intertextual *vinaya* comparisons. The fragment in question contains variations of the *naiḥsārgika pātayantika* section, written by the same scribe on obverse and reverse. One side more closely resembles the Theravāda *pāṭimokkha*, the other the Sārvāstivāda *prātimokṣa*. A marginal insertion made by the scribe clearly indicates that he had compared the two versions. Strauch proposes that this sort of intertextual comparison and analysis was part of a "process of harmonization" resulting eventually "in the emergence of generally accepted and supraregionally used canons with a codified and authoritative textual shape" (2014, 825). From the perspective of contemporary *vinaya* scholars, reading comparatively allows for better-informed interpretations of various details, affords a glimpse of innovation in particular local traditions of the type Hüsken and Kieffer-Pülz argue to be necessary and inevitable, and, as Strauch's study suggests, may in fact mimic the reading practices ancient monastic scholars themselves employed.

In light of Blackburn's notion of textual community, Hüsken and Kieffer-Pülz's observations regarding contemporary *vinaya* reception, and current best practices in the field, I suggest that historical analyses of *vinaya*

30. Kieffer-Pülz observes, "In order to learn about law from the *Vinaya*, we have to be aware that there is not just one vinaya, but several, and they stem from distinct schools, from different time periods, from different regions, and were adapted to their environments to different degrees" (2014, 61). Clarke avers, "If . . . we are interested in providing a balanced and nuanced picture of Indian monastic Buddhism, it seems certain that we will need to take the evidence provided by all extant monastic codes seriously, and this in turn will mean that the *Vinayas* other than the Pāli will warrant much more attention than the cursory glances they have so far been given" (2009, 38). Schopen writes, "We need no longer be implicitly or explicitly concerned primarily with the question of what Buddhist monasticisms originally were. We might be equally—and probably more fruitfully—concerned with what at given places and given points in time they had become" (Schopen 2000b, 86; quoted in Clarke 2009, 38n131).

texts should *also* involve reading against and for other "texts," *including* non*vinaya* Buddhist traditions, gendered representational traditions circulating regionally, modes of storytelling, and other formal and informal legal traditions pertinent to female status and female virtue whenever possible. In the case of the *Mahāsāṅghika-Lokottaravādin Bhikṣuṇī-vinaya* community, shared texts may have included female *vinaya* traditions, male *vinaya* traditions, *sūtra* traditions, and also other texts, practices, or oral teachings not located in the Buddhist canon. When we read in this manner, we become more attuned to complex social dynamics, acts of interpretation and adaptation, or differences of opinion within the community that may be reflected in the text. We also develop a better understanding of the redactors' knowledge of and sensitivity to widespread gendered customs and codes.[31]

As an example of reading the *Mahāsāṅghika-Lokottaravādin Bhikṣuṇī-vinaya* as a record of a textual community dynamically sourcing a range of oral and written texts, let us consider the first *gurudharma*, which requires a nun, even though she be ordained for one hundred years, to honor the feet of a monk with her head (*śirasā padā vanditavyā*),[32] though

31. Blackburn's "textual community" is related to what Richard Lariviere calls "customary practice." Lariviere, a specialist in Hindu legal traditions, argues that, while *dharmaśāstra* texts participate in a fiction about themselves regarding their ancient or timeless origins, in fact, they should be thought of as "records of custom." In other words they record the way of life of people living in various regions of ancient India at some certain time. Lariviere observes, "That the dharma literature is a record of custom is obfuscated by the fact that the idiom of all the dharma literature is one of eternality and timelessness. This means that there are no contemporaneous references which can help us to establish the chronology of these ideas, nor is there admission that custom and practice changed and evolved over time. It is further obfuscated by the fact that the dharma literature clings to the claim that all of its provisions can be traced directly or indirectly to the Veda, the very root of dharma" (2004, 612). A parallel rhetoric in the Buddhist canonical tradition is its assertion that all *vinaya* precepts were handed down by the Buddha himself during his lifetime. In a recent article, Timothy Lubin further explores the importance of custom in Hindu law, writing, "Passages from the *Baudhāyanaśrautasūtra* and numerous *gṛhyasūtras* show that already in these rulebooks established practices of particular social groups were accepted as a valid authority in certain contexts where explicit textual warrant was lacking, and that a further distinction was there made between the general norms of experts and the valid particular norms of locality or social group" (2016, 669).

32. Roth 1970, 17, §13.

he be ordained but one day. Again, a full reading of this rule would require (at minimum) a detailed comparison with other sectarian *vinaya* traditions, but for the sake of briefly exploring Blackburn's hermeneutic in relationship to our nuns' *vinaya*, only a reading against *dharmaśāstra* will be undertaken here. This reading is supported by the fact that the *Mahāsāṅghika-Lokottaravādin Bhikṣuṇī-vinaya* text uses similar vocabulary to *dharmaśāstra* on this topic, including the words *abhivādana* for respectful greeting, *añjali* for a cupped hand gesture, and *pratyutthāna* for the action of rising from one's seat to receive a respected guest. For instance, the commentary for *gurudharma* 1 describes the respectful greeting required of nuns as *abhivādana-vandana-pratyutthāñjalī-karma samīcī-karma* (Roth 1970, 22, §§19–21). The verb *pratyutthihenti* also appears in the story of Sthūlanandā and Jetā cited earlier (Roth 1970, 285–286, §247). This shared vocabulary suggests that the redactors of this *vinaya* were aware of traditions surrounding ritualized gestures of salutation of the type also codified in *dharmaśāstra* texts.

The *dharmasūtra* literature goes into some detail on *abhivādana*, the greeting required for superiors, including one's *ācārya* and one's parents.[33] This form of greeting requires a bent posture and the utterance of an appropriate phrase. It some cases, it includes the clasping of feet. In its description of *guru abhivādana*, the *Āpastamba Dharmasūtra* gauges the proper depth of the bow according to caste; a brahman does not bend at all, while a *śūdra* must bend "very low" (I.5.16; Olivelle 2000, 33). There is no need, the *Gautama Dharmasūtra* submits, to greet women other than one's mother, paternal uncle's wife, and sisters, except when returning from a journey (6.7; Olivelle 2000, 135). The *Baudhāyana* rules that a student past puberty need not greet his own brother's wives or the younger wives of his teacher (1.3.33; Olivelle 2000, 203). The *Gautama* states, "Some say there is no restrictive rule (*niyama*) about salutation (*abhivādata*) between husband and wife" (6.6; Olivelle 2000, 135). Regarding this, Julia Leslie points out that, were a rule to exist, it would govern the wife's salutation, not the husband's, as "a superior never salutes an inferior" (1989, 163). The wife's use of *guru abhivādana* would be problematic, however, because it requires reciting "I am (insert initiation name), sir!" Women, of course, do not receiving initiation names as they do not undergo the ritual of *upanāyana*.

33. *Manusmṛti* 2.117–133, *Āpastamba Dharmasūtra* 1.5.12–22, *Gautama Dharmasūtra* 6.1–11, *Baudhāyana Dharmasūtra* 1.3.35–34.

Namaskāra, bowing with hands joined in *añjali*, is another form of honorific greeting, associated in particular with venerating deities, honoring illustrious persons such as ascetics, and, in medieval legal commentary, wives ritually greeting their husbands (Leslie 1989, 162). In the brahmanic context, the connection made in later commentaries between wifehood and the ritual of *namaskāra* is sensible since women do not receive the special name at initiation that is supposed to be used in the *guru abhivādana* greeting and because a "good woman should always worship her husband like a god" (*Manusmṛti* 5.154; Olivelle 2005, 146). References to *namaskāra* do not occur frequently in the *dharmasūtra*s or in *Manusmṛti*.[34] The nominal *namaskāra* or various forms of *namas* √*kṛ* do, however, appear elsewhere in contemporaneous literature such as the *Mahābhārata* as well as in older Vedic texts such as the *Atharva-veda*.

In *gurudharma* 1, nuns, no matter how senior, must bow, head-to-feet, to any monk, no matter how junior. They are given a line to recite upon greeting a monk, just as Vedic students must utter a scripted greeting when meeting their teacher. In place of "I am (insert initiation name), sir!" that forms part of the *guru abhivādana* (*Āpastamba-dharmasūtra* 1.5.12; Olivelle 2000, 33), they are to say, "I honor the feet of all of the noble ones" (Roth 1970, 22, §21). *Gurudharma* 1 appears to improvise on the *abhivādana* salutation, and, in requiring them to greet monks head-to-feet, slotted nuns into the *śūdra* category. *Gurudharma* 1 may also draw on a *namaskāra* style of salutation, this time slotting the nuns in the wife's or propitiator's role vis-à-vis male monastics. An implicit reference to *namaskāra* occurs in the Pāli commentary to *garudhamma* 1. There the Buddha declares the necessity of *garudhamma* 1, using the excuse that followers of other ascetic sects will never bow to a woman, no matter how senior.

If we posit, then, that *gurudharma* 1 seems to be participating in the social logic and gestural traditions also described in these various *dharmaśāstra* contexts, we can speculate that it does so to establish a much-needed beachhead for socially vulnerable and ritually ambiguous nuns by analogizing them to *śūdra*s and wives and propitiators of ascetics (even though they may in fact be high caste, are no longer functioning as

34. Gautama advises avoiding both *abhivādana* and *namaskāra* while wearing one's shoes (9.45; Olivelle 2000, 141). Manu ordains that those who have suffered loss of caste due to heinous crimes should go without being honored (*nirnamaskāra*) (*Manusmṛti* 9.239; Olivelle 2005, 202).

wives and are themselves ascetics). It is important here to note that, for *dharmaśāstra* lawgivers, gender does not always take precedence over age.[35] For instance, sons are required to venerate their mothers. In this sense, then, *gurudharma* 1 departs from dominant *dharmaśāstra*-style logic in giving gender hierarchical precedence over age *in every case*. This innovation results logically from the intersectionality of the ritualized social positions (coded by gender, renouncer status, and seniority) legislated by the *gurudharma* 1 tradition. While wives in the *dharmaśāstra* system eventually become senior women and therefore hierarchically superior to some men, *śūdra*s never gain the upper hand over those of superior class,[36] and lay propitiators are never honored over ascetics, no matter how senior. Since nuns are analogized to wives, *śūdra*s, and propitiators simultaneously by the extremity of the *gurudharma* 1 salutation ritual, their social inferiority as women intensifies exponentially, as it were.

Making gender an indelible mark of social and ritual inferiority in this way, even in the case where the woman is so much older and an ascetic to boot, is unprecedented and may explain why the Buddha is depicted as making an extra effort to be clear and explicit regarding the unusual practice of having senior women bow to junior men. He specifies that all nuns, whether young, old, or middling, must respectfully salute all monks, whether young, old, or middling. He follows this explanation, which both clarifies and emphasizes, with a concession toward older or sicker nuns for whom a full head-to-foot gesture of respect is not physically possible (Roth 1970, 22, §§19–21).

The brief preliminary analysis of *gurudharma* 1 in relationship to brahmanic salutation rituals offered here approaches the text neither as a faithful description of actual behaviors, nor as a straightforward call for male privilege, nor as an expression of the Buddha's original vision for his community, but rather as the imprint of dynamic processes of social negotiation and interpretation taking place within ancient nuns' communities and between male and female *saṅgha*s. By being analogized to wives, social inferiors, and propitiators of ascetics vis-à-vis familiar rituals of salutation

35. *Āpastamba Dharmasūtra* 1.13.2–4 defines superiority in a very general sense as people of higher classes and those who are older.

36. *Gautama* 6.10 notes that a householder (who would be a bath graduate) need not formally greet an eighty-year-old *śūdra* (Olivelle 2000, 135).

and veneration, female ascetics—who occupy an ill-defined and controversial social position—are provided with a stable and unthreatening social footing within the communities of Buddhist ascetics, non-Buddhist ascetics, and laypeople alike, albeit at cost to their status. The additional commentary offered, ostensibly by the Buddha, regarding this unusual rule, and the concessions made toward elderly or unwell nuns, might be taken as evidence of female resistance to being made to ritually perform gender inferiority even beyond what is customary. In fact, the *Pāli-vinaya* tradition records such resistance in *Cullavagga* 10. There, Mahāpajāpatī, a senior woman in an elite household, accepts all the eight rules to be respected on behalf of herself and the five hundred Sakya women as conditions of initiation into the order. She raises questions only about the first, submitting, "It were well, Lord, if the Lord would allow greeting, standing up for, salutation and the proper duties between monks and nuns according to seniority" (Horner 1958, 5: 358). As was alluded to earlier, the Lord answers in the negative, referencing his need to be in step with "the followers of other sects" who will not "carry out greeting (*abhivādanaṃ*), standing up for (*paccuṭṭhānaṃ*), salutation (*añjalikammaṃ*) and proper duties towards women" (Horner 1958, 5: 358; Oldenberg 1880, 2: 258).

Feminist History: The Ancient Tampon

Reading nuns' *vinaya* texts to learn about the ancient nuns' lives necessitates responsiveness to their multiple modalities and a greater level of transparency and intentionality regarding the hermeneutic employed in any given interpretation than has been customary in the scholarly literature. Ideally, any such historical reading would take into account not just the principles of irrelevance and counterargument but also the historically layered and rhetorically complex nature of the text, and its dynamic status as a practice. It would do so not just implicitly but also explicitly, with some justification for the hermeneutical principles applied. I would like to offer a short reading of a small *Mahāsāṅghika-Lokottaravādin Bhikṣuṇī-vinaya* text, engaging previous work on similar material by Hüsken, in order to provide an example of how the reading practices I suggest might work as a suite to illuminate new perspectives on early Buddhist female monasticism.

Bhikṣuṇī prakīrṇaka 15 says that the nuns ruined bedding and seat cushions when they experienced their menstrual periods every month.

The Lord allowed them to "to wear a little cloth shaped like an axle pin (*ānīcolaka*) for the purpose of protecting the bedding and seating" (Roth 1970, 309, §268). Given the reference to its axle-pin shape, and a warning included in the text not to push it in too far, I interpret this device to be a roll of fabric worn like a modern-day tampon. This rule is located in the *prakīrṇaka* section, which corresponds to the *skandhaka* sections of *Pāli-vinaya*.[37] The *Pāli-vinaya* also contains a prescription to wear the *ānīcolaka* (P. *āṇicolaka*), also located in the *skandhaka* section of the text, specifically, in the *Cullavagga*.[38] A roughly corresponding rule from the *Mūlasarvāstivāda-vinaya*, located in the *prayaścittika* section of the *prātimokṣa vibhaṅga*, prescribes a cloth tied on with a string, but not one shaped "like an axle pin."[39]

Another rule in the *Pāli-vinaya*, located in the *pāṭimokkha* itself (*Pācittiya* 47) says, "When a nun uses the household cloth without relinquishing it, it is an offense requiring expiation."[40] *Āvasathacīvara*, the relevant Pāli term, is translated here as "household cloth," following Hüsken, who argues that *āvasatha* refers to a roadside lodging where ascetics stay overnight. She suggests, then, that the *āvasathacīvara* is a publicly kept menstrual cloth to be used by visiting nuns, washed, and relinquished to another nun (Hüsken 2001, 86–87).[41] Hüsken further proposes that *āvasathacīvara* is, at least in the context of this rule, a nod to brahman practice, which requires the menstruating wife to use a "stained cloth" (*malavadvāsas*) for three days and wash it on the fourth, signaling to her husband the return of her sexual availability (2001, 89–90). For Hüsken, then, the original function of the *āvasathacīvara* was ceremonial more than practical, designed to set the minds of ritually observant lay hosts at ease

37. Several rules that are found in the *prātimokṣa* proper of other *vinaya*s are moved to the *prakīrṇaka* section of the *Mahāsāṅghika-Lokottaravādin Bhikṣuṇī-vinaya*.

38. Horner interprets *āṇicolaka* to mean a "pin and a little cloth," rather than an axle-pin-shaped cloth (i.e., a tampon). The Pāli text mentions a thread tied around the thigh or hip to keep the *āṇicolaka* in place and makes no mention of inserting the *āṇicolaka* inside (Horner 2013, 5: 374).

39. Derge Kangyur 'dul wa (Vol. 9) Ta 299a7–299b.6.

40. My translation with reference to I. B. Horner's translation and Hüsken 2001.

41. In the commentary we encounter again Thullanandā (S. Sthūlanandā), who annoys her fellow nuns when she fails to relinquish the *āvasathacīvara* after the prescribed three days. Oldenberg, 3: 303, 20–25. Horner, 3: 198.

when potentially menstruating nuns came to stay. In other words, she argues that lay hosts wished visiting nuns to follow menstrual conventions, even though, as celibate ascetics, their sexual availability should not have been in question (Hüsken 2001, 95).

The idea of the "household cloth" as such is missing from the *Mūlasarvāstivāda-vinaya*, though there *is* a rule about relinquishing communally owned menstrual cloths.[42] Similarly, the *Mahāsāṅghika-Lokottaravādin Bhikṣuṇī-vinaya* does not reference the "household cloth" as such, although it does mention relinquishing communally owned menstrual rags in a passage about where and how nuns should wash their menstrual cloths (*prakīrṇaka* 18; Roth 1970, 310, §271). Interestingly, this passage and the several that come just before regarding laundry feature lay anxieties around the polluting quality of female blood.[43]

These small differences between various *vinaya* texts on the inglorious subject of female hygiene might reasonably be read as evidence of various Buddhist textual communities making adaptations in response to practical problems within the community and social pressures coming from the wider social environment. It seems that, at different points and in different places, Buddhist monastic communities formally incorporated two devices into their disciplinary system—the *ānīcolaka* (*āṇicolaka*) and the *āvasathacīvara*—both different from, but in one case functionally cognate with, the *malavadvāsas* of brahman menstrual law. As is customary in *vinaya* writings, these innovations are attributed to the Buddha; however, from a historical point of view, the Buddha is not likely to be responsible for introducing these innovations. Male monastic lawyers may have conceived and negotiated these provisions for nuns' monthly bleeding independently, but this also seems unlikely, especially in the case of the *ānīcolaka*, as it requires greater knowledge of female anatomy and reproductive functioning. It seems far more likely that the nuns themselves developed the practices these rules prescribe, as they inevitably possessed knowledge of the ritual sensitivities and pragmatic concerns surrounding menstruation that would have fallen outside of the experience of male monastics. These practices could then have been codified by monastic lawyers, perhaps in consultation with senior female monastics.

42. Here, Sthūlanandā stars again. *Prāyaścittika* 171 at Derge Kangyur 'dul wa (Vol. 9) Ta 299b.6–300a.6.

43. See Langenberg 2013, 92–93, for a translation of this series of rules.

Arguably, support for this analysis can be found in Timothy Lubin's careful study of custom as a legal principle in the Brahminic *dharmaśāstra* tradition, which we may take as contiguous with and contemporaneous to Buddhist law. Lubin's research finds that where "official textual warrant" is lacking, the customary practices of certain groups (especially qualified males of the brahman caste) could be counted as authoritative (2016, 669). However, Lubin observes, "valid custom is not merely a matter for learned, male Brahmins to pronounce on. In some contexts, at least, women and other social groups are acknowledged as authorities in ceremonial practice. This is particularly true in the case of ceremonies with relevance to women" (2016, 683). Although Lubin's research concerns Brahminic and not Buddhist law, at the very least it shows that women exercised legal authority in certain, albeit narrow, domains in ancient India.

Taking up Finnegan's imperative that we consider the literary qualities of *vinaya*, what do we observe about the rhetorical surface of our menstrual text? What mood or tone is deployed? Do we see the workings of culturally constituted gender representation in this text? While the story of Gartodara's mother is played for laughs, and the Sthūlanandā story exaggerates secondary sexual features in a misogynist manner, the menstrual text in question assumes a flat affect. The advice given is practical and straightforward and there is no engagement of humor, gender representation, or, notably, the poetics of disgust (a highly developed symbolic language in Indian Buddhism).[44] On this last point, this *vinaya* passage stands in contrast to Buddhist *sūtra* and *śāstra* texts eloquent on the subject of polluting and foul female reproductive fluids (Langenberg 2016; Langenberg 2017). It seems that this rule, whose narrative framing is limited to the statement that menstruating nuns "ruined the bedding and seating," is focused on practical management, not narrative representations of gender, blood taboos, or the venting of male sexual cathexis. Indeed, it is remarkable in its unremarkableness. This is more suggestive of a mature female than a male priestly voice.[45]

44. It could, perhaps, be argued that a hint of disgust underlies the term *vraṇamukha*, the term used in this text for vagina. *Vraṇamukha* can refer not only to the vagina but also to a wound, the anus, or a leprous scab.

45. I want to emphasize that it is, of course, common for women to participate in the politics of representation and reinscribe male-authored fantasies about the female body. The point made here, however, is that they are somewhat less likely to do so than male ascetics, especially when concerned with the practical management of their bodies.

The *Mahāsāṅghika-Lokottaravādin Bhikṣuṇī-vinaya* text differs from the parallel *Pāli-vinaya* text in the notable addition of further guidance: "Pushing it in too shallowly is not suitable but neither is pushing it in too deeply in order to dispel the passion of desire. On the contrary, it should be pushed into the orifice loosely. Whichever nun inserts it too deeply, or too shallowly, in that way slaking her lust, commits a gross sin" (Roth 1970, 309, §268). This bit of moralizing, which could be an intratextual reference to rules about what constitutes sex located at *pārājika* I (the rule prescribing celibacy for monks and nuns), is possibly the interpolation of scholarly redactors interested in the articulation of monastic sexual virtue and the elaboration of *vinaya* law. These words of caution may also represent the application of more general *vinaya* principles regarding sexual transgression to menstruation by certain, exceedingly prudent, members of the nuns' community.

The process of conceiving and articulating a thoughtful and transparent hermeneutic in relationship to a particular text is inevitably a reflexive and even paradoxical one. As one thinks about and seeks to understand a text on its own terms, questions related to both translation and interpretation that did not exist previously gradually emerge as important, even decisive. Consider the Sanskrit terms *prasrāvamarga* (path of urine/fluid) (P. *passāvamagga*) and *vraṇamukha* (orifice or, literally, "wound opening"), both of which have been translated simply as "vagina" by scholars (including myself). *Prasrāvamarga* appears in the *pārājika* I section containing the most important rules governing sexuality. *Vraṇamukha* also appears in *pārājika* I, but only as a general word for "orifice." *Vraṇamukha* recurs, this time signifying vagina, in the *prakīrṇaka* passage about menstruation just discussed, but there *prasrāvamarga* drops out.[46]

Attention to the historically layered and rhetorically complex nature of the *vinaya*, and the diverse points of view contained therein, compels, I argue, a more careful look at these two terms. Conversely, a more nuanced translation of these two terms deepens one's sense of this *vinaya*'s rhetorical complexity. In fact, these two terms do not both simply refer in a straightforward way to what, in biomedicalized English, one would term "the vagina," or at least not precisely in the same way. Consider, for instance, that in the *sekhiya* (comportment) section of the Pāli *vinaya*,

46. *Vraṇamukha* appears in at least one other *prakīrṇaka* passage from the same text, a text describing a nun who, sitting cross-legged, is entered vaginally by a snake (Roth 1970, 302, §255). This is not an exhaustive list of references.

with its several training rules about proper urination, *passāva* (the Pāli for *prasrāva*, the first element in the compound word *prasrāvamarga*) refers to urine.[47] Elsewhere in Pāli sources, *passāva* is paired with *vacca* to mean urination and defecation.[48] In Sanskrit medical texts such as the *Caraka-saṃhitā* and Vāgbhāṭa's *Aṣṭāṅgahṛdaya*, the word *prasrāva* (literally, flowing forth) also refers to urine while the *prasrāvakaraṇa* is the urethra. Faxian's Chinese translation of the *Mahāsāṅghika Bhikṣuṇī-vinaya* renders the term *prasrāvamarga* appearing in *pārājika* 1 (translated into English literally) as "small action route." Hirakawa translates this into English as "urinary tract" (Hirakawa 1982, 104).[49] Édith Nolot, who translated the *Mahāsāṅghika-Lokottaravādin Bhikṣuṇī-vinaya* into French, is not too interested in this ambiguity and simply asserts that "vagina" (*le vagin*) is clearly what is meant (despite the typical use of *prasrāva* for urine) (Nolot 1991, 62n9). I wonder, however, if the terminology used in *pārājika* 1 may actually indicate some confusion about female orifices and their functions among its (presumably male) authors and transmitters. Such confusion is not unknown in other elite premodern religious texts, Buddhist or other.[50]

47. For instance *sikkhāpada* 75 from the *sekhiyakaṇḍa* of the *bhikkhu-vibhaṅga* reads: *na udake uccāraṃ vā passāvaṃ vā kheḷaṃ vā karissāmīti sikkhā karaṇīyā.*

48. DN i.70; MN i.83; J. i.5; ii.19.

49. I am grateful to Andrew Chittick for this insight into Faxian's Chinese translation of this passage. In another *vinaya* text of the *Mahāsāṅghika-Lokottaravādins*, the *Abhisamācārikā*, *praśvāsakuṭi* is used to mean "urinal." In his comparative study of this text, Maulichand Prasad suggests that *praśrāvakuṭi* is what is meant (Prasad 1984, 89). See also Handy 2016, 139–192.

50. Cabezón describes a passage from the *Dharmaskandha Sūtra* positing the existence of five species of worms inhabiting the "urinary tract of women" that "constantly eat away at the women's bodies," causing them to become "very excited with passion" and to "never have their fill of sex" (2017, 125n328). *Maitri Upaniṣad* 3.4 includes a reference to human beings being born from the *mūtradvāra* (literarally, "door for urine"). Hume translates this term as "urinary opening." Olivelle translates it as "urinary canal." Neither comments on the anatomical misunderstanding. In her intellectual and religious memoir, Haviva Ner-David writes vividly about the strange experience of being an observant woman studying *niddah* (the term for female purity laws in Judaism) in an orthodox setting and coming across a passage in which the revered Talmudic commentator, Rashid, confidently (but incorrectly) asserts that the urethra and the vagina are connected by a tube (Ner-David 2000, 155). This is not an exhaustive list of examples.

As mentioned, the menstrual rule allowing nuns to use a "little cloth shaped like an axle pin" (*ānīcolaka*) discussed above refers to the vagina by the word *vraṇamukha*, not *prasrāvamarga* (Roth 1970, 309, §268). This word, which translates literally as "wound opening" seems to come closer to identifying an orifice from which blood could flow, although in another *Mahāsāṅghika-lokottaravādin* context—a disciplinary text governing the toileting habits of monks—it is used to refer rather to the anus.[51] As mentioned, in the *pārājika* 1 rule of the same Middle-Indic *bhikṣuṇī-vinaya* tradition, it is also used as a general word for "orifice," of which there are three (all forbidden for intercourse): the anus, the *prasrāvamarga*, and the mouth. In any case, and especially since they occur as words for female reproductive parts at two very different moments in the composite *bhikṣuṇī-vinaya* text—one of great disciplinary significance (the *pārājika*) and the other from a lesser section on "miscellanea" (*prakīrṇaka*)—the words *prasrāvamarga* and *vraṇamukha* should be treated differently and not simply homogenized using the biomedicalized English term "vagina."

More to the point, it is at least possible, given the flat tone and practical content of the *prakīrṇaka* passage, not to mention the difference in status between these two textual moments, that the shift in vocabulary may actually be the product of differently gendered points of view. Indeed, the female community is likely to have possessed practical knowledge about their own bodies, including the fact that urine and blood flow from different orifices, leading them to prefer the less specific (and possibly bloodier) *vraṇamukha* over the misleading *prasrāvamarga* when discussing menstruation. I would further argue that the creators of the *prakīrṇaka* text seem likely to have been knowledgeable monastic women working within a complex social-ritual environment to resolve disciplinary issues related to their female bodies and communities. The more accurate use of terminology is one piece of evidence supporting such a view.

Although I would not want to make too much of it, it is also worth noting that the term, *ānīcolaka*, bears the diminutive *-ka* suffix that Stephanie Jamison has identified as a marker of "women's language" in the *Ṛg Veda* and other early Indic texts, including Buddhist texts in Middle-Indic languages (of which our *Mahāsāṅghika-lokottaravādin Bhikṣuṇī-vinaya*

51. Karashima 2012, 153, §18.16. Elsewhere in the Pāli canonical literature (MN 75 at i.506), the term is used to refer to a leper's sores. This is not an exhaustive list of references.

is one) (Jamison 2008; Jamison 2009). For instance, in comparing the *Therīgāthā* (that famous collection of verses attributed to the first female disciples of the Buddha) with the *Theragāthā* (the parallel male collection), Jamison observes that "the female verses employ the *-ka* forms more densely than the men's even in fairly neutral contexts" (2009, 324). In part, this is so because women's speech is colloquial speech, compared to the higher registers of formal language associated with the masculine, and with men. The suffix, *-ka*, is a marker of colloquial registers of speech. Jamison also draws connections between the *-ka* suffix and "highly marked contexts, namely those describing women's bodies" (Jamison 2009, 324). Regardless of the specific applicability of Jamison's discoveries about "women's language" in Middle-Indic literature to our menstrual text, her work provides an important model for a reading strategy that pays attention to affective tone and stylistic register, thus helping to reveal something about the "secret secret [and gendered] lives of texts." As I hope I have convinced you, the little axle-pin-shaped cloth has its own secrets to tell.

I contend, then, that this humble little text about ancient "tampons," read in the context of other *vinaya* treatments of the issue as well as contiguous traditions, affords an intriguing glimpse of an ancient nuns' community that was agentive (though perhaps in a narrow sphere), possessed of a savvy social intelligence, relatively unconcerned with ritual pollution (except in as much as it affected nun-lay relations), and able to work collaboratively with each other and with monastic lawyers to manage practical and ritual problems.[52] Such monastic women—resourceful, innovative, diplomatic—are a far cry from the religiously subservient nuns of whom Schopen, and others, are weary. Taken together with other texts about monastic women living within (but also seeking to rupture?) culturally inscribed codependencies with male partners, disciplined around (but also disregarding?) circulating tropes of acceptable feminine physicality, performing (but also resisting?) ritualized subordination, we start to piece together a fuller picture of ancient female communities on the ground. Still, these ascetic women of long ago are only available to us through the application of an intentional and transparent hermeneutic, not through a naïve historiography cloaked in philological rigor. And we catch but a glimpse—eyes, feet, stray words, disconnected limbs in one of Picasso's

52. Alice Collett's chapter in this volume on the term *antevāsinī* and what it tells us about gender segregation in the early community supports this last point.

cubist portraits—not a clear view of a well-lighted group as in, say, one of Vermeer's detailed and rational tableaus.

References

Berkwitz, Stephen C. 2009. "Materiality and Merit in Sri Lankan Buddhist Manuscripts." In *Buddhist Manuscript Cultures: Knowledge, Ritual and Art*, edited by Stephen C. Berkwitz, Juliane Schober, and Claudia Brown, 35–50. London: Routledge.

Bka' 'gyur (sde dge par phud). 1976–1979. Tibetan Buddhist Resource Center W22084, 103 vols. Delhi: Delhi Karmapae Chodhey Gyalwae Sungrab Partun Khang. http://tbrc.org/link?RID.W22084.

Blackburn, Anne M. 1999. "Looking for the *Vinaya*: Monastic Discipline in the Practical Canons of the Theravāda." *Journal of the International Association of Buddhist Studies* 22, no. 2: 281–310.

———. 2012. "The Text and the World." In *The Cambridge Companion to Religious Studies*, edited by Robert A. Orsi, 151–176. Cambridge: Cambridge University Press.

Cabezón, José Ignacio. 2017. *Sexuality in Classical South Asian Buddhism*. Somerville, MA: Wisdom Press.

Clarke, Shayne Neil. 2009. "Monks Who Have Sex: *Pārājika* Penance in Indian Buddhist Monasticism." *Journal of Indian Philosophy* 37: 1–43.

———. 2014. *Family Matters in Indian Buddhist Monasticisms*. Honolulu: University of Hawai'i Press.

Collins, Steven. 1990. "On the Very Idea of the Pali Canon." *Journal of the Pali Text Society* 15: 89–126.

———. 1998. *Nirvana and Other Buddhist Felicities*. Cambridge: Cambridge University Press.

de Jong, J. W. 1974. "Notes on the *Bhikṣuṇī-vinaya* of the Mahāsāṅghikas." In *Buddhist Studies in Honour of I. B. Horner*, edited by Lance Cousins, 63–70. Dordrecht: D. Reidel.

Finnegan, Diana Damchö. 2009. "'For the Sake of Women, Too': Ethics and Gender in the Narratives of the Mūlasarvāstivāda Vinaya." PhD dissertation, University of Wisconsin-Madison.

Frauwallner, Erich. 1956. *The Earliest Vinaya and the Beginnings of Buddhist Literature*. Rome: Instituto Italiano per il Medio ed Estremo Oriente

Hallisey, Charles. 1990. "Apropos to the Pāli Vinaya as a Historical Document: A Reply to Gregory Schopen." *Journal of the Pali Text Society* 15: 197–208.

Handy, Christopher Aaron. 2016. "Indian Buddhist Etiquette and the Emergence of Ascetic Civility." PhD dissertation, McMaster University.

Heim, Maria. 2014. *The Forerunner of All Things: Buddhaghosa on Mind, Intention, and Agency*. New York: Oxford University Press.

———. 2018. *The Voice of the Buddha: Buddhaghosa on the Immeasurable Words*. New York: Oxford University Press.

Hirakawa, Akira. 1982. *Monastic Discipline for the Buddhist Nuns: An English Translation of the Chinese Text of the Mahāsāṃghika-Bhikṣuṇī-Vinaya*. Patna: Kashi Prasad Jayaswal Research Institute.

Horner, I. B., trans. [1938–1966] 2012–2014. *The Book of the Discipline (Vinaya-pitaka)*. Vols. 1–4. Bristol: Pali Text Society.

Hüsken, Ute. 1997. "A Stock of Bowls Requires a Stock of Robes: Relations of the Rules for Nuns in the Theravāda Vinaya and the Bhikṣuṇī-Vinaya of the Mahāsāṅghika-Lokottaravādin." In *Untersuchungen zur Buddhistischen Literature: Zweite Folge, Gustav Roth zum 80*, 201–238. Göttingen: Vandenhoeck & Ruprecht.

———. 1999. "Rephrased Rules: The Application of Monks' Prescriptions to the Nuns' Discipline in Early Buddhist Law." *Bukkyō Kenkyū* 28: 19–29.

———. 2001. "Pure or Clean?" *Traditional South Asian Medicine* 6: 85–96.

Hüsken, Ute, and Petra Kieffer-Pülz. 2012. "Buddhist Ordination as Initiation Ritual and Legal Procedure." In *Negotiating Rites*, edited by Ute Hüsken and Frank Neubert, 255–276. Oxford: Oxford University Press.

Jamison, Stephanie. 2008. "Women's Language in the Rig Veda?" *Indologica: T. Y. Elizarenkova Memorial Volume*, Book 1, edited by L. Kulikov and M. Rusanov, 153–165. Moscow: Russian State University for the Humanities.

———. 2009. "Sociolinguistic Remarks on the Indo-Iranian *-ka* Suffix: A Marker of Colloquial Register." *Indo-Iranian Journal* 52: 311–329.

———. 2011. "The Secret Life of Texts." *Journal of the American Oriental Society* 133, no. 1: 1–7.

Karashima, Seishi. 2012. *Die Abhisamācārikā Dharmāḥ: Verhaltensregeln für buddhische Möche der Mahāsāṃghika-Lokottaravādins*. Bd. 1. Tokyo: International Research Institute for Advanced Buddhology, Soka University.

Kieffer-Pülz, Petra. 2014. "What the *Vinayas* Can Tell Us about Law." In *Buddhism and Law: An Introduction*, edited by Rebecca Redwood French and Mark A. Nathan, 46–62. Cambridge: Cambridge University Press.

Lammerts, Christian. 2014. "Genres and Jurisdictions: Laws Governing Monastic Inheritance in Seventeenth-Century Burma." In *Buddhism and Law: An Introduction*, edited by Rebecca Redwood French and Mark A. Nathan, 183–197. Cambridge: Cambridge University Press.

Langenberg, Amy Paris. 2013. "Mahāsāṅghika-Lokottaravādin Bhikṣuṇī Vinaya: The Intersection of Womanly Virtue and Buddhist Asceticism." In *Women in Early Indian Buddhism: Comparative Textual Studies*, edited by Alice Collett, 80–96. New York: Oxford University Press.

———. 2016. "Buddhist Blood Taboo: Mary Douglas, Female Impurity, and Classical Indian Buddhism." *Journal of the American Academy of Religion* 84, no. 1: 157–191.

———. 2017. *Birth in Buddhism: The Suffering Fetus and Female Freedom.* Abingdon-on-Thames: Routledge.

———. 2020. "On Reading Buddhist Vinaya: Feminist History, Hermeneutics, and Translating Women's Bodies." *Journal of the American Academy of Religion* 88, no. 4: 1121–1153.

Lariviere, Richard W. 2004. "*Dharmaśāstra*, Custom, 'Real Law,' and 'Apocryphal' *Smṛtis*." *Journal of Indian Philosophy* 32: 611–627.

Leslie, Julia, trans. 1989. *The Perfect Wife* (*Strīdharmapaddhati*). New York: Penguin Books.

Levman, Bryan Geoffrey. 2014. "Linguistic Ambiguities, the Transmissional Process, and the Earliest Recoverable Language of Buddhism." PhD dissertation, University of Toronto.

Lubin, Timothy. 2016. "Custom in the Vedic Ritual Codes as an Emergent Legal Principle." *Journal of the American Oriental Society* 136, no. 4: 668–687.

Mrozik, Susanne. 2006. "Materializations of Virtue: Buddhist Discourses on Bodies." In *Bodily Citation: Religion and Judith Butler*, edited by Ellen T. Armour and Susan M. St. Ville, 15–47. New York: Columbia University Press.

———. 2007. *Virtuous Bodies: The Physical Dimensions of Morality in Buddhist Ethics*. New York: Oxford University Press.

———. 2009. "A Robed Revolution: The Contemporary Buddhist Nun's (*Bhikṣuṇī*) Movement." *Religion Compass* 3, no. 3: 360–378.

Muldoon-Hules, Karen. 2017. *Brides of the Buddha: Nuns' Stories from the Avadānaśataka*. Lanham, MD: Lexington Books.

Nattier, Jan. 2003. *A Few Good Men: The Bodhisattva Path according to The Inquiry of Ugra (Ugraparipṛcchā)*. Honolulu: University of Hawai'i Press.

Ner-David, Haviva. [2000] 2014. *Life on the Fringes: A Feminist Journey toward Traditional Rabbinic Ordination*. Jerusalem: Ben Yehuda Press.

Nolot, Édith. 1991. *Règles de Discipline des Nonnes Bouddhistes*. Collège de France, Publications de L'institute de Civilisation Indienne, Fascicule 60. Paris: Diffusion de Boccard.

Ohnuma, Reiko. 2013. "Bad Nun: Thullanandā in Pāli Canonical and Commentarial Sources." *Journal of Buddhist Ethics* 20: 17–66.

Oldenberg, Hermann. 1880. *Vinaya-piṭaka*. Vol. 2. Bristol: Pāli Text Society.

Olivelle, Patrick, ed. 2000. *Dharmasūtras: The Law Codes of Āpastamba, Gautama, Baudhāyana, and Vasiṣṭha*. Delhi: Motilal Banarsidass.

———. 2005. *Manu's Code of Law: A Critical Edition and Translation of the Mānava-Dharmaśāstra*. Oxford: Oxford University Press.

Pollock, Sheldon. 2009. "Future Philology? The Fate of a Soft Science in a Hard World." *Critical Inquiry* 35: 931–961.

Prasad, Maulichand. 1984. *A Comparative Study of the Abhisamācārikā: Abhisamācārikā-Dharma-Vinaya of the Ārya Mahāsāṃghika-Lokottaravādins and the Pali Vinaya of the Theravādins*. Patna: Kashi Prasad Jayaswal Research Institute.

Prebish, Charles. 1996. "Śaikṣa-Dharmas Revisited: Further Considerations of Mahāsāṅghika Origins." *History of Religions* 35, no. 3: 258–270.

Roth, Gustav, ed. 1970. *Bhikṣuṇī-Vinaya Including Bhikṣuṇī-Prakīrṇaka and a Summary of the Bhikṣu-Prakīrṇaka of the Ārya-Mahāsāṃghika-lokottaravādin*. Patna: K. P. Jayaswal Research Institute.

Schopen, Gregory. 1991. "Archeology and Protestant Presuppositions in the Study of Indian Buddhism." *History of Religions* 31: 1–23.

———. 1997a. "If You Can't Remember, How to Make It Up: Some Monastic Rules for Redacting Canonical Texts." In *Bauddhavidyāsudhākaraḥ: Studies in Honour of Heinz Bechert on the Occasion of His 65th Birthday*, edited by P. Kieffer-Pülz and J.-U. Hartmann, 571–582. Swisttal-Odendorf: Indica et Tibetica Verlag.

———. 1997b. "On Monks, Nuns, and 'Vulgar' Practices: The Introduction of the Image Cult into Indian Buddhism." In *Bones, Stones, and Buddhist Monks: Collected Papers on the Archaeology, Epigraphy, and Texts of Monastic Buddhism in India*, 238–257. Honolulu: University of Hawai'i Press.

———. 2000a. "Hierarchy and Housing in a Buddhist Monastic Code: A Translation of the Sanskrit Text of *Śāyanānavastu* of the *Mūlsarvāstivāda-vinaya*—Part One [from the Sanskrit]." *Buddhist Literature* 2: 92–196.

———. 2000b. "The Good Monk and His Money in a Buddhist Monasticism of 'The Mahāyāna Period.'" *The Eastern Buddhist* 32, no. 1: 85–105.

———. 2004. "The Suppression of Nuns and Ritual Murder of Their Special Dead." In *Buddhist Monks and Business Matters: Still More Papers on Monastic Buddhism in India*, 329–359. Honolulu: University of Hawai'i Press.

———. 2007. "The Learned Monk as a Comic Figure: On Reading a Buddhist Vinaya as Indian Literature." *Journal of Indian Philosophy* 35: 201–226.

———. 2008. "On Emptying Chamber Pots without Looking and the Urban Location of Buddhist Nunneries in Early India Again." *Journal Asiatique* 296, no. 2: 229–256.

———. 2009. "The Urban Buddhist Nun and a Protective Right for Children in Early North India." In *Pāsādikadānam: Festschrift für Bhikkhu Pasadika*, edited by M. Straube, 359–380. Marburg: Indica et Tibetica Verlag.

———. 2010. "On Incompetent Monks and Able Urbane Nuns in a Buddhist Monastic Code." *Journal of Indian Philosophy* 38: 107–131.

———. 2014a. "On the Legal and Economic Activities of Buddhist Nuns: Two Examples from Early India." In *Buddhism and Law: An Introduction*, edited by Rebecca Redwood French and Mark A. Nathan, 91–114. Cambridge: Cambridge University Press.

———. 2014b. "The Buddhist Nun as an Urban Landlord and a 'Legal Person' in Early India." In *Buddhist Nuns, Monks, and Other Worldly Matters: Recent Papers on Monastic Buddhism in India*, 119–130. Honolulu: University of Hawai'i Press.

Strauch, Ingo. 2014. "Looking into Water-pots and Over a Buddhist Scribe's Shoulder: On the Deposition and the Use of Manuscripts in Early Buddhism." *Asia* 68, no. 3: 797–830.

Tournier, Vincent. 2012. "The *Mahāvastu* and the *Vinayapiṭaka* of the Mahāsāṅghika-lokottaravādins." *ARIRIAB* 15: 87–104.

Witkowski, Nicholas. 2017. "*Pāṃśukūla* as a Standard Practice in the *Vinaya*." In *Rules of Engagement: Medieval Traditions of Buddhist Monastic Regulation*, edited by Susan Andrews, Jinhua Chen, and Cuilan Liu, 263–311. Hamburg University Buddhist Studies Series 9. Bochum: Projektverlag.

Yao, Fumi. 2015. "The Story of Dharmadinnā: Ordination by Message in the Mūlasarvāstivāda *Vinaya*." *Indo-Iranian Journal* 58: 216–253.

Part II

Translators

Chapter 4

Translating the Theravāda Commentaries

Why, How, for Whom?

Oskar von Hinüber

If Buddhist tradition is taken at face value, the history of the commentaries on the Theravāda *Tipiṭaka*, which have been handed down in the Mahāvihāra in Anurādhapura, is largely a history of translation. As described in the *Mahāvaṃsa*, Mahinda arrived in Ceylon and started to convert King Devanaṃpiya Tissa (247–207) and his entourage by preaching no. 27 *Cūlahatthipadūpamasuttanta*, MN I 175–184.[1] Then he addressed a still larger assembly and turned to the *Petavatthu* and to the *Vimānavatthu* followed by the *Saccasaṃyutta* (SN V 414–477) in order to first raise emotion in the audience and then to calm it again.[2] Having thus prepared his listeners, Mahinda explains that *nibbāṇa* is the only and ultimate goal beyond all emotion and change. While the commentary to these *Mahāvaṃsa* verses points out that this is a well-planned instruction in three steps, it is silent on the obvious linguistic question: How was Mahinda understood? Which language did he use?

1. According to Mhv. XIV 22 = Dīp. XII 57.

2. According to Mhv. XIV 58 = Dīp. XII 84 explained in the *Mahāvaṃsa* commentary as *saṃvegaṃ janetuṃ . . . assāsetuṃ*, Mhv-ṭ. I 338, 8ff.

The linguistic problem is, however addressed in connection with the commentaries in the much later and well-known story of Buddhaghosa at the beginning of the first continuation of the *Mahāvaṃsa* composed by Dhammakitti during the reign of King Parakkamabāhu I (1153–1186). Already in India the Thera Revata recognizes Buddhaghosa's exceptional abilities and asks him to translate the commentaries on the canon back into Pāli, which were extant in Ceylon as translated into Sinhala by Mahinda. They were, however, inaccessible in India, not only because of their language, but first of all because no commentaries existed in India to explain the canonical texts:

pālimattaṃ idh' ānītaṃ	*natthi aṭṭhakathā idha*
. . .	
Sīlahaḷaṭṭhakathā suddhā	*Mahindena matīmatā*
. . .	
katā Sīhaḷabhāsāya	*Sīhaḷesu pavattati*
taṃ tattha gantvā sutvā taṃ	*Māgadhānaṃ niruttiyā*
parivattehi sā hoti	*sabbalokahitāvahā* (Mhv. XXXVII 228–230)

Only the canonical text is handed down here (i.e., in India), there is no commentary here. . . . The pure Sīhaḷa commentary created by the wise Mahinda in the Sīhaḷa language continues to exist in Ceylon. Go there, hear it and translate[3] it into the language of Magadha (i.e., Pāli). The whole world will benefit from it.

3. Translations are rarely mentioned in ancient Indian literature. Some examples are collected in von Hinüber 2007, 115ff., on the vocabulary used to express the idea of "translating" non-Buddhist texts. Cf. also Slaje 2005, 23n97 (*bhāṣāviparyayāt*). Neryosang (13th c.?) uses the verb *ava-tṝ* (to translate): *idaṃ . . . pustakaṃ mayā nairiosaṃgena dhavalasutena pahalavījaṃdāt saṃskṛtabhāṣāyāṃ avatāritaṃ* (. . . this book was translated by me, Nēryōsang, the son of Dhavala, from the Pahlavī-Zand into the Sanskrit language) (oral communication by Daniel Sheffield, Princeton University, during the 224th Annual Meeting of the American Oriental Society at Phoenix, AZ, March 14–17, 2014; cf. Spiegel 1861, 2). In selected Buddhist Central Asian languages the act of translating is expressed in the following ways: In Khotanese the verb *byūh-* (to change, to translate) is used: *hvatanau yi haṃjsäte byūhä sarvasatvānu*

This late tradition, written down about seven hundred years after Buddhaghosa's lifetime, is of course in accordance with the verses introducing and concluding various commentaries by Buddhaghosa, which are in all likelihood *the* or, at any rate, a source of this story.

There are three different sets of introductions to the respective commentaries on the three parts of the *Tipiṭaka*. All stress the fact that the following texts are translations of an older version despite remarkable differences between the introductions to the commentary on Buddhist law, the *Samantapāsādikā*, on the one hand, and those to *Suttanta* and *Abhidhamma* texts on the other.

Only the introduction to the *Samantapāsādikā* strongly underlines the "international" character of this commentary by referring explicitly to monks of other countries (*dīpantare*, Sp. 2, 10* [verse 8]) who are unable to understand the language current in Ceylon. Moreover, the *Sīhaḷa-Mahā-aṭṭhakathā* draws material also from foreign commentaries such as the *Andhaka-aṭṭhaka*, a commentary from Āndhrapradeś, mentioned implicitly in these verses only (*Kurundināmādisu*, Sp. 2, 18* [verse 10]). Unfortunately, nothing is said on the language in which these commentaries from India were written. Although there was an awareness of the South Indian Dravidian languages of the Indian east coast in Ceylon at the time as shown in the famous story on the "Ursprache" preserved in the *Sammohavinodanī* (Vibh-a. 387 = Paṭis-a. I 5),[4] the commentary on the *Vibhaṅga*: If the mother speaks the *damilabhāsā* and, hearing her first, a child picks up Tamil. Hearing the father speaking first in the *andhakabhāsā*, the child picks up Telugu, which is probably one of the oldest references to this language. If the child hears neither father nor mother, the language will be *māgadhabhāsā*, that is, Pāli. This, if not Pāli,

hätāyä, Book of Zambasta 23, 2 (cf. 23, 372) "I intend to translate it into Khotanese for the welfare of all beings" (Emmerick 1968); for Bactrian epigraphical evidence can be adduced ιωναγγο οασο . . . αριαο ωσταδο (a Greek edict . . . put into Aryan) (line 3), Sims-Williams 2004, 53–68; for the Uigur evidence, cf. Röhrborn 1990, 67–73, cf. also *Zeitschrift der Deutschen Morgenländischen Gesellschaft* 162 2012, 243 with n4. Tibetan translations are discussed by, for example, Hahn 2007, 123–149, and Seyfort Ruegg 2016, 193–265, who very marginally also discusses Theravāda evidence. Translations into Chinese are discussed, for example, by Nattier 2008, 19–27; the reflections on translation by Chinese translators themselves are edited and translated by Cheung 2006.

4. On the views of Buddhists and Jains on the "original language," cf. von Hinüber 2001, §2ff.

might have been the language of the *Andhaka-aṭṭhakathā* on Buddhist law.[5]

The relevant verses from the introduction to the *Samantapāsādikā* read:

saṃvaṇṇanā Sīhaḷadīpakena
vākyena esā pana saṅkhaṭattā
na kiñci atthaṃ abhisaṃbhuṇāti
dīpantare bhikkhujanassa yasmā
tasmā imaṃ pālinayānurūpaṃ
saṃvaṇṇanaṃ dāni samārabhissaṃ
. . .
saṃvaṇṇanaṃ tañ ca samārabhanto
tassā[6] *Mahāaṭṭhakathaṃ sarīraṃ*
katvā Mahāpaccariyaṃ tatheva
Kurundināmādisu vissutāsu
vinicchayo aṭṭhakathāsu vutto
yo yuttaṃ atthaṃ apariccajanto . . . (Sp. 2, 7*–19*, verses 8–11)

Because this commentary is composed in the language of the island of Ceylon, it is of no use to the monks in the other island (the Indian subcontinent). Therefore, I am going to begin[7] this commentary following the rules of the sacred text.[8] . . . And, beginning this commentary, I have made the (Sīhaḷa) Mahā-aṭṭhakathā its body, without discarding suitable opinions, which are presented as the decisions in the commentaries Mahāpaccarī, the famous Kunrundī etc.

This approach of the anonymous author of the *Samantapāsādikā* described in simple *Triṣṭubh* verses is quite different from the path followed by Buddhaghosa in his commentaries on the *Suttapiṭaka*. For he mentions neither monks from other countries, whom he had in mind,

5. On research on the *Andhaka-aṭṭhakathā*, see von Hinüber 1996, §210ff. and Kieffer-Pülz 2010, 147–235.

6. E[e] w.r. *tasmā*.

7. This would, in Sanskrit terminology, refer to the *śāstrārambha*, cf. Slaje 2008 [rev.: Cox 2009, 400ff.; Rocher 2009, 511ff.; Grahelli 2014, 161–165].

8. The contrast to *Sīhāḷadīpakena vākyena* seems to indicate that the commentator also has in mind the language of the canonical text here.

nor any text used other than the one brought by Mahinda and translated by him into Sinhala. In other words, he strictly follows the orthodoxy of the Mahāvihāra in Anurādhapura. If the author of the *Samantapāsādikā* "internationalizes" his text by using Pāli, Buddhaghosa in contrast "nationalizes" his commentaries by gradually superseding the international *bhāṇavāra* tradition while focusing on the Mahāvihāra-Theravāda as he states in verses in the more elaborate *āryā*-meter:

> *. . . aṭṭhakathā*
> *Sīhaḷadīpaṃ* ***pana ābhatātha*** *vasinā Mahā-****Mahindena***
> *ṭhapitā Sīhaḷa****bhāsāya dīpavāsīnam*** *atthāya*
> ***apanetvāna tato*** *haṃ Sīhaḷab****bhāsaṃ*** *manoramaṃ* ***bhāsaṃ***
> ***tantinayānu****cchavikaṃ* ***āropento*** *vigata****dosaṃ*** . . . (Sv. 1, 15*–20*, verses 6–8)[9]

> The commentary was brought to the Island of Ceylon and established in the Sīhaḷa language by Master Mahā-Mahinda for the sake of the inhabitants of the island. Having removed the Sīhāḷa language from it (the commentary), and having raised (it) to the lovely language, adequate to the rules of the tradition, free from blemishes . . .

The equally anonymous commentaries on the *Abhidhammapiṭaka* composed at the initiative of, but not by Buddhaghosa, follow the same principles.[10] Their introductory plain *śloka*s are clearly based on Buddhaghosa's *āryā*-verses at the beginning of the *sutta* commentaries:

	aṭṭhakathā
ābhatā pana *therena*	***Mahindena*** *tam uttamam*
yā dīpaṃ ***dīpavāsīnaṃ***	***bhāsāya*** *abhisaṅkhatā*
apanetvā tato bhāsaṃ	*Tambapaṇṇivāsinaṃ*
āropayitvā *nid****dosaṃ***	***bhāsan tantinayānu****gaṃ* (Dhs-a. 1, 28*–2, 2*, verses 13–15)

9. Words used again in the introduction to the *Abhidhamma* commentaries are printed in bold.

10. The origin of the various commentaries is discussed in greater detail in von Hinüber 2013/2014 [2015a], 353–387.

The motive behind these translations is to raise the commentaries to the same linguistic status as the canonical texts by the use of Pāli as an appropriate language.

In sum: All Pāli commentaries on the *Vinayapiṭaka*, the four great *Nikāyas* of the *Suttapiṭaka* excluding the *Khuddakanikāya* commentaries and the *Abhidhamma* commentaries, are at least according to the tradition translations. Despite these rather strong indications it must be asked whether we can accept the tradition as a fact. Luckily, the tradition is supported by immediate evidence, however slim.

Helmer Smith (1882–1956) pointed out in his seminal review article on Wilhelm Geiger's (1856–1943) *Etymological Dictionary of the Sinhalese Language* (1941; Smith 1950, 177–223) that there are some quotations in old Sinhalese from the *heḷaṭuvā* and the *maha aṭuvā* (that is, the *Sīhaḷa-aṭṭhakathā* and the *Mahā-aṭṭhakathā*) preserved in the *Dhampiya Aṭuvā Gätapadaya* ascribed to King Kassapa V (929–939).[11] These immediate traces of a commentary in Sinhala Prakrit confirm the tradition.[12]

There is still one more point to support this. Some of the explanations in the extant Pāli *Aṭṭhakathā* do not make much sense as they stand, if, for example, *aṇuṃ thūlan* (DN I 223, 8*) *ti khuddakaṃ mahantaṃ* Sv. 393, 3 or *uppannaṃ hotī* (DN I 244, 10*) *ti jātaṃ hoti* Sv. 395, 9 (HPL §231). However, they do make sense in a bilingual commentary, in a commentary resembling what is later a *sannaya* in Ceylon or a *nissaya* in Southeast Asia (HPL §203). For the word *aṇu* (small, minute) does not survive in Sinhala, and, though *thūla* (large, fat) does, it soon became a homophone with *tulya* (equal), both developing into Sinhala *tul*.[13] Therefore, these glosses may be explanations taken over from the old *Sīhaḷa Aṭṭhakathā*, where they were indeed useful.

Even if we can be fairly confident that a commentary in old Sinhala Prakrit did exist once, the question remains whether it can be dated back to the time of Aśoka, when Mahinda is supposed to have come to Ceylon. Here, we are again confronted with the general problem that almost all texts, whether canonical scripture or commentary, grew over an extended period. Therefore, we are usually at best only able to define approximately the date

11. Cf. HPL 262 (introduction).

12. In light of this evidence, the skepticism expressed by Ole Holten Pind (1992, 135–156), particularly 138, does not seem to be justified.

13. Geiger 1941, s.v. 961. *tul*[1] and 962. *tul*[2] and Turner 1966, 193. *aṇu-*[2].

at which a certain text was closed and when the final version, which we have, came into the existence. For the Theravāda commentaries that is the time of Buddhaghosa. However, we are also able to search for roots of the texts reaching deep into the past, as done for canonical Pāli, for example, by Heinrich Lüders (1869–1943; Lüders 1953) or by Erich Frauwallner (1898–1974) for the Theravāda chronicles when he traced the sources of *Dīpavaṃsa* and *Mahāvaṃsa* back to Indian material (Frauwallner 1984).

Similarly, there are traces of rather old explanations in the commentaries, which in all likelihood came from India to Ceylon at an early date. For it is a priori necessary, if not imperative, that the canonical texts were explained in one way or the other when Buddhism was brought to Ceylon, irrespective of the language that Mahinda may have used. Therefore old explanations are expected, but difficult to trace and impossible to search systematically in the extant commentaries. One such case is possibly, as pointed out more than once already, the explanation of the rare technical word *giñjaka*, which occurs only in one single formula mentioning a particular type of a building, the *giñjakāvasatha* at Nādika/Ñātika in Magadha, where the Buddha stayed also during his last wandering described in the *Mahāparinibbānasuttanta*:

> *tatra sudaṃ bhagavā Nādike viharati giñjakāvasathe* (DN II 91, 21 = II 94,15)
> At that time, the Lord was staying at Nādika in the *giñjaka* house.

This sentence is repeated a couple of times in the *Vinaya*- and *Suttapiṭakas*.[14] The explanation of the word *giñjaka* as *iṭṭhakāmaye āvasathe*, Sv. 543, 11 = Ps. II 235, 6 = Spk. III 281, 8 = AN-a. III 351, 23 ≠ Spk. II 75, 3, "in a house made of bricks" could hardly be found in Ceylon. For, as Jules Bloch (1880–1953) pointed out far back in 1951 the word *giñjaka* survives in new Indo-Aryan languages, however only in the language of the peasants of Bihar as *pan-giñjā* designating a kind of brick. Recently, a new reference to *giñjakiya* in an inscription dated to the first century BC came to light in Deorkothar (Madhyapradeś) (von Hinüber and Skilling 2013). Although the second part of the word is lost, it seems certain that

14. Altogether there are fifteen references: one each in the *vinaya* and in the *Majjhimanikāya*, three in the *Aṅguttaranikāya*, and five each in the *Dīgha*- and *Saṃyuttanikāya*.

again a kind of building is meant. Because of the geographic distribution of the *giñjaka-*, it is highly unlikely that any native monk in Ceylon could have known the meaning of this rare word belonging to the language of artisans living in the northeastern part of Central India.

Other instances, which point to explanations originating from Northern India, are "etymologies" such as the one used to elucidate the word *yantaka* in *anujānāmi yantakaṃ sūcikaṃ*, Vin. II 148, 23 by *yaṃ yaṃ jānāti taṃ yantakaṃ*, Sp. 1216, 12 "whatever he knows is a *yantaka*" (i.e., bolt of the door). As is well known, in contrast to almost all other Prakrits, initial *y-* does not develop into *j-* in Sinhala (Geiger 1938, 79, §77.1). Therefore, this "etymology" could hardly have been invented in Ceylon, but it does make sense in the linguistic environment in Northern India.

Another example is far less straightforward and not entirely clear. It occurs in the *vinaya* in the introduction to the fifth *Saṃghādisesa*, where a matchmaking is described. After the go-between praised the boy in front of the prospective bride's parents, they answer:

> *ete kho, bhante, amhe na jānanti ke vā ime kassa vā ti, kismiṃ viya kumārikāya vatthuṃ* (Vin. III 135, 15–17)
>
> They (that is the groom's parents) do not know us, honoured sir, nor who we are, nor to whom we belong, nor what, as it were is the girl's property. (Horner [1938] 2006, 229)

The last part, *kismiṃ viya kumārikāya vatthuṃ*, cannot be construed grammatically.[15] Somewhat hesitatingly I. B. Horner, therefore, refers to the correct reading *vattuṃ* for *vatthuṃ* and thus improves her translation in a note, "we should be ashamed to speak thus for the girl('s sake)," following the commentary: *kismiṃ viyā ti kicchaṃ viya kileso viya, hiri viya amhākaṃ hotī ti adhippāyo*, Sp. 552, 28ff. This is a strange explanation "in what (loc.) means 'as it were with difficulty, distress.' The idea is 'we are, as it were, ashamed.'" It is difficult, if not impossible to understand immediately, why there is a locative and why *kismiṃ* is explained by *kic-*

15. This sentence is misunderstood also as "nor what is the young girl's property" in Bailey and Mabbett 2003, 221.

cham.[16] It is perhaps possible to find an explanation if the original wording of this idiom was slightly different, reading *kicchi* instead of *kismiṃ*. The word *kicchi* is the old eastern Middle Indic form corresponding to Sanskrit *kiṃcit*, which was alien to the western Middle Indian languages as shown by the inscriptions of Aśoka, where, as in the Girnār version, the word *kicchi* of Aśoka's administrative language is regularly replaced by *kiṃci*. If *kicchi viya kumārikāya vattuṃ* is read, the translation is straightforward: "what on earth shall we say concerning the girl?" Grammar[17] and meaning are as smooth as is the explanation *kicchi viyā ti kicchaṃ viya*.[18] Perhaps the sound of *kicchi* easily evoked *kicchaṃ*, because even the meaning fits. This assumption, however, presupposes that this gloss is fairly old and originated at a time when the form *kicchi* still was found in this eastern idiom only to be misunderstood in the end in western India. For only the western *kiccha* sounds similar to eastern *kicchi*, in contrast to the corresponding eastern *kasira*.[19] Why the substitute *kismiṃ*, which is otherwise used in the language of the *vinaya* only as an adjective as in *kismiṃ vatthusmiṃ*, while the interrogative pronoun is *kimhi*, is unclear. If this guess should prove to be correct, this could add another trace of a fairly ancient comment on a text of the *Tipiṭaka*.

---

16. Parallel explanations of *kismiṃ viya* followed by an infinitive, which occurs only rarely and only in the language of the introductions to *vinaya* rules, are perhaps everywhere ultimately based on eastern *kicchi* (?): *kismiṃ viyā ti kiṃsu viya, kileso viya*, Sp. 665, 7 (ad Vin. III 211, 9); *kismiṃ viyā ti kīdisaṃ viya lajjanakaṃ viya*, Sp. 819, 18 (ad Vin. IV 79, 6; *kismiṃ viya* is replaced by *kathaṃ* in the parallel version at J. I 477, 13), cf. *kiṃ viya abbhutaṃ*, Th. 552 "what indeed is strange in that?" (Norman [1969] 2007), or, in a non-Buddhist text, *kim iva . . . kathayati*, *Śiśupālavadha* XVI 31, "why should (a truly great man) point to . . ." (Dundas 2017) explained as *kim iva katham iva* by Vallabhadeva and *kim arthaṃ, na kathayati* by Mallinātha.

17. For *kiṃ* c. inf. cf. CPD s.v. *aparajjhati* ad DN I 91, 10.

18. The subcommentary on Sp. 665, 7 elaborates: *kismiṃ viyā ti ettha kismiṃ viyā ti nipātavasena, samānatthaṃ kiṃsu viyā ti nipātapadan ti āha* **kiṃsu viyā** *ti, kiṃ viyā ti attho, dukkhaṃ viyā ti adhippāyo. tenāha* **kileso viyā** *ti-ādi*, Sp-ṭ. B[e] II 401, 26–402, 2 "*kismiṃ viya*: here, *kismiṃ viya* is used as a particle, a synonym is the particle *kiṃsu viya*. (Therefore the commentary says) *kiṃsu viya*. The meaning is *kiṃ viya*. The idea is "quite painful." Therefore (the commentary) says "almost a distress." On the various shades of the meaning of *iva*, cf. Brereton 1982, 443–450.

19. In Pāli *kicchena kasirena* exist side by side in the formula *kicchena kasirena* (3+4).

To sum up, there is some direct and indirect evidence supporting the assumption that old explanations of the canonical texts were brought from India and were translated into Sinhalese. This immediately entails the question how this was done. For as pointed out more than once, the commentaries were by no means simple translations, because Buddhaghosa and his team took the opportunity to restructure and modernize the texts. It may suffice to draw attention to only one such instance from the beginning of the *Samantapāsādikā*, where the anonymous commentator himself draws the attention to changes in the arrangement of the older material, on which he based his commentary:

> *ettha pana ṭhatvā sabba-aṭṭhakathāsu pabajjā ca upasaṃpadā ca kathitā. mayaṃ pana yathāṭhitapālivasen'eva Khandhake kathayissāma*
>
> At this point lower and higher ordination is described in all commentaries. We, however, shall explain it in the Khandhaka, where it is placed in the scriptures.

After pointing out that matters that should be dealt with in the *Khandhaka* or in the *Parivāra* commentaries rather were occasionally explained by the *aṭṭhakathācāriyas*, the earlier commentators, already in the commentary on the *Vinaya-Vibhaṅga*, this paragraph concludes:

> *evaṃ hi kathīyamāne palikkamen'eva vaṇṇanā katā hoti* (Sp. 206, 18–24)
>
> For, by this method of explanation the commentary is structured in such a way that it closely follows the canonical text.

These and other remarks show that the new commentary tries to improve upon the structure of its predecessor. All this would only make sense if the monks at the time knew and also continued to use the old *Aṭṭhakathā*, a situation that seems to have prevailed over a long period. For, as mentioned earlier, Kassapa V could still quote from the *Sīhaḷa Aṭṭhakathā* in the tenth century. Indeed, it is usually believed that the old *Sīhaḷa Aṭṭhakathā* finally fell out of use and was gradually lost approximately at the time of the reforms of Parakkamabāhu I during the twelfth century (cf. HPL §374).

So far, evidence, however slim, is available on the history of the commentaries, of their past, as it were, when looking back from the period of Buddhaghosa into the time of their origin and development. Looking into the future from the same point, again from the times of Buddhaghosa, is as difficult as any prediction. For how to find those monks, who were supposed to use the commentaries outside the Mahāvihāra, even outside Ceylon in India and perhaps beyond in *dīpantare*?

Seen from Anurādhapura, Buddhist monks in the north, that is South India, and perhaps also Southeast Asia, may be the target audience of the author(s) of the *Samantapāsādikā*. In contrast to Ceylon, however, during the centuries before and after Buddhaghosa, no textual evidence can be adduced as a guide when looking for fellow Theravādins in South India.[20] However, it is evident from the introductory and concluding verses to the *Nikāya* commentaries that Buddhaghosa himself obviously had various connections to South India. For he explicitly mentions at the end of his commentary on the *Aṅguttaranikāya*, the *Manorathapūraṇī*, that he was asked to compose this text by a Thera named Jotipāla, who lived together with Buddhaghosa "in Kāñcī and other places" (. . . *Jotipālena / Kañcīpurādisu mayā pubbe saddhim vasantena*, AN-a. V 98, 2*). That Kāñcī was a famous seat of Buddhist learning is of course well known.[21]

The intention of the *Samantapāsādikā* to reach out to foreign monks by using Pāli implies that Pāli was used also in South India. This is of course likely because all great commentators, Buddhaghosa himself and his contemporary Buddhadatta, later Dhammapāla and much later again Vajirabuddhi, who seems to have known Kāñcī quite well, had South Indian connections or were South Indian. Unfortunately, the Buddhist textual tradition of South India is lost almost completely, whether in Pāli or Sanskrit. Very few Buddhist texts in Tamil remain, as does the late and isolated manuscript of the *Mañjuśrīmūlakalpa* from Kerala.[22]

Still, there are some very faint echoes of Pāli perhaps in ancient South Indian inscriptions, if we read the form *ayirahaṃgha: ayirasaṃgha* in an

---

20. Indirect evidence is perhaps provided by the "Pāli" texts that are found in early Southeast Asia, but written by monks from India. They are most likely roughly contemporary to Buddhaghosa according to Falk 1997, particularly 84, 91 (5th c.). The results of Falk are summarized and anticipated in Stargardt 1995.

21. For details, see von Hinüber 2015b, n27.

22. For Tamil texts, see Monius 2015, 813–818, and on the *Mañjuśrīmūlakalpa*, von Hinüber 2015b, 943–958, particularly 949b.

inscription from Nāgārjunakoṇḍa with the typical Pāli "Umlaut" written *ayi* to express /ä/ (von Hinüber 2001 §147). This is desperately slim evidence. However, there is also the impressive donation to the Theriyas at Nāgārjunakoṇḍa under the Śātavāhana King Māḍhariputta Siri Puḷumāvi (ca. 225–240), when a Cetiyaghara is donated to the *theriyānaṃ taṃbapaṃṇakānaṃ suparigahe* "for the possession (acquisition) by the Theriyas from Tambapaṇṇi."[23] Although the designation Theriya for the Buddhist school that is normally called Theravāda is seldom used, it still seems to be an old name confirmed once an *āryā*-verse in the *nigamana* of the *Sumaṅgalavilāsinī* is metrically restored:

> *Dāṭhānāgena saṃgha(t)therena theriyavaṃsena*[24]
> — — | — — | ⏑ — ⏑ | — — | ⏑ — ⏑ | ⏑ | — — | ⏑

Both names, Theravāda and Theriya, were obviously used side by side and are equally old as suggested by the *Dīpavaṃsa*, where the *Mahāsaṃgītikā (= Mahāsāṃghikā) bhikkhū*, Dīp. V 32 are opposed to:

> *visuddha-**Theravādamhi** puna bhedo ajāyatha*
> *Mahiṃsāsakā* . . .
> . . . *Vajjiputtakavādamhi* (Dīp. V 45ff.)

While Theriya is formed like Mahāsāṃghika, Theravāda follows the alternative pattern found in school names such as Sarvāstivāda.[25]

The Theriyas mentioned in the Nāgārjunakoṇḍa inscription boast to have pervaded almost the whole Buddhist world: *Kasmīra-Gaṃdhāra-Cīna-Cilāta-Tosali-Avaraṃta-Vaṃga-Vanavāsi-Yavana-Damila-(Palura)-Taṃbapaṃṇidīpa-pasādakānaṃ* (Vogel 1929/1930, 22) by activities as *pasādaka*s "missionaries." This is repeated slightly more modestly in a second inscription accompanying a donation of a Buddhapāda made under

23. Vogel 1929/1930, 1–37, 22ff. = Tsukamoto 1996, II. Naga 41.2—The meaning of *parig(r)aha* is discussed by von Hinüber and Skilling 2016, 25–28.

24. The text of the *nigamana* is edited by von Hinüber 1995, 129–133 = von Hinüber 2009, 62–66; the text was republished in von Hinüber 2018 in a metrically restored form. The wording quoted here is one of the possible restorations of this verse.

25. The history of the name Theravāda is discussed by Perreira 2012, cf. also Skilling 2009.

the Ikṣvāku ruler Vīrapuruṣadatta (240/250–265/275): *theriyānaṃ vibhajavādānaṃ Kasmīra-Gaṃdhāra-Yavana-Vanavāsa-Taṃbapaṃnidīpa-pasādakānaṃ Mahāvihāravāsinaṃ* (Tsukamoto 1996, II Naga 50.1).

This presence of Theriyas or Theravādins in large parts of India reaching up to the far north is indeed confirmed by a fragment of a manuscript of the Theravāda *Vinaya* preserved in Nepal, by translations of Theravāda texts into Tibetan between 800 and 1300 or by the use of the *Vimuttimagga* in Sena Bengal (HPL §250; cf. now also Stuart 2017, xvii and 241).

In the South there is perhaps some more evidence on Theravādins now. The *cetiya* excavated at Kanaganahalli between 1996 and 1999 is widely known in the meantime (Poonacha 2011 [2013]; von Hinüber and Nakanishi 2014). There are about 300 to 320 new inscriptions in common western Middle Indic mixed with some terms surviving from the Mauryan administrative language, but there is no connection to Pāli as the language of the Mahāvihāra Theravāda. At the beginning of a short fragment, a so far overlooked name of a school was recognized by A. Griffiths and V. Tournier (oral communication): *mahāvinase(l)i[* (von Hinüber and Nakanishi 2014, II.5, 9) "of the Mahāvinaseli(yas)" should be read instead as *mahāvinase(pa).i.*

As usual, the indirect evidence again proves to be rather weak. Still, two images could be mentioned together with their inscriptions as discussed in a recent article.[26] In the excavation report the first inscription is connected to an image showing the transport of relics:

> *aya majhimo sacanāmo aya ca dudubhisaro* (III.3, 2)
>
> The venerable Majjhima Saccanāma and the venerable Dundubhissara.

Therefore, the scene seen in the accompanying image was interpreted as the transport of the relics of Majjhima and Dundubhissara. This, however, was an error as Monika Zin has demonstrated (Zin 2018, 89). Luckily, however, only the names, particularly Dundubhissara, are important, because he is mentioned as one of the missionaries sent to the Himalayas only in the surviving Theravāda tradition. Of course, a rather strong warning is

26. Von Hinüber 2016, 7–20, particularly 12ff.

necessary when using this *argumentum e silentio*: Other traditions simply may have been lost.

The same is true for a second instance. This time, however, image and inscription do belong together. The unusual image is a representation of acrobats: *lakhako meyakathālikā* (IV.6) corresponding to Pāli *laṃghako Medakathalikā* (the acrobat Meyakathālikā). The correct interpretation of this image was found by the Venerable Anālayo, who referred to a corresponding story in the *Satipaṭṭhāna-Saṃyutta* in the *Mahāvagga* of the *Saṃyuttanikāya* (SN V 168, 17–169, 3). Although there are parallels to the story in texts of various Buddhist schools, only Theravāda preserves the very unusual name in the older Pāli form Medakathalikā as one of the extremely rare feminine names for a man. This strange fact is duly pointed out by the commentary to the *Saṃyuttanikāya*.[27]

These may be hints to Theravāda presence at Kanaganahalli, which was an important Buddhist center from the time of Aśoka as underlined by the fragment of one of the rock edicts found at Sannati in the immediate vicinity of Kanaganahalli and remains so through the Śātavāhana period, as shown by epigraphical evidence. Moreover, there may be evidence, slim again, this time for Theravāda literature. For an image is labeled by an inscription as a scene from the *Velāmajātaka*. This could be based on the text of one of the three *Jātaka*s, which are lost in the Theravāda collection, but obviously still known in Kanaganahalli: *jātaka velāmiya* (III.1, 5) "Velāmajātaka" (von Hinüber 1998, 117).

The form of the title corresponds to *jātaka vesatariya* (III.1, 14) for *Vessantara-jātaka*. This type of title was current also in Theravāda literature before the *Jātaka-atthavaṇṇanā* was created on the basis of the earlier *Aṭṭhakathā* in Pāli well after Buddhaghosa and without any translation being involved as far as is known. Buddhaghosa, too, still knew and occasionally quoted from the older version the Pāli *Jātaka-Aṭṭhakathā*.[28]

If all this evidence, vague as it may be in detail, is taken together, perhaps the contours of those Theravāda or Theriya monks living in *dīpantare* or South India emerge as shadows from the fog of history.

This finally may answer the three questions put forward in the title: The commentaries were translated to modernize the texts in old Sinhala

27. Story and image (no. LXXXVI in Poonacha, 2011 [2013]) are discussed in von Hinüber 2016, 18ff.

28. Lüders 1941, 145; HPL §114n190, and von Hinüber 1998, 11.

Prakrit linguistically by giving them, at the same time, a new and better structure. The *vinaya* commentary reached out to monks living outside Ceylon and sought to internationalize the Mahāvihāra position, in contrast to the *nikāya-* and *abhidhamma*-commentaries, which were created together with the *Visuddhimagga* in the first place for the Mahāvihāra monks themselves to reassure them of the orthodoxy of their views. The eventual spread of Mahāvihāra Theravāda to Southeast Asia shows that the admirable intellectual achievements of Buddhaghosa and others bore rich fruit as their work laid a very firm fundament on which many later generations of Theravāda monks were able to build successfully.

References

Bailey, Greg, and Ian Mabbett. 2003. *The Sociology of Early Buddhism*. Cambridge: Cambridge University Press.

Brereton, Joel P. 1982. "The Particle *iva* in Vedic Prose." *Journal of the American Oriental Society* 102: 443–450.

Cheung, Martha. 2006. *An Anthology of Chinese Discourse on Translation. Volume One. From the Earliest Times to the Buddhist Project*. Manchester, UK: St. Jerome; Kinderhook, NY: InTrans.

Cox, W. 2009. Review: Walter Slaje (ed.). 2008. *Śāstrārambha. Inquiries into the Preamble in Sanskrit*. Abhandlungen für die Kunde des Morgenlandes Band LXII. Wiesbaden: Harrassowitz Verlag. *Journal of the Royal Asiatic Society* 19: 400–401.

Dundas, Paul, ed. and trans. 2017. *Magha: The Killing of Shishupala*. Murty Classical Library of India. London: Harvard University Press.

Emmerick, Ronald E. 1968. *Book of Zambasta: A Khotanese Poem on Buddhism*. London: Oxford University Press.

Falk, Harry. 1997. "Die Goldblätter aus Śrī Kṣetra." *Wiener Zeitschrift für die Kunde Südasiens* 41: 53–92.

Frauwallner, Erich. 1984. "Über den geschichtlichen Wert der alten ceylonesischen Chroniken." In *Nachgelassene Werke I. Aufsätze, Beiträge, Skizzen*, edited by Ernst Steinkellner, 7–33. Österreichische Akademie der Wissenschaften. Philosophisch-historische Klasse. Sitzungsberichte, 438 Bd. Vienna: Verlag der Österreichischen Akademie der Wissenschaften.

Geiger, Wilhelm. 1938. *A Grammar of the Sinhalese Language*. Colombo: The Royal Asiatic Society, Ceylon Branch.

———. 1941. *An Etymological Glossary of the Sinhalese Language*. Colombo: The Royal Asiatic Society, Ceylon.

Grahelli, A. 2014. Review: Walter Slaje (ed.). 2008. *Śāstrārambha. Inquiries into the Preamble in Sanskrit.* Abhandlungen für die Kunde des Morgenlandes Band LXII. Wiesbaden: Harrassowitz Verlag. *Indo-Iranian Journal* 57: 161–165.

Hahn, Michael. 2007. "Striving for Perfection: On the Various Ways of Translating Sanskrit into Tibetan." *Pacific World: Journal of the Institute of Buddhist Studies*, 3rd Series 9: 123–149.

Hinüber, Oskar von. 1995. "The Nigamanas of the Sumaṅgalavilāsinī and the Kaṅkhāvitaraṇī." *Journal of the Pali Text Society* 21: 129–133. Reprinted in: *Kleine Schriften I & II*, edited by Harry Falk and Walter Slaje, 62–66. Wiesbaden: Harrassowitz Verlag, 2009.

———. 1996. *A Handbook of Pāli Literature* [HPL]. Indian Philology and South Asian Studies 2. Berlin: Walter de Gruyter.

———. 1998. *Entstehung und Aufbau der Jātaka-Sammlung.* Akademie der Wissenschaften und der Literatur, Mainz. Abhandlungen der geistes- und sozialwissenschaftlichen Klasse 7. Stuttgart: Franz Steiner Verlag.

———. 2001. *Das ältere Mittelindisch im Überblick.* Zweite Auflage, Österreichische Akademie der Wissenschaften. Philosophisch-historische Klasse. Sitzungsberichte, 467. Band. Vienna: Verlag der Österreichischen Akademie der Wissenschaften.

———. 2007. "Buddhistische Kommentare aus dem alten Indien: Die Erklärung des Theravāda-Kanons." In *Kommentarkulturen: Die Auslegung zentraler Texte der Weltreligionen; Ein vergleichender Überblick*, edited by Peter Walter and Michael Quisinsky, 99–115. Beihefte zum Saeculum, Bd. 3. Köln: Böhlau.

———. 2013/2014 [2015a]. "Building the Theravāda Commentaries: Buddhaghosa and Dhammapāla as Authors, Compilers, Redactors, Editors and Critics." *Journal of the International Association of Buddhist Studies* 36, no. 1–2: 353–387.

———. 2015b. "Manuscripts and Printing: South, Southeast and Central Asia." In *Brill's Encyclopedia of Buddhism Vol. I*, edited by Jonathan Silk, 943–958. Leiden: Brill.

———. 2016. "Buddhist Texts and Buddhist Images. New Evidence from Kanaganahalli (Karnataka/India)." *Annual Report of the International Research Institute for Advanced Buddhology at Soka University* 19: 7–20. Reprinted in: *Kleine Schriften III*, edited by Harry Falk, Haiyan Hu-von Hinüber, and Walter Slaje, 1571–1588. Wiesbaden: Harrassowitz Verlag, 2019.

———. 2018. "Two Notes on Pāli Metre." *Journal of the Pai Text Society* 33: 115–122.

Hinüber, Oskar von, and Maiko Nakanishi. 2014. "Kanaganahalli Inscriptions." *Annual Report of the International Research Institute for Advanced Buddhology at Soka University* 17 Supplement.

Hinüber, Oskar von, and Peter Skilling. 2013. "Two Buddhist Inscriptions from Deorkothar (Dist. Rewa, Madhya Pradesh)." *Annual Report of the International Research Institute for Advanced Buddhology at Soka University* 16: 13–26.

———. 2016. "An Inscribed Kuṣāṇa Bodhisatva from Vadnagar." *Annual Report of the International Research Institute for Advanced Buddhology at Soka University* 19: 21–28.

Horner, I. B., trans. [1938] 2006. *The Book of the Discipline (Vinaya-Piṭaka) Vol. I: Suttavibhaṅga.* Lancaster: Pali Text Society.

Kieffer-Pülz, Petra. 2010. "Zitate aus der Andhakaṭṭhakathā in den Subkommentaren."*Studien zur Indologie und Iranistik* 27: 147–235.

Lüders, H. 1941. *Bharhut und die buddhistische Literatur.* Abhandlungen für die Kunde des Morgenlandes XXVI, 3. Leipzig: Deutsche Morgenländische Gesellschaft.

Lüders, H. 1953. *Beobachtungen über die Sprache des buddhistischen Urkanons: Aus dem Nachlass herausgegeben von Ernst Waldschmidt.* Abhandlungen der Deutschen Akademie der Wissenschaften zu Berlin. Klasse für Sprache, Literatur und Kunst, Jahrgang. 1952, No. 10. Berlin: Akademie Verlag.

Monius, Anne E. 2105. "Local Literatures: Tamil." In *Brill's Encyclopedia of Buddhism*, Vol. 1, edited by Jonathan Silk, 813–818. Leiden: Brill.

Nattier, Jan. 2008. "A Guide to the Earliest Chinese Buddhist Translations." *Bibliotheca Philologica et Philosophica Buddhica* 10: 19–27.

Norman, K. R., trans. [1969] 2007. *The Elders' Verses I: Theragāthā.* Lancaster: Pali Text Society.

Perreira, Todd LeRoy. 2012. "Whence Theravāda? The Modern Genealogy of an Ancient Term." In *How Theravāda Is Theravāda? Exploring Buddhist Identities*, edited by Peter Skilling et al., 443–571. Chiang Mai: Silkworm Books.

Pind, Ole Holten. 1992. "Buddhaghosa: His Works and Scholarly Background." *Buddhist Studies / Bukkyō Kenkyū* 21: 135–156.

Poonacha, K. P. 2011 [2013]. *Excavations at Kanaganahalli (Sannati, Dist. Gulbarga, Karnataka).* Memoirs of the Archaeological Survey of India 106. Delhi: Archaeological Survey of India.

Rocher, Ludo. 2009. Review: Walter Slaje (ed.). 2008. *Śāstrārambha. Inquiries into the Preamble in Sanskrit.* Abhandlungen für die Kunde des Morgenlandes Band LXII. Wiesbaden: Harrassowitz Verlag. *Journal of the American Oriental Society* 129, no. 3: 511–512.

Röhrborn, Klaus. 1990. "Zur Werktreue der alttürkischen Übersetzung der Hsüan-tsang-Biographie." In *Buddhistische Erzählliteratur and Hagiographie in türkischer Überlieferung*, edited by Jens Peter Laut and Klaus Röhrborn, 67–73. Veröffentlichungen des Society Uralo-Altaica Bd. 27. Wiesbaden: Otto Harrassowitz.

Seyfort Ruegg, David. 2016. "On Translating Buddhist Texts: A Survey and Some Reflections." In *Cross-Cultural Transmission of Buddhist Texts: Theories and Practice of Translation*, edited by Dorji Wangchuk, 193–265. Indian and Tibetan Studies 5. Hamburg: Department of Indian and Tibetan Studies, Universität Hamburg.

Sims-Williams, Nicholas. 2004. "The Bactrian Inscription of Rabatak: A New Reading." *Bulletin of the Asia Institute* 18: 53–68.

Skilling, Peter. 2009. "Theravāda in History." *Pacific World: Journal of the Institute of Buddhist Studies*, 3rd Series 11: 61–93.

Slaje, Walter. 2005. "Kaschmir im Mittelalter und die Quellen der Geschichtswissenschaft." *Indo-Iranian Journal* 48, 1: 1–70.

———, ed. 2008. *Śāstrārambha: Inquiries into the Preamble in Sanskrit*. Abhandlungen für die Kunde des Morgenlandes Bd. 62. Wiesbaden: Harrassowitz Verlag.

Smith, Helmer. 1950. "Wilhelm Geiger et le vocabulaire du singalais classique." *Journal Asiatique* 238: 177–223.

Spiegel, Friedrich. 1861. *Neriosengh's Sanskrit-Uebersetzung des Yaçna*. Leipzig: Wilhelm Engelmann.

Stargardt, Janice. 1995. "The Oldest Known Pali Texts, 5th–6th Century: Results of the Cambridge Symposium on the Pyu Golden Pali Text from Śrī Kṣetra, 18–19 April 1995." *Journal of the Pali Text Society* 21: 199–213.

Stuart, Daniel M. 2017. *The Stream of Deathless Nectar: The Short Recension of the Amatarasadhārā of the Elder Upatissa—A Commentary on the Chronicle of the Future Buddha Metteyya with a Historical Introduction*. Materials for the Study of the Tripiṭaka Volume 12. Bangkok: Fragile Palm Leaves Foundation and Lumbini International Research Institute.

Tsukamoto, Keisho. 1996. *A Comprehensive Study of the Indian Buddhist Inscriptions: Part 1—Text, Notes and Japanese Translation*. Kyoto: Heirakuji-Shoten.

Turner, R. L. 1966. *A Comparative Dictionary of the Indo-Aryan Languages*. London: Oxford University Press.

Vogel, Jean Philippe. 1929/1930. "Prakrit Inscriptions from a Buddhist Site at Nagarjunakonda." *Epigraphia Indica* 20: 1–37.

Zin, Monika. 2018. *The Kanaganahalli Stūpa: An Analysis of 60 Massive Slabs Covering the Dome*. Delhi: Aryan Books International.

Chapter 5

The Impact of Nineteenth-Century Missionary Translations of Theravāda Buddhist Texts

Elizabeth Harris

In the introduction to this volume, Alice Collett surveys the field of translation studies and both in discussing the field and its now postcolonial guise, and in her more detailed introductions to the chapters, she touches on the issues of colonialism and orientalism. Translation of Buddhist texts, as with other religiuous texts, has been critiqued as an enterprise of colonial appropriation, in my own previous work as well as that of many others. However, in this chapter I seek to explore some aspects of the work of orientalists more deeply.

My thesis in this chapter is that nineteenth-century missionary translators of Pāli and Sinhala Buddhist texts should be given more importance in accounts of orientalist representations of Buddhism, Buddhist modernism, and the translation of Buddhism into the West. To argue this thesis, I will focus on three Wesleyan Methodist missionary Indologists in nineteenth-century Sri Lanka, then Ceylon, who were either involved in the translation of texts or the compilation of dictionaries, which I would argue is a form of translation: Benjamin Clough (1791–1853), Daniel J. Gogerly (1792–1862), and Robert Spence Hardy (1803–1868). First, I will make some theoretical observations about the act of translation in the context of orientalism. Second, I will offer biodata for my three translators and some reflections on the ideological/religious underpinning of their work. Third, I will summarize their translation skills, focusing on one publication or one dimension of their work. Finally, I will offer three reasons for the importance of their work: their chronological priority within nineteenth-century orientalism, their capacity to nuance orientalist studies, and the impact of their work on orientalists and the growth of Buddhist modernism when it broke free from missionary agendas. The chapter builds on previous research into the impact of evangelical Protestant missionaries in the Buddhist majority areas of Sri Lanka (Harris 2006; Harris 2010; Harris 2012; Harris 2014).

The Act of Translation in the Context of Orientalism

Translation is an act of interpretation, shaped by historical context, sociopolitical considerations, and the knowledge and preconceptions of the translators. It can be characterized by "contest, concealment, duplicity, hidden agendas and manipulation conditioned by power relationships" (Harris 2010, 178). This is not to say that accurate translations are impossible but rather that they are not context-neutral. Clough, Gogerly, and Spence Hardy were products of the missionary movement nurtured by the Evangelical Revival at the end of the eighteenth century, and the imperialist assumption that the British had a right to direct and shape learning in their foreign territories. Their translations were conditioned by this. Nevertheless, their sense of imperial ownership did not preclude awareness of scholarly precedent in Sri Lanka or that Sri Lankan Buddhists were heirs to a sophisticated scholarly tradition (Harris 2006, 33–34; Harris 2012).

Sujit Sivasundaram isolates Alexander Johnston (1775–1849), chief justice in Sri Lanka between 1811 and 1818, and John D'Oyley (1774–1824), the first British Resident in Kandy, as the most important early orientalists in Sri Lanka (Sivasundaram 2013, 95–134). I agree with him, although I would add Joseph de Joinville, an early civil servant who wrote one of the first nineteenth-century accounts of Sri Lankan Buddhism, drawing on Sinhala texts (Joinville 1801; Harris 2006, 20–54; De Estève and Fabry 2012). More significant than this, however, is Sivasundaram's argument that the scholarship of these early orientalists joined a lineage that extended back to the eighteenth-century Kandyan revivalist Saranamkara (Sivasundaram 2013, 96–105). Citing the agency of the Sri Lankan monastic *saṅgha* within the development of British orientalism and contesting postcolonial writers who have represented the relationship between the precolonial and the colonial as one of radical rupture, he argues for continuity between the two periods. In this he builds on the work of Ananda Guruge, Donald Lopez, J. J. Clarke, Charles Hallisey, Ann Blackburn, and myself (Guruge 1984; Lopez 1995; Clarke 1997; Hallisey 1995; Harris 2006; Blackburn 2010). For instance, I argued in 2006 that orientalist representations of Sri Lankan Buddhism arose from "an interactive and reciprocal relationship" between Westerners and Asian Buddhists (Harris 2006, 4), although it was not, of course, a power-neutral one. The representations that resulted were neither the creations of the West nor the creations of Asia, and they were marked by a radical multiplicity (Harris 2006, 4).

Clarke has suggested that this multiplicity can still be embraced by the concept of an orientalist family (Clarke 1997, 10). In 2006, I agreed with him only if it was recognized that this family was dysfunctional and internally argumentative (Harris 2006, 4) and I still hold this position. In turning my gaze onto missionary translations, therefore, I am highlighting one branch of this turbulent orientalist family, which drew on eighteenth-century and precolonial precedents.

Biodata for Clough, Gogerly, and Spence Hardy

Benjamin Clough was from Bradford in West Yorkshire. He arrived in Sri Lanka in 1814, as a member of the first group of Wesleyan Methodist missionaries, and stayed until 1837 (Small 1968, 613). When this first group dispersed to carefully chosen towns on the island, Clough remained in Galle, where the group had touched land, at first preaching to the military, and Dutch and Portuguese Christians. He also started to learn Sinhala. Relationships with indigenous Sri Lankans began when a Mahā Mudeliyiar (local administrator under the British), Abraham Dias Abeysinhe Amarasekera, his name suggesting that he received Christian baptism under the Dutch, gave him property for a school and a home. The chronicler of the early Wesleyan Methodist mission to Sri Lanka, William Harvard, claimed that curious Buddhist monks visited this house to ask Clough questions about Christianity (Harvard 1823, 170–171; Harris 2012, 285).

Clough did not stay long in Galle. By August 2015, he had been appointed to Colombo (Harvard and Clough 1816, 115). In effect, he seems to have maintained a presence in both towns. Significant is that he joined

Harvard in visiting Buddhist *vihāras* in the Colombo region to converse with monks about Buddhism, writing to his home committee in 1816:

> Mr Harvard and myself have been labouring the last six or eight months to find out, if possible, what the system is, and what the main pillars are that support it. . . . We have spent much of our time in conversing in a quiet way, with the most learned priests we could meet with. (Clough 1816, 398; quoted in part in Harris 2006, 21)

He added, however, that "they [the monks] carry us through such labyrinths of confusion and nonsense, that we are sometimes ready to despair of effectually succeeding" (Clough 1816, 398). Nevertheless, this did not prevent him from pulling together what he thought he had learned at this point—February 1816. Buddhists were atheists. *Nibbāna* was annihilation, despite the fact that "their descriptions of *this place* are almost endless." Buddhists believed in "an infinite number of worlds," the "eternity of matter," and a system whereby "virtue and vice, of necessity, punishes itself," the greatest punishment being, "an almost endless transmigration through the bodies of beasts, birds, fishes and reptiles" (Clough 1816, 398–399). Clough also heard much about the *dēvālāya* system, namely, the worship of deities, but concluded that it was separate from Buddhism, involved the worship of the devil since he confused it with exorcist ceremonies, and was extremely strong, to the extent that children were dedicated to the devil (Clough 1816, 398–399). In 1833, he expanded on this by stressing that "sentient existence" within Buddhism is seen to have "so much of misery inseparably united to it, that it is regarded as an evil from which all ought to seek emancipation" (Clough 1833, 279). This became the basis of the early missionary representation of Buddhism.

Clough's scholarly works that related to Buddhism included a Sinhala-English dictionary in two volumes. In 1821 (Clough 1821), the English to Sinhala volume was published. The second volume, Sinhala to English, followed in 1830 (Clough 1830). In 1824, he completed a Pāli grammar and vocabulary, started by the civil servant William Tolfrey. This was effectually a translation of the Pāli grammar, the *Bālāvatāra*, with additions from the Pāli lectionary, the *Abhidānappadīpikā*, and another grammatical text, the *Dhātumanjūsā* (Clough 1824, iv). It represented Pāli through a form of Sinhala script, although Clough's explanations transliterated it into Roman lettering, using a rough diacritical system. He also translated part of the ceremony connected with *upasampadā* (higher ordination) and some of the monastic rules found in the *Khandhaka*, published through the Royal Asiatic Society in London, on the committee of which he served (Clough 1834), and wrote a pamphlet on the Buddhist Vihāra, published in a collection of missionary writings (Clough 1833).

He influenced and was influenced by Rasmus Kristian Rask (1787–1832), the Danish comparative linguist who stayed in Sri Lanka from November 1821 to August 1822 (Nordstrand 1974, 70) and referred to him in his Pāli grammar (e.g., Clough 1824, 7). In this chapter, I will focus on volume 2 of his Sinhala-English dictionary (Clough 1830).[1]

Daniel John Gogerly was born in 1792 and arrived in Sri Lanka in 1818 to supervise the Wesleyan Methodist printing press.[2] He was ordained in 1823. He then stayed in Sri Lanka until his death in 1862, without returning to Britain, rising to a leadership position within the mission. He married four times and had two children, one of whom married a Sinhala woman, which means there are Sri Lankan Gogerlys to this day.

Gogerly began to learn Pāli and collect Pāli texts in the 1830s when he was in Dondra, near Mātara on the south coast of Ceylon, within an almost totally Buddhist culture. He eventually possessed almost a complete *Tipiṭika* in manuscript form (Harris 2006, 62). I argued in 2010 that it was the strength of Buddhism in the south of Sri Lanka that prompted Gogerly to study Pāli, together with "the conviction that the monastic Sangha would only take Christianity seriously if Christians took Buddhism seriously, in terms of its texts and traditions" (Harris 2010, 180).

We are told by Spence Hardy that Gogerly, at first, had to be persuaded to publish his translations (Harris 2006, 62), although this was not true for his articles on Buddhism, including a pivotal one, published in

1. The dictionary was revised by George Baugh, Robert Tebb, and Bartholomew Gunasekera for publication in the early 1890s (Clough 1892). The revisers stated, "We have not altered anything for altering's sake; and the quaint language and curious definitions of the original are largely left untouched, while at the same time vigilance has been exercised to ensure accuracy throughout." But they did add quite a lot. Additions were made particularly to words relating to Buddhism to reflect the missionary understanding of Buddhism at that point in the century after the scholarship of Gogerly.

2. For a fuller account of his life, see Harris 2010.

1838, in which he presented his "discovery" of *anattā*, which he translated as no-soul (Gogerly 1838). Eventually, however, his translations appeared in *The Friend* and the *Journal of the Ceylon Branch of the Royal Asiatic Society*. Significantly, they were not disseminated widely in the West. Their main impact was on British residents in Sri Lanka and Sri Lankans educated in English. Only in 1908, long after the founding of the Pali Text Society, was his output collected and published in Sri Lanka and England by Arthur Bishop (1908).

In addition to a translation of the first eighteen *vagga*s of the *Dhammapada* that I examined in 2010 (Harris 2010), Gogerly published selections from the *Cariyāpiṭaka* relating to almsgiving, selections from *sutta*s chanted during a *Paritta* ceremony, selections from the *Jātaka*, extensive sections of the *Vinaya*, and the *Pāṭimokkha*. From the *Dīghanikāya*, he published translations of the *Brahmajālasutta* (DN 1), the *Sigālakasutta* (DN 31), and the *Mahāsatipaṭṭhānasutta* (DN 22). And from the *Majjhimaikāya*, he published translations of the *Verañjakasutta* (MN 42), the *Mahādhammasamādānasutta* (MN 46), the *Raṭṭhapālasutta* (MN 82), and the *Cūḷakammavibhaṅgasutta* (MN 135).

That Gogerly was cognizant of a much larger selection of texts is shown in his articles on Buddhist belief and practice. For instance, "An Outline of Buddhism," a paper he gave in 1861 (Bishop 1908, 1: 15), refers to the *Aggaññasutta*, the *Parinibbānasutta*, the *Saṃyuttanikāya*, the *Aṅguttaranikāya*, the *Abhidhammapiṭaka*, and the *Milindapañha* (Gogerly 1870, included in Bishop 1908, 1: 15–44). The Royal Asiatic Society in London holds handwritten notes by Gogerly on the sections of the *Aṅguttaranikāya*. In this chapter, I will concentrate on his translation of the *Cūḷakammavibhaṅgasutta* (Bishop 1908, 2: 492–502).

Robert Spence Hardy was born in Lancashire but moved to York as a teenager to live with his maternal grandfather, Robert Spence, a supporter of Wilberforce. He brought Spence into his name because of this. Gifted with a facility for words, after leaving school, he gained an apprenticeship with the *Yorkshire Gazette*. His vocation changed when he met Wesleyan Methodist advocate of missionary work Thomas Coke (1747–1814) at Spence's house. Attracted to the idea of such work, he was ordained in 1825 and traveled to Sri Lanka in the same year. In 1830, he returned to Britain, visiting several countries on the way, including India, Egypt, Jerusalem, Cyprus, Greece, and Italy—a Victorian "gap" year. He married in Britain and returned to Ceylon in 1835. This time he stayed thirteen years, returning to Britain in 1848 because of his wife's ill-health. He returned again in 1863 and remained until 1865 (Harris 2014, 84–86, drawing on Coplans 1980).

As was Clough, Spence Hardy became fluent in spoken and written Sinhala. He also became an avid collector of manuscripts. He was able to read before the Ceylon Branch of the Royal Asiatic Society in 1848 a list of 467 books available in Sinhala, Pāli, and Sanskrit (Harris 2006, 64; Spence Hardy 1847). In addition to numerous articles and editorials in the Colombo-based journal he founded, *The Friend*, he authored four major books on Buddhism. Two were published when he was living in England: *Eastern Monachism* (Spence Hardy 1850) and *A Manual of Buddhism in Its Modern Development* (Spence Hardy 1853). *The Sacred Books of the Buddhists Compared with History and Modern Science* was published in Colombo in 1863 (Spence Hardy 1863), in Sinhala in 1865, and in England under a slightly revised name in 1866 (Spence Hardy 1866). *Christianity and Buddhism Compared* was published posthumously (Spence Hardy 1874).

Barbara Coplans (1980) has argued that Spence Hardy's first two books were innovative enough to merit a comparison with Weber in that Spence Hardy sought to study Buddhism as a thing in itself and was interested in Buddhism as lived. When compiling them, for instance, he rejected the study of Pāli in favor of the Sinhala texts (Coplans 1980, 242–246), since he believed they could reveal "the sentiments, and illustrate the manners of the present race of priests" (Spence Hardy 1850, viii; cited in Harris 2006, 64). So, with the expertise of a convert to Christianity from the Buddhist monastic *saṅgha*, he poured over ola leaf manuscripts in Sinhala, including *sūtra sannayas*, eighteenth-century Sinhala commentaries on the Pāli texts, originating from the Kandyan Kingdom (Blackburn 2001, 107–138). Later in his life, he wanted to learn Pāli and was helped by a pupil of Gogerly, David de Silva, since, at that point in the nineteenth century, he could find no *bhikkhus* willing to teach a Christian missionary (Spence Hardy 1866, viii; cited in Harris 2006, 64).

In this chapter, I will focus on *A Manual of Buddhism*, since he compiled this largely from his translations of Sinhala Buddhist texts, which included: Sinhala versions of the *Jātaka*, the *Visuddhimagga*, the *Milindapañha*, portions of the *Suttapiṭaka*, the *Pūjāvaliya*, the *Saddharmālankāraya*, the *Saddharmaratnāvaliya*, the *Amāvatura*, the *Thūpavamsa*, the *Rājavaliya*, and *sūtra sannayas*.

The Ideological and Religious Underpinning of Their Work

All of these missionaries were men of their time, united in the conviction that Buddhism was false and that it would eventually be superseded by Christianity. Clough became known for his incisive preaching, which, as early as 1815, provoked the monks at Kälani Mahā Vihāraya to send a petition to the British administration suggesting that religions should not abuse each other (Harris 2006, 197). Such "abuse," however, was seen as necessary by Clough, who wrote in 1833 that if Ceylon were rid of Buddhism and exorcist ceremonies—"these lying vanities"—and embraced Christianity, then it "would become one of the most happy and delightful regions on earth"(1833, 281).

Clough's Sinhala-English and English-Sinhala dictionary, however, did not explicitly carry this agenda. In the two volumes, Clough attempted to be fair to Buddhism and also Hinduism, as he understood them. He sought to inform rather than to berate. He certainly undertook a remarkable amount of research into the religions of Sri Lanka for volume 2. It is significant, for instance, that Clough demonstrated knowledge of dimensions of Buddhism that would be downplayed by later Buddhist modernists, such as devotion to the material reality of texts.

Gogerly also wrote in different registers, from the polemical to the apologetic, and from the argumentative to the broadly descriptive, in order to persuade Buddhists of the superiority of Christianity. His translations, however, were, again, in a league apart from his other writings, although they shared his overall missionary agenda (Harris 2010). Gogerly, for instance, wrote that Buddhism in the Matara area rendered people "earthly, sensual and devilish," despite the "morality" of Buddhist precepts and the "refinement" of Buddhist metaphysics, with the result that they were chained to "the Prince of Darkness" and were in need of the liberation that Christianity could bring (1837, 46–47).

One aim of his translations, therefore, was to reveal to Buddhist practitioners inconsistencies between their traditional Buddhist practice and the Pāli texts, which he thought would aid evangelization. In addition, as I explained in 2010, there were at least three other objectives, namely, "to correct the misconceptions about Buddhism that were present among missionaries and other non-Buddhists; to highlight differences between Christianity and Buddhism at the level of belief in order to demonstrate the superiority of Christianity; to inform" (Harris 2010, 182). I added:

> The first and third of these sprang from Gogerly's genuine desire to be just to Buddhism through his mastery of Pāli. The second, however, lay in tension with these. It sprung from a missionary mindset that continually asked: "What in Buddhism competes with Christianity so hindering conversion? What in Buddhism can be used to show the superiority of Christianity?" (Harris 2010, 182)

Spence Hardy was utterly convinced of the superiority of British culture and the providential ordination of Britain to Christianize the East. There is ample evidence of this in his editorials in *The Friend*. For instance, in 1841, he urged his readers to remember that "it is now almost universally received as an established truth, that God has given to our nation [Britain] her extensive colonies and possessions, that we may enlighten the people under our sway by imparting to them the religion of Christ" (Spence Hardy 1841b, 223). Buddhism, for Spence Hardy, was idolatry and idolatry was the greatest offense against God, with the power to send souls into an eternal hell. In 1839 he joined a short-lived Wesleyan Methodist mission in Kandy, where he witnessed the support given to Buddhist institutions by the British administration in accordance with the 1815 Kandyan Convention, which John D'Oyley had negotiated with the Kandyans, when Britain took control of the previously independent kingdom. This led him to write, in 1839, a short polemical treatise, *The British Government and the Idolatry of Ceylon*, which argued for freedom of religion but against any link between the government and such "idolatry" (Spence Hardy 1839).

His rhetoric can be illustrated through an act of imagination, when Spence Hardy placed himself above Sri Lanka and, looking down on its religious practice, wrote this:

> Could we be transported, like our blessed Master, to some mount of universal vision, how should we be confounded at the numberless pollutions and puerilities of idol worship. A thousand temples would be seen, consecrated to impurity and lust; and the shouts of myriads would be heard, ascending before the shapes of blasphemy and horror, whose very invention must have been infernal; while abominations would be witnessed, hallowed as divine, which, had they been but human, would

> have scattered pestilence and death around them, and been everywhere shunned and execrated as the destroyers of mankind. (Spence Hardy 1841a, 171; Harris 2018, 28–29)

A Manual of Buddhism, however, belonged to a different league of writing. The implicit premise behind it was that the translations offered would speak for themselves and prove Buddhism to be irrational, unscientific, idolatrous, and uninspired. He, therefore, explained that his task was to "impart information" rather than take the role of "expositor or controversialist" (Spence Hardy 1853, 358). That some of his critical comments were placed in footnotes rather than in the main text underscores this. That he was willing to praise Buddhism, albeit with a theological caveat, is demonstrated in his statement that the Buddha could have been "the means of producing a moral revolution more important in its results, and more extensive in its ramifications, than any other uninspired teacher, whether of the eastern or western world" (Spence Hardy 1853, 358). I would agree with Coplans that it shows Spence Hardy, at this point in his Indological career, to be close to Weber. Nevertheless, the balance of the book feeds into the premise that he believed that the translations alone would prove Buddhism to be irrational. For it was a book that was predominantly narrative, focusing on cosmology and the biographies of Buddha Gotama and some previous buddhas, namely, those parts of Buddhism that Spence Hardy believed were the most incompatible with scientific thought. Only after page 358 does Spence Hardy pass to the ontology of Buddhism and, finally, its ethics.

Summary of Their Lexical and Translation Work

As with the biographical material, I will examine the three missionaries chronologically, beginning with Clough.

Benjamin Clough

Volume 2 of Clough's Sinhala-English dictionary (Sinhala into English), of necessity, had to engage with Buddhism, because Sinhala overflows with words connected with Buddhism, most appropriated from Pāli and Sanskrit. What is remarkable about Clough's 1830 dictionary is the level of his understanding of the religions of Sri Lanka. Gone is the rather fumbling, incredulous tone of his 1816 letter, when he had been engaging seriously with the Buddhist monastic *saṅgha* for only a few months. By 1830, he was able to point out which Sinhala words derived from Pāli and Sanskrit, and to offer lengthy interpretations of their meaning. Between 1816 and 1830, however, there had been some high-profile conversions of Buddhist monks, as a result of the Wesleyan Methodist mission, for example, the controversial Kapugama Dhammakhandha, who was baptized as George Nadoris de Silva (1768–1843; Young and Somaratne 1996, 53–56). Some of the sophistication of the dictionary could be due to conversations with one of these, although errors of understanding are certainly present, in line with the missionary construction of Buddhism in the 1820s, for instance, that Buddhists believed in the transmigration of the soul. Philosophy from the Pāli texts, data from Sinhala texts, and information about popular practice and material religious culture are all present.

If I had been one of Clough's missionary colleagues and had read the dictionary from beginning to end, I would have been introduced to many key concepts in Buddhism. The defilements (*klesha*; P. *kilesa*), for instance, were described in this way:

> Pain; affliction or distress; pain from disease, anguish; worldly occupation, care, trouble; wrath, anger; lust, passion, evil, pollution, defilement; the sinful corruptions of all the *senses* and *spiritual faculties* of man; according to the doctrines of Buddhism, *klesha* is the source of all the miseries to which existence in any stage is subject; and so long as it exists in any degree either in man or any sentient being it binds him to *existence* which is considered a calamity; the destruction of *klesha* is therefore considered the sole object of a buddhist's religious life; hence without any reference to a *supreme being*, all the *laws*, *precepts*, *rites* and *ceremonies* of *Buddhism* have a regard only to the entire destruction of *klesha*; this object accomplished, the soul or sentient faculty in man, or any higher order of being, escapes from existence, and obtains *nirwani* or *annihilation*. (Clough 1830, 154)

I would have read about the five and the ten precepts and the ten good deeds (*dasa kusula kamma*). I would also have learned much about the

Buddha. Under the definition of *dāna* (generosity), I would have read that the Buddha as *bodhisatta* "gave more flesh from his own body to feed the poor, than the bulk of this earth, and blood more than there is water in the sea" (Clough 1830, 265; see also 220). I would have discovered that one epithet of the Buddha indicated that he was "the religious instructor of the gods" (Clough 1830, 272) and that the Buddha knew "three things, viz, impermanency of matter, existence of sorrow in all things, annihilation of the spirit" (Clough 1830, 191). In connection with the *Pansiya Jatika Pota* (the Sinhala version of the *Jātaka*), I would have read that the book was so sacred that Buddhists "will offer to it and worship it" (Clough 1830, 209).

As for meditation, I would have learned that the practice of *jhāna*, Clough preferring to link this to the Sanskrit form, *dhyāna*, was "that profound and abstract consideration which brings its object fully and undisturbedly before the mind, and is the favourite religious exercises of the *buddhistical ascetics*, and practised chiefly with a view to freeing the soul from all evil propensities" (Clough 1830, 194) and would even have seen an early formulation of the Four Noble Truths: "1 That sorrow is connected with existence in every state: 2 that men are attached to existence only by sensual desire: 3 the means conducing to complete subjugation of the passions: 4 the state preparatory to "*nirwana*," in which the passions are subjected, & every attachment to a continuance of existence destroyed" (Clough 1830, 194).

Much in Clough's representation is a reasonably accurate translation of the Sinhala Buddhist understanding, except for the representation of *nibbāna*, which the missionaries were convinced implied complete annihilation, and transmigration. *Nibbāna* is represented as something that happened at death:

> The *summum bonum* of *buddhism*, viz. the entire destruction of all the passions, the total cessation of all the animal functions, the extinction of every particle of the vivifying principle, the final emancipation of the soul or sentient faculty, exemption from further transmigration, escape from every state of existence, *annihilation*! (Clough 1830, 329)

Other entries, however, described it less polemically as "the state of the final emancipation of the soul from all existence, before which period sorrow cannot be destroyed, it being inherent in every state of existence" (Clough 1830, 276). Sarcasm also entered occasionally, as with his explanation of *dāgäba*, when he explained that "*dágabs*" contained relics taken from the ashes of the Buddha's burnt body: "Every temple has its *dágab*, and every *dágab* has a portion of these bones; so that at this rate of calculation *Buddha* must have had tolerably large bones!" (Clough 1830, 264–265).

DANIEL J. GOGERLY

With his translation of the *Cūḷakammavibhaṅga Sutta* (The Shorter Discourse on Action, *Majjhima Nikāya* iii 202–206), Gogerly sought to inform people about Buddhism's answer to "the unequal distribution of prosperity and adversity in the present state," namely, the principle of *kamma*, which he described as "an occult power, an irresistible fate, resulting from the merit or demerit of actions performed in a previous state of existence" (Bishop 1908, 2: 492) and translated as "conduct" in the discourse. His implicit agenda, therefore, was to evoke the superiority of the concept of forgiveness in Christianity, and his implicit assumption, that this could be done without modifying or manipulating the meaning of the discourse. Some sentences were paraphrased to diminish repetition, a tendency present in all his translations. Customary elements were cut, such as *Ehi passiko*—thus have I heard—at the beginning. The final paragraph, describing, in a poetic but standardized way, the brahmin student's response, was reduced to once sentence, "When Gotama ended the discourse, Subha warmly expressed his admiration, and embraced the Buddhist faith." The discourse's nuanced presentation of the planes of being considered *duggati* (woeful or deprived) were reduced to one category, hell.

Nevertheless, the translation incisively conveyed the original sense of the text, namely, that violence, anger, envy, disrespect, meanness, pride, and an unwillingness to learn about wholesome action led to rebirth in a deprived state or a human birth with low status, while their opposites led to a heavenly rebirth or a prosperous human rebirth. It compares well with more contemporary translations by I. B. Horner (1993) and Bhikkhu Ñāṇamoli and Bhikkhu Bodhi (1995).

ROBERT SPENCE HARDY

To give an indication of Spence Hardy's translation skills in *A Manual of Buddhism*, I will briefly touch on cosmology and the biography of the Buddha. Cosmologically, the reader was introduced to: innumerable world systems that are subject to destruction and renovation (Spence Hardy 1853,

2–3); the mountain Maha Meru with its surrounding rocks and oceans and the "sacred continent" of "Jambudwípa" (1853, 4–19); the dimensions of the sun and moon, and their movement (1853, 20–24); the heavens and "the places of torment" (1853, 26–28); the process of the destruction of worlds and the renovation of similar worlds (1853, 28–35). Detailed measurements and statistics were given for each. Only in a footnote at the end did Spence Hardy judge his material: "The whole of his cosmogony, and of his astronomical revelations, is erroneous; and there are statements in nearly every deliverance attributed to him upon these subjects which prove that his mind was beclouded by like ignorance with other men" (1853, 35). Spence Hardy introduced his Buddha biography in this way:

> Of this matter the greater part may be a mass of mere absurdity, with as little of interest as would be presented by the detail of a consecutive series of the dreams of a disturbed sleep; but it is probable that nearly every incident is founded on fact; and if we were in possession of some talismanic power that would enable us to select the true and reject the false, a history might be written that would scarcely have an equal in the importance of the lesson it would teach. (1853, 139)

What followed was a tour de force, stretching from page 138 to page 386. There was little attempt to find a historical Buddha. Spence Hardy included almost every possible narrative from his sources and footnotes linked these to other mythologies, for instance, those of ancient Greece, the narratives of Islam, and Egypt. The last chapter on the Buddha concerned the "dignity, virtues and powers" of a Buddha (1853, 358–386), and ranged across the Buddha's appearance and stature, his way of walking, the marks on his body denoting his Buddhahood, his way of eating, his kindness, his mode of preaching, and his "supernatural endowments," namely, his knowledge and wisdom. However, as with the cosmology, a judgmental note creeps in at one point, when Spence Hardy claims his translations show proof of a "prostration of intellect" that had nothing to do with the divine (1853, 359–360).

The Impact of These Translations

I pass now to the three reasons for my argument that these missionary translators of Pāli and Sinhala texts should be allowed a stronger voice in accounts of orientalist representations of Buddhism. My first argument is an argument from chronology in that their work was published prior to the usual suspects among nineteenth-century orientalists such as Robert Childers (1838–1876), Edwin Arnold (1832–1904), T. W. Rhys Davids (1843–1922), Max Müller (1823–1900), and Wilhelm Geiger (1856–1943). Volume 2 of Benjamin Clough's dictionary was the first of its kind. Rasmus Rask left a Sinhala syllabary when he departed from Sri Lanka in August 1822, but it was never published. Before Clough, several Westerners had attempted to write about Buddhism or compile information from texts, for example De Queyroz (1930), Robert Knox (1681), Francis Buchanan in Myanmar (1799), Mahony (1801), Joinville (1801), John Davy (1821), and William Harvard (1832). Not one, however, had, at least in the nineteenth century, attempted a dictionary that, by necessity, had to pinpoint the exact meaning of individual words connected with Buddhism. Spence Hardy was equally the first to translate and publish Sinhala Buddhist texts connected with Buddhist cosmology and the Buddha biography, except for Joseph Joinville. He was not, however, the first to draw from Sinhala historical chronicles. In the British period, George Turnour was the first to do this systematically, in the 1830s, although he had several precursors, such as Diogo do Couto, François Valentijn (1666–1727), Mahony, and Joinville.[3] As for D. J. Gogerly, he was translating and publishing Pāli texts well before those who were based in Europe had started. By 1860, only Viggo Fausböll's 1855 Latin translation of the *Dhammapada* was readily available in the West. Gogerly's first translation was published in 1839—selections from Pirit or *parittam* (Gogerly 1839). The strengths and biases of these authors, therefore, reached Westerners, some of them resident in Sri Lanka, before the work of later classic orientalists.

The second argument concerns the capacity of these translators to nuance orientalist studies through their insistence that Buddhism on the ground was much more than a rational philosophy. At the beginning, I stressed that orientalist representations of Buddhism embodied a radical multiplicity. This multiplicity can be mapped on a spectrum, with those who represented Buddhism as a rational and positive philosophy at one end, and those who represented it as nihilistic, irrational, superstitious, and in league with demonism at the other. My translators and the missionaries who were influenced by them, although they were willing to praise some aspects of Buddhism, were at the nihilistic end of this spectrum,

3. I examine this history in detail in Harris 2018.

representing a strand of thinking about Buddhism that penetrated into the twentieth century and that is still present among those evangelical Christians who represent Buddhism as spiritually threatening and demonic.[4] The refrain of the missionary successors to Clough, Gogerly, and Spence Hardy, aware of the growing appeal of Buddhism in the West, was: "But we know what Buddhism is on the ground—and it isn't what you think it is" (Harris 2006, 107–109). I have quoted before these words said by Wesleyan Methodist missionary in Sri Lanka Thomas Moscrop, when speaking to an audience in Birmingham in 1894 of those attracted by the loveliness of Buddhism:

> But they do not know what we know, that nine tenths of the Buddhist temples in Colombo have their demon shrines, covered by the same roof and allowed of the priests, even that of the Buddhist High Priest himself—shrines with dark recesses containing demon images which call forth the deepest awe and worship of the people. (Moscrop 1894, 286)

In the twentieth century, disciples of Edward Said such as Philip Almond (1988) were in danger of essentializing both the Victorian needs that orientalist representations of Buddhism met and the representations of Buddhism that circulated in nineteenth-century Britain. The antidote to such essentializing is the evangelical missionaries, who demonstrate that orientalism was a dialogical, relational, and even conflict-riven field. Moreover, as I have argued elsewhere, Buddhist modernism owes as much to the missionary representation of Buddhism as nihilistic and irrational, which Asian Buddhists countered point for point drawing on their own awareness of the Pāli texts, as to scholars in the West who positioned themselves at the philosophical end of the spectrum (Harris 2006, 198–204).

My third and last argument lies on the other side of the coin from my second. It is that the translation work of these scholars broke free of their missionary agenda, influencing both other orientalist scholars and nonscholarly inquirers into Buddhism. Both Spence Hardy and Gogerly

4. See for instance Victor Hafichuk within an article on the dangers of Buddhism: "Either Jesus Christ is the One and Only Way to God or He is not. If He is, then all other ways lead astray to darkness and destruction, because in Him and Him only is life" (Hafichuk n.d.).

adopted a more explicitly negative stance on Buddhism as their writing career progressed. This is most obvious in the work of Spence Hardy, who certainly could not be compared to Weber in his polemical later works, but it was also present in Gogerly's work, for instance, in 1861 when he presented Buddhist cosmology as doctrine for the first time in order to demonstrate the irrationality of Buddhism (Harris 2006, 74). One reason for this was that they both had evidence that their translations were feeding into the European freethought discourse in a positive way. Clough, as early as 1816, had pointed out that Buddhist monks, when disputing the Bible or defending their own religion, made "use of the same arguments that our philosophical gentry in England do to defend the same Atheistical cause" (1816, 399). As synergy developed between the Sri Lankan monastic *saṅgha* and Western freethought movements as the century developed, so synergy developed between the translations of Clough, Gogerly, and Spence Hardy, and Western thinkers who were attracted to Buddhism. In this context, the translations leapt out of their missionary framework to feed an orientalist imaginaire that represented Buddhism as positive and rational. Paradoxically, they were then employed to promote an antimissionary agenda.

In Sri Lanka, for instance, Gogerly's translations from the *Dhammapada* influenced William Knighton (d. 1900), secretary of the Ceylon Branch of the Royal Asiatic Society, when he presented Buddhism as a "philosophical religion" with a sophisticated ethical core that could allow it to stand alongside Christianity "in its civilizing and humanizing influence" (Harris 2006, 76–85). And Rhys Davids, writing forewords to Gogerly's collected works in 1907, could claim that he was "the greatest Pali scholar of his age" (Harris 2010, 179; quoting Bishop 1908, 2: vii). The scholarship of these missionaries, therefore, was employed and appreciated within contexts that repudiated the missionary agenda and from which emerged what has been termed Buddhist modernism.

In Conclusion

Clough, Gogerly, and Spence Hardy were typical orientalists in that they sought to exert power over knowledge. They worked principally in the first half of the nineteenth century, believing that their work would serve proselytization, by uncovering facts about Buddhism that would prove the superiority of Christianity. The fruit of their labor, however, left a more complex legacy. On one hand, their work fed into a representation of Buddhism as negative soteriology that continues within some Christian contexts. On the other hand, however, their work was foundational in the development of nineteenth-century orientalism and Buddhist modernism. It is also significant that Spence Hardy's stress on narrative and Clough's uncovering of materiality have a remarkably contemporary ring. These missionaries are worth revisiting.

References

Almond, Philip C. 1988. *The British Discovery of Buddhism*. Cambridge: Cambridge University Press.

Bishop, Arthur S., ed., 1908. *Ceylon Buddhism: Being the Collected Writings of Daniel John Gogerly*. 2 vols. Colombo: Wesleyan Methodist Bookroom; London: Kegan Paul, Trench, Trübner and Co.

Blackburn, Anne M. 2001. *Buddhist Learning and Textual Practice in Eighteenth-Century Lankan Monastic Culture*. Princeton: Princeton University Press.

———. 2010. *Locations of Buddhism: Colonialism and Modernity in Sri Lanka*. Chicago: University of Chicago Press.

Buchanan, Francis. 1799. "On the Religion and Literature of the Burmas." *Asiatick Researches* 6: 136–308.

Clarke, J. J. 1997. *Oriental Enlightenment: The Encounter between Asian and Western Thought*. London: Routledge.

Clough, Benjamin. 1816. "Extract of a Letter from Mr Clough to Mr Buckley, *Point de Galle*, Feb 12, 1816." *Methodist Magazine* 39: 397–400.

———. 1821. *A Dictionary of the English and Singhalese, and Singhalese and English Languages under the Patronage of the Government of Ceylon in Two Volumes*. Vol. 1. Colombo: Wesleyan Mission Press.

Clough, Benjamin. 1824. *Compendious Pali Grammar, with a Copious Vocabulary in the Same Language*. Colombo: Wesleyan Mission Press.

———. 1830. *A Dictionary of the English and Singhalese, and Singhalese and English Languages under the Patronage of the Government of Ceylon in Two Volumes*. Vol. 2. Colombo: Wesleyan Mission Press.

———. 1833. "The Vihara of Buddha in Ceylon." In *The Missionary; or Christian's New Year Gift*, edited by William Ellis, 277–289. London: Seeley and Sons; Simpkin and Marshall; and Holdsworth and Ball.

———. 1834. "The Ritual of the Budd'hist Priesthood, Translated from the Original Pálí Entitled Karmawákya." In *Miscellaneous Translations from*

Oriental Languages, vol. 2. London: Published for the Oriental Translation Fund by Richard Bentley.

———. 1892. *A Sinhalese-English Dictionary New and Enlarged Edition*. Kollupitiya: Wesleyan Mission Press.

Coplans, Barbara A. R. 1980. "Methodism and Sinhalese Buddhism: The Wesleyan Methodist Encounter with Buddhism in Ceylon 1814–1864 with Special Reference to the Work of Robert Spence Hardy." Unpublished thesis, University of Leeds.

Davy, John. 1821. *An Account of the Interior of Ceylon and Its Inhabitants with Travels in That Island*. London: Longman, Hurst, Rees, Orme & Brown.

De Estève, Marie-Hélène, and Philippe Fabry. 2012. *Eudelin de Jonville: Some Notions about the Island of Ceylon / Quelques notions sur L'isle de Ceylan*. Colombo: Viator.

De Queyroz, Fernão. 1930. *The Temporal and Spiritual Conquest of Ceylon*. Colombo: Government Printer.

Gogerly, Daniel J. 1837. "*Quarterly Letter* dated 30 October 1837 from Dondra." In *Extracts from Quarterly Letters Addressed to the Secretaries of the Wesleyan Missionary Society by Ministers of the South Ceylon District*, 46–51. Colombo: Wesleyan Mission Press.

———. 1838. "On Transmigration." *The Friend* 2, no. 3: 41–48; 2, no. 4: 61–69; 2, no. 5: 85–94.

———. 1839. "On Budhism—Pirit." *The Friend* 2, no. 10: 185–192; 2, no. 11: 205–213; 2, no. 12: 225–231; 3, no. 1: 1–7; 3, no. 2: 21–26.

———. 1870. "An Outline of Buddhism." *Journal of the Ceylon Branch of the Royal Asiatic Society 1867–1870*; reprinted in Bishop 1908, 1: 15–44.

Guruge, Ananda. 1984. *From the Living Foundations of Buddhism: Sri Lankan Support to Pioneering Western Orientalists*. Colombo: Ministry of Cultural Affairs.

Hafichuk, Victor. n.d. "Buddhism Examined from a Godly and Biblical Perspective." www.thepathoftruth.com/falsehood-exposed/buddhism.htm.

Hallisey, Charles. 1995. "Roads Taken and Not Taken in the Study of Theravāda Buddhism." In Lopez 1995, 31–61. Chicago: University of Chicago Press.

Harris, Elizabeth. 2006. *Theravāda Buddhism and the British Encounter: Religious, Missionary and Colonial Experience in Nineteenth Century Sri Lanka*. Abingdon: Routledge.

———. 2010. "Manipulating Meaning: Daniel John Gogerly's Nineteenth Century Translations of the Theravāda Texts." *Buddhist Studies Review* 27, no. 2: 177–195.

———. 2012. "Memory, Experience and the Clash of Cosmologies: The Encounter between British Protestant Missionaries and Buddhism in Nineteenth Century Sri Lanka." *Social Sciences and Missions* 25, no. 3: 265–303.

———. 2014. "Two Western Indologists in Nineteenth Century Sri Lanka: Daniel John Gogerly and Robert Spence Hardy." In *Methodism in Sri Lanka: Visions and Realities 1814–2014*, edited by G. P. V. Somaratne, 81–128. Colombo: Wesley Press.

———. 2018. *Religion, Space and Conflict in Sri Lanka: Colonial and Postcolonial Contexts*. Abingdon: Routledge.

Harvard, William. 1823. *A Narrative of the Establishment and Progress of the Mission to Ceylon and India Founded by the Late Rev Thomas Coke under the Direction of the Wesleyan-Methodist Conference*. London: W. M. Harvard.

Harvard, William, and Benjamin Clough. 1816. "Extract from a Letter from the Missionaries, Messrs. Harvard and Clough, to the Missionary Committee, Colombo, Aug. 26, 1815." *Methodist Magazine* 39: 115–120.

Horner, I. B., trans. [1959] 1993. "Discourse on the Lesser Analysis of Deeds." In *The Collection of the Middle Length Sayings*, 248–253. Oxford: Pali Text Society.

Joinville, J. 1801. "On the Religion and Manners of the People of Ceylon." *Asiatick Researches* 7: 307–444.

Karunaratna, Charles Winston. 1999. *Buddhism and Christianity in Colonial Ceylon (The British Period, 1796–1948)*. Ilford: Self-published.

Knox, Robert. 1681. *An Historical Relation of the Island of Ceylon in the East Indies*. London: Robert Chiswell.

Lopez, Donald S. Jr., ed., *Curators of the Buddha: The Study of Buddhism under Colonialism*, Chicago: University of Chicago Press.

Mahony, Captain. 1801. "On Singhala, or Ceylon, and the Doctrines of Bhoodha from the Books of the Singhalais." *Asiatick Researches* 7: 32–56.

Moscrop, Thomas. 1894. "Christianity and Buddhism in South Ceylon: A Missionary Speech." *Monthly Literary Register* II New Series 12: 285–287.

Ñāṇamoli and Bodhi, trans. 1995. "The Shorter Exposition of Action." In *The Middle Length Discourses of the Buddha*, 1053–1057. Boston: Wisdom.

Nordstrand, Ove K. 1974. "A Note on Rasmus Rask and the Ceylonese Manuscripts at the Library of the Wesleyan Mission, Colombo, in 1822." *Journal of the Sri Lanka Branch of the Royal Asiatic Society* 18: 70–73.

Sivasundaram, Sujit. 2013. *Islanded: Britain, Sri Lanka and the Bounds of an Indian Ocean Colony*. Chicago: University of Chicago Press.

Small, Walter, J. T. 1968. *A History of the Methodist Church in Ceylon 1814–1964*. Colombo: Wesley Press.

Spence Hardy, Robert. 1839. *The British Government and the Idolatry of Ceylon*. Colombo: Wesleyan Mission Press.

———. 1841a. "Idolatry." *The Friend* 4, no. 9: 171–172. (Signed "McAll.")

———. 1841b. "On Duty." *The Friend* 4, no. 12: 221–226.

———. 1848. "On the Language and Literature of the Singhalese." *Journal of the Ceylon Branch of the Royal Asiatic Society* 1, no. 2: 99–104.

———. 1850. *Eastern Monachism: An Account of the Origin, Laws, Discipline, Sacred Writings, Mysterious Rites, Religious Ceremonies and Present Circumstances of the Order of Mendicants Founded by Gotama Buddha*. London: Partridge and Oakley.

———. 1853. *A Manual of Budhism in Its Modern Development*. London: Partridge and Oakley.

———. 1863. *The Sacred Books of the Buddhists Compared with History and Modern Science*. Colombo: Wesleyan Mission Press.

———. 1866. *The Legends and Theories of the Buddhists Compared to History and Science*. London: Williams and Norgate.

———. 1874. *Christianity and Buddhism Compared*. Colombo: Wesleyan Methodist Book Room.

Young, Richard F., and G. P. V. Somaratne. 1996. *Vain Debates: The Buddhist-Christian Controversies of Nineteenth Century Ceylon*. Publications of the De Nobili Research Library 23. Vienna: University of Vienna.

Chapter 6

Words or Terms?

Models of Terminology and the Translation of Buddhist Sanskrit Vocabulary

Ligeia Lugli

Buddhist Sanskrit texts, like most texts, can be conceived as networks of words woven together by complex lexical, semantic, and pragmatic relations. An understanding of these relations, and of the many factors that influence the meaning and use of words in context, is key to the translation of these texts. This may sound obvious. Yet, I had occasion to discover that many translators of Buddhist literature conceptualize their translation task rather differently.

As part of my lexicographic work on Buddhist Sanskrit vocabulary, I had, at some point, to interview the prospective audience of the lexical resource I was working on.[1] Since the resource was mainly aimed at translators of Buddhist Sanskrit texts, most of the interviewees were scholars and students actively engaged in the translation of such texts. The interviews were enlightening. Among other things, they revealed a fundamental discrepancy between the interviewers' and interviewees' conceptualization

1. The interviews were held in 2015 at the Mangalam Research Center (Berkeley, CA) and online, as part of the development of the Buddhist Translators Workbench (https://www.mangalamresearch.org/buddhist-translators-workbench/).

of the language of Buddhist sources. While my colleagues and I were talking of Buddhist Sanskrit words and vocabulary, our interlocutors were consistently referring to Buddhist Sanskrit terms and technical terminology. They appeared to hold what I call a "terminological view" of the Buddhist lexicon, whereby much of the Buddhist vocabulary (notably the segment that proves the most resistant to rendition in English) is taken to have a highly specialized and stable meaning that is best understood (and translated) not so much through the study of its behavior in context, but rather through mastery of, quite specifically, abhidharmic definitions.

Fascinated by this discrepancy in the conceptualization of the Buddhist Sanskrit lexicon, I gave some thought to the difference between words and terms and the impact any conceptualization of that difference may have on translation.

Models of Terminology and Their Impact on Translation

Terminology is a specialized subset of the general language. As such, it calls for specialized translation. Generally speaking, translating terminology requires a level of precision and consistency that is neither necessary nor advisable in the translation of most nonspecialized texts. Yet, just how different terminological translation should be from nonspecialized translation ultimately depends on how greatly we take terms to differ from general language words.

For most of the twentieth century, Western scholars in the fields of terminology and specialized translation regarded terms to be fundamentally different from words.[2] Contrary to words in the general language, whose meaning is largely "fuzzy" and context dependent, terms typically designate well-defined concepts that have a precise function and taxonomic position within a system of knowledge.[3]

2. The fields of terminology and specialized translation are closely related. Theoretical work on terminology first began in response to the needs of translators working on technical texts and it is no coincidence that Eugene Wüster, the father of terminology as an academic discipline, was actively engaged in technical bilingual lexicography (see Faber-Benítez 2009, 111).

3. See Cabré (2010, 357) and Bowker and Hawkins (2006, 79): "The concepts that make up specialized fields of knowledge are designated by lexical items known as terms."

An example may serve to illustrate this difference and how it affects translation. Let us contrast the word "friend" with the term "diabetes." Depending on the context, "friend" can mean, among other things, someone one likes to spend time with, an ally in war, a romantic partner, or a mere acquaintance. The boundaries between these various concepts are not clearly delineated. Where the concept of friend starts, and that of acquaintance ends, is largely a matter of personal interpretation. Moreover, if one wants to express the prototypical meaning of the word "friend," that is, the idea of someone one wants to spend time with or talk to, there are a plethora of near-synonyms one can choose from depending on the communicative situation, register, or semantic nuance one wishes to convey. One can for example choose the words "buddy" or "mate" over "friend." Thus, to render the word "friend" accurately in another language, translators have to pay great attention to context. In most cases, they have to keep adapting their rendition of this word throughout the text, in order to convey the various meanings it takes in different sentences. No translator would stick to one single translational equivalent to render all the different meanings that a word like "friend" acquires in different contexts.

The translation of the term "diabetes" is an entirely different matter. "Diabetes" refers to a well-defined family of diseases that occupies a specific position in medical taxonomy. Moreover, the term "diabetes" stands in a biunivocal relationship with the concept it expresses. It only refers to one medical concept and, in medical discourse, this medical concept can only be expressed with the name "diabetes." Lexical choice in this case is not influenced by the multitude of factors that usually inform word selection in everyday language. Regardless of context, collocational patterns, or communicative situation, one would have to use the term "diabetes" to refer to the homonymous family of diseases.

The tasks of the translator in this case is to find an equivalent expression in the target language for the medical concept expressed by the term "diabetes." Once a suitable equivalent is found, it has to be consistently adopted throughout the entire text, to ensure precision and avoid the ambiguities that lexical variation might bring about. This task is not without its challenges. To make sure they select the appropriate equivalent, translators need to be well acquainted with the definition of a term in a discipline and make sure that it matches the definition of the equivalent term in the target language. In some cases, the target language may lack an exact equivalent and translators would have to decide how to fill the terminological gap. Overall, however, in the case of "pure terms" like "diabetes," terminological translation is a straightforward, if not mechanical, matching exercise. Alas, as it often happens with seemingly straightforward things, this view of terminology and terminological translation has turned out to be often unrealistic.

Only a minority of terms behave as neatly as "diabetes." "Diabetes," is, so to speak, a prototypical term. More specifically, "diabetes" fulfills the requirements of the General Theory of Terminology (also called "classical model of terminology" in this chapter). According to this theory, a lexical item qualifies as a term only if it stands in biunivocal relation with its referent and is unambiguously defined.[4] In other words, this model of terminology views terms as radically different from general language words.

Current Model of Terminology

Over the last couple of decades, a growing body of evidence has emerged against the General Theory of Terminology. It is now generally agreed that the distinction between words and terms is far from clear-cut, with terms being subject to much of the same fluidity as words. The current model of terminology is articulated, with minor differences, within a variety of theoretical frameworks. Prominent theories include sociocognitive, communicative, and frame-based theories of terminology.[5] Regardless of their individual flavor, all current theories agree that terms are dynamic and stand on a continuum with general language words.

Three main points emerge from the ever-growing literature on the subject. First, specialized concepts, which are the referents of terms, are dynamic, multifaceted, and often tolerant of a degree of vagueness. To begin with, they are subject to diachronic change, as they develop together with the fields of knowledge to which they pertain.[6] They are also subject to contextual change. They are conceptualized differently depending on the field in which they occur, with different aspects of the same specialized concept being foregrounded in different contexts.[7] This is all the more

4. See Bowker and Hawkins 2006, 83.

5. For an overview of these theories, see Faber-Benítez 2009, 112ff.

6. See ten Hacken 2015 and Dury 1999.

7. This phenomenon is often referred to as multidimensionality or perspectivization; see Rogers 2004, Antia et al. 2005.

frequent when a concept is underspecified and thus allows for a degree of reinterpretation in different environments (Freixa 2006, 64). Faber-Benítez and León-Araúz (2016) offer a fine example of this phenomenon. They propose that the oscillatory movement that constitutes the prototypical aspect of the concept of "wave" is fundamentally underspecified. It can apply to anything that follows an oscillatory movement pattern. This underspecification allows the concept of "wave" to become associated with different specialized concepts in different fields, for example, with electromagnetic waves in physics and surface waves in marine ecology (Faber and León-Araúz 2016, 9). Thus, words denoting broad, underspecified concepts like "wave" are likely to acquire different terminological realizations in different contexts, especially when compounded with other words that serve to specialize their meaning (e.g., the adjective "electromagnetic").

Second, terms behave much more like general language words than was previously thought. Style and register affect specialized prose, creating terminological variation and alternations between terms and general language expressions that approximate the same specialized concept (e.g., "cardiovascular disease" can be replaced by "heart condition" in some contexts).[8] Furthermore, like general language words, terms are not exempt from being used metaphorically or developing semantic extensions that result in terminological polysemy.[9]

Finally, words and terms stand on a semantic continuum. As the example of "wave" mentioned earlier illustrates, most terms are but general language words that acquire specialized meanings in certain contexts. These contexts are not always easy to identify and some ambiguity as to the terminological status of an expression may arise. Faber and León-Araúz (2016), for example, argue that the verb "to dissipate" in the domain of meteorology (e.g., in the sentence "the cyclone has dissipated") is related to the terminological value of this verb in thermodynamics, where it specifically refers to the dispersion of energy. However, they note that the verb can also be read in its general language sense of "to dissolve

8. See Bowker and Hawkins 2006 and Fernández-Silva, Freixa, and Cabré 2011.

9. Terminological polysemy differs from the polysemy of words in the general language, insofar as it rarely gives rise to ambiguity. The different terminological realizations of a single word typically pertain to different domains of knowledge. The use of "virus" in computer science, for example, is a metaphorical extension of the biological application of the same term, but the two uses are not likely to generate much semantic ambiguity as they typically occur in very different contexts.

gradually."[10] Cases like this call for reconceptualizing terminology as a graded phenomenon. Terms and words stand on a cline of specialization, with some instantiations being closer to "classical" terms and some closer to general language use.

This renders the categorization of word instantiations as terminological somewhat problematic.[11] Recent definitions of terms emphasize the function that terms serve in context rather than their intrinsic lexico-semantic properties. A leading terminologist, M. T. Cabré, writes:

> Linguistically, terms are lexical units of language that activate a specialized value when used in certain pragmatic and discursive contexts. The special value results in a precise meaning recognized and stabilized within expert communities in each field. From a cognitive point of view, terms constitute conceptual units representing nodes of knowledge which are necessary and relevant in the content structure of a field of specialty and which are projected linguistically through lexical units. All the conceptual nodes together constitute the conceptual structure of the field. (2010, 357)

In this model of terminology, the challenge for terminologists is to identify words that "can acquire terminological value, to account for how this value is activated [and] to explain the relations of these units with other types of sign" (Cabré 2010, 357). This complicates the work of translators as well, as the task of terminological translation becomes more nuanced than it used to be within the classical model of terminology.

IMPACT ON TRANSLATION

In a paradigm where terms and words blur into one another, consistency and conceptual precision, the bedrocks of terminological translation within the classical model of terminology, become potential sources of inaccuracy. To consistently render all instances of "wave" in a text with a

10. Faber and León-Araúz 2016, 6–7.

11. For an outline of the difficulties of distinguishing between words and terms, or specialized and nonspecialized vocabulary, and a survey of attempts to arrive to such distinction, see Pearson 1998, 16–28.

translation that conveys the precise meaning of the word in physics may quickly lead to inaccuracy if, in fact, the source text moves across domains of knowledge; for example, by referring to waves in the context of both physics and ecology. The same applies if the source text moves across registers. For example, if a physics textbook intersperses highly specialized scientific demonstrations with nonspecialized examples accessible to the general reader.

Translators need to assess very carefully whether each instance of a word possesses terminological value and to what degree this value departs from the general language. Failure to distinguish between terminological and general language instances of the same word inevitably results in a distortion of the register of the source text. Overconsistent and overspecialized renditions risk making the translated version sound more scientific than the original (cf. Olohan 2013, 428). This problem is especially acute when renditions are less transparent than the original. For in this case the translated text will prove less accessible to a general audience than the source text intended to be.

To retain the level of accessibility of source text, a translation should strive to convey the same degree of continuity between terminological and general language uses that a word has in the source language. Thus, if a physics textbook switches between highly specialized explanations of electromagnetic waves and widely accessible examples linking some electromagnetic phenomenon to sea waves, a translation should capture the continuity between the terminological and general language applications of the word "wave."

This may not always be achievable in practice. Different languages may link general language and terminological expressions differently. If a language uses radically different expressions for the general and specialized concept of "wave," it may be impossible to preserve the same level of lexical cohesion and semantic transparency in translation. Depending on the case, translators will have to decide whether to prioritize the preservation of lexical cohesion or the accurate rendition of register. In cases where some level of wordplay is involved, lexical cohesion may prove the better choice. In other instances, it may be preferable to maintain the same register and level of specialization as the source text.

All this is very difficult to achieve in any kind of translation. It proves especially difficult in the translation of ancient Buddhist texts. A number of factors contribute to this increase in difficulty. The most obvious is, perhaps, the unavailability of native speakers to help us judge how natural or specialized an expression may sound in a given context. This difficulty is compounded with the cultural distance between present-day English and classical Buddhist languages. Such distance makes it likely that we will encounter in Buddhist texts words that have no equivalent in English (lexical gaps). Concepts that were salient in the ancient Buddhist world and may have been neatly expressed by a single word (lexicalized) in the languages of that world are not prominent in the conceptual landscape of the modern West and are therefore not lexicalized in contemporary English. The very nature of the texts, too, adds a layer of complexity to the task of translation. The hermeneutic and intertextual dynamics at play in much of Buddhist literature often call for the preservation of lexical cohesion in the translated text.[12] Finally, as Griffiths noted in his much-quoted article on Buddhist Hybrid English, many translators lack sufficient knowledge of the source languages and their conceptual landscape to be able to render Buddhist terminology adequately (1981, 19). I would add that they often also neglect to evaluate the terminological status of individual word instantiations with sufficient delicacy.

Consistency and accuracy have perhaps been overemphasized in the field of Buddhist translation.[13] The repeated adoption of overspecialized renditions, stemming, perhaps, from interpreting segments of the Buddhist vocabulary through a classical model of terminology, has surely contributed the rise of unidiomatic English translations.

A large-scale survey of the Buddhist lexicon is needed to determine to what extent Buddhist terms may fit the classical model of terminology and, hence, require highly consistent and precise renditions. A cursory look at the words[14] I had the good fortune of studying in my lexicographic work suggests that the classical model of terminology may not be the best fit for the Sanskrit Buddhist lexicon. Several terms follow the pattern highlighted by Faber-Benítez and León-Araúz (2016), whereby terminological specializations of a polysemous word arise when an otherwise underspecified word is compounded with specifying lexical items (e.g., *rūpaprasāda*, *śraddhānusarin*).

12. See Ñāṇamoli [1956] 2011, l–li.

13. See Ñāṇamoli [1956] 2011, l–li; Norman 1984 and the following section in this chapter.

14. For a list of these words see Lugli 2019.

In what follows I am going to focus on a single case study on the Sanskrit word *saṃjñā* and show how different models of terminology affect the rendition of this word in Buddhist contexts.

Case Study: *Saṃjñā*

Saṃjñā is a prominent word in the Buddhist lexicon. It refers, among other things, to a key doctrinal concept, the *saṃjñāskandha*. Not surprisingly, its English rendition is a matter close to the heart of many scholars, translators and Buddhist followers alike. Alas, *saṃjñā* is extremely difficult to translate. Many a learned footnote, dense with elucubrations on its possible renditions and their various shortcomings, testifies to this translational difficulty.

It is not my ambition to offer yet another essay on how this word should or could be rendered in English. I merely intend to problematize the discussion on the terminological translation of this word. I will first show that much of the academic debate on the translation of *saṃjñā* is tinged with a version of the "terminological view" of the Buddhist Sanskrit lexicon. In this case, a view that aligns with the classical model of terminology insofar as it conceptualizes the translational challenges posed by *saṃjñā* exclusively in terms of terminological precision and consistency of rendition. I will then evaluate to what extent the use of *saṃjñā* in the sources is terminological and whether this word fits the classical or current model of terminology better. Finally, I will conclude by proposing that we move away from framing the translation of *saṃjñā* as a terminological problem and treat *saṃjñā* as a lexical gap instead.

THE ACADEMIC DEBATE ON *SAṂJÑĀ*

Most students of Buddhist texts will struggle with the translation of the word *saṃjñā* at some point in their career. Fortunately, there is no shortage of exquisitely researched pieces of secondary literature to which they can refer in their struggle. Here, I wish to revisit six pieces that guided my own understanding of this word in my studies: Vetter (2000, 24–26), Skilling (1994, 477ff.n31), Deleanu (2006, 481n41), Seyfort Ruegg (1973, 76–77n2) and (1995, 146), and the brief discussion in Gyatso (1992, 7).

Much of the discussion in these contributions revolves around a critique of the once-favored translation of this word with "perception."[15] The reasons adduced against rendering *saṃjñā* (or its Pāli cognate *saññā*) with "perception" are various, but they tend to cluster around three issues.

First, "perception" is regarded as an imprecise translation that does not exactly match the cognitive function expressed by *saṃjñā*. Vetter and Deleanu highlight that "perception" suggests a rather simple processing of sensorial inputs, which does not accommodate the complexity of the cognitive process that *saṃjñā* denotes.[16] In a similar vein, Gyatso and Skilling emphasize that perception fails to convey the discriminative nature of the cognitive function expressed by *saṃjñā*.

Second, the rendition of *saṃjñā* with "perception" risks introducing terminological inconsistencies. Seyfort Ruegg (1995) and Gyatso point out that "perception" is best used to render the term *pratyakṣa*, which occupies a very different position in the Buddhist conceptual taxonomy and should not be confused with *saṃjñā*.[17]

Finally, "perception" does not cover the full semantic range *saṃjñā* has in context. Skilling highlights the difficulty of finding a single English word that matches the variety of contexts in which *saṃjñā* occurs and he provisionally accepts "perception" as a viable translation option. Vetter and Deleanu prefer to dispense with this problematic rendition and propose "ideation" as a translation term capable of approximating the different meanings of *saṃjñā* (Vetter 2000, 25; Deleanu 2006, 481).

All the aforementioned scholars would probably agree that *saṃjñā* is polysemous and therefore not a term in the classical sense (see the following section). Yet, their discussion of the translation of this word seems to presuppose a view of *saṃjñā* that is consonant with the classical model of terminology, especially in regard to the insistence on precision and consistency of rendition.

The preoccupation with the semantic imprecision of "perception," for instance, points to an understanding of *saṃjñā* as a term consistently denoting a specific type of cognitive activity, which must be rendered with utmost precision in translation. Seyfort Ruegg's and Gyatso's concern

15. See especially Seyfort Ruegg 1995, 146; Vetter 2000, 24–25; Gyatso 1992, 7.

16. See Vetter 2000, 24–25.

17. See Seyfort Ruegg 1995, 146; Gyatso 1992, 7.

over the possible conflation of *saṃjñā* with *pratyakṣa* in English translations is explicitly framed as a problem of terminological coherence and standardization, which, again echoes the classical ideal of consistency of rendition.[18] Finally, this ideal of consistency is clearly behind Deleanu's and Skilling's quest for a single one-word equivalent that would match all senses of *saṃjñā*.

There is no doubt that translations should accurately render the meaning of the source text and that a degree of consistency in the choice of renditions is desirable (although not necessarily at the level of individual words!). Yet, to consistently choose a rendition that sounds specialized, such as apperception (Seyfort Ruegg 1973), ideation (Deleanu 2006; Skilling 1984), or perception-as (Gyatso 1992),[19] risks creating a translation that sounds more "jargony" and technical than the source text.

It is true that the contributions considered here are mostly concerned with *saṃjñā* in reference to the *saṃjñāskandha*, which is a term and indeed needs to be rendered consistently (see the following section). Still, the specialized status of *saṃjñā* appears to be taken for granted in the literature and little attention is given to possible fluctuations in the level of specialization that this word undergoes in context. The attitude of some authors toward definitions is significant in this regard.

Several studies take abhidharmic definitions of the *saṃjñāskandha* as their point of reference. Some scholars compare these definitions with contemporary lexicographic definitions of the English words they choose to translate *saṃjñā* and use such definitional comparison as a test of translational accuracy.[20] This definition-matching practice decontextualizes both the Sanskrit and the English word. This is justifiable only if one takes

18. See especially Gyatso: "Buddhologists are still very much engaged in the project of arriving at satisfactory translations and interpretation of primary texts, where the problem of which Western word should render a Buddhist technical term is frequently a vexing one: the translation of many of the most foundational concepts is still not standardized" (1992, 33).

19. Gyatso glosses *saṃjñā* with "perception-as," rather than translating it, and explains her decision with this phrase: "*saṃjñā* is what might be termed perception-as; it consists of assigning an object a label, classifying it in a category, seeing it as something and so forth . . ." (1992, 7).

20. See Deleanu 2006, 481; Skilling 1994, 477 and 479.

the terminological meaning of *saṃjñā* to be unaffected by context, as the classical model of terminology would predict.[21]

Few of the studies considered here acknowledge the effect that contextual variation has on the semantic value of *saṃjñā* (Seyfort Ruegg 1973; Skilling 1994). They too, alas, appear to neglect the translational plasticity required to represent the specialized and nonspecialized uses of *saṃjñā*. Seyfort Ruegg (1973), for instance, emphasizes the continuity between the various senses of this word in the conceptual domains of cognition and language. Still, he confines his discussion to the philosophical discourse, so he does not address the connection between the specialized and nonspecialized meanings of *saṃjñā*; nor does he mention the translational challenge that conveying this connection in English would pose (Seyfort Ruegg 1973, 77n2). Skilling (1994), by contrast, widens the lexical study of *saṃjñā* to cover nonphilosophical material. He is perhaps the only one, among the authors considered here, to highlight the relationship between the abstract cognitive sense that *saṃjñā* has in *abhidharma* and the everyday meanings it expresses in narrative contexts. He is also the only one to warn the reader of the shortcomings of adopting too specialized a rendition for this word (Skilling 1994, 477n31). Still, frustratingly, he strives to find a single one-word English rendition that would accommodate both specialized and nonspecialized applications of the word.

Overall, little attention is devoted to teasing out the difference between the translational requirements of *saṃjñā* as the name of a *skandha* and *saṃjñā* in other contexts. Even less attention is paid to the degree of semantic specialization that *saṃjñā* has in the compound *saṃjñāskandha*.

To what extent this is merely an oversight or the result of a conscious reading of *saṃjñā* through the lens of the classical model of terminology is hard to tell. In either case to disregard the differences and similarities between the specialized and nonspecialized applications of *saṃjñā* is bound to have consequences in translation. Notably, it is likely to result in misrepresentation of the register and level of accessibility of the text.

It is therefore crucial to tease out when *saṃjñā* functions as a term, when it behaves as a general language word, and which intermediate degrees of specialization it might have in between these two poles.

To this end, I have drawn on my ongoing lexicological research on *saṃjñā* and surveyed over six hundred concordance lines with a view to

21. On the relative limitations and usefulness of definitional approaches to terminology, see ten Hacken 2015.

evaluate to what extent different models of terminology may fit the use of this word in context.[22] This research is based on two Sanskrit corpora,[23] a corpus of Buddhist texts dating approximately from the first half of the first millennium CE and a reference corpus of non-Buddhist texts from a similar period.[24] Both corpora comprise different genres and text-types. The Buddhist corpus includes *śāstra*s of various scholastic affiliations, Mahāyāna *sūtra*s, *avadāna*, and literary texts such as the works of Aśvaghoṣa.[25] The reference corpus includes religio-philosophical and political *śāstra*s, extracts from the epics and works by Kālidāsa.[26] Both corpora are still being adjusted for balance[27] and the results discussed here are based only on a preliminary qualitative study of the corpus data.

22. My current research of *saṃjñā* is part of the project "Lexis and Tradition," funded by the British Academy through the Newton International Fellowship program. The dataset used for this study is available on Zenodo (10.5281/zenodo.3402506). I am grateful to Roberto García for helping me with the collection and semantic annotation of part of the concordances for *saṃjñā*. Any inaccuracy in the interpretation and analysis of these citations is, of course, solely mine.

23. In this chapter, I use the words "corpus" and "corpora" in their Corpus Linguistics sense, that is, to refer to "large collections of [electronic] texts used for computer-assisted linguistic analysis" (Meyer 2002, ix). The corpora used for this study, however, are rather small, totaling just over one and half million words (the corpus size in words is estimated from character count to control for the effect of different compounding styles among the texts included in the corpus).

24. The periodization of the texts is obviously only tentative, as the exact chronology of the sources is unknown.

25. The Buddhist corpus used for this study includes the following texts: *Abhidharmakośabhāṣya*, *Arthaviniścayasūtra*, *Aśokāvadana*, *Aṣṭasāhasrikāprajñāpāramitā*, *Bhāvasaṃkranti*, *Bhaiṣajyaguruvaiḍūryaprabharājasūtra*, *Bodhisattvabhūmi*, *Buddhacarita*, *Daśabhūmikasūtra*, *Kāśyapaparivartasūtra*, *Jātakamalā*, *Madhyāntavibhāgabhāṣya*, *Mahāyānasūtrālaṃkāra*, *Mūlamadhyamakakārikā*, *Pañcaskandhaka*, *Ratnāvalī*, *Rāṣṭrapālaparipṛcchāsūtra*, *Ratnagotravibhāga*, *Saddharmapuṇḍarīkasūtra*, *Saundarananda*, *Samādhirāja*, *Sarvadharmāpravṛttinirdeśa*, *Suvarṇavarṇāvadāna*, *Trisvabhāvanirdeśa*, *Triṃśikā*, *Vajracchedikā*, *Vigrahavyāvartanī*, *Vimalakīrtinirdeśasūtra*, *Viṃśatikā*.

26. The reference corpus includes: *Abhijñānaśākuntalam*, *Arthaśāstra*, *Mahābhārata* (1–9), *Manusmṛti*, *Meghadūta*, *Nyāyasūtrabhāṣya*, *Pañcatantra*, *Rāmāyaṇa* (2), *Vaiśeṣikasūtrabhāṣya*, *Yogasūtra*.

27. For an overview of the concept of balance in corpus design, see Hardie and McEnery 2011, 10–13.

SAṂJÑĀ: A TERM OR A WORD?

Corpus research is hardly needed to determine that *saṃjñā* is not a term in the classical sense. As it is well known, this word is highly polysemous. In the corpora used for this study, it takes at least seven different senses, meaning, in turn, 1) signal, 2) name, 3) technical term, 4) a high number, 5) notion, 6) a form of cognitive construal, and 7) being conscious.[28] The contexts and discourses in which this word occurs are equally wide ranging, spanning warfare, cosmology, argumentation, storytelling, and Buddhist doctrine. Even if we consider only its uses in specialized Buddhist texts and confine our analysis to *abhidharma* literature, we find that this word undergoes a variety of semantic permutations. In fact, within the corpora used for this study, the text in which *saṃjñā* displays the richest polysemy is the *Abhidharmakośabhāṣya*.[29] To limit the investigation to attestations where *saṃjñā* refers to the conceptual domain of cognition, which is the focus of the academic debate on the translation of *saṃjñā*, does not completely eliminate *saṃjñā*'s polysemy either; although it does reduce it. In the *Abhidharmakośabhāṣya* alone *saṃjñā* expresses at least three meanings in this conceptual domain: the cognitive state of being conscious, the cognitive process of conceptual construal, and the content of such construal in the form of a notion or awareness of something. Try

28. For the sake of simplicity, I adopt here a conservative view of polysemy as a collection of different discrete senses. Yet, an alternative model of polysemy would probably fit *saṃjñā* better, given that its various senses are all very closely related conceptually. Polysemy can be viewed as a form of semantic underspecification, insofar as different contexts highlight different aspects of a broad, vague concept, or as a series of conceptual extensions of a prototypical core meaning (for a brief summary of current theories of polysemy and an explanation of the relationship between polysemy and semantic underspecification, see Falkum and Vicente 2015). The underspecification model may provide a better description of *saṃjñā*'s semantic behavior. Regardless of which model of polysemy we choose, the fact that *saṃjñā* undergoes noticeable semantic permutations in different contexts disqualifies it from being classified as a term in the classical sense.

29. In the *Abhidharmakośabhāṣya* the word takes up the unusual meaning of "a large number" alongside its typical Buddhist senses of "name," "notion," and "cognitive construal" and its meanings of "signal" and "being conscious," widely attested outside of Buddhist sources. The extreme polysemy of *saṃjñā* in this text is partly due to the coexistence of multiple discourses in this text. However, a degree of polysemy is registered even in specialized passages pertaining to strictly doctrinal *abhidharma* discourse; see, for example, *Abhidharmakośabhāṣya* (Pradhan 1983, 330) and note 37 in this chapter.

as we might, *saṃjñā* is not amenable to the monosemy required by the classical model of terminology.[30]

The current model of terminology, being tolerant of polysemy, seems a better fit for *saṃjñā*. Still, strictly speaking, this word is not a term from the point of view of current terminology theories either. According to current theories, a word functions as a term insofar as it refers to specific nodes within a field of knowledge.[31] Within the sources considered for this study, *saṃjñā* in itself does not seem to correspond to any specific node in the Buddhist system. However, as discussed in the previous section, the current model of terminology views terms as originating through a process of specification and formalization of a general language meaning. This process, the model expects, is often realized through lexical compounding. This fits the case of *saṃjñā* well. *Saṃjñā* does indeed refer to items in the Buddhist doctrinal taxonomy when it is used in combination with other words, typically *skandha* and (*caitasika*) *dharma*.[32] It is important to specify that in these cases the actual terms that denote specialized Buddhist concepts are the multiword expressions *saṃjñā* + *skandha* and *saṃjñā* + *dharma*. *Saṃjñā* on its own may retain

30. The corpus used in this study is too small to indicate whether *saṃjñā* may fulfill the other requirement of the General Theory of Terminology, that is, that a term is not used interchangeably with other near-synonyms. I have so far identified only one case where *saṃjñā* is substituted by a similar word in a location that typically features *saṃjñā*. *Saundarananda* contains a variation on the canonical string *aśubhe śubhasaṃjñā* where *saṃjñā* is replaced with the semantically related verb √*kḷp* (*Saundarananda* VIII.54: *śubhatām aśubheṣu kalpayan*; cf. *Aṣṭasāhasrikāprajñāpāramitā*; Wogihara 1932, 334: *anitye nityam iti duḥkhe sukham iti anātmany ātmeti aśubhe śubham iti vikalpya saṃkalpya utpadyate saṃjñāviparyāsaś cittaviparyāso dṛṣṭiviparyāsaḥ*). Extensive onomasiological research is needed to gauge how interchangeable *saṃjñā* and semantically related words might have been and how entrenched *saṃjñā* was vis-à-vis competing expressions. A graphical visualization of the distribution of *saṃjñā*'s senses over the corpus can be found in *A Visual Dictionary and Thesaurus of Buddhist Sanskrit* (Lugli et al. 2019–) *sub voce saṃjñā*.

31. See Cabré (2010, 357), quoted earlier in this chapter.

32. In the Sanskrit Buddhist corpus used for this study *saṃjñā* also displays other terminological realizations. When paired with the words *bhāvinyā* and *anvarthā*, *saṃjñā* functions as a specialized term that signifies specific types of word-referent relations. This use is well attested in the *Abhidharmakośabhāṣya*, where it appears to pertain to the specialized domain of hermeneutics and argumentation. However, since this terminological application of *saṃjñā* is not characteristically Buddhist, I will not discuss it in this chapter.

the terminological power of these multiword expressions if it is clear from the context that the words *skandha* and *dharma* are implied. This can be considered as a case of terminological specification of a more general word-sense, similar to the case illustrated in the previous section by the examples of the expressions "wave" and "electromagnetic wave."[33]

How close the analogy between the term *saṃjñāskandha* and a term like "electromagnetic wave" might be depends on how specialized and transparent we take *saṃjñā* to be in the string *saṃjñā + skandha*. In the expression "electromagnetic wave," "wave" is both specialized and transparent. It is specialized because it refers to a specific node in the field of physics; it is transparent because its application in physics is sufficiently close to the prototypical general language use of the word to be intelligible to a nonspecialized audience (understanding the specifying modifier "electromagnetic," by contrast, requires some degree of specialized knowledge on the part of the audience). Exactly how specialized and transparent *saṃjñā* is in itself, in isolation from the terms *skandha* and *dharma*, is difficult to determine.

Corpus data can help us in this regard. Here I will limit my discussion of corpus data to attestations in which *saṃjñā* expresses a form of cognitive process, which is the word-sense activated in the multiword expressions *saṃjñā + skandha* and *saṃjñā + dharma*.

The corpora used for this study suggest that *saṃjñā* in this word-sense is likely to be situated at the lower end of the terminological cline.[34] It might have enjoyed some degree of specialization, but it remained close to nonspecialized uses and its terminological application in combination with *skandha* was probably semantically transparent, being but a formalization of a widely used nonspecialized sense. Here is why.

The use of *saṃjñā* in the sense of a cognitive process displays a degree of specialization insofar as it seems to have a Buddhist flavor, with non-Buddhist sources preferring the sense of cognitive state.[35] This signals

33. See note 9 in this chapter.

34. I paraphrase here M. Rogers's expression "cline of 'terminess' " (Rogers 2015).

35. The two senses can be clearly distinguished on syntactic grounds by the presence or absence of an object governed by *saṃjñā*. The difference in the semantic distribution of *saṃjñā* in the Buddhist and reference corpora may be simply due to a discrepancy in the topics covered in the two sets of texts. A systematic onomasiological study is needed to determine whether non-Buddhist sources tend to use different words to lexicalize the same concept that *saṃjñā* + object expresses in Buddhist texts.

that this use might have been characteristic of the Buddhist discourse; but it does not warrant that it had a specialized terminological value in Buddhist sources. To determine to what extent this word-sense may have possessed a degree of terminological specialization, we should consider the level of specialization of the contexts in which it occurs and the degree of precision of the concept it refers to.

Canonical references to *saṃjñāviparyāsa*, typically instantiated in the construction "x-loc y-acc (*iti*) *saṃjñāviparyāsa*" and signifying a mistaken interpretation of reality, may be regarded as providing a specialized context for the use of *saṃjñā* (at least as far as the phrase *saṃjñāvipāryasa* is concerned). However, this use seems too close to nonspecialized occurrences of *saṃjñā* in narrative contexts to justify a terminological reading.[36] Sentences like *gṛhapaterantike pitṛsaṃjñāmutpādayet* ("he would regard the householder as a father," *Saddharmapuṇḍarīka*; Kern and Nanjio 1970, 107), *vismṛtaśatrusaṃjñas* ("forgetting that he used to consider him an enemy," *Jātakamalā*; Hanisch 2005, xxv, 8), or *sa pārthivāntaḥpurasaṃnikarṣaṃ* (. . .) *dhīro vanasaṃjñayeva* ("He remained composed in the female quarters as if these were a place of austerity to him" (*Buddhacarita*; Johnston 1935, 1: 51), all of which occur in nonspecialized contexts, are semantically identical and syntactically related to the prototypical canonical use of *saṃjñāviparyāsa*. The same use is also attested in the topos of mistaking a rope for a snake (e.g., *Abhidharmakośabhāṣya*, 375: *rajjvām iva sarpasaṃjñā*), which, even though it occurs in specialized doctrinal contexts, is unlikely to have a specialized meaning, due to the everyday nature of the image around which the analogy pivots. All in all, it seems that *saṃjñā* in the sense of cognitive process or cognitive construal (i.e., take something for / regarding something as) is not technical. The use of this word is likely to have sounded rather idiomatic to an audience familiar with the use of *saṃjñā* in Buddhist narrative texts but with no specialized knowledge of Buddhist doctrine or *abhidharma*.

36. It might be worth noting, incidentally, that the *Abhidharmakośabhāṣya* remarks that the canonical string *saṃjñāviparyāsaḥ cittaviparyāso dṛṣṭiviparyāsa* is subject to the vagaries of linguistic convention—an assertion that may be taken to signal a perceived lack of terminological precision in these phrases (see *Abhidharmakośabhāṣya*; Pradhan 1983, 283: *yat tarhi sūtre uktam "anitye nityam iti saṃjñāviparyāsaḥ cittaviparyāso dṛṣṭiviparyāsa" iti / dṛṣṭir evātra viparyāsaḥ saṃjñācitte tu tadvaśāt // V.9 // dṛṣṭiviparyāsavaśād eva tatsaṃprayukte saṃjñācitte viparyāsāv uktau / vedanādayo 'pi kasmān noktāḥ / lokaprasiddhyā / loke hi viparyastasaṃjño viparyastacitta iti prasiddhaṃ na punar viparyastavedana iti /*).

This meaning of *saṃjñā* is likely to have remained transparent even in highly specialized contexts. A look at the definition of the *saṃjñāskandha* in the *Abhidharmakośabhāṣya*, for example, shows that this terminological application of *saṃjñā* stands on a continuum with the nonspecialized uses of the word in narrative texts. The *Abhidharmakośabhāṣya* defines *saṃjñā* in relation to the *saṃjñāskandha* as the process of identifying the characteristics of objects and exemplifies it with the construal of something as blue or yellow or of someone as friend or foe.[37] This is but a formalization and specification of the nonterminological use of *saṃjñā* in narrative contexts, where *saṃjñā* is used in the fundamentally identical sense of to consider someone as an enemy, or as a father, and so on. Thus, while the string *saṃjñā* + *skandha* functions as a term, the meaning of *saṃjñā* in this string is close to its nonspecialized meaning.

This allows for some fluidity between terminological and general language uses of *saṃjñā*. In the *Abhidharmakośābhāṣya*, for example, a highly specialized discussion on experience in the immaterial realm (*arūpyadhātu*) clearly connects the terminological use of *saṃjñā* as one of the *skandha* with the general use of *saṃjñā* as awareness of something—a meaning that is attested outside of Buddhist sources, too.[38]

So, in keeping with the current model of terminology, the boundary between terminological and nonterminological uses of *saṃjñā* is fuzzy. Even clearly specialized expressions such as *saṃjñā* + *skandha* are best conceived as standing on a terminological cline rather than as being neatly separated from general language uses. By virtue of this continuum between its specialized and nonspecialized applications, in most contexts *saṃjñā* is likely to have been semantically transparent and to have sounded idiomatic to an audience not especially trained in the Buddhist system. A good translation of this word should aim to convey a similar level of transparency and idiomaticity.

---

37. *Abhidharmakośabhāṣya*; Pradhan 1983, 10: *saṃjñā nimittodgrahaṇātmikā // I.14 // yāvannīlapītadīrghahrasvastripuruṣamitramitrasukhaduḥkhādinimittodgrahaṇamasau saṃjñāskandhaḥ/*. Cf. *Pañcaskandhaka*; Steinkellner and Li 2008, 4: *saṃjñā katamā | viṣayanimittodgrahaṇam |*.

38. See, for example, *Abhidharmakośabhāṣya*; Pradhan 1983, 330: *katham idānīṃ sukhasvabhāvāṃ vedanāṃ duḥkhataḥ paśyanti / yathā rūpasaṃjñādīny api duḥkhataḥ paśyanti / [. . .] āryāṇāṃ ca rūpārupyopapattau kathaṃ duḥkhasaṃjñā pravarteta {Y. pravartate} / na hi punas teṣāṃ duḥkhavedanāhetuḥ skandhā bhavanti/*. Cf. *Mahābhārata* VII.49: *nihatāḥ pṛtanāmadhye mṛtasaṃjñā mahābalāḥ*.

From Terminological Problem to Lexical Gap

Interpreting *saṃjñā* through the current model of terminology does not make the task of translating it any easier. Quite the opposite. As mentioned in the previous section, the current model of terminology, being more nuanced than its predecessor, adds layers of complexity to the task of terminological translation. It does however present some advantages. Besides providing a more accurate representation of the behavior of *saṃjñā* in context, the current model of terminology helps us reprioritize our translational desiderata. By highlighting that *saṃjñā* acquires varying degrees of specialization in different instantiations, this model reveals that the quest for a single translation equivalent is unrealistic, if not outright misleading. By showing the continuity between the meaning formalized in abhidharmic definitions and the broader use of the word in nonspecialized discourse, it also deemphasizes the importance of finding a precise rendition that would match these definitions in favor of crafting translations able to convey *saṃjñā*'s fluctuations in register and meaning.[39]

Thus, the current model of terminology helps us shift our attention from definitional minutiae to the main translational challenge that *saṃjñā* poses: *saṃjñā* corresponds to a lexical gap in English.

Saṃjñā is difficult to render in English not because it is a specialized term that refers to a precise and doctrinally sophisticated concept, but because this concept is not lexicalized in English. The problem is twofold.

First, there is no English word that covers the whole semantic spectrum of *saṃjñā*. This is a very common phenomenon, as lexical polysemy is rarely aligned across languages (anisomorphism).[40] It is also a much-discussed issue within the debate on the rendition of *saṃjñā*, as it impacts translation of this word on several levels. It hinders the rendition of lexical cohesion, making it difficult to convey the relationship between different semantic realizations of *saṃjñā* throughout a text or across texts. Perhaps more importantly, it risks introducing in the translation conceptual distinctions alien to Sanskrit sources. As Seyfort Ruegg (1973) notes, there is some conceptual continuity in Buddhist philosophy between the concepts *saṃjñā* expresses in the domain of language (designation) and in

39. Cf. Skilling 1994, 477n31.

40. For an accessible study of anisomorphism, see Adamska-Sałaciak 2013.

the domain of cognition (notions, conceptual construal).[41] This continuity is difficult to render in English for want of lexical items that can similarly connect these domains.

Second, there is no single English word that expresses the concept of "taking something for," "construing something as," or "thinking of something in terms of," which is the sense from which the specialized use of *saṃjñā* in Buddhist literature arises. This, too, is a very common phenomenon. Different languages lexicalize concepts differently and foreground different aspects of them. This is in no way limited to specialized vocabulary. A typical example of this phenomenon in translation and linguistics literature is the absence of words in English to differentiate between maternal and paternal uncles, a difference that is lexicalized, for example, in Polish and Arabic.[42] While the lack of an equivalent in the target language surely makes translation harder, this problem is manageable if we overcome the (unhealthy) desire to map each noun of the original text to a single noun in the translated text.

A common translation strategy to deal with lexical gaps is to craft phraseological renditions (circumlocution).[43] While phraseological renditions are often used in the translation of Buddhist texts, they tend to be regarded in the field as a last resort to be adopted only once the quest for the perfect equivalent has failed. It is my contention that phraseological rendition is theoretically sound and should be the strategy of choice in translating *saṃjñā* and other words that have no identifiable counterpart in English. Circumlocution offers a great advantage over solutions like neologism and borrowing—both of which have been adopted for rendering *saṃjñā*, which is sometimes left untranslated or glossed with quasi-neologisms such as "perception-as."

41. See Seyfort Ruegg 1973, 77. Seyfort Ruegg's wording ("même si les valeurs de 'notion' et de 'nom' sont à considérer comme deux acceptions distinctes du mot sanskrit saṃjñā") suggests that there is an actual division in the semantic spectrum of *saṃjñā*. However, such division may be an artifact of looking at the meaning of this word through the lens of languages like French and English. These languages lexicalize the conceptual space differently from Sanskrit and force the speaker to differentiate between the meanings that *saṃjñā* expresses in the domains of language and cognition; cf. note 28 in this chapter.

42. See, for example, Farghal 2015, 67; Wierzbicka 2016, 72.

43. For a summary of translation strategies recommended for dealing with lexical gaps, see Rogers 2015, chapter 5.

Contrary to translation "equivalents" made of individual nouns or nominal compounds (e.g., ideation or perception), phraseological renditions enjoy some plasticity, especially at the level of syntax. They include different parts of speech which can be adjusted to retain the semantic transparency and idiomaticity of the source text. Just to illustrate the principle, and with no intention of suggesting a specific rendition, let us revisit the main argument adduced against rendering *saṃjñā* with "perception" in the literature. The authors considered earlier are dissatisfied with the semantic imprecision of this word. *Saṃjñā* means "perception-as" rather than perception tout court, some note. This shortcoming could be overcome simply by switching from the noun "perception" to variations of the verbal of phrase "to perceive as" (e.g., "perceiving something as," "perceived as," "one who perceives something as," and so on). This phrase has the advantage of sounding idiomatic in English, because it is sufficiently malleable to fit different syntactic contexts, and also of being semantically transparent. It could also, if the context allows, be manipulated to capture at least some of the lexical cohesion of a source text. This could be done, in theory, by exploiting either lexical or syntactical similarities. Lexically, a phraseological rendition of *saṃjñā* containing the string "to perceive as" could be deployed to echo cases where *saṃjñā* is translated, for example, with "perception" or with cognates such as "misperception" or "apperception." Syntactically, it could be used to link to cases where *saṃjñā* is rendered with verbs of cognition that govern a similar complementation pattern, like "to consider as," "to regard as," "to construe as," which may better fit the register or meaning of *saṃjñā* in other contexts. Most importantly, the flexibility of phraseological rendition can help us convey the different registers and level of specialization that are found in the source texts.

To frame the translation of *saṃjñā* as a lexical gap problem, rather than as a terminological problem, frees us from the constraints of classical terminological translation. It affords us a measure of creativity, which the most talented of us can use to weave translations that are as intelligible to contemporary readers as the source texts were intended to be to their audiences.

Conclusion

The case study illustrates that translators of Buddhist texts can benefit from staying abreast of advances in the fields, not only of Buddhist and translation studies but also linguistics. The adoption of corpus methods and current terminology theories (and more generally lexico-semantic theories) can help us rethink the way we conceive of the Buddhist Sanskrit vocabulary and the way we approach its translation. To consider key Buddhist expressions as general language words that may acquire terminological value under certain conditions can lend some fluidity to our translations and help us move one step away from the notorious clumsiness of Buddhist Hybrid English. Much more work needs to be done to understand the level of specialization, idiomaticity, and semantic transparency of the vocabulary of Sanskrit Buddhist texts. A larger scale study is also needed to estimate how representative *saṃjñā* may be of the behavior of Buddhist terminology in general. In the meantime, only very broad suggestions about translation practice can be gleaned from the single case study on *saṃjñā*.

References

Adamska-Sałaciak, Arleta. 2013. "Equivalence, Synonymy, and Sameness of Meaning in Bilingual Dictionary." *International Journal of Lexicography* 26, no. 3: 329–345.

Antia, Bassey, Gerhard Budin, Heribert Pitch, Margaret Rogers, Klaus-Dirk Schmitz, and Sue Ellen Wright. 2005. "Shaping Translation: A View from Terminology." *Meta* 50, no. 4. https://doi.org/10.7202/019907ar.

Bowker, Lynne, and Shane Hawkings. 2006. "Variation in the Organization of Medical Terms." *Terminology: International Journal of Theoretical and Applied Issues in Specialized Communication* 12, no. 1: 79–110.

Cabré, Maria Teresa. 2010. "Terminology and Translation." In *Handbook of Translation Studies, Vol. 1*, edited by Yves Gambier and Luc von Doorslaer, 356–365. Amsterdam: John Benjamins.

Deleanu, Florin. 2006. *The Chapter on the Mundane Path (Laukikamārga) in the Śrāvakabhūmi: A Trilingual Edition (Sanskrit, Tibetan, Chinese), Annotated Translation, and Introductory Study*. Vol. 2.

Dury, Pascaline. 1999. "Étude comparative et diachronique des concepts ecosystem et écosystème." *Meta* 44, no. 3: 485–499.

Faber-Benítez, P. 2009. "The Cognitive Shift in Terminology and Specialized Translation." *MonTI* 1: 107–134.

Faber-Benítez, Pamela, and Pilar León-Araúz. 2016. "Specialized Knowledge Representation and the Parameterization of Context." *Frontiers in Psychology* 7: 196.

Falkum, Ingrid L., and Augustin Vicente. 2015. "Polysemy: Current Perspectives and Approaches." *Lingua* 157: 1–16.

Farghal, Mohammad. 2015. *Contextualizing Translation Theories: Aspects of Arabic–English Interlingual Communication*. Newcastle upon Tyne, UK: Cambridge Scholars.

Fernandez-Silva, Sabela, Judit Freixa, and Maria Teresa Cabré. 2011. "A Proposed Method for Analysing the Dynamics of Cognition through Term Variation." *Terminology: International Journal of Theoretical and Applied Issues in Specialized Communication* 17, no. 1: 49–73, doi:10.1075/Term.17.1.04fer.

Freixa, Judit. 2006. "Causes of Denominative Variation in Terminology: A Typology Proposal." *Terminology: International Journal of Theoretical and Applied Issues in Specialized Communication* 12: 51–77.

Griffiths, Paul. 1981. "Buddhist Hybrid English: Some Notes on Philology and Hermeneutics for Buddhologists." *Journal of the International Association of Buddhist Studies* 4, no. 2: 17–132.

Gyatso, Janet. 1992. *In the Mirror of Memory: Reflections on Mindfulness and Remembrance in Indian and Tibetan Buddhism*. Albany: State University of New York Press.

Hanisch, Albrecht, ed. 2005. *Āryaraśūras Jātakamālā: Philologische Untersuchungen zu den Legenden 1 bis 15*. Marburg: Indica et Tibetica Verlag.

Hardie, Andrew, and Tony McEnery. 2011. *Corpus Linguistics: Method, Theory and Practice*. Cambridge: Cambridge University Press.

Johnston, E. H. 1928. *The Saundarananda of Aśvaghoṣa*. Oxford: Oxford University Press.

———. 1935. *The Buddhacarita: Acts of the Buddha*. Calcutta: Baptist Mission Press.

Kern, H., and Bunyiu Nanjio, eds. 1970. *Saddharmapuṇḍarīka*. Osnabrück: Biblio Verlag.

Khoroche, Peter. 1987. *Towards a New Edition of Āryaśūra's Jātakamālā*. Bonn: Indica et Tibetica.

Lugli, Ligeia, Bruno Galasek-Hul, and Luis G. Quiñones-Martinez. 2019. *A Visual Dictionary and Thesaurus of Buddhist Sanskrit*. mangalamresearch.shinyapps.io/VisualDictionaryOfBuddhistSanskrit/. https://doi.org/10.5281/zenodo.3716014.

Meyer, Charles. 2002. *English Corpus Linguistics: An introduction*. Cambridge: Cambridge University Press.

Montero-Martínez, Silvia, and Pamela Faber. 2009. "Terminological Competence in Translation." *Terminology: International Journal of Theoretical and Applied Issues in Specialized Communication* 15, no. 1: 88–104.

Ñāṇamoli, Bhikkhu, trans. [1965] 2011. *The Path of Purification*, 3rd online ed. Colombo: Buddhist Publication Society.

Norman, K. R. 1984. "On Translating from Pali." *One Vehicle*: 77–87.

Olohan, Maeve. 2013. "Scientific and Technical Translation." In *The Routledge Handbook of Translation Studies*, edited by Francesca Bartrina and Carmen Millan-Varela, 425–437. London: Taylor and Francis.

Pearson, Jennifer. 1998. *Terms in Context*. Amsterdam: John Benjamins.

Pradhan, Prahlad. 1983. *The Abhidharmakośa of Vasubandhu*. Patna: K. P. Jayaswal Research Institute.

Rogers, Margaret. 2004. "Multidimensionality in Concept Systems: A Bilingual Textual Perspective." *Terminology: International Journal of Theoretical and Applied Issues in Specialized Communication* 10: 215–240.

———. 2015. *Specialised Translation: Shedding the "Non-literary" Tag*. Palgrave Studies in Translating and Interpreting. London: Palgrave Macmillan.

Seyfort Ruegg, David. 1973. *Le traité du tathāgatagarbha de Bu ston rin chen grub: Traduction du De bžin gšegs pa'i sñin po gsal žin mdzes par byed pa'i rgyan*. Paris: École française d'Extrême-Orient.

———. 1995. "Some Reflection on the Place of Philosophy in the Study of Buddhism." *Journal of the International Association of Buddhist Studies* 18, no. 2: 145–182.

Skilling, Peter. 1994. *Mahāsūtras: Great Discourses of the Buddha*. Oxford: Pali Text Society.

Steinkellner, Ernst, and Xuezhu Li, eds. 2008. *Vasubandhu's Pañcaskandhaka*. Beijing: China Tibetology Publishing House; Vienna: Austrian Academy of Sciences Press.

ten Hacken, Pius. 2015. "Terms and Specialised Vocabulary: Taming the Prototypes." In *Handbook of Terminology*, vol. 1, edited by Hendrik Kockaert and Frieda Steurs, 14–33. Amsterdam: John Benjamins.

Vetter, Tilmann. 2000. *The "Khandha Passages" in the Vinayapiṭaka and the Four Main Nikāyas*. Wien: Verlag der Oesterreichischen Akademie der Wissenschaften.

Wierzbicka, Anna. 2016. "New Perspectives on Kinship: Overcoming the Eurocentrism and Scientism of Kinship Studies through Lexical Universals." In *Routledge Handbook of Linguistic Anthropology*, edited by Nancy Bonvillian, 62–79. New York: Routledge.

Wogihara, Unrai, ed. 1932. *Abhisamayālaṃkār'ālokā Prajñāpāramitāvyākhyā (Commentary on Aṣṭasāhasrikā-prajñāpāramitā) by Haribhadra, Together with the Text Commented on—Part 1*. Tokyo: Toyo Bunko.

Part III

Words

Chapter 7

Translation and Historical Context

Interpretations of *Antevāsinī*

Alice Collett

This chapter is the first in the volume of applied examples, or case studies, which take up some of the same themes discussed already but explore them from the point of view of a specific example. In this chapter, I examine the term *antevāsinī*, comparing its appearance in Indian inscriptions with the use of the word in Buddhist *vinaya* literature. The chapter takes up themes explored so far by Collett Cox, Amy Langenberg, and Ligeia Lugli. The question is not how to translate the word *antevāsinī*—or its masculine counterpart *antevāsin*—in a literal, word-for-word sense, as it invariably means "pupil" or "student." The problem is, instead, exactly what we mean by "pupil" or "student"; that is, do we understand it as a narrow technical term or a word with a range of meanings? The problem relates to three issues that have already been discussed in the volume. First, to the question of how texts become constituted, and the extent to which we see a text as having "multiple forms as historical instances" (Cox, chapter 1).[1] Also, in comparing the epigraphic data with *vinaya* textual

1. In relation to early texts of Indian Buddhism, that they are layered through having undergone processes of evolution is not a new observation. Such observations have been noted for some time with, for instance, von Hinüber's remarks, following Schlingloff

sources, I evince an approach advocated by Langenberg in chapter 3 of this volume—that *vinayas* should be read intertextually—and also revisit her question of the extent to which it is appropriate to consider *vinaya* texts as reflections of social reality. Finally, I take up some points from the last chapter that are elucidated by an examination of an apparently technical term that is not static, not always used in ways that demand adherence to an exacting technical definition.

In *vinaya* literature, *antevāsin/ī* is part of a fourfold classification of defined roles that relate to ordination and become delineated through formal monastic procedures. According to extant *vinayas*, an individual wishing to join the Order has a *pabbajjā* ordination and becomes a novice (*sāmanera/ī*) and a pupil (*antevāsin/ī* or *saddhivihārikin/ī*) with both a preceptor (*upajjhāya/ā*) and a teacher (*ācariya/ā*).[2] After a period of two years, the novice takes full or higher ordination (*upasampadā*) and becomes a monk or nun (*bhikkhu/nī*). According to the *vinayas*, this formal process happens in gender-segregated communities; that is, male novices have male preceptors and teachers and female novices have female preceptors and teachers. The problem with the word *antevāsinī* arises because there is a striking disjoint between the parameters of what a female pupil is and does according to the texts and the data in the inscriptions. In the early Buddhist epigraphic record, there is a noticeable frequency with which women are recorded in inscriptions with male teachers; that

(1964) in his *A Handbook of Pāli Literature* that certain of the *vinaya* origin stories in the Pāli *Vinaya* may be spurious (1996, 13). Also, in the last few decades, several scholars show, through a comparison of rules in different *vinayas*, that the idea of a novice period prior to full ordination is something that developed over time, and this has particular implications for nuns. For example, Ann Heirman, in two articles (1997 and 2011) discusses first some discrepancies with regard to the novice period in that some stories related as the origin of monastic code do not take account of the idea of a probationary period (1997, 80); then second, and more fully, other discrepancies between different *vinayas* with regard to the inception of the nuns' Order, which again indicate—in some cases more than others—problems with the idea of a probationary period (2011, 603–611). Another example is In Young Chung's article, published in the *Journal of Buddhist Ethics* in 1999, in which, through a comparative analysis of monastic rules of different schools, existing in different languages, she problematizes the idea of the novice period.

2. There are some variations to this, for instance, *upajjhāyā* is sometimes rendered *upajjhā*, and *saddhivihārinī* as *saddhivihārikā*. In this chapter, all Old and Middle Indic words that require standardization are standardized to Pāli.

is, the women are pupils (*antevāsinī*) of a male monastic. According to the formal structures presented to us in *vinaya* literature, this should not happen. But the epigraphic record suggests, to the contrary, that it was commonplace.[3] Thus, to understand *antevāsinī* as it appears in inscriptions as the technical term for a female pupil within the gender-segregated monastic schema prescribed by the extant *vinaya* literature is problematic.

In order to address this issue, I will first outline some of the basic parameters of the idea of an *antevāsin/ī* in *vinaya* literature. Next I will provide some background on scholarship that has explored the relationship between texts and epigraphy, and I will examine the extent to which the material evidence suggests that early communities had comprehensive knowledge of the *vinaya*. Finally, I will focus on the word *antevāsinī* itself and discuss how the epigraphic evidence problematizes a reading of the word as a static technical term.

Antevāsin/ī in *Vinaya* Literature

The section of *vinaya* literature that deals with the role of an *antevāsin/ī* is the *Mahākkhandaka*—more usually known as the *Pravrajyāvastu*—section of the *Skandhaka*, or *Vinayavastu*, the part that deals with rules governing communal behavior. Wijayaratna (1990, 137–140) provides a summary of the section in the Pāli *Vinaya*—which is in the *Mahāvagga* and *Cullavagga*—that outlines and delineates the roles and expectations of both preceptor (*upajjhāya/ā*) and co-resident disciple (*saddhivihārin/ī*) and teacher (*ācariya/ā*) and pupil (*antevāsin/ī*).[4] The passages in both the *Mahāvagga* and *Cullavagga* are identical to one another—essentially a repeat—and also identical in terms of the relationship they delineate between preceptor and co-resident disciple and teacher and pupil.[5] One of the features of the relationship that highlights the level of intimacy

3. Following presentation of the paper for this chapter at the conference, I was asked about the issue of the *bhikkhunovādata*, the "monk advisor to nuns." I have addressed this question in Collett 2015.

4. Vin. I 25, 7–24 and Vin. II 222–230. Also see Langenberg (2013) for a recent outline of the development of ordination processes.

5. That is, the same passages are repeated four times; twice for a preceptor and disciple and twice for a teacher and pupil, once each in the *Mahāvagga* and once each in the *Cullavagga*.

expected is that the teacher and pupil should regard one another in familial terms, that is (as per the male configuration in the text), a teacher should regard his pupil as a son, and the pupil should regard his teacher as his father (*ācariyo . . . antevāsikamhi puttacittaṃ upaṭṭhāpessati antevāsiko ācariyamhi pitucittaṃ upaṭṭhāpessati* Vin. I 61). Frauwallner notes that this section in all extant *vinayas* is "essentially the same with the exception of the usual deviations due to different traditions and of isolated amplifications and developments" (1956, 71). However, the Mūlasarvāstivāda and Mahāsāṃghika *Vinayas* do not, according to Frauwallner, stipulate the father-son aspect of the relationship.

The core of the relationship between pupil and teacher is training. The teacher is encumbered with duties not solely to teach about doctrine but also to act as a role model and caregiver. The teacher should impart knowledge, but knowledge about communal life and community etiquette as much as doctrine and practice. The teacher must also ensure the material needs of the pupil are met, and nurse them when sick. The pupil must themselves act as servant to the teacher, and gain the teacher's permission before performing certain actions and duties. However, the relationship is described as more reciprocal and less hierarchical than it appears on the surface; the pupil also has the right to offer advice to the teacher, and to correct mistakes.

Two particular dimensions of the roles I want to draw attention to concern other aspects of the expected intimacy between pupils and teachers. The *antevāsin/ī* is expected to assist their teacher with bathing and dressing. The two sections of the Pāli on this are as follows:

> If the teacher wishes to enter the village, his inner clothing should be given (to him), the inner clothing (that he is wearing) should be received (from him) in return, the girdle should be given (to him); having folded them (into two or four folds), the outer robes are to be given (to him). (Horner [1951] 2007, 4: 60)[6]
>
> If the teacher wishes to bathe, he [the *antevāsin*] should prepare a bath. . . . If the teacher wishes to enter a heated room . . . taking a chair for the heated room, having gone close behind the teacher, having given him the chair for the heated room, having

6. *sace ācariyo gāmaṃ pavisitukāmo hoti, nivāsanaṃ dātabbaṃ, paṭinivāsanaṃ paṭiggahetabbaṃ, kāyabandhanaṃ dātabbaṃ saguṇaṃ katvā saṃghāṭiyo dātabbā* . . . Vin. I 46 (changing forms of *upajjhāya* to *ācariya* as per instruction I 61).

received his robe, he [the *antevāsin*] should lay it to one side. (Horner [1951] 2007, 4: 61–62, with one change)[7]

Another indication of the closeness expected in the relationship comes via etymology. *Antevāsin/ī* and *saddhivihārin/ī* are cognate terms, and the difference between the two roles is not entirely clear. Etymologically, both derive from the notion that a pupil or student would be expected to live with their teacher or preceptor. Horner translates *saddhivihārin/ī* as "one who shares a cell," although she does not bring to bear the etymology of *antevāsin/ī* in her translation choices for this word, which she translates variously as "pupil" or "novice." Drawing from the *Śatapatha Brāhmaṇa* (and elsewhere), Monier-Williams translates *antevāsin/ī* as "a pupil who dwells near or in the house of his teacher" (1999 [1899], 43), which Cone practically replicates (2001, 153) in her translation of the Pāli. *Anta* means "inner" or "near," and combined with a form of the common verb √*vas* has the primary meaning of "dwell with or near."

Given the above, it is difficult to imagine the male-female teacher-pupil relationships recorded in the inscriptions were understood to be relationships that adhered to these parameters of the pupil's role as laid out in the *vinaya*s. The idea of a female novice attending to the teacher's personal bodily needs, including helping him dress and undress, is implausible, as is the idea that a female novice lives with her male teacher.[8]

7. *sace ācariyo nahāyitukāmo hoti, nahānaṃ paṭiyādetabbaṃ . . . sace ācariyo jantāgharaṃ pavisitukāmo hoti . . . jantāgharapīṭhaṃ ādāya ācariyassa piṭṭhito-piṭṭhito gantvā jantāgharapīṭhaṃ datvā cīvaraṃ paṭiggahetvā ekamantaṃ nikkhipitabbaṃ* . . . Vin. I 47 (changing forms of *upajjhāya* to *ācariya* as per instruction I 61). PED and Cone prefer to translate *jantāghara* as a heated room, that is, in which a fire is kept, perhaps similar to a steam room, rather than Horner's choice of "bathroom."

8. Here we need to be attuned to the ambiguity with regard to *anta*. If a female novice lives *with* her male teacher, this is problematic, but if the intention is simply to communicate a more generic proximity, that is less problematic. Buddhists were not, of course, the first nor the only religious group to delineate a pedagogic relationship, and neither was it—as in most societies—solely a religious habit. For example, the longer version of Asoka's Minor Rock Edit II enjoins appropriate conduct toward occupational apprentices (*antevāsin/aṃtevāsīni*) (Falk 2006, 57), and both Brahmanical and Jain literature focus on teacher-pupil relations, sometimes using these same words, but not consistently. Hara (1979) traces the concept of the religious teacher (*ācārya*) in Sanskrit works (as a preface to *guru*) noting it first in the Vedas and then the *Upaniṣads*. In some of the excerpts mentioned, the pupil of the *ācārya* is an *antevāsin*, but not always. But Hara also notes that, according to Brahmanic tradition, the pupil would be expected to live in the house of the teacher (*ācārya-kula*) during their period of studentship (1979, 94).

Texts and Epigraphs

Since the first epigraphers began to decipher Indian Buddhist inscriptions, the question of the relationship of the epigraphic record to extant Buddhist texts was a ubiquitous one. The first epigraphers identified several verse and prose extracts from texts that appear in inscriptions, and in the century or so since then others have also come to light. As well as this, early epigraphers identified possible textual parallels by syntax alone. For example, Konow notes of an inscription from Sārnāth that

> . . . though I have not found the exact quotation, I do not doubt that the passage cut on the stone is meant as a quotation from the Canon. Our inscription, therefore, furnishes a valuable epigraphical proof from the existence of a Pāli Canon in the second or third century AD. (1907/1908, 292)

The inscription reads:

1. *catt[ā]r imāni bhikkhave ar[i]yasaccāni*
2. *katamāni cattāri dukkha[ṁ] dikkhavē arā(ri)yasacca[ṁ]*
3. *dukkhasamudaya ariyaya(sa)ccaṁ dukkhanirōdhō ariyasaccaṁ*
4. *dukkhanirōdha-gāminī ca paṭipadā ari[ya*]saccaṁ*[9]

Konow was correct; the quote appears in a *Saṃyuttanikāya* passage (V 433), concerning a teaching that took place at Sāvatthī:

> *cattār' imāni bhikkhave ariyasaccāni. katamāni cattāri. dukkham ariyasaccaṃ dukkhasamudayaṃ ariyasaccaṃ dukhanirodhaṃ ariyasaccaṃ dukkhnirodhagāminī paṭipadāyaariyasaccaṃ*
>
> Monks and all present, there are four noble truths. What four? The noble truth of suffering, the noble truth of the origin of suffering, the noble truth of the cessation of suffering, and the noble truth of the way leading to the cessation of suffering.[10]

9. I have updated Konow's orthography.

10. See Collett and Anāyalo (2014) on the vocative *bhikkhave*. Here we argue that the translation of *bhikkhave* has more breadth to it than usually assumed, and we discuss the differentiation with regard to regularity of its occurrence.

The most common verse from texts found in inscriptions is the well-known "*ye dhammā hetuppabhavā . . .*" formula, that elucidates the doctrine of *paṭicca-samuppāda* (see Boucher 1991).[11] Others include three verses found at Swat from the *Mahāparinibbānasutta* and *Dhammapada* (Bühler 1896–1897, 133–135), and more recently, Skilling (1991) identified a verse known from several texts in an inscription from Andhra Pradesh.[12] As well as verses, there are other clues that composers of inscriptions had knowledge of Buddhist texts. For instance, in a coauthored article published in 1984 Salomon and Schopen discuss a phrase found on three inscriptions that describe relics as being deposited in "a previously unestablished place" (*apradiṭhavitaprave pateśe*) for the purpose of "the merit of Brahmā" (*brammapuň[o]*). This, they say is a "passage taken over from a canonical Buddhist text, or (that)—at the very least—there is clear textual authority for the expressions" (1984, 116). In much of his work, Schopen also highlights other ways that the epigraphic record correlates with the Mūlasarvāstivāda *Vinaya*. To take just two examples, in a chapter from his second edition of collected papers (2004, 21), he notes that monks are called *trepiḍaka*s, "those who know the Three Baskets," and that monks have "co-residential pupils" (*sārdhaṃvihārin*).[13] Both of these terms are used extensively in the Mūlasarvāstivāda *Vinaya*, and the latter of the two is one of the terms used in *vinaya* literature alongside *antevāsinī*. Both these words are clerical titles, used to designate role and status. The use of such titles in inscriptions does broadly correspond to their usage in Buddhist *vinaya* and other literature. For both monks and nuns, the most popular terms used are *bhikkhu, bhikkhunī, ayya/ā, thera/therī, pabbajaka/*pabbajikā, bhandata*, and for designated roles that identify a skill or attribute *tepiṭaka/ā, bhānaka, vinayadhāra, suttantaka/ikā* (with various spellings). In his introduction to the Bhārhut volume of *Corpus Inscriptionum Indicarum*, Lüders (1963, 3) notes that there is a "great

11. *ye dhammā hetuppabhavā tesāṃ hetuṃ tathāgato, āha tesāñ cayo nirodho evaṃvādī mahāsamaṇo 'ti.* "Those *dhammas* which arise from a cause, the Tathāgata has declared their cause, and that which is the cessation of them. Thus the great renunciant has taught" (Boucher 1991, 6).

12. In literature extant in Sanskrit and Pāli, the verse appears in *Dhammapada*, verse 191; *Samyuttanikāya* II 185.23; *Itivuttaka* 17.22–18.2; *Theragāthā* verse 1259; *Therīgāthā* verses 186, 193, 310, and 321; *Udānavarga* 6.

13. Now also in Doris Srinivasan's edited collection (2007, 287–331).

variety is to be found in ecclesiastical titles"[14] appearing in inscriptions. However, apart from some regional variation, no significant difference has as yet been unearthed between textual and epigraphic usage.[15]

Antevāsinī

In 2013, then 2014, von Hinüber and Skilling, then Salomon and Marino, published articles on two important inscriptions from Deorkothar. These inscriptions do not directly correspond to any canonical textual passages but are similar in form and structure. The inscriptions record lineages of monks that go back to the time of the Buddha, employing, singularly, the term *antevāsin* to denote this. Deorkothar Inscription 1 is as follows:

1. bhagavato budha(sa) [*sakamunisa* ***ātevāsi*** *dhamamitra dhamamitrasa* **ātevāsi**]
2. utaramitro utaramitrasa **(ā)[tevāsi** *dhamamitra dhamamitrasa* **ātevāsi**]
3. bhaḍu bhaḍusa **ātevāsi** nā(ṃ)di(nu)[tara nāṃdintarasa **ātevāsi** upasako]
4. upasakasa **ātevāsi** savajayo (sa)va[jayasa **ātevāsinā**]
5. dhamadevena kokuḍikena bahusutiye(na) [thabho kārāpito +++++++]
6. usapito thabho ācariyena kasi[

14. The titles and combinations he notes are as follows: *aya* (*ārya*), *bhadata* (*bhadanta*), *bhānaka* (*bhāṇaka*), combination of *bhadamta* with *aya*, combination of *aya* with *bhānaka*, combination of *bhadata* with *bhānaka*, combination of *aya* with *sutaṁtika* (*sutrantikā*), combination of *aya* with *peṭaki* (*peṭakin*), combination of *aya* with *aṁtevāsi* (*antevāsin*), combination of *bhadata* with *satupadāna* (*sṛishṭopādāna*), combination of *bhadata* with *aya*, *bhānaka*, and *navakamika* (*navakarmika*), *bhatudesaka* (*bhaktoddeśaka*), *paṁchanekāyika* (*pañchanaikāyika*), *bhikhunī* (*bhikshunī*), *bhicchunī*.

15. Of the twenty-five monks who are mentioned on Bhārhut inscriptions, none of them are given the title *bhikkhu*. The most common title is instead *ayya*. The nuns, however, are never called *ayya*, instead the usual *bhikkhunī* is used. This appears to be something particular to Bhārhut.

Translation:

> Lord Buddha's [**pupil**] . . . Uttaramitra, Uttaramitra's **pupil** . . . Bha(ṃ)ḍu, Bha(ṃ)du's **pupil** Nāṃdinuttara, Nāṃdinuttara's **pupil** . . . Upasaka, Upasaka's **pupil** Sarvajaya, [by] Sarv[jaya's **pupil**] Dhammadeva from Kokuḍi, a member of the Bahusutiya school, [a column was made] . . . erected was the column of *ācariya* Kasi[. . .[16]

In the inscriptions, *antevāsin* is used to denote pupillage, and von Hinüber and Skilling consider that it is being used here in a way that accords with technical *vinaya* terminology. They say: "In a Buddhist inscription, one expects *antevāsin* to have the sense of the well-known technical term of Vinaya law, denoting a novice who lives together with his teacher (*ācarya* or *ācariya*, Vin. I 60, 26–29): that is to say, as a 'pupil' " (2013, 16).[17] Here I want to challenge this assertion. With regard to *antevāsinī* as it appears in inscriptions to indicate male-female teacher-pupil relations, we cannot understand it "to have the sense of the well-known technical term of Vinaya law, denoting a novice who lives together with [the] teacher" if, when doing so, we expect the behavior of the *antevāsinī* to fully conform to *vinaya* prescriptions.

As noted earlier, understood as a technical *vinaya* term, an *antevāsinī* is part of a fourfold classification of clearly delineated gender-segregated roles relating to ordination, and the relationship between novices or pupils and their teacher and preceptor, according to the texts, is a close one. But inscriptions tell a different story. Inscriptions by women who describe themselves as pupils of male monastic teachers range over a four-hundred-year period, dating from the second century BCE to the second century CE. This was not a regional phenomenon, as the inscriptions are found in a geographical spread ranging from the western coastal sites, to Sāñcī in central Madhya Pradesh, Mathurā in the north, Amarāvatī in Andhra

16. My bold, von Hinüber and Skilling 2013, 15 and 17. Reconstructed passages are placed within square brackets. Within the brackets, reconstructions that are based on the extant fragments are placed in roman type, while hypothetical reconstructions are placed in italics (2013, 15). Salomon and Marino (2014, 33–34) disagree with the translation of Kokuḍi as a place-name and instead understand it as a reference to an early Buddhist school—called (variously) Kukkutika, Kaukkuṭika, and so forth.

17. Salomon and Marino (2014) use student rather than "pupil."

Pradesh, and Kanaganahalli in the south (see Collett 2015 for more on these inscriptions).

It is this dislocation that gives rise to the problem. How are we to understand different sources that appear to be telling us conflicting details about what it means to be an *antevāsinī* in early Buddhist communities? I will lay out the discussion taking up some of the theoretical, historical, and hermeneutical issues already delineated in parts 1 and 2 of this volume and relating them to translation of so-called technical *vinaya* terms.

The first issue to address is the extent to which it is apposite to consider *antevāsinī* as a technical term in each instance, and if so, to seek to identify what type of technical term it is. Understanding terminology as functioning in the manner espoused by the classical model of terminology—pace Lugli—as a static technical term, *antevāsinī* would be required to mean exactly the same in all instances, which it palpably does not. However, if we adhere instead to newer theorizing about the function of terms in a language, that is, that they are dynamic and adaptive, it remains possible to understand *antevāsinī* as a term, but a term that governs discrete sets of behaviors in the distinct source language contexts in which it is utilized. Other epigraphic evidence from the period is suggestive of the possibility that regional teachers had a group of students around them, as is suggested by the etymology of the contemporaneous corpus title that derives from *upa-ni-√ṣad*—meaning "to sit down near to (the teacher)" and the evidence of Gotiputa, a prominent Buddhist teacher, known from inscriptions in the Sāñcī area, who acquired the designation "the light of Sāñcī" (*kākanava pabhāsana*; Willis 2001, 221).[18] Pupils of such teachers would still act via the broad parameters of the basic semantic range of "pupil"; they would be ones who receive instruction from a teacher. They may also, as would be typical in this ancient North Indian milieu, fulfill an expectation of some level of service required in the role, but just what the service was would not necessarily be exactly the form of service prescribed in the *vinayas*. For example, services pupils perform for their teachers need not extend to help with dressing and bathing.

Second, attributing a more dynamic nature to *antevāsinī* as a term can be justified by closer scrutiny of the texts. Evidently, even the *vinaya* texts themselves do not consistently stick to static *vinaya* terminology.

18. *Kākanava* is the old name for the Sāñcī *stūpa*. Here Willis (2001) also lists the pupils (*antevāsin*) of Gotiputa.

The evidence demonstrates that the technical terms are not fully formed at each point during the (long) period of composition of *vinaya* texts. I will use the *bhikkhunīvibhaṅga* of the Pāli *Vinaya* to highlight this. As discussed earlier, the word *antevāsin* appears in the *Mahāvagga* and *Cullavagga* passages that outline and delineate the role of *antevāsin*. Here it appears in its male form. The word *antevāsinī*, however, is barely used at all in the origin stories of the *bhikkhunīvibhaṅga*. The preference is to formulate it as the compound *antevāsibhikkhunī*, such as in this brief preamble to *pācittiya* 11:

> Now at that time a man, a relative of a nun who was a pupil of Bhaddā Kāpilānī, set out from a village for Sāvatthī on some business. (Horner [1942] 2004, 263)

> *Tena kho pana samayena bhaddāya kāpilāniyā* ***antevāsibhikkhuniyā*** *ñātako puriso gāmakā sāvatthiṃ agamāsi kenacid eva karaṇīyena* (Vin. IV 268)

Or the pupils of Thullanandā (*pāc.* 27), for whom robe distribution was held up:

> Now at that time, the nuns who were pupils of Thullanandā had gone out. (Horner [1942] 2004, 296)

> *Tena kho pana samayena thullanandāya bhikkhuniyā* ***anetvāsibhikkhuniyo*** *pakkantā honti* (Vin. IV 284)

Here, the compound *antevāsibhikkhunī* cannot be being used to indicate that the person being referred to is a novice, otherwise they would not be called a *bhikkhunī*. The uncompounded *antevāsinī* appears in the old commentary now included with the main *vinaya* text, but only once in an origin story. Similarly, the word *saddhivihārinī*, co-resident pupil, does not occur in the origin stories for the *Pāṭimokkha* rules. Instead a cognate is used—*sahajīvinī*—which the old commentary clarifies is a synonym for *saddhavihārinī*, as in the following example of *pācittiya* 34:

> Now at that time the nun Thullanandā, when the one she lives with was sick, neither attended to her nor made any effort to have her attended to.

> *Tena kho pana samayena Thullanandā bhikkhunī dukkhitaṃ sahajīviniṃ n'eva upaṭṭheti na upaṭṭāpanāya ussukaṃ karoti* (Vin. IV 291)

And the old commentary tells us:

> *The one she lives with* means: co-resident pupil.
> *sahajīvinī nāma saddhivihārinī vuccati* (Vin. IV 291)[19]

Third, the term preceptor (*upajjhā/upajjhāyā*) is not always used where one might expect it, and instead *pavattinī* is used, and again, the old commentary specifies this is a synonym for *upajjhā* (see Vin. IV 326, *pavattinī nāma upajjhā vuccati*).

Like *antevāsinī*, in inscriptions, this word for preceptor does not conform to *vinaya* prescriptions. According to the *vinaya* texts, an *antevāsinī* would have a female preceptor (*upajjhā/upajjhāyā*), but there exist inscriptions that record both 1) females with male preceptors and 2) females in male-female teacher-pupil relations in which the term for female preceptor is used. In the following example, from Kanaganahalli, again noted by von Hinüber and Nakanishi, a nun uses the term *upajjhāya* for her male teacher, that is, she specifically calls him "my preceptor."

> *siddha || na(mo) bhagavato samasabudhasa adh(ā)lakamahā*
> *ce[t]iyasa (ra)ño vāseṭhi(p)uta siri pulumāvisa*
> *savachare 30 5 gi(m)h(ā)na pakhe 2 10 koroku(la)na*
> *bhikhuniye dhamasiriyāya agarak(o) paṭasa*
> *tharo ca deyadhama saha a(māpitū)hi saha ca m(e)*
> *upajāehi bhayata varanabhutihi saha ca bhayata*
> *(s)ihehi savasatāna ca hitasughatha* (2014, 31)

> Success! homage to the Lord, the perfectly Enlightened One, of the great Addhālaka Caitya. In the year 35 of King Vāseṭṭhiputta Siri Pulumāvi (Vāsiṣṭhiputra Śrī Pulumāvi), in the 2nd half-month of the summer, (on the) 10th (day). An *agaraka* and a covering with slabs are the pious gift of the nun from the Koro family, Dhamasiri (Dharmaśrī), together with my parents and my teacher,

19. See also Vin. IV 325, 326.

> the Venerable Varanabhūti, and the Venerable S(ī)ha (Siṃha) and for the well-being and happiness of all beings. (2014, 31)[20]

From Amarāvatī is an inscription that records a male-female-female lineage, which includes the word for female preceptor:

> *vinayadhirasa aya-punavasusa atevāsiniya uvajhāyinī samuḍiyāya atevāsiniya malaṃyā pāḍakā dāna[ṃ]* (*em.* Burgess [1886] 1996, 37)
>
> Gift of footprints by Malā, pupil of the female preceptor Samuḍiyā, pupil of Venerable Punavasu, a *vinayadhāra*.

The fluidity of these apparent technical terms in both sets of sources engenders further issues, already highlighted by Cox and Langenberg in this volume. First, what exactly do we understand *vinaya* "texts" to be in this context, and second, how did these early communities use the *vinaya* "texts" that were available to them? Certainly it is the case that these same communities in which male-female teacher-pupil relations existed knew some form of *vinaya*. Inscriptions that record such relationships also feature monastics who apparently were well versed in *vinaya* literature. These are the individuals with clerical titles designating roles that identify them as ones who knew the Buddhist corpus, or the *vinaya*. Two of these designated roles are 1) *tepiṭaka*, that is, one who knows the *tipiṭaka*, and 2) *vinayadhāra*, one who knows the *vinaya*. We have several inscriptions that tell us that monks and nuns in direct teacher-pupil relations with one another were themselves *tepiṭaka*s or *vinayadhāra*s. Three of these inscriptions concern the monk Bala and his female disciple Buddhamitrā. This inscription is from the Caubārā mounds at Mathurā:

> *mahārajasya devaputrasya huv[e]ṣkasya saṃ 30 3 gṛ 1 di 8 bhīkṣhusya balasya [t]repiṭakasya antevā[si]nīy(e) [bhi]kṣuṇīye tre(piṭi)[kā]ye buddha[mi]trāy[e] bhāgineyīye bhikhuṇīye dha-*

20. "It is remarkable that the nun Dhammasiri refers to her teacher by using *me*, and, moreover, that she had a personal (*me*: my) male teacher (*upajāehi* [*upadhyāyaiḥ*] . . ." (von Hinüber and Nakanishi 2014, 32). They go on to comment that "*upajjhā* (fem.) does not exist in Pāli," but this is not the case (see above).

> *nava[t]īye bodhi[s]atvo p[r]atithā[p]i(to) [mā]dh[u]ravaṇake sahā mātāpitihi . . .*
>
> In the year 33 of the *mahārāja devaputra* Huveṣka, in the 1st (month) of the hot season, on the 8th day, a bodhisattva was set up at Madh[u]ravaṇaka by the nun Dhanavatī, the sister's daughter of the nun Buddhamitrā, who knows the Tripiṭaka, the female pupil of the monk Bala, who knows the Tripiṭaka, together with her father and mother . . . (Lüders 1961, 55; also see Bloch 1905–1906, 181)

The one other inscription—quoted already—that provides similar evidence is that of Samuḍiyā, female pupil of Punavāsu, a *vinayadhāra*. In this case, we have a named *vinayadhāra* recorded as the teacher of a female pupil. And, interestingly, this is the very inscription where we have the only instance of the word for preceptor (*upajjhayā*) used for a female. These inscriptions then, tell us that individuals apparently well versed in *vinaya* code engaged in male-female teacher-pupil relations.[21]

The next question, then, must be, to what extent did those conferred with titles that declare them to be well versed in *vinaya* and other matters actually know the canon(s) and/or aspects of it? If we assess this question in relation to a *vinayadhāra*, there are well-attested passages (with parallels in different traditions) that delineate and define who and what a *vinayadhāra* is expected to be. The following is Shizuka Sasaki and Nobuyuki Yamagiwa's translation of a fifth-century manuscript fragment of the passage, which they ascribe to the Mahāsāṃghika *Vinaya* (2006):

> He knows it is so. . . . Possessed of these fourteen qualities he is a *Vinayadhara*, the foremost among *Vinayadhara* except for the Tathāgatha Arhat and Samyuksaṃbuddha. Indeed, Monks, you should consider the Elder Upāli who is possessed of these

21. Interestingly, as Schopen (2004, 247–8) notes, it is only in the inscription of Buddhamitrā's maternal niece, the nun Dhanavatī, that we come to know of the male-female teacher-pupil relationship between Bala and Buddhamitrā. The inscriptions of Bala and Buddhamitrā themselves are silent on this. Also, the *vinayadhāra* himself, Punavāsu, is not the person who made the inscription that tells us of his teacher-pupil relationship with Samudiyā, and neither is she, the preceptor, the one, but rather it is recorded by her pupil.

> fourteen qualities as the foremost of the *Vinayadhara* except for the Tathāgatha Arhat and Samyuksaṃbuddha. Elder Upāli, Monks, knows what is an offence, knows what is not an offence, (knows what is) a serious offence, (knows what is a slight offence), knows concealment, knows non-concealment, knows confessing, knows non-confessing, knows rehabilitation (knows non-rehabilitation, . . .) . . . Possessed of five qualities he is a *Vinayadhara*. What are the five qualities? He lives controlled by the moral conduct under the *Prātimokṣa*, he is possessed of right conduct and resort, he sees danger even in the slightest faults, he trains himself by undertaking the precepts of training, conduct of body and conduct of speech . . . (2006, 190, internal references removed)[22]

Although such passages at firsthand suggest a comprehensive knowledge is expected of a *vinayadhāra*, the focus here is on the *Pāṭimokkha*, rather than other parts of the *vinaya*s that delineate and define organization roles, such as *antevāsinī*. And, interestingly, in the *Pāṭimokkha*, although there are many rules pertaining to some aspect of relationships between men and women and/or monks and nuns, there is no prescription against a monk being a teacher to a nun. As noted earlier, the organization of the monastic community along gender-segregated lines is formulated in the *Mahākkhandaka/Pravrajyāvastu* section of *vinaya*s, not the *Pāṭimokkha*. So questions remain as to what exactly constituted *vinaya* in these communities, including the extent to which the *Pravrajyāvastu* was known, or even formulated. And pertaining to this is also the question of how

---

22. Sasaki and Yamagiwa (2006) note how this closely parallels passages in other *vinaya* and other texts, such as the Pāli: "A monk is possessed of the seven qualities of an expert in Discipline: if he knows what is an offence, if he knows what is not an offence; if he knows what is a slight offence, if he knows what is a serious offence; if, possessed of moral habit, he lived controlled by the control of the *Pāṭimokkha*; if, possessed of right conduct and resort, seeing danger in the slightest faults, he, undertaking them, trains himself in the rules of training; if he is one who acquires at will, without trouble, without difficulty, the four meditations that are of the purest mentality, abiding in ease here and now; and if, by the destruction of the cankers, he, having realised here and now by his own super-knowledge the freedom of mind and the freedom through wisdom that are cankerless, enters and abides in them" (Horner [1938] 1966, 6: 218).

vinaya—whatever it was—was used. Langenberg surveys examples of ways in which *vinaya* has been utilized in Buddhist communities throughout history other than as a simple compendium of rules that should govern behavior. The above quote delineates some aspects of the expectation of a *vinayadhāra* and is suggestive of a status as a respected advisor. And if the concatenation of their knowledge is to advise on whether an action is "an offense" or not, well, a male monastic having female pupils is not. According to extant *Pravrajyāvastu*s it would be nonnormative, and problematic to the extent that canonical prescriptions concerning community organization were being disavowed. And we are again, pace Langenberg, faced with the question of the extent to which *vinaya*s *prescribe* ideas about how the community should be operating or *describe* social reality. If it is the former and not the latter, then we need to revisit assumptions about early Buddhist communities being segregated along gender lines.

If *antevāsinī* is a fluid, dynamic technical term, that in the epigraphic context refers to female pupils who receive instruction from male monastic teachers, and if we understand text-as-process, we need to hold the real possibility that either the *Pravrajyāvastu* was not known, or not formulated at this time, which challenges us to reconsider the matter of the early monastic community being segregated along gender lines. As well as this epigraphic data there is textual evidence that calls into question whether this was always the case. In my 2013 volume, following on from insights of I. B. Horner, I explore this question in relation to the structure of the extant *Vinaya* in Pāli:

> As noted by Horner . . . the extant structure to the Pāli *Vinaya*, with the nuns' rules after those for monks, may not have been the original structure. Horner asserts this on the basis of two pieces of evidence: a fragment of a Tibetan text and the (mis) placement of the indeclinable *pi*. Further evidence for her argument comes at the beginning and end of most sections of the extant nuns' *Suttavibhaṅga*. With the exception of the first section on *pārājika*s, each section both begins and ends with a summary line or passage which details the rules to be recited or which have been told. For example, the concluding paragraph in the nuns' *pārājika* section—concluding the telling of four *pārājika*s, as the four the nuns share with monks do not appear—the text reads: "Told, Venerable Ones, are the eight offenses involving defeat" (*udditṭhā kho ayyāya aṭṭha*

> *pārājikā dhammā*, Vin. IV, 222). At the beginning of the section on *saṅghādisesa* rules we find: "Venerable Ones, these seventeen rules come up for recitation" (*ime kho pan' ayyāyo sattarasa saṃghādisesā dhammā uddesaṃ āgacchanti*, Vin. IV, 223), and to conclude that section, "Told, Venerable Ones, are the seventeen *saṅghādisesa* rules" (*uddiṭṭhā kho ayyāyo sattarasa saṃghādisesā dhammā*, Vin. IV, 242), when, in fact, only ten rules have been detailed, as the seven that apply to both monks and nuns have not been repeated. In the extant Pāli *Vinaya*, it is not stated which of the seven missing *saṅghādisesa* rules for nuns are the seven that they share with monks, but Buddhaghosa does enumerate these in his commentary to the Pāli *Vinaya*. (Collett 2013, 66)

Further, in my 2016 monograph, I note some interesting features of the structure of the extant *Thera-Therīgāthā* that also suggest this text may not have originally been configured the way it currently is, along gender lines, with the monks' verses first followed by the nuns (Collett 2016, 162–165). The evidence—linguistic, intertextual, and content based—points to a possibility that the verses were originally grouped by family.

Conclusion

In conclusion, in this chapter I have looked at the word *antevāsinī* as it appears in inscriptions and discussed translation issues in relation to it. These issues do not arise from a question of literal verbatim translation as "pupil" or "student" but rather in relation to the parameters of pupillage as understood by the classification *antevāsinī*. Although *antevāsinī*—and its masculine counterpart *antevāsin*—have come to be understood as a clearly delineated role of a pupil in the monastic schema relating to ordination, examination of the different parameters of meaning as evinced by its use in epigraphs has brought up questions. As I stated at the onset, my aim was to evaluate *antevāsinī* in relation to theoretical, historical, and hermeneutical principles already examined in this volume. In relation to Lugli's survey of terminology theory, given the varying uses of *antevāsinī* in the two contexts I have highlighted, if we want to continue to understand it as a technical term, in all instances, we need to acknowledge the dynamics of that, to not be constricted by classical ideas about terminology—that a term overarchingly refers to one and the same thing—but that the parameters of the technical application need to be nuanced to the developing environments of an adaptive religious tradition. Next, the context of the appearance of the term in inscriptions potentially problematizes a notion that *vinaya*s are indeed a reflection of social reality. And if we couple that with an awareness of texts-as-processes, that change and adapt over time, we are able to grant some latitude so that our dynamic term can be referring to idiosyncratic types of pupils in the different contexts in which it is used. All this adds up to, and elucidates, the ways in which the vicissitudes of translation practice impact how we understand social reality in a historical milieu. Here, the question could hardly be a more pivotal one—was the early Buddhist community always segregated along gender lines?

References

Bloch, T. 1905–1906. "Two Inscriptions on Buddhist Images." In *Epigraphia Indica* 8: 179–82. Calcutta: Office of the Superintendent of Government Printing.

Boucher, Daniel. 1991. "The *Pratītyasamutpādagātha* and Its Role in the Medieval Cult of the Relics." *Journal of the International Association of Buddhist Studies* 14, no. 1: 1–27.

Bühler, Georg. 1896–1897. "Three Buddhist Inscriptions in Swāt." *Epigraphia Indica* 4: 133–135.

Burgess, J. A. S. [1886] 1996. *The Buddhist Stupas of Amaravati and Jaggayyapeta in the Krishna District, Madras Presidency, Surveyed in 1882. With Translations of the Aśoka Inscriptions at Jaugada and Dhauli, by Georg Bühler*. Archaeology Survey of Southern India 4. New Delhi: Archaeological Survey of India.

Burgess, J. A. S., and Bhagwanlal Indraji. 1881. *Inscriptions from the Cave-Temples of Western India with Descriptive Notes, &c.* Archaeological Survey of Western India, Reports, Old Series 10. Bombay: Government Central Press.

Chung, In Young. 1999. "A Buddhist View of Women: A Comparative Study of the Rules for *Bhikṣuṇī*s and *Bhikṣu*s Based on the Chinese Prątimokṣa." *Journal of Buddhist Ethics* 6: 29–105.

Collett, Alice. 2013. "Pāli Vinaya: Reconceptualising Female Sexuality in Early India." In *Women in Early Indian Buddhism: Comparative Textual Studies*, edited by Alice Collett, 62–79. South Asia Research. New York: Oxford University Press.

———. 2015 "Women as Teachers and Disciples in Early Buddhist Communities: The Evidence of Epigraphy." *Religions of South Asia* 9, no. 1: 28–42.

———. 2016. *Lives of Early Buddhist Nuns: Biography as History*. New Delhi: Oxford University Press.

Collett, Alice, and Anālayo. 2014. "*Bhikkhave* and *Bhikkhu* as Gender-inclusive Terminology in Early Buddhist Texts." *Journal of Buddhist Ethics* 21: 760–797.

Falk, Harry. 2006 *Aśokan Sites and Artefacts. A Source-Book with Bibliography*. Mainz am Rhein: Philipp von Zabern.

Frauwallner, Erich. 1956. *The Earliest Vinaya and the Beginnings of Buddhist Literature*. Rome: Instituto Italiano per il Medio ed Estremo Oriente.

Hara, Minoru. 1979. "Hindu Concepts of Teacher: Sanskrit *Guru* and *Ācārya*." In *Sanskrit and Indian Studies: Essays in Honour of Daniel H. H. Ingalls*, edited by M. Nagatomi, B. K. Matilal, J. M. Masson, E. C. Dimock, 93–118. Dordrecht: Springer.

Hallisey, Charles. 2015. *Therigatha: Poems of the First Buddhist Women*. Cambridge, MA: Harvard University Press.

Heirman, Ann. 1997. "Some Remarks on the Rise of the *bhikṣunīsaṃgha* and on the Ordination Ceremony for *bhikṣunī*s according to the Dharmaguptaka *Vinaya*." *Journal of the International Association of Buddhist Studies* 20, no. 2: 33–85.

———. 2011. "Buddhist Nuns: Between Past and Present." *Numen* 58, nos. 5–6: 603–631.

Hinüber, Oskar von. 1996. *A Handbook of Pāli Literature*. Indian Philology and South Asian Studies 2. Berlin: Walter de Gruyter.

Hinüber, Oskar von, and Maiko Nakanishi. 2014. "Kanaganahalli Inscriptions." *Annual Report of the International Research Institute for Advanced Buddhology at Soka University* 18, Supplement: 1–197.

Hinüber, Oskar von, and Peter Skilling. 2013. "Two Buddhist Inscriptions from Deorkothar (Dist. Rewa, Madhya Pradesh)." *Annual Report of the International Research Institute for Advanced Buddhology at Soka University* 16: 13–26.

Horner, I. B., trans. [1938–1966] 2012–2014. *The Book of the Discipline (Vinaya-piṭaka)*, Vols. 1–4. Bristol: Pali Text Society.

Jyväsjärvi, Mari. 2007. "Parivrājikā and Pravrajitā: Categories of Ascetic Women." *Indologica Taurinensia* 33: 73–92.

Konow, Sten. 1907–1908. "Two Buddhist Inscriptions form Sārnāth." *Epigraphia Indica* 9: 291–293. New Delhi: Archaeological Survey of India.

Langenberg, Amy Paris. 2013. "Scarecrows, Upāsakas, Fetuses, and Other Child Monastics in Middle-Period Indian Buddhism." In *Little Buddhas: Children and Childhoods in Buddhist Texts and Traditions*, edited by Vanessa R. Sasson, 43–74. New York: Oxford University Press.

Lüders, H. 1912. *A List of Brahmi Inscriptions: From the Earliest Times to about AD 400 with the Exception of Those of Asoka*. Appendix to *Epigraphia Indica* 10. Calcutta: Office of the Superintendent of Government Printing.

———. 1961. *Mathurā Inscriptions*. Edited by K. L. Janert. Göttingen: Vandenhoeck & Ruprecht.

———. 1963. *Bhārhut Inscriptions*. Revised and supplemented by E. Waldschmidt and M. A. Mehendale. *Corpus Inscriptionum Indicarum* 2, pt. 2. Ootacamund: Government Epigraphist for India.

Norman, K. R. 1969. *Elder's Verses I, Theragāthā*. London: Pali Text Society.

———. 1994. "A Philological Approach to Buddhism." In *The Buddhist Forum, Vol. V: The Bukkyō Dendō Kyōkai Lectures 1994*. London: Routledge.

Salomon, Richard, and Gregory Schopen. 1984. "The Indravarman (Avaca) Casket Inscription Reconsidered: Further Evidence for Canonical Passages in Buddhist Inscriptions." *Journal of the International Association of Buddhist Studies* 7, no. 1: 107–123.

Salomon, Richard, and Joseph Marino. 2014. "Observations on the Deorkothar Inscriptions and Their Significance for the Evaluation of Buddhist Historical Traditions." *Annual Report of the International Research Institute for Advanced Buddhology at Soka University* 17: 27–39.

Schopen, Gregory. 2004. *Buddhist Monks and Business Matters: Still More Papers on Monastic Buddhism in India*. Honolulu: University of Hawai'i Press.

Senart, E. 1902–1903. "Inscriptions at the Caves at Karle." In *Epigraphia Indica* 7: 47–75. Calcutta: Office of the Superintendent of Government Printing.

———. 1905–1906. "The Inscriptions in the Caves at Nāsik." In *Epigraphia Indica* 8: 59–97. Calcutta: Office of the Superintendent of Government Printing.

Shah, Kirit K. 2001. *The Problem of Identity: Women in Early Indian Inscriptions*. New Delhi: Oxford University Press.

Shizuka Sasaki and Nobuyuki Yamagiwa. 2006. "A Vinaya Fragment on the Qualifications of a Vinayadhara." In *Buddhist Manuscripts Vol. III*, edited by Jens Braavig et al., 189–193. Oslo: Hermes.

Sims-Williams, Nicholas. 1998. "Further Notes on the Bactrian Inscription of Rabatak, with an Appendix on the Names of Kujula Kadphises and Vima Taktu in Chinese." *Proceedings of the Third European Conference of Iranian Studies Part 1: Old and Middle Iranian Studies*. Wiesbaden: Reichert.

Skilling, Peter. 1991 "A Buddhist Verse Inscription from Andhra Pradesh." *Indo-Iranian Journal* 34, no. 4: 239–246.

———. 1993. "A Note on the History of the Bhikhunī-sangha (II): The Order of Nuns after the Parinirvāṇa." *World Fellowship of Buddhists Review* 30: 29–49.

Srinivasan, Doris, ed. 2007. *On the Cusp of an Era: Art in the Pre-Kuṣāṇa World*. Vol. 18. Leiden: Brill.

Wijayaratna, Mohan. 1990. *Buddhist Monastic Life: According to the Texts of the Theravada Tradition*. Cambridge: Cambridge University Press.

Willis, Michael. 2001. "Buddhist Saints in Ancient Vedisa." *Journal of the Royal Asiatic Society* 11, no. 2: 219–228.

Chapter 8

Translating the *Tīrthika*

Enduring "Heresy" in Buddhist Studies*

C. V. Jones

Introduction

When we translate Buddhist texts from Indian sources (or, frequently, from earlier translations of them) a great many Indic words defy direct one-to-one rendering into English or other twenty-first-century languages. Some of these are to some or other degree technical terms that require careful contextualization. An example might be *dharma*/*dhamma*, which when not referring to Buddhist "teaching" or "law" (posing another well-known challenge for translators) refers to "phenomena" or "elements of experience" as explored by different traditions of *abhidharma*.[1] Terms such as *dharma* often go untranslated, on the assumption that readers—apart from those taking early steps into the study of Buddhism—are aware of to what the author or translator is referring. Other Indic terms are

*Aside from insightful suggestions by the editor, portions of this chapter benefited from valuable feedback from Paul Dundas, Claire Maes, and Perry Schmidt-Leukel, to whom I am very grateful.

1. See, for example, Gethin (2004), as well as other essays collected in Olivelle (2009), and that of Lugli in this volume.

less immediately dependent upon understanding the technicalities of the worldview or system in which they play a part, and are more readily rendered into what translators take to be adequate, if not always perfect, expressions drawn from the target language. But such translations have sometimes been too hastily plucked from their Western linguistic and cultural context and, in marriage to an Indic word, rob the latter of some of its original sense.

One such Indian expression is the Sanskrit *tīrthika*, or otherwise *tīrthya*, and with it the closely related *tīrthakara*. These are cognate with the Pāli *titthiya* (also *titthakara*), which is widely attested in the literature of the Pāli Buddhist tradition.[2] These terms share a common etymological basis in the Indic root √*tṝ*, meaning "to cross over"; a *tīrtha*, well known in the context of India's tradition of sacred bathing sites, is a crossing point of a river, or otherwise a ford, or simply a shallow point at some source of water. *Tīrthika/tīrthya* refers to a category of person, and so these terms (with the exception perhaps of *tīrthakara*, about which more later) might be rendered very literally as "one who pertains to a ford." In the context of Indian Buddhist literature, with some ancient overlap with other Indian religious traditions, a *tīrthika* is someone who pertains to a figurative "ford" between the world of transmigration (*saṃsāra*) and some kind of liberation from it; hence, a *tīrthika* is a practitioner, or perhaps teacher, of some or other proposed route out of rebirth.

In Western treatment of Indian Buddhist works we very often find *tīrthika* or cognate expressions translated as "heretic," implying perhaps that the figurative *tīrtha* to which such a practitioner relates, that is, their understanding of liberation and how it is achieved, is some "heresy" that deviates from the correct path to *nirvāṇa* as taught in the Buddha's *sad-dharma*. No doubt in most Indian Buddhist sources, proper to either the "early" tradition (represented by literature including the Pāli *nikāya*s and Chinese *āgama*s) or to the Mahāyāna, the term *tīrthika* is one of abuse: persons labeled as such are considered deluded or outright perverse in thought and/or practice. But a large question mark hangs over whether the English "heretic" captures the nuances of this and related expressions across the different Buddhist and wider Indian contexts in which we find them.

2. I will often use the term *tīrthika* to stand for all of these expressions, although when exploring one or another particular literary context I shall revert to, for example, *titthiya* or *tīrthakara* as appropriate.

The English "heresy"—of which some "heretic" is an exponent—has its origins in the Greek *hairesis*, which meant either a choice or inclination, sometimes between philosophical school or system. The term was employed by classical authors to refer to Stoicism or Epicureanism as discrete philosophical "sects," and in the mid-first century, by authors such as Josephus, to refer to Jewish denominations such as the Sadducees and Pharisees (McGrath 2009, 36–39). This usage appears to have carried no obviously negative connotations. The picture begins to change in the Greek New Testament, although very often, in particular throughout the book of Acts, the Greek *hairesis* still refers simply to groups or factions united by a common opinion or doctrine.[3]

Any neutrality did not survive long into the Christian tradition. A pejorative use of the word seems to be well established by the second century CE, during which time the Church became concerned with matters of orthodoxy and the expulsion of views—"choices" of position—that were deemed unacceptable. Late in the second century, the Church Father Irenaeus composed his *Adversus Haereses*, which challenged the legitimacy of (foremost, among other trends) Gnostic thinking that had taken root in the early Church. Importantly, Irenaeus's targets were specifically the Gnostics who were Christians themselves, who made competing claims to represent the authentic form of his own tradition (Vallée 1981, 9–40). In other words, a key feature of heresy in this formative context was some claim to a shared religious or intellectual heritage: Christian heretics, such as the second century Marcion or third-fourth century Arius, were as such by virtue of claiming to espouse the correct account of the figure of Christ and his nature, but also failing to have this account accepted by the majority of (or most authoritative among) the faithful.[4] A heretic is

3. For example, Acts: 5.17, 15.5, 24.5 and 14, 26.5, 28.22; also 1 Cor. 11.18. A more accusatory tone is discernable already in Gal. 5.20 and 2 Peter 2.1, in which the language of *hairesis* has become associated with worldly vices or the "false teacher" (*pseudodidaskalos*), who is condemned in the strongest terms.

4. Some Christian heresiological works conflated true "heretics" with other groups: see Cameron (2007, 348–350). St. John the Damascene's seventh-century *Heresies in Epitome* drew heavily from the fourth-century *Panarion* by Epiphanius, but to that earlier doxography of Greek and Jewish sects added Islam imagined as a brand of heresy devised from Arian readings of the Christian Bible. The characterization of Islam as a kind of Christian heresy continued into the twentieth century in, for example, Belloc's 1938 tract, mentioned below.

hence some manner of "enemy within," adhering to a heterodox, potentially divisive position within the parameters of one's own tradition. This usage is well established a millennium later, when Aquinas describes heresy as "a species of infidelity, attaching to those who profess faith in Christ yet corrupt his dogmas" (Gilby 1975, 82–83). It survived into the twentieth century, and was expressed succinctly by Hilaire Belloc (1938, 4) in his highly polemical *Great Heresies*: "Heresy is the dislocation of some complete and self-supporting scheme by the introduction of a novel denial of some essential part therein."[5]

This very brief sketch of the Western notion of heresy should be kept in mind as we proceed. As far as we understand the ideas, practices, and status proper to so-called *tīrthika*s, translation in terms of "heresy" or "heretics" misrepresents their origins, the manner in which these individuals would have identified themselves (i.e., not as advocates of any supposed teaching of the Buddha), and moreover the manner in which Buddhists in one or other context imagined them. The established place of this translation in the lexicon of "Buddhist English" reflects the influence of distinctly Christian vocabulary in the articulation of Indian intellectual history to Western audiences.[6] As part of ongoing critical reflection on the appropriateness of Western terminology in the translation and transmission of Buddhist literature, this choice of language warrants reconsideration.[7]

After a review of how the term *tīrthika* has been translated both by Western scholarship and by historical transmitters of Buddhist works into other Asian languages, this chapter will explore some specific examples of Buddhist literature that concern themselves with who a *tīrthika* is and, from a Buddhist perspective, the status of his or her ideas and practices. A thorough survey of occurrences of the expression *tīrthika* and its cognates across the breadth of Indian Buddhist literature is far

5. Moreover: "The denial of a scheme wholesale is not heresy, and has not the creative power of heresy. It is of the essence of heresy that it leaves standing a great part of the structure it attacks" (Belloc 1938, 7).

6. A subtly different problem to that addressed by Griffiths (1981) in his still very pertinent discussion of "Buddhist Hybrid English."

7. Assessments of the early influence of Christian vocabulary in the translation of Buddhism, in particular in the pioneering work of the Rhys Davids, include those by Collett (2006) and Snodgrass (2007). A good discussion of the Orientalist context of early Western imaginings of Buddhism—"in a manner that reflects specifically Western concerns, interests and agendas"—is that by King (1999, 144–160).

beyond the scope of this chapter. I will hence draw upon some short but illuminating discussions of the *tīrthika* that belong to different periods and genres of Buddhist writing, in order to highlight the inadequacy of the language of "heresy" in relation to it. It is evident that by the middle of the first millennium Buddhist systematizers had a clear idea of who precisely warranted the label *tīrthika*, and it is here that we shall start. We then move back through literary history via texts that are witnesses to earlier periods of Buddhist composition, in which the picture may not be so clear but talk of "heresies" appears less appropriate still. This leads us eventually back to the "late-Vedic" climate of the mid–first millennium BCE, in which Buddhism first emerged, and amid which it is possible to hypothesize that the origins of the term *tīrthika* are fundamental to a central and enduring opposition in Indian religious thought: between the attainment of worldly ends, via the practice of ritual, and escape from the world through ascetical renunciation.

Translations Old and New

Western dictionaries of Indic language have been important propagators for the language of heresy apropos of *tīrthika* and related terms. The dictionary of the Pali Text Society, edited by T. W. Rhys Davids and William Stede ([1921] 1959, 302b) renders the Pāli *titthiya* as first "an adherent of another sect" but second "an heretic"; a *titthiyasāvaka* (Skt. *tīrthyaśrāvaka*) is defined simply as "a follower of an heretic sect."[8] No less important, and interesting for the further detail that it provides, must have been Franklin Edgerton's 1953 dictionary of Buddhist Hybrid Sanskrit. In his entry for *tīrthika*, Edgerton translates it as precisely "heretic" (and reserves for *tīrthakara* the more appropriate, if also ultimately inaccurate, "heresiarch"). His entry for *tīrthika* is in part occupied with a challenging occurrence of this term in the *Mahāvastu*, to which we will return later. But despite acknowledging that the expression was "originally neutral" and referred to the "adherent (or founder) of (any) religion," Edgerton concludes, "Otherwise, and very often, *tīrthika* alone means *heretic* simply" (Edgerton 1953,

8. More cautiously, they render *titthakara* as " 'ford-maker,' founder of a sect." I. B. Horner, in her translations of the Pāli *Vinaya* literature, avoids this terminology in favor of, for example, "followers of other sects" (Horner [1940] 2004, 303); see also Maes (2015, 174–176).

254b). Edgerton nevertheless identifies that an important nuance of this Indic term is suggested by the frequent occurrence in Buddhist literature of *anyatīrthika/-tīrthya* (P. *aññatitthiya*), that is, "*tīrthika*s who are other (to us)" together with *paratīrthika*, or—subtly different—*kutīrthika* (perhaps "deficient" or "contemptible" *tīrthika*s). These expressions, for which Edgerton provides several sources, capture the sense that persons called *tīrthika*s were indeed other to the Buddhist *saṅgha*, but also invite the idea, perhaps in the very early history of Buddhism, that to warrant the label *tīrthika* was not, by that expression on its own, so terrible.

Further examples that Edgerton provides highlight problems with a crude rendering of *tīrthika* and related terms with the language of heresy. In various works (Edgerton cites the *Saddharmapuṇḍarīka*, *Lalitavistara*, and *Mahāvastu*) we find the compound *śramaṇa-brāhmaṇa-tīrthika-gaṇika*, which Edgerton takes as evidence that the category *tīrthika* excludes *brāhmaṇas*.[9] While the reality may have been more complicated than this, such a distinction would prove the shakiness of Edgerton's rule; it is likely that for many Buddhist authors the *tīrthika* was not an adherent of just "any religion" that contradicted what was taught by the Buddha.[10]

9. More diverse lists of different kinds of renunciants appear in many other Buddhist sources. A particularly early list appears in both the *Sattajaṭilasutta* (SN 3.11, I 77) and *Udāna* (Steinthal 1885, 65): *jaṭila, nigaṇṭha, acelaka, ekasāṭaka, paribbājaka*. Another early and lengthy example is in the *Aṅguttaranikāya* (AN III 276.31–277.1: *ājīvaka, nigaṇṭha, muṇḍasāvaka, jaṭilaka, paribbājaka, māgaṇḍika, tedaṇḍika, aviruddhaka, gotamaka, devadhammika*); a further list is preserved in the Sanskrit *Lalitavistara* (Vaidya 1958, 276.15–16: *caraka-parivrājaka-vṛddhaśrāvaka-gautama-nirgrantha-ājīvika-* . . .): see Schlingloff (1994, 71) regarding the latter two of these lists.

10. The antiquity of *śramaṇa-brāhmaṇa* as a true dichotomy is questioned in recent and important work by Nathan McGovern (e.g., 2019), who contests that the title *brāhmaṇa* was not originally the preserve of Vedic ritualists to the exclusion of ascetical renunciants (i.e., *śramaṇas*: Buddhist, Jain, or otherwise). My position is that those who were definitely successful in securing the label *brāhmaṇa* for themselves alone—that is, exponents and developers of Vedic tradition—were not commonly described by Buddhists as *tīrthika*s, nor were they themselves invested in the language of fords (*tīrtha*s) that was used by exponents of ascetical renunciation. An interesting group in this picture are the *jaṭila(ka)*s, or "matted-hair ascetics," who performed fire sacrifices and washed themselves at sources of water (possibly some literal *tīrtha*?) in pursuit of purity (*Udāna* 1.9 [Steinthal 1885, 6]). For another consideration of the *jaṭila* tradition see McGovern (2019, 113–121). In the *Mahāvagga* (Vin. I 71), *jaṭila*s are classified apart from *titthiya*s; not, in other words, members of a renunciant order or group that might be designated a *tīrtha*.

Although a *tīrthika* operated outside of the Buddhist *saṅgha*, the range of those to whom this referred was perhaps not so broad as to encompass exponents of all ideas or practices to which Buddhism objected. A pertinent question, in short, is whether a "religious teacher" who does not pertain to some manner of *tīrtha*—however we understand to what this term refers—would have been called a *tīrthika*.[11]

Of course Edgerton is not alone in his reliance on the language of "heresy" in this context: many influential authors in the history of Buddhist studies have employed the same terminology. The glossary in Conze et al. (1954) defines *tīrthika* as (foremost) "heretic," while Nakamura (1987; also 1955) used the same English translation when writing specifically about Buddhist awareness of rival doctrines. Indeed this choice of language dates back to a very early period in the study of Buddhism in the West: Eugène Burnouf (e.g., 1876, 145) favored "les hérétiques," which was maintained throughout the work of other prominent Francophone scholars, including Sylvain Lévi (e.g., 1911, 7) and Étienne Lamotte (e.g., 1958, 21).[12] In this century, among more recent works that are intended as introductions to the study of Buddhism, John Strong (2001, 107) takes a considered approach when he describes the famous six *tīrthakaras* of the *Śrāmaṇyaphalasūtra* as "six heretical teachers (various kinds of non-Buddhists)." The thesis of this chapter is that a retirement of this still widely known choice of language—which Strong, quite reasonably, chooses to further clarify, and

11. Much rides, of course, on what we take to be a proponent or teacher of a "religion" in pre-modern India: whether this expression should be limited to pursuit of some or other account of liberation (*mokṣa*), or understood to include also the complex ritual world of Brahmanical sacrifice. It certainly appears that *tīrthikas* were characterized as having concerns beyond the mundane. A source in Edgerton's discussion of the term is the *Saddharmapuṇḍarīka*, which after a list of what it calls *anyatīrthikas* (*caraka-parivrājaka-ājīvaka-nirgrantha*) lists separately "persons adept at worldly spells" (*lokāyatamantradhāraka*) and persons associated with "worldly practices" (*lokāyatika*: often understood to refer to traditions of disputation or sophistry), both of which may describe parties who may have been Brahmanical but not interested in liberation from rebirth (Kern and Nanjio [1908–1912] 1970, 276.2–3).

12. An interesting contrast can be made with early German translations by Karl Eugen Neumann, throughout whose translation of the *Majjhimanikāya* we find for *aññatitthiya* the translation "andersfährtige Pilger," or "pilgrims of another path" (e.g., 1922, 145). Neumann had earlier rejected the category of heresy (Ketzerei) with relation to persons who espouse (erroneous) views, and asserted that "the Indian does not know such a concept at all" (1911, 79n231).

which lingers in other twenty-first-century discussions of Buddhist literature—is by now overdue.[13]

Not all modern authors have relied on the translation "heretic," and alternative renderings resemble approaches that were favored by Buddhist translators in earlier centuries. Sometimes *tīrthika* has been translated using language that communicates those to whom it must have referred: teachers or practitioners of rival religious or philosophical systems that were extraneous to the Buddhist fold. Cristina Scherrer-Schaub (1999, 71) and after her Vincent Eltschinger (2013, 12n38, 36n3) have rendered *tīrthika* with "allodox": that is, some proponent of a system of thought that is other to Buddhism.[14] This captures not only the fact that the Indic *tīrthika* appears often in compound form preceded by *anya-* but also the sense of *tīrthika* rendered into Chinese with either *waidao* 外道, "(a proponent of) an extraneous path," or *yidao* 異道, "(a proponent of) a different path."[15]

Another attested rendering of *tīrthika* into English is "forder."[16] This is a more literal reading of the term and follows the approach taken by Tibetan translators where they rendered this and related expressions with *mu stegs pa* or *mu stegs can* (or, in a contracted form, simply *mu stegs*). These Tibetan expressions are calques: *mu* refers to some limit or boundary (it can render the Sanskrit *koṭi*), while *stegs* designates a platform or bridge; with the nominalizing (*pa*) or possessive suffix (*can*) we arrive at "one who

13. It is not my position that most contemporary authors or teachers in the field of Buddhist studies still rely on the translation "heretic" for *tīrthika* without any further qualification. But there is a risk that materials for the study of Buddhism that preserve this translation blur distinctions between European notions of heresy and the ways in which Indian Buddhist authors conceptualized traditions other than their own.

14. I see an important distinction between the neologism "allodox" and the English "heterodox," despite them having roots in similar Greek terms. The latter is better established in English with reference to ideas that are "not orthodox," that is, are not accepted or standard within a given tradition or framework. The benefit of allodox—if, of course, it becomes widely accepted and understood—is a stress on the challenging alterity of the *tīrthika*, who might propound alternative responses to concerns shared with Buddhists (see also note 43, below). For considerations apart from "allodox," see also Eltschinger 2012, 30n4.

15. I believe that the English "extraneous" does a double service: these traditions not only find their origins outside of the Buddha's teaching but are normally thought to be irrelevant in light of the (true, i.e., *sad-*)*dharma*.

16. For example, in translations by Hopkins (e.g., 1975, 28n10).

pertains to a platform at some limit," or a "ford" established at a bank for the purpose of crossing. An explanation of this translation is provided by the ninth-century *sGra sbyor bam po gnyis pa*, which unpacks content in the great lexicon of Tibetan Buddhist translation, the *Mahāvyutpatti*:

> In the manner that one constructs a platform from the shore for entering floodwaters, one who practices various customs/teachings (*chos*: Skt. *dharmas*), such as asceticism, yoga and so forth, constructs a platform for entering the floodwaters of *nirvāṇa*, so is called a "forder" (*mu stegs can*: Skt. *tīrthika*).[17]

An interesting nuance of this explanation is that the construction of a ford is understood in terms of the practice proper to some or other religious adept: the adept makes the ford, for themselves. This may not be entirely true to earlier Indian understanding of the category *tīrthika*, which is not quite the same as the *tīrthakara/tīrthaṅkara*, or "the maker of a ford," who is the founder of some or other tradition of renunciation (i.e., *tīrtha*).

Our Tibetan translators, as well as contemporary authors who employ the language of "fords," imply that *tīrthika*s are not necessarily just any "religious" teacher or practitioner outside of the parameters of the Buddhist *saṅgha*. It must refer to individuals who make their goal some kind of liberation; that is, the use of some figurative *tīrtha*. Keeping in mind the distinction observed by Edgerton, the Indic *tīrthika* might have not so naturally referred to *brāhmaṇas*, if by this we mean ritualists whose priority was often not liberation from the world and the established social order so much as correct activity within them in accord with Vedic prescriptions.[18] One way of articulating this is that *tīrthika* refers to some renunciant who has as their aim some absolute "break" from the world. The fact that both the Buddha and those whom Buddhist authors deemed *tīrthika*s had a common interest in an end to transmigration is an important dimension of the latter term, one which, as we shall see, even

17. *mtsho'i 'gram nas mtshor 'jug pa'i stegs 'cha' ba dang 'dra bar dka' thub dang rnal 'byor la sogs pa chos sna tshogs spyod cing mya ngan las 'das pa'i mtshor 'jug pa'i stegs 'cha' bas na mu stegs can zhes bya /* (Ishikawa 1990, 97 [entry no. 293]). It is noticeably strange that this passage seems to identify *nirvāṇa* with the floodwaters; we might have expected a dative particle to make clear that the floodwater is crossed *to reach* liberation.

18. See note 10 in this chapter.

permitted the idea that the work of (*anya*)*tīrthika*s in the world might not be entirely without merit.

Commentarial Literature and the *Tīrthika* as "Opponent"

Indian Buddhist commentators and systematizers identified the expression *tīrthika* with rival schools of thought and practice. Many authors emphasized doctrinal differences: Buddhaghosa's fifth-century *Samantapāsādikā* glosses *aññatittha* with *aññaladdhi* "another view/doctrine," and so also *aññatitthiya* with *aññaladdhika*: "a person with a view/doctrine different (to our own)" (Takakusu and Nagai 1966, 1034). From perhaps the same century, Vasubandhu's *Abhidharmakośabhāṣya* attacks the views of the Sāṃkhya and Vaiśeṣika systems, and does so most directly in his appendix to the main text (his *Pudgalaviniścaya*), where *tīrthika* is taken to refer to non-Buddhists who hold a person or self to have independent existence (*svabhāva*) apart from the five aggregates (Pradhan 1967, 461.14–16). *Tīrthika* might then be a general term for anyone—Sāṃkhya, Vaiśeṣika, or otherwise—who subscribes to such a view, although crucially Vasubandhu does not include here the Pudgalavādins, who are a primary target in this work, and both belonged to the Buddhist *saṅgha* while holding misguided views about personhood (*pudgala*). Confronting forms of *pudgalavāda* position (as something more akin to "heresy," i.e., a contentious stance *within* the Buddhist tradition) was a noticeable concern of Buddhist authors until roughly the sixth century (Priestley 1999, 48–52), after which time Dignāga and other authors began to give greater attention to the arguments of non-Buddhist philosophies that were perhaps, by this period, more important targets for sustained criticism.[19]

Buddhist commentators in the early centuries of the Common Era often took the defining feature of *tīrthika*s to be some or other wrong-

19. There are earlier systematic refutations of non-Buddhist ideas, although these do not always clearly identify real-world targets. For example, the refutation of various "allodoxies" (*paravādas*) in the *Yogācārabhūmiśāstra* (see Eltschinger 2013–2014), perhaps completed around the start of the fourth century, targets views that we commonly associate with Sāṃkhyas, Vaiśeṣikas, and "orthodox" Brahmanism. Only briefly does this content of the text refer by name to *tīrthyas* (*bāhyastīrthyas*: "*tīrthya*s outside [of our tradition]"), and specifically in its introduction to refutations of erroneous views of a permanently existing self (Bhattacharya 1957, 129.5–9; Eltschinger 2013–2014, 208). Although it is very likely that persons targeted by apologetic works such as this

minded view or belief, often regarding the existence or nature of the self. Whereas earlier in Buddhist literature we find rejection of many different ways of thinking about selfhood (e.g., in the *Mahāniddesa*: *sattassa narassa māṇavassa posassa puggalassa*, etc.; La Vallée Poussin and Thomas 1916, 127.22–24), we encounter in some commentarial sources a distinction between the innate (*sahaja*) conception of the self, proper to worldly persons (*pṛthagjana*; *laukika*), and views about the self that are speculative (*vikalpita*; *parikalpita*) and proper to *tīrthikas* (Eltschinger 2013, 271–275). Here the *tīrthika* is associated with false doctrines rather than simply the naïve views of everyday persons, although the other dimension of the *tīrthika*—being extraneousness to the Buddhist tradition—is not always explicitly stated. Could someone within the *saṅgha*, who expressed views commonly associated with those outside of it, be described as a *tīrthika*?

One perspective on this issue is provided by the commentary (*vyākhyā*) to the *Ratnagotravibhāga* (henceforth, RGVV), a lengthy work that unpacks challenging aspects of Mahāyāna Buddhist teaching (foremost, how to understand what is meant by *tathāgatagarbha*, otherwise "Buddha-nature"), likely produced in the fifth century. We can here compare the Sanskrit version of the text, in its edition by E. H. Johnston (1950), with a Chinese translation produced in 511 CE by Ratnamati 勒那摩提 (*Jujing yisheng baoxing lun* 究竟一乘寶性論: T. 1611) and an eleventh century Tibetan translation (e.g., text no. 5526 in the Peking edition of the Tengyur; no. 4025 in the Derge edition). At one juncture the RGVV categorizes different beings in accord with how they should be taught in order for them to progress toward comprehension of that which is ultimate (in this context called *dharmakāya*). This begins with a threefold distinction between 1) persons with desire for existence (*bhavābhilāṣin*), 2) those with desire for extinction (*vibhavābhilāṣin*), and 3) those with desire for neither (*tadubhayānabhilāṣin*), the third of which describes a bodhisattva (Johnston 1950, 27.17–18).[20] The first category is divided further: 1a) those who are of the lineage that is not for *nirvāṇa* (*aparin-*

would have been considered *tīrthikas*, there is a subtle distinction to be made between this label and another that becomes more prominent in later apologetical literature, in which Buddhist authors confront rival "scholars of reasoning or logic": so-called *tārkikas*.

20. This echoes the older Buddhist discernment of three types of craving (*tṛṣṇā*): for pleasure (*kāma*), existence (*bhāva*), and extinction (*vibhāva*). The idealized bodhisattva is here someone who has let go of the last of these, which continues to hinder *tīrthikas* as much as other Buddhists.

irvāṇagotraka), who are said to desire *saṃsāra* over *nirvāṇa*, and 1b) those of this *dharma* (*ihadhārmika*)—that is, within the Buddhist *saṅgha*—who possess this same desire and are hostile to the Mahāyāna (Johnston 1950, 28.1–2). A distinction is then made between both of these and 2) those who want for an end to existence (*vibhāva*), which includes 2ai) "other" religious teachers or practitioners who are extraneous to the *dharma* (*itobāhya . . . anyatīrthya*; Johnston 1950, 28.6–7).

The Sanskrit and Tibetan forms of the RGVV list these *anyatīrthya*s to include "ascetics" (*caraka*s; Tib. *tsa ra ka*), "wanderers" (*parivrājaka*s; Tib. *kun tu rgyu*) and "(Jain?) mendicants" (*nirgrantha*s; Tib. *gcer bu pa*) (Johnston 1950, 28.6–7; with minor emendation after Schmithausen 1973, 142). These proposed English translations attempt simply to draw out different connotations of each Indic term; it is unlikely that these terms were intended to evoke, here or in other Buddhist works, anything like specific classes of non-Buddhist.[21] Similar and often longer lists occur elsewhere—for example, in the *Vimalakīrtinirdeśa* (Taishō University 2006, 33 [20a1]) and *Saddharmapuṇḍarīka* (see note 11 in this chapter)—and not much precision may have been intended by them, so much as undiscriminating reference to all manner of non-Buddhist renunciants whose views should always be opposed. An informative variant is preserved in the Chinese translation of the RGVV—that is, the oldest form of the text available to us—in which the text glosses *tīrthya*s (外道) to refer very specifically to the Sāṃkhyas (僧佉), Vaiśeṣikas (衛世師), and Nirgrantha-Jñātaputras (尼揵陀若提子: T. 1611[31]828c19–22).

The RGVV then explains that these *tīrthya*s desire extinction but lack any method for achieving it (*anupāyapatita*), although this describes also 2aii) some members of the *saṅgha* (again called "of this *dharma*"; Johnston 1950, 28.7–8). These are Buddhists who cling to views of personhood (*pudgaladṛṣṭi*),[22] and who lack faith in the highest truth (*paramārthānadhimukta*), as well as monks whose pride in their understanding of emptiness means that they too do not correctly understand

21. There is stronger reason to believe that *nirgrantha* designated proponents of the Jain tradition specifically, regarding which see Balbir (2000, 1–4).

22. Again the Chinese version of the RGVV treats us to a further detail and identifies as an example of those committed to views of personhood the Vātsīputrīyas (犢子等): one of the Buddhist *nikāya*s that subscribed to the contentious *pudgalavāda* position (T. 1611[31]828c22).

the content of the Mahāyāna (Johnston 1950, 28.8–11). The *tīrthya*s and wrong-minded Buddhists, grouped together but still *distinct from* one another, are finally contrasted with 2b) persons who do have a means for liberation (*upāyapatita*): that is, the *śrāvaka*s and *pratyekabuddha*s, who for all of their limitations (not being on the path of the bodhisattva) nevertheless have "proceeded fixed to what is right" (*samyaktvaniyāmam avakrāntāḥ*; Johnston 1950, 28.13–14).

What is most revealing about category 2aii)—that is, persons without a means for attainment, but nevertheless "of this *dharma*"—is that the RGVV condemns them for "having faith (in the *dharma*), but behaving like those above (i.e., *tīrthya*s), and otherwise clinging to wrong views" (*ihadhārmikāś ca tatsabhāgacaritā eva śrāddhā api durgṛhītagrāhiṇaḥ*; Johnston 1950, 28.7–8). Moreover, those who have no faith in emptiness—which, we are told, is no better than having erroneous views about personhood—"are no different from *tīrthika*s" (*śūnyatānadhimukto nirviśiṣṭo bhavati tīrthikair*; Johnston 1950, 28.9–10). This demonstrates, somewhat ironically, that these individuals "within the *dharma*" indeed *are* different to *tīrthya*s: the comparison is clearly intended as a slur, and would be meaningless if persons within the *saṅgha* could, literally speaking, be deemed *tīrthika*s. Hence the RGVV exemplifies that the *tīrthika* is necessarily someone outside of the Buddhist tradition, to whom someone with erroneous views within the *saṅgha* might nevertheless be disparagingly compared.

Narrative Literature and the *Tīrthika* as "Obstacle"

Generalizations about *sūtra* texts and commentarial *śāstra* literature are risky, but in contrast to commentarial works that use the term *tīrthika* to refer to persons harboring certain views, the colorful narratives of Mahāyānist *sūtra* literature frequently understand *tīrthika*s to be simply obstacles to the *dharma*, or an affront to the influence of the *dharma* comparable to the "great adversary," Māra. A likely early example of this is found in most versions of the *Aṣṭasāhasrikā-prajñāpāramitā*, in which the deity Śakra protects the Buddha and his audience from a hundred *anyatīrthika*s, who approach the congregation with hostile intent (*pratihatacitta*) and a desire to undermine the Buddha's teaching (Vaidya 1960, 38.22–39). Immediately after this, Māra himself conjures an army of minions and intends to disrupt the Buddha more forcibly, but is once again deterred by Śakra in exactly the same fashion.

Here and elsewhere in Mahāyānist *sūtra* compositions the *tīrthika*s represent a challenge to the Buddha's promotion of the *dharma* in the world; there is little interest in disproving their ideas or practices, let alone converting them.[23] But unlike the mythical Māra, the literary *tīrthika*s must have evoked for a Buddhist audience very tangible opposition in the world from teachers or religious adepts who sought to discredit the *dharma* and its exponents. In the mythic-narrative context of Mahāyānist *sūtra*s the particular views of literary *tīrthika*s do not seem to matter. Their significance is rather their impact in *saṃsāra*: they are obstacles to the influence of the Buddha and perpetuity of the *dharma*, embodying doctrines or practices that must be rejected or quashed.[24] The *tīrthika* is presented as an obstruction to the *dharma*, rather than as an exponent of any persuasive alternative or meaningful challenge to Buddhist teaching.

Some Mahāyānist works make particularly creative claims about the role played by *tīrthika*s and confront their existence by having them explained away in terms of the activities of the Buddha or bodhisattvas. Particularly bold is the *Bodhisattvagocaropāyaviṣayavikurvāṇanirdeśasūtra* (henceforth, BGVNS), which explores the varieties of ways that advanced bodhisattvas can affect the world. The text also circulated under a number of shorter titles: for example, the later of its two Chinese translations (produced by Bodhiruci 菩提流支 in the sixth century) suggests something like the Indic title **Mahāsatyakanirgranthaputranirdeśa/-vyākaraṇa* (T. 272: *Da sazheniqianzi suoshuo jing* 大薩遮尼乾子所說經), while a reference in the Sanskrit *Śikṣāsamuccaya* preserves the name *Satyaka-parivarta*.[25] The

23. A similar perspective appears in numerous *jātaka* stories preserved in Pāli and Sanskrit. For example the *Mahāpadumajātaka* (Fausbøll 1963a, 187.5–6) compares the influence of *tīrthika*s after the appearance of the Buddha to that of fireflies after the dawn, whereas the *Cullahaṃsajātaka* (Fausbøll 1963b, 334–354) recounts the Buddha's need to outdo rival teachers in a show of his miraculous power. In many more instances the *tīrthika*s and their fall from authority are referenced only to affirm the dominance of the Buddha and his teaching.

24. An interesting accusation is made in the *Saddharmapuṇḍarīka*, which imagines that Mahāyānist monks will be admonished by Buddhist opponents for speaking/teaching what is proper to *tīrthya*s (*tīrthyavāda*; Kern and Nanjio 1970, 273.3; compare also Kumārajīva's Chinese translation: T. 262[9]36c10: 謂是邪見人 / 說外道論議). The text insinuates that its exponents will be accused of circulating ideas that belong outside of the *dharma*, which would be expected among the ranks of those called *tīrthika*s.

25. Bendall 1897–1902, 165.17: *āryasatyake parivartte*; regarding the likely names of the Indian text, see Silk 2013, 158–160.

primary speaker of the text is indeed a mendicant named Satyaka, who is referred to throughout as a *nirgrantha*.[26] This likely intends the same literary Saccaka who speaks with the Buddha in two texts preserved in the Pāli canon: the *Cūḷasaccakasutta* (MN 35, I 227) and *Mahāsaccakasutta* (MN 36, I 237). A lengthy portion of the BGVNS concerns Satyaka's instruction of the king Caṇḍapradyota, which as Zimmermann (2000) has explored constitutes a Buddhist critique of non-Buddhist *arthaśāstra* literature. But the twist in the tale—although predictable to students of Mahāyānist *sūtra*s in general—is that the *nirgrantha* Satyaka, who extols throughout the merits of the Buddhist *dharma*, is in fact an advanced bodhisattva (Jones 2016, 150–153).

Satyaka's affiliation to any particular non-Buddhist tradition is unclear: commonly the term *nirgrantha*(*putra*) is taken to refer to followers of the Jain tradition, although as Jamspal (2010, 143–147) points out the BGVNS understands Satyaka to be clothed (so is no member of anything like the Digāmbara Jain tradition), and—in his disputations with the king—he appeals to the authority of the Vedas. At any rate he is no member of the Buddhist *saṅgha*, and although the king respectfully refers to Satyaka as a *brāhmaṇa*, denoting perhaps his status at birth, the Buddha himself describes the wandering mendicant as precisely a *tīrthika* (Tib. *mu stegs can*), who has amassed a great number of followers. The ensuing revelation, that Satyaka is in fact a bodhisattva, is an unusual one. Although Mahāyānist texts are full of instances of bodhisattvas taking on unexpected forms, they are not so frequently said to take on the guise of non-Buddhist teachers specifically.[27] The BGVNS extends this narrative device to provide an explanation for the existence of *tīrthika*s in general,

26. Regarding the Tibetan text, see Jamspal 2010; moreover, Silk 2013.

27. Another (and likely earlier) instance is found in the *Vimalakīrtinirdeśa* (Taishō University 2006, 77 [46b7]), in which the bodhisattva might "follow the way of *tīrthika*s, [but] becomes [the correct] *tīrtha* [for them]" (*tīrthikagatiṃ ca gacchati, tīrthabhūtaś ca bhavati*; compare, in Kumārajīva's Chinese, T. 475[14]549a24–25). However this does not extend to the claim also made in the BGVNS that *tīrthika*s *in general* must be the work of bodhisattvas or the Buddha. Otherwise it is works of the *tathāgatagarbha* tradition—notable for attempting to make sense of similarities between what they teach (in some instances, explicitly, a Buddhist account of the self) and what is expounded by rival systems—that go so far as to declare that promulgators of ostensibly non-Buddhist teachings are created (**nirmita*) by the Buddha or bodhisattva(s) (see Jones 2016).

and so challenges an audience's expectations not just about the activities of bodhisattvas but the status or value of non-Buddhist teachers in the world. At one stage the Buddha declares that there are in fact no *tīrthika*s in his Buddha-field (i.e., our world), but that those who appear to be as such exist only by his power, for his (salvific) purposes:

> That place [i.e., the Buddha-field] does not generate *tīrthika*s and such like them. Why is that? Mañjuśrī, in my Buddha-field the presence of *tīrthika*s and *nirgrantha*s in every case is due to the sustaining power of the Tathāgata, for the purpose of displaying the range of [his] inconceivable skill-in-means.[28]

In other words there are no "true" *tīrthika*s, in the sense of *genuinely* extraneous teachers of other paths, but any persons who appear to be as such are there only by the will and power of the Buddha. The text goes on to explain that these *tīrthika*s cultivate the perfection of insight, employ skill-in-means, and are empowered by the Buddha to develop other sentient beings.[29] Accompanying verses affirm that the apparent power of these *tīrthika*s, like that of Satyaka, are part of skillful displays by powerful bodhisattvas.[30] The purpose of this claim must be twofold: to laud the creative power of the Buddha and bodhisattvas, but also to explain away the existence of non-Buddhist institutions and systems, and their effects in the world, in such a fashion that they pose no threat to the authority of Buddhist *dharma*. To return to the central matter of this chapter: if an audience of the BGVNS could make sense of the claim that at least some *tīrthika*s in the world were in fact bodhisattvas—such that their teachings must contribute, in some unfathomable fashion, to the spread of the *dharma*—are we happy to understand that the defining feature

---

28. T. 272(9)326c24–26: 彼處不生諸外道等。何以故? 文殊師利, 我佛國土有諸外道、尼乾子等, 皆是如來住持力故, 為欲示現不可思議方便境界。Compare also material at T. 271([9]326c24–327a2, and in Tibetan translation Derge no. 146 (*mdo sde, pa*), 97a3–6; Q.813 (*mdo sna tshogs, nu*), 53a4–7.

29. See T. 272(9)326c26–327a2. See also Silk 2013, 176–177; Jones 2016, 152–153.

30. T. 272(9)327c10–11: 外道大神通 / 皆自在菩薩 / 汝當知方便 / 示現如是相。 Compare also T. 271(9)306c5–6, and in Tibetan translation Derge no. 146 (*mdo sde, pa*), 98b4–5; Peking no. 813 (*mdo sna tshogs, nu*), 54b6–7.

of a *tīrthika* is adherence to something that we might term, in English, "heresy"?

The implication in the *sūtra* is that some "*tīrtha*" that a *tīrthika* may promote could play a positive role in the spread of the *dharma*. This does not serve to promote non-Buddhist teachings, but does make space for them in the mysterious activities of buddhas and bodhisattvas. Such an idea has some precedent outside of Mahāyānist literature, although it is uncommon to find the position that the bodhisattva (normally Śākyamuni himself, in a previous existence) became, by name, a *tīrthika* or *tīrthakara* specifically.[31] A notable exception is found in the *Mahāvastu*: a text of the Mahāsāṃghika tradition, which lauds bodhisattvas taking on different forms for specific purposes. Upon attaining the eighth stage (*bhūmi*) of a bodhisattva's progress "[bodhisattvas] become *tīrthikas*[32] who destroy existence (*bhavasūdana*); henceforth, they condemn worldly pleasures and extol cessation."[33] Edgerton's discussion of the term *tīrthika* (discussed earlier) identified this passage as a "corruption," rejecting the idea that the *Mahāvastu* could have used the term *tīrthika* to refer to anything other than a "heretic."[34] But the text is coherent: the purpose of this stage in the bodhisattva's career is to introduce to the world some notion of an end to rebirth, preempting the emergence of a Buddha who will then teach the correct path toward *nirvāṇa*. By suggesting that the bodhisattva, in the guise of a *tīrthika*, can fulfill such a role, persons designated as *tīrthikas* are polemically accorded a subordinate place in the many and varied soteriological strategies of buddhas and bodhisattvas.

Whereas the Mahāyānist BGVNS paints a picture of a world inhabited by *tīrthikas* who are in fact devices of the Buddha or his bodhisattvas, the

31. The bodhisattva is more often reported to have become a *brāhmaṇa* associated with the introduction of different practices, including forms of meditation, into the world: for example, in the *Mahāgovindasutta* (DN 19, II 220–252).

32. J. J. Jones's translation (1949, 84) renders *tīrthikas* with "ascetic pilgrims," likely meaning to associate them with the observance of literal *tīrthas*—that is, sacred sites at rivers—as discussed later.

33. *ataḥ prabhṛti tīrthikā vā bhavanti bhavasūdanāḥ / ataḥ prabhṛti kucchanti kāmāṃ śaṃsanti nirvṛtiṃ //* (Senart 1882, 106.8–9).

34. Senart (1882, 460), in his notes to the *Mahāvastu*, expresses something similar and suggested emendation of *vā* to *na* in the passage quoted (see previous note). I am grateful to Claire Maes for bringing this to my attention.

Mahāvastu articulates that on his way to buddhahood a bodhisattva will first appear as a *tīrthika* to introduce the very idea of an end to transmigration, before later articulating the (*sad-*)*dharma* when he emerges as a fully realized Buddha. In these literary contexts, it makes little sense to believe that a bodhisattva could be characterized by opinions, views, or ambitions—that is, internal states—that would be accurately described as "heretical," and yet he indeed becomes what Buddhism calls a *tīrthika*. In various literary contexts, the defining characteristic of the literary *tīrthika* is what he *teaches*, or at any rate embodies, in the world: an apparent alternative to the Buddhist path, which for some Buddhist authors was best confronted by reducing their appearance and activities to the expedient devices of bodhisattvas.

Early Buddhism and the First "Fords"

More often than not it is difficult for us to discern with clarity who in the real world (if indeed anyone specific) the literary *tīrthika*s were intended to evoke, although they were certainly 1) extraneous to the Buddhist fold, 2) obstacles to the authority of the Buddha's teaching, and 3) associated with alternative (erroneous) accounts of liberation. As we step further back in literary history, we find that sources for the "early" Buddhist tradition—representative of Buddhist literature prior to the advent of the Mahāyāna—are sometimes clearer in their understanding of who was or was not a *tīrthika* (or P. *titthiya*). In the Pāli tradition it is clearer still that "heretic" is an unsuitable translation. On at least one occasion in the Pāli *nikāya*s, in the *Soṇadaṇḍasutta* (DN 4, I 116), it is taken for granted that the Buddha himself can be considered a *titthakara*: "Indeed, Sirs, the ascetic Gotama, being the head of an order, of a congregation, the teacher of a congregation, is acknowledged as best of the various *titthakaras*."[35] This scarcely makes sense if the final term in this description is understood to mean, after Edgerton, "a heresiarch." It could be argued that because this line is delivered not by a Buddhist but by the *brāhmaṇa*

35. DN I 116.16–18: *samaṇo khalu bho gotamo saṃghī gaṇī gaṇācariyo puthu-tittha-karānaṃ aggam akkhāyati*. Translation modified from that found in Rhys Davids ([1899] 1956, 149).

Soṇadaṇḍa (by whom the Buddha could have been considered a perverter of the supposedly "catholic" Vedic social hierarchy) Gotama might be something like a "heretic" from a conservative Brahmanical perspective.[36] However in the context of the *sutta* the term *titthakara* appears no more loaded than others used in the same refrain (e.g., *gaṇācariya*: "teacher of a congregation"); Soṇadaṇḍa simply recognizes that the Buddha is "one who produces a *tittha*." The same language is found in surviving forms of the *Śrāmaṇyaphalasūtra* (e.g., DN 2), which is well known for its account of the six non-Buddhist teachers who provide unsatisfactory answers to questions posed by King Ajātaśatru.[37] Elsewhere in Pāli literature the use of *aññatitthiya* implies that there is room to compare the Buddhist order with communities of "other" *titthiyas*. In the *Cullavagga*, in response to the pleas of Ānanda and Mahāpajāpatī Gotamī to permit the ordination of women into the *saṅgha*, the Buddha refers to the position of women among communities of *aññatitthiyas*, that is, in other religious groups, as a guiding precedent (Oldenberg 1880, 257–258; Chakravarti 1987, 32).

Behind all of this lies the figurative *tittha* that is established by some *titthakara* or "ford-maker," which presupposes an important metaphor shared by Buddhist, Jain, and other traditions that owe their origins to the *śramaṇa* tradition of renunciation that was prevalent in Magadha during the late Vedic period. This basic metaphor conceptualizes the tumult of transmigration as a flood (P./Skt. *ogha*; Ardhamāgadhī *oha*), which in Jain literature, for example the *Āyāraṅgasutta*, is that which the renunciant looks to cross, and for which a *tīrthaṅkara* (such as, in our current age, Mahāvīra) has revealed a means of traversal.[38] The flood metaphor is also found throughout what are considered to be relatively early materials in the Pāli Canon. The *Suttanipāta* recounts many interactions between the Buddha and various renunciants, *brāhmaṇas*, and deities whose common interest

36. Gotama could have been categorized as a *nāstika*: a "naysayer" regarding the existence (or at least prominence) of the Vedic gods and sacrifices. Another common term in Brahmanical literature is *vedabāhya*, "outside the Vedas," which again has connotations of externality rather than of "heresy" per se. For more on these terms, which belong to a period of Indian literature later than what is preserved in these Pāli sources, see Doniger O'Flaherty (1983, 109–111).

37. DN I 47.15–18. In fine studies of the six teachers featured in this narrative and others, both Vogel (1970) and MacQueen (1988) refer to them as "heretics."

38. See Jacobi 1882: 1.2.3, §6; 1.2.6, §3; 1.6.1, §6; II.16 v. 10.

is the means over the flood of "birth and aging, pain and lamentation."[39] The very first *sutta* collected in the *Saṃyuttanikāya* is the *Oghataraṇasutta* (SN 1), or "discourse regarding crossing the flood." It is noteworthy that elsewhere in the *suttas* (and throughout Buddhaghosa's commentaries on these materials) this flood is glossed to be "fourfold," consisting of desire (*kāma*), becoming (*bhāva*), views (*diṭṭhi*), and ignorance (*avijjā*), rather than simply the singular "flood" of the *Suttanipāta*.[40]

This shift away from "crossing the flood" to "overcoming (several) floodwaters" parallels what was likely a very deliberate distancing of Buddhist terminology away from the language typical of their *śramaṇa* rivals, who continued to invest importance in the metaphor of the flood, the identification of the correct means across it (*tittha*), and the teacher who establishes such a crossing (*titthakara*). Jain texts reserve the title *tīrthaṅkara* exclusively for their own teachers who (re)establish the Jaina *tīrtha* in the world—Pārśva, Mahāvīra, and others before them—and denied it to their opponents, foremost of whom was the Ājīvika figurehead Makkhali Gosala, whose followers considered *tīrthaṅkara* to be the appropriate title for their own master (Basham 1951, 27–28, 79; Balcerowicz 2016, 39, 315–316).[41] Whereas Buddhist authors ceased to consider the Buddha in these terms, Jainism retained this language at its very core and understood the *tīrtha* that some *tīrthaṅkara* (re)establishes in the world to refer foremost to the Jain community—both renunciate and lay, male and female—which, like the Buddhist *saṅgha*, is the institution through which liberation can be achieved (Dundas 2002, 20).[42]

---

39. *Pārāyanavagga*, v. 1056: *jātijaraṃ sokapariddavañ ca* (Andersen and Smith 1913, 203). Further relevant verses from the *Suttanipāta* include 173; 178; 219; 471; 495; 538; 771; 779; 823; 945; 1059; 1064; 1069–1070; 1081–1083; 1092–1093; 1096; 1145, for which see Andersen and Smith (1913) or translations in Bodhi (2017).

40. See, for example, SN IV 257–258; V 59. In the second of these passages, the four floods (along with other obstacles) are not for "crossing," but instead should be "known, understood, destroyed, abandoned" (*abhiññāya . . . pariññaya . . . parikkhayāya . . . pahānāya*).

41. Jain literature also confronts what it calls *annautthiyas* (*anyatīrthikas*), referring to Ājīvikas or other rivals, as reflected in fragments of the *Viyāhapannatti* (Skt. *Vyākhyaprajñapti*): see Deleu (1977); Balcerowicz (1997, 205–206).

42. For a short history of the *tittha* in Jain commentarial literature—in which it is sometimes also used to refer to the Jain canon of scriptures—see Balcerowicz (1997, 203–206). Here Balcerowicz glosses *tīrthika*, and so forth, as " 'a thinker,' 'an adept,' viz. someone more engaged and experienced in one's own religious system" (1997, 205).

It appears then that the language of *tīrthas* was presumed by early Buddhist tradition but was, over time, virtually abandoned. This was likely part of a gradual move to distance Buddhism and its language from their most proximate rivals or competitors.[43] Notably, early Buddhist accounts of the Buddha's dealings with persons designated as *titthiyas* or *tittha-karas* are for the most part distinct from his interactions with figures representative of the Vedic socioritual order.[44] Pāli Buddhist sources do not use the language of "fords" in reference to figures representative of Vedic authority, and so it seems that in this literary context a Brahmanical ritualist was not, without belonging to an institution concerned with how to achieve liberation from rebirth, someone who would naturally be categorized as a *tīrthika*.[45]

This distinction is supported by the absence of the central flood metaphor—or any investment in a "ford" across it—in early Brahmanical sources themselves. An early reference to a literal *tīrtha* is recorded in the *Taittirīyasaṃhitā* of the Black Yajurveda, in which a sacrificer purifies himself in water after the performance of the Soma ritual, freeing himself from fetters associated with the deity Varuṇa (Parpola 2003, 523; also Eck 1981, 327). However with the exception of this rite the lack of interest in bathing sites in the Vedas—that is, reference to literal *tīrthas*—is disproportional to the tremendous importance of pilgrimage to sacred fords (*tīrthayātrā*) in Brahmanical literature of later centuries (see Jacobsen 2018). Works of the Brahmanical tradition that develop and

43. Regarding the "othering" of renunciate traditions outside of the Buddhist *saṅgha*, with particular focus on the Pāli *Vinaya* literature, see Maes (2016). Buddhist eschewal of the language of *tīrtha*/*tīrthikas* can be considered part of a response to what Maes discusses as the "proximate other" (after Jonathan Z. Smith): that is, (in the Buddhist context) traditions of renunciation that made competing claims about liberation and how to approach it, whose exponents lived and operated in ways comparable to members of the Buddhist *saṅgha*.

44. For a recent overview of *suttas* dealing with representatives of Vedic authority, see Nichols (2015).

45. Occasionally in Pāli sources we find instances where "*śramaṇas* and *brāhmaṇas*" (i.e., *samaṇabrāhmaṇa*) are qualified as being "of various sects" (*nānātitthiya*: e.g., in the *Pāṭhikasutta* [DN III 16–17]; also DN I 179; MN II 2; and the *Udāna* [Steinthal 1885, 66–67: *nānātitthiyā samaṇabrāhmaṇā* . . .]). This usage may simply intend that some within the group belong, by birth, to the category *brāhmaṇa*; they may not be proponents of Brahmanical ideas.

defend the Vedic sacrifice and Brahmanical culture surrounding it make little use of the language of *tīrtha*s, or of the root √*tṝ* in anything like the sense of a "passing over" from rebirth.[46] And while we do encounter *tīrtha* in the sense of "the correct/prescribed manner" (e.g., at the very end of the *Chāndogya-upaniṣad*: 8.15.1; e.g., Olivelle 1998, 286–287), the *tīrtha* understood as a means out of perpetual transmigration does not appear important to Brahmanical works that are accepted to have originated before the start of the Common Era.

Still little is made of literal *tīrtha*s in the early *dharmasūtra* and *dharmaśāstra* literature, although the *Mānava-dharmaśāstra* (3.130 [Olivelle 2005, 115, 472]) does confirm that a *brāhmaṇa* himself could be considered a *tīrtha* when he is of good lineage and learned in the Vedas, and so is someone fit to receive gifts (Parpola 2003, 542). This is the curious sense of *tīrtha* as "one who is worthy": perhaps the *brāhmaṇa* who, by virtue of his birth and learning, is at the intersection of the gods and the world. Kane (1953, 581–582) observed that the later literature of the *dharmaśāstra* tradition devoted more attention to the value of literal *tīrtha*s than to any other topic, and during the gradual composition of the *Mahābhārata* (foremost its *Tīrthayātrāparvan*), perhaps in the earliest centuries of the Common Era, pilgrimage began to surpass sacrifice as the most efficacious means out of rebirth (Kane 1953, 561–564). As Ensink (1979) writes, in the Brahmanical epics and Purāṇas the different forms of Vedic sacrifice are used as yardsticks for the benefits obtained by bathing at *tīrtha*s, implying that the attribution of soteriological value to these loci was less established, but gaining in importance such that it would eventually eclipse the value of the classical Vedic sacrifice. Buddhist literature of

46. Exceptions may be in the *Bṛhadāraṇyaka-upaniṣad* (4.4.23): that he who knows the self passes over (*tarati*) evil, and it over him; but this does not explicitly refer to any "passing over" from transmigration. Closer are lines in the *Chāndogya-upaniṣad* (7.1.3) and *Muṇḍaka-upaniṣad* (3.2.9), which speak of traversing (*tarati*) sorrows—in the latter this is said to be toward immortality (*amṛta*)—while the *Kaṭha-upaniṣad* (1.17) mentions the crossing over of birth and death (*tarati janmamṛtyū*) for one who properly understands Vedic ritual (regarding all of these passages, see Olivelle 1998). Eck (1981, 329–332) provides a longer list of instances in which the *Saṃhitā*s, *Brāhmaṇa*s, and *Upaniṣad*s invest importance in the verb √*tṝ*, although I am not convinced that in so many of these the sense is much more than simply "to traverse," without any clear relation to the flood/ford metaphor central to the *śramaṇa* traditions.

the early Common Era includes Aśvaghoṣa's *Buddhacarita* (perhaps second century), which makes several references to *tīrtha*s as sites associated with purification, and has the mendicant Bodhisattva Siddhārtha criticize the view that allegedly sacred waters can cleanse the bather of past evils (v. 730–731 [Olivelle 2008, 196–197]).[47]

It is very likely that veneration of literal *tīrtha*s across India predated Brahmanical interest in them. Asko Parpola has hypothesized that use of literal fords in South Asian ritual may date back as far as the Indus Valley Civilization and the famous "Great Bath" at Mohenjo-Daro (Parpola 2003, 525–526); Brahmanical authors may have been very late to accommodate into their tradition the importance that some populations of India invested in sites of sacred water here or there across the Indian landscape.[48] However, we must keep in mind that the fords of the *śramaṇa* milieu, fords produced by *tīrthakara*s, are nothing without the flood that they are supposed to traverse. Our Buddhist and Jain authors, with origins in Magadha and, perhaps significantly, the floodplains of the Ganges and its tributaries, imagine fords not for entering sacred water but for crossing its dangerous, fast-flowing currents.

The importance of a figurative *tīrtha*—established in the world by some *tīrthakara*—is absent from works of the Vedic tradition and its preoccupation with socioritual order. A distinction between the label *brāhmaṇa* and persons belonging to some *tīrtha* may not have been hard and fast (see note 10 in this chapter), but neither the Brahmanical tradition itself nor Buddhist authors who opposed it seem to have readily referred to Vedic ritualists as, by name, *tīrthika*s. We cannot then suppose that in all Buddhist literary contexts *tīrthika* could refer to just any "religious" adept outside of the Buddhist fold; it designated renunciants who were occupied

47. At this juncture the Chinese translation of the *Buddhacarita* (T. 192[4]13b8) refers to non-Buddhists (諸外道) who observe the purifying power of water, where the reference in Indian material underlying this translation may have been simply to *tīrtha*s—that is, literal fords (and not figurative "forders")—that are sources of water considered to have some sacred status. There is also clear reference to the sacredness of literal *tīrtha*s in *jātaka* literature, for example, the *Juṇhajātaka* (Fausbøll 1963a, 96.8) in which a list of the virtues of the monk Ānanda includes his having dwelt at *tīrtha*s (*titthavāsa*).

48. Regarding which see also Nath (2007).

with the specific problem of transmigration, the seemingly inescapable current of death and rebirth, and how to leave it.[49]

Conclusion

Much more could be said about attitudes toward those called *tīrthika*s in different Buddhist sources, but what is clear is that talk of "heretics" and their respective "heresies" is out of place when we render these sources into English. The fact that Buddhist authors used *tīrthika* pejoratively—including in instances where the *tīrthika* is imagined to have some subordinate function in the promotion of Buddhist *dharma*—does not mean that we should burden our studies or translations with the language of "heresy." The sense that *tīrthika*s belonged to different traditions of renunciation, and the fact that over time this language became (for Buddhists) so derogatory, is undoubtably analogous to what became of the Greek *hairesis*. In the context of writing about Buddhism, the English term "heretic" is so loaded with pejorative connotations, and of specifically *intra*sectarian dispute, that this translation cannot, today, be of much use to us.

What, then, will do? Translations in terms of either "allodoxy" or "fording" both have their merits: the first communicates the "otherness" of *tīrthika*s, but does an injustice to the Buddha himself as the originator of some figurative *tīrtha*; the second captures neatly the central metaphor of this language but lacks the frequent dismissiveness with which the term *tīrthika* was used by the majority of Buddhist authors. These problems exist in part because the pejorative flavor of this language increased over the centuries. The sense that the Buddha was a *tīrthakara* may have been dropped well before the advent of the Mahāyāna, although in years closer to the Buddha's death it may not have been quite so contentious to have described Śākyamuni himself in just such terms.[50] Translating *tīrthika* in terms of "non-Buddhist adepts or teachers" is for the most part accurate;

49. An interesting complication, in the *Aṅguttaranikāya* (AN I 173), is the Buddha's identification of three fundamental beliefs of renunciant orders, or perhaps (literalistically) "sites upon which a ford is built" (*titthāyatanāni*): that all experiences come about because of past actions, or by the creative work of a supreme deity (*issara*: Skt. *īśvara*), or without any prior cause.

50. Exceptions remain. The eighth-century *Tattvasaṅgraha* by Śāntarakṣita states that the Tathāgata "is head of all those makers of *tīrtha*s" (*sarvatīrthakṛtāṃ . . . sthito*

it should however be understood that what was promoted by a *tīrthika* was some account of a means out of transmigration and not—as was the priority of many *brāhmaṇas*—observance of Vedic prescriptions and the heavily ritualized worldview associated with them.

Even as we lack a simple, one-word translation for *tīrthika*, one dimension of this term and its context deserves further emphasis. As noted earlier, in Jain tradition the *tīrtha* created by a *tīrthaṅkara* does not refer exclusively to teachings about liberation, so much as to the (re) construction in the world of the religious community that pursues and preserves these teachings. Translated into the language of the Buddhist tradition, the *tīrtha* of any Indian *tīrthakara* referred not foremost to a master's *dharma* but rather to his *saṅgha*. As such, a "ford-maker" is the founder of a group: an order or organization of renunciants; the "ford" is the institution to which a mendicant is affiliated. The defining feature of any such organization is some or other response to the problem of transmigration, imagined as a flood that can be crossed only by entry into that institution: that is, entry into that *tīrtha*.[51] In short, we should keep in mind that the "ford" metaphor seems to have referred, perhaps originally, to community rather than to creed.[52]

However we choose to translate these terms, closer investigation of how they were used leads us to some important distinctions that should be kept in mind when we discuss the religious landscape(s) of classical India.

---

mūrdhni tathāgataḥ) (see Eltschinger 2013, 217). This was surely not intended to laud the authority of any other *tīrthakṛts*, but preserves the idea that the Buddha's is one (although the only true) *tīrtha* among many, and that he himself is a manner of *tīrthakara*.

51. The most famous account of "crossing water" in early Buddhist literature is undoubtedly the simile of the raft, featured in the *Alagaddūpamasutta* (MN 22, I 130–142). In the simile, that which is crossed over is a "great expanse of floodwater" (*mahantaṃ udakaṇṇavaṃ*), although the Buddha does not dwell on either the "flood" or "ford" so much as the key lesson of the simile: the danger of attaching oneself to teachings. The simile is perhaps an implied critique of the language of "fording" altogether, in which the means across the flood is an *instrument*, rather than some fixed "site" or sacred locus (i.e., *tīrtha*) to which one might remain attached. For further accounts of crossing waters in Buddhist literature, see Maes (2015, 194–207).

52. One might consider the *tīrtha* to be a "sect," so *tīrthika* a "sectarian," but this suffers from the connotation that "sectarianism" arises through dissent. as groups split from an orthodox or mainstream position or institution (see Dundas 2002, 45). See also Balcerowicz (1997), regarding *tīrtha* and the no-less-fraught category "religion."

Very obviously there is a difference to be observed between the *tīrthika* and a *tīrtha(ṅ)kara*, the former referring to proponents of some other community or institution but not, necessarily, their founding authorities. Moreover, not all "non-Buddhist" religious adepts would be naturally called *tīrthika*s: some rivals to the Buddha's authority—preservers of the Brahmanical sacrifice and proponents of a social order associated with it—were not all so concerned with finding a passage out of transmigration, nor affiliated to groups that made this their primary concern. Aside from the no-less complex history of literal *tīrtha*s in India, the figurative *tīrtha* appears to be a product of the world of ascetic renunciation in Magadha, in which Buddhism forged an identity in contrast to other orders of mendicancy that responded to the same problem, the "flood" of suffering over which an ascetic sought passage.

As is so often the case with the reconstruction of Indian religious history, our available literature provides only small and opaque windows onto what people did or thought in the environments of our authors. When trying to articulate for contemporary audiences the world about which Indian authors wrote, we would do well not to distort matters through the too-easy application of terminology drawn from Western religious history. Accordingly, the language of heresy should be avoided when describing figures—real or imagined—whose defining feature seems to have been their commitment to alternative accounts of liberation, and moreover to institutions associated with them, that were extraneous to Buddhism.

References

Andersen, Dines and Smith, Helmer, eds. 1913. The *Sutta-nipāta*. London: H. Frowde for the Pali Text Society.

Balbir, Nalini. 2000. "Jain-Buddhist Dialogue: Material from the Pāli Scriptures." *Journal of the Pali Text Society* 26: 1–42.

Balcerowicz, Piotr. 1997. "Jaina Concept of Religion." Contributions on Oriental Traditions (On Non-Monotheistic Religions). *Dialogue and Universalism* 11–12: 197–215.

———. 2016. *Early Asceticism in India: Ājīvikism and Jainism*. Abingdon: Routledge.

Basham, A. L. 1951. *History and Doctrines of the Ājīvikas: A Vanished Indian Religion*. London: Luzac.

Belloc, Hilaire. 1938. *The Great Heresies*. London: Sheed and Ward.

Bendall, Cecil, ed. 1897–1902. *Çikshāsamuccaya—A Compendium of Buddhistic Teaching Compiled by Çāntideva, Chiefly from Earlier Mahāyāna-sūtras*. Bibliotheca Buddhica 1. St Pétersbourg: Imperial Academy. Rpt.: 1952. 'S-Gravenhage: Mouton & Co.

Bhattacharya, Ramkrishna. 2011. *Studies on the Cārvāka/Lokāyata*. London: Anthem Press.

Bhattacharya, Vidhushekhara, ed. 1957. *The Yogācārabhūmi of Ācārya Asaṅga*, part 1. Calcutta: University of Calcutta.

Bodhi, Bhikkhu, trans. 2017. *The Suttanipāta: An Ancient Collection of the Buddha's Discourses Together with Its Commentaries*. London: Wisdom / Pali Text Society.

Burnouf, Eugene. 1876. *Introduction a l'Histoire du Buddhisme Indien*. 2nd ed. Paris: Maissoneuve.

Cameron, Averil. 2007. "Jews and Heretics: A Category Error?" In *The Ways That Never Parted: Jews and Christians in Late Antiquity and the Early Middle Ages*, edited by Adam Becker and Anette Yoshiko Reed, 345–360. Tübingen: Mohr Siebeck.

Chakravarti, Uma. 1987. *The Social Dimensions of Early Buddhism*. Delhi: Oxford University Press.

Collett, Alice. 2006. "Buddhism and Gender: Reframing and Refocusing the Debate." *Journal of Feminist Studies in Religion* 22, no. 2: 55–84.

Conze, Edward, I. B. Horner, David Snellgrove, and Arthur Waley. 1954. *Buddhist Texts Through the Ages*. Oxford: B. Cassirer.

Deleu, Jozef. 1977. "Lord Mahāvīra and the *Anyatīrthikas*." In *Mahāvīra and His Teachings*, edited by Upadhye et al., 188–194. Bombay: Bhagavāna Mahāvīra 2500th Nirvāṇa Mahotsava Samiti.

Doniger O'Flaherty, Wendy. 1983. "The Image of the Heretic in the Gupta Purāṇas." In *Essays on Gupta Culture*, edited by Bardwell L. Smith, 107–153. Delhi: Motilal Banarsidass.

Dundas, Paul. 2002. *The Jains*. 2nd ed. London: Routledge.

Eck, Diana L. 1981. "India's *Tīrthas*: 'Crossings' in Sacred Geography." *History of Religions* 20, no. 4: 323–344.

Edgerton, Franklin. 1953. *Buddhist Hybrid Sanskrit Grammar and Dictionary, Vol. 2: Dictionary*. New Haven: Yale University Press.

Eltschinger, Vincent. 2012. "Apocalypticism, Heresy and Philosophy." In *World View and Theory in Indian Philosophy*, edited by Piotr Balcerowicz, 29–85. Delhi: Manohar.

———. 2013. *Buddhist Epistemology as Apologetics: Studies on the History, Self-understanding and Dogmatic Foundations of Late Indian Buddhist Philosophy*. Vienna: Verlag der Österreichischen Akademie der Wissenschaften.

———. 2013–2014. "The *Yogācārabhūmi* against Allodoxies (*paravāda*): 1. Introduction and Doxography." *Wiener Zeitschrift für die Kunde Südasiens* 55: 191–234.

Ensink, Jacob. 1979. "Hindu Pilgrimage and Vedic Sacrifice." In *Ludwik Sternbach Felicitation Volume*, part 1, edited by J. P. Sinha, 105–118. Lucknow: Akhila Bharatiya Sanskrit Parishad.

Fausbøll, V., ed. 1963a. *The Jātaka Together with Its Commentary*. Vol. 4. London: Pali Text Society, by Luzac and Company.

———, ed. 1963b. *The Jātaka Together with Its Commentary*. Vol. 5. London: Pali Text Society, by Luzac and Company.

Gethin, Rupert. 2004. "He Who Sees Dhamma Sees Dhammas: Dhamma in Early Buddhism." *Journal of Indian Philosophy* 32: 513–542.

Gilby, Thomas, ed. and trans. 1975. *Summa Theologiae: Latin Text with English Translation, Introduction, Notes, Appendices and Glossaries*. Vol. 32. London: Blackfriars in conjunction with Eyre and Spottiswoode.

Griffiths, Paul J. 1981. "Buddhist Hybrid English: Some Notes on Philology and Hermeneutics for Buddhologists." *Journal of the International Association of Buddhist Studies* 4, no. 2: 17–32.

Hopkins, Jeffrey, with Lati Rimpoche and Anne Klein. 1975. *The Precious Garland and the Song of the Four Mindfulnesses*. London: Allen and Unwin.

Horner, I. B. trans. [1940] 2004. *The Book of the Discipline (Vinaya-Piṭaka), Vol. III (Suttavibhaṅga)*. Oxford: Pali Text Society.

Ishikawa, Mie, ed. 1990. *A Critical Edition of the sGra sbyor bam po gnyis pa: An Old and Basic Commentary on the Mahāvyutpatti*. Tokyo: Toyo Bunko.

Jacobi, Hermann, ed. 1882. *The Âyâraṃga Sutta of the Çetâmbara Jains*. London: Pali Text Society.

Jacobsen, Knut A. 2018. "Pilgrimage: *tīrthyayātrā*." In *Hindu Law: A New History of Dharmaśāstra*, edited by Patrick Olivelle and Donald R. Davis Jr., 335–346. Oxford: Oxford University Press.

Jamspal, Lozang, trans. 2010. *The Range of the Bodhisattva, A Mahāyāna Sūtra (Ārya-Bodhisattva-gocara): The Teachings of the Nirgrantha Satyaka*. New York: American Institute of Buddhist Studies.

Johnston, E. H., ed. 1950. *The Ratnagotravibhāga Mahāyānottaratantraśāstra*. Patna: Bihar Research Society; rpt. in Prasad, H. S. 1991. *The Uttaratantra of Maitreya*. Delhi: Sri Satguru.

Jones, C. V. 2016. "A Self-Aggrandizing Vehicle: *Tathāgatagarbha*, *Tīrthika*s, and the True Self." *Journal of the International Association of Buddhist Studies* 39: 115–170.

Jones, J. J., trans. 1949. *The Mahāvastu*. Vol. 1. London: Luzac.

Kane, P. V. 1953. *History of Dharmaśāstra*. Vol. 4. Poona: Bhandarkar Oriental Research Institute.

Kern, Henrik and Nanjio Bunyio [1908–1912] 1970. *Saddharmapuṇḍarīka*. Saint Petersburg: Commissionnaires de l'Académie Impériale des Sciences. Rpt. Osnabrück: Biblio Verlag.

King, Richard. 1999. *Orientalism and Religion: Postcolonial Theory, India and "The Mystic East."* New York: Routledge.

Lamotte, Étienne. 1958. *Histoire du Bouddhisme Indien*. Louvain: Publications universitaires, Institut orientaliste.

La Vallée Poussin, Louis de, and E. J. Thomas, eds. 1916. *Niddesa*. Vol. 1. London: H. Milford for the Pali Text Society.

Lévi, Sylvain., trans. 1911. *Mahāyānasūtrālaṃkāra: Exposé de la doctrine du grand véhicule le système yogācāra*. Vol. 2. Paris: Librairie Honoré Champion.

MacQueen, Graeme. 1988. *A Study of the Śrāmaṇyaphala-Sūtra*. Wiesbaden: Harrassowitz.

Maes, Claire. 2015. "Dialogues With(in) the Pāli Vinaya. A Research into the Dynamics and Dialectics of the Pāli Vinaya's Ascetic Other, with a Special Focus on the Jain Ascetic Other." PhD dissertation, Universiteit Gent, Belgium.

———. 2016. "Flirting with the Other: An Examination of the Process of Othering in the Pali Vinaya." *Bulletin of the School of Oriental and African Studies* 3, no. 3: 535–557.

McGovern, Nathan. 2019. *The Snake and the Mongoose: The Emergence of Identity in Early Indian Religion*. New York: Oxford University Press.

McGrath, Alister. 2009. *Heresy: A History of Defending the Truth*. London: SPCK.

Nakamura Hajime. 1955. "Upaniṣadic Tradition and the Early School of Vedānta as Noticed in Buddhist Scripture." *Harvard Journal of Asiatic Studies* 18, no. 1/2: 74–104.

———. 1987. *Indian Buddhism: A Survey with Bibliographical Notes*. Delhi: Motilal Banarsidass.

Nath, Vijay. 2007. "Purāṇic *Tīrtha*s: A Study of Their Indigenous Origins and Transformation (Based Mainly on the *Skanda Purāṇa*)." *Indian Historical Review* 34, no. 1: 1–46.

Neumann, Karl Eugen. 1911. *Die Reden Gotamo Buddho's aus der Sammlung der Bruchstücke Suttanipāto des Pāli-Kanos*. Munich: Piper.

———. 1922. *Die Reden Gotamo Buddho's aus der Mittleren Sammlung Majjhimanikāyo des Pāli-Kanons*. Vol. 1. Munich: Piper.

Nichols, Michael. 2015. "Bowing to the Buddha: The Relationship between Literary and Social Dialogue in the Nikāyas." In *Dialogue in Early South Asian Religions: Hindu, Buddhist and Jain Traditions*, edited by Brian Black and Laurie Patton, 174–190. Surrey: Ashgate.

Oldenberg, Hermann., ed. 1880. *The Vinaya Piṭakaṃ. Vol. 2. The Cullavagga*. London and Edinburgh: Williams and Norgate.

Olivelle, Patrick., ed. and trans. 1998. *The Early Upaniṣads: Annotated Text and Translation*. New York: Oxford University Press.

———, ed. and trans. 2005. *Manu's Code of Law: A Critical Edition and Translation of the Mānava-Dharmaśāstra*. Oxford and New York: Oxford University Press.

———, ed. and trans. 2008. *Life of the Buddha*, by Aśvaghoṣa. New York: New York University Press.

———. 2009. *Dharma: Studies in Its Semantic, Cultural and Religious History*. Delhi: Motilal Banarsidass.

Parpola, Asko. 2003. "Sacred Bathing Place and Transcendence: Dravidian *Kaṭa(vuḷ)* as the Source of Indo-Aryan *Ghāṭ*, *Tīrtha*, *Tīrthaṅkara* and *(Tri) vikrama*." In *Jainism and Early Buddhism: Essays in Honor of Padmanabh S. Jaini, Part 1*, edited by Olle Qvarnström, 523–574. Fremont, CA: Asian Humanities Press.

Pradhan, Prahlad, ed. 1967. *Abhidharmakośabhāṣyam of Vasubandhu*. Patna: K. P. Jayaswal Research Institute.

Priestley, Leonard. 1999. *Pudgalavāda Buddhism: The Reality of the Indeterminate Self*. Toronto: Centre for South Asian Studies, University of Toronto.

Rhys Davids, T. W. [1899] 1956. *Dialogues of the Buddha*. Part 1. London: Luzac and Company.

Rhys Davids, T. W., and William Stede. [1921] 1959. *The Pali Text Society's Pali-English Dictionary*. London: The Pali Text Society.

Scherrer-Schaub, Cristina. 1999. "Translation, Transmission, Tradition: Suggestions from Ninth-Century Tibet." *Journal of Indian Philosophy* 27, no. 1/2: 67–77.

Schlingloff, Dieter. 1994. "Jainas and Other 'Heretics' in Buddhist Art." In *Jainism and Prakrit in Ancient and Medieval India: Essays for Prof. Jagdish Chandra Jain*, edited by N. N. Bhattacharyya, 71–82. New Delhi: Manohar.

Schmithausen, Lambert. 1973. "Philologische Bemerkungen zum *Ratnagotravibhāga*." *Wiener Zeitschrift für die Kunde Südasiens und Archiv für indische Philosophie* 15: 123–177.

Senart, Émile, ed. 1882. *Le Mahāvastu: Texte sanscrit publié pour la première foi et accompagné d'introductions et d'un commentaire*. Vol. 1. Paris: Société Asiatique.

Silk, Jonathan. 2013. "The Proof Is in the Pudding: What Is Involved in Editing and Translating a Mahāyāna Sūtra?" *Indo-Iranian Journal* 56: 157–178.

Snodgrass, Judith. 2007. "Defining Modern Buddhism: Mr. and Mrs. Rhys Davids and the Pāli Text Society." *Comparative Studies of South Asia, Africa and the Middle East* 27, no. 1: 186–202.

Steinthal, Paul., ed. 1885. *The Udâna*. London: Pali Text Society.

Strong, John. 2001. *The Buddha: A Short Biography*. Oxford: Oneworld.

Suzuki, D. T., ed. 1958. *The Tibetan Tripitaka: Peking Edition*. Vol. 144. Tokyo-Kyoto: Tibetan Tripitaka Research Institute.

Taishō shinshū daizōkyō 大正新脩大藏經, edited by Takakusu Junjirō 高楠順次郎 and Watanabe Kaigyoku 渡邊海旭. Tokyo: Taishō shinshū daizōkyō kankōkai/Daizō shuppan, 1924–1932. Via the CBETA [Chinese Buddhist Electronic Text Association] Online Reader, August 2019, https://www.cbeta.org/node/4977.

Taishō University, the Study Group on Buddhist Sanskrit Literatur, eds. 2006. *Vimalakīrtinirdeśa: A Sanskrit Edition Based upon the Manuscript Newly Found at the Potala Palace*. Tokyo: Taishō University Press.

Takakusu, J., and M. Nagai, with K. Mizuno, eds. 1966. *Samantapāsādikā: Buddhaghosa's Commentary on the Vinaya Piṭaka*. London: Pali Text Society, by Luzac and Company.

Vaidya, P. L., ed. 1958. *Lalitavistara*. Darbhanga: Mithilāvidyāpīṭha.

———, ed. 1960. *Aṣṭasāhasrikā Prajñāpāramitā*. Darbhanga: Mithilāvidyāpīṭha.

Vallée, Gérard. 1981. *A Study in Anti-Gnostic Polemics: Irenaeus, Hippolytus, and Epiphanius*. Studies in Christianity and Judaism 1. Waterloo, Ontario: Wilfred University Press, for the Canadian Corporation for Studies in Religion.

Vogel, Claus. 1970. *The Teachings of the Six Heretics*. Deutsche Morgenländische Gesellschaft. Wiesbaden: Kommissionverlag F. Steiner.

Zimmermann, Michael. 2000. "A Mahāyānist Criticism of *Arthaśāstra*: The Chapter on Royal Ethics in the *Bodhisattva-gocaropāya-viṣaya-vikurvaṇa-nirdeśa-sūtra*." *Annual Report of the International Research Institute for Advanced Buddhology at Soka University* 3: 177–211.

Chapter 9

Translating *Paṭicca-samuppāda* in Early Buddhism

Dhivan Thomas Jones

This chapter addresses the issue of how to translate the term *paṭicca-samuppāda*, which relies on the use of Prakrit and Sanskrit grammatical forms for which there are no exact English equivalents, and which expresses a core Buddhist concept for which there is no exact philosophical equivalent outside of Buddhist teachings.

Introduction

Among the specialized terms in early Buddhist teachings, *paṭicca-samuppāda* should count as one of the most important, since it designates a concept identified with the *dhamma* itself. The Buddha is reported to have said, "Who sees *paṭicca-samuppāda* sees the *dhamma*; who sees the *dhamma* sees *paṭicca-samuppāda*,"[1] suggesting an internal relationship between *paṭicca-samuppāda* and the teaching (*dhamma*) as a whole. A well-known exchange in the Pāli canon between Ānanda and the Buddha about *paṭicca-samuppāda* further suggests its significance:

1. Spoken by Sāriputta in MN 28, PTS I 191, who attributes the saying to the Buddha: *yo dhammaṃ passati so paṭiccasamuppādaṃ passati*. Anālayo (2011, 198) reports an MĀ parallel to this saying.

> "It is wonderful, lord, it is marvelous, how deep and profound is this *paṭicca-samuppāda*, though to me it seems quite plain."
>
> "Do not say that, Ānanda, do not say that. This *paṭicca-samuppāda* is deep and profound. It is from not understanding and penetrating this *dhamma* that people have become like a tangle of string covered in mold and matted like grass, unable to escape from *saṃsāra* with its miseries, disasters, and bad destinies."[2]

In this exchange, Ānanda's understanding of *paṭicca-samuppāda* as profound, but nevertheless not difficult for him to understand, suggests a concept of general application. The Buddha's response, however, implies an understanding of *paṭicca-samuppāda* as a concept with a specific application to the human condition as entangled in suffering (*dukkha*) and the round of rebirth (*saṃsāra*) due to immersion in craving (*taṅhā*).[3] This specific application is spelled out many times in the early Buddhist teachings, in the form of the standard formula of the twelve *nidāna*s, from ignorance (*avijjā*) to aging-and-death (*jarā-maraṇa*).

A translation of the term *paṭicca-samuppāda* therefore needs, on the one hand, to communicate a general concept of profound significance that is nevertheless not too difficult to understand and, on the other hand, a concept that when applied to the human condition, in the form of the twelve *nidāna*s, reveals the very workings of *saṃsāra*. These rather demanding criteria have led to a range of translations into English. The entry on *paṭicca-samuppāda* in the pioneering *Pāli-English Dictionary* (PED), for instance, lists: " 'arising on the grounds of (a preceding cause),' happening by way of cause, working of cause & effect, causal chain of causation;

---

2. This exchange forms the introduction to the *Mahānidāna-sutta* at DN 15 (PTS II 55), and is also found at SN 12.60 (PTS II 92): *acchariyaṃ bhante abbhutaṃ bhante. yāva gambhīro cāyaṃ bhante paṭiccasamuppādo gambhīrāvabhāso ca atha ca pana me uttānakuttānako viya khāyatī'ti. mā hevaṃ ānanda avaca mā hevaṃ ānanda avaca. gambhīro cāyaṃ ānanda paṭiccasamuppādo gambhīrāvabhāso ca. etassa ānanda dhammassa ananubodhā appaṭivedhā evamayaṃ pajā tantākulakajātā kulagaṇṭhikajātā muñjapabbajabhūtā apāyaṃ duggatiṃ vinipātaṃ saṃsāraṃ nātivattati.*

3. This interpretation relies on the Buddha's discussion of craving (*taṅhā*) at AN 4: 199 (PTS II 211–113), in it is said that this world has become "like a tangle of string covered in mold and matted like grass, unable to escape from *saṃsāra* with its miseries, disasters, and bad destinies" through craving.

causal genesis, dependent origination, theory of the twelve causes."[4] As we shall see, the authors of PED have provided, first, an accurate literal transcription of the term in their rendering "arising on the grounds of (a preceding cause)," before venturing several more or less domesticated translations. One of these, "dependent origination," has remained a popular choice among scholars and practitioners seeking a succinct translation, while the related translation "dependent arising" has since become equally popular. The translation "conditioned co-production," coined by Edward Conze, still retains a loyal following.[5] Variations on these choices include "dependent co-arising" and "interdependent co-arising," translations which imply various degrees of commitment to the interpretation of *paṭicca-samuppāda* in terms of interconnectedness.

It might seem as a consequence that any translation of *paṭicca-samuppāda* is no more than a matter either of preference or of ideological commitment. However, in this chapter, I will argue that "dependent arising" is the most exact and appropriate translation of *paṭicca-samuppāda*, at least as the term is used in early Buddhism prior to the development of *Abhidharma*. My argument will depend on two lines of investigation. The first is the analysis of the component words *paṭicca* and *samuppāda* and of their combination in the "syntactical compound" of *paṭicca-samuppāda*. The second line of investigation is into the conceptual metaphors implied by these words, which communicate the concept of causation, or better, how experience works, through metaphors of movement. Additionally, I will show how the early Buddhist discourses illustrate *paṭicca-samuppāda* by means of agricultural comparisons, a consideration that again favors the translation "dependent arising."

Analyzing the Expression *Paṭicca-samuppāda*

Paṭicca-samuppāda is made up of two words, *paṭicca* and *samuppāda*, together forming a compound;[6] and while *samuppāda* can be translated

4. PED 394.

5. See, for example, Conze 1953, 48; Conze 1956, 152; and especially Conze 1962, 156f.; Lamotte 1980.

6. The hyphen in *paṭicca-samuppāda* is a convenience to show that the expression is a compound. In Pāli texts it is not usually hyphenated.

straightforwardly, *paṭicca* is more difficult to put into English, being an absolutive that can be translated "because of" as well as "dependent on." The combined expression *paṭicca-samuppāda* is not straightforward either, since *paṭicca-samuppāda* is a so-called "syntactical compound," an irregular grammatical construction without parallel in English. Nevertheless, the meaning of *paṭicca-samuppāda* can be completely unpacked through analysis, and this should be the basis on which to decide how to translate it.

The compound expression *paṭicca-samuppāda* is evidently a specialized term, meaning that it refers unambiguously to a particular concept. The words of which the compound is composed, however, have a range of meanings in Pāli, and in order to correctly understand the compound, we need to determine the particular contextual meanings of its component words. To illustrate with a simple parallel: the compound *buddha-vacana* is a Buddhist term composed of two words. While the word *buddha*, on its own, may refer to the Buddha, Śākyamuni, it may also refer to past or future *buddhas*, or indeed to any awakened being, and may in the broadest sense simply be understood as the past participle of the verb *bujjhati*, "understand."[7] Likewise, the word *vacana* can mean "speaking" as well as "language" in a more technical sense.[8] However, the compound term *buddha-vacana* expresses the single concept of "word of the Buddha,"[9] relying on the specific meanings of *buddha* as Śākyamuni and *vacana* as "utterance."

The Meaning of the Word *Samuppāda*

The word *samuppāda*, forming the second part of the compound expression *paṭicca-samuppāda*, is an action noun derived from the verbal root *pad*, with the prefixes *sam-* and *ud-*. The root *pad* forms the finite verb *pajjati*, but this is only attested once in the Pāli canon, in an instance Rhys

7. See PED 488, which separates the general from the applied meaning.

8. See PED 592.

9. Buswell and Lopez 2013, *The Princeton Dictionary of Buddhism*, s.v. *buddhavacana*, 155: "those teachings accepted as having been either spoken by the Buddha or spoken with his sanction."

Davids and Stede describe as "doubtful."[10] But we can say that the root *pad* means "go," "go to,"[11] and that the prefix *ud-* means "up" or "out."[12] Hence *uppajjati* means "goes up," "arises," and by extension, "comes into being," "appears," "is born," and so forth.[13] This verb commonly appears in the Pāli canon in analytic descriptions of experience, when it can be translated "arises." Talking to King Pasenadi of Kosala, for instance, the Buddha is reported to have said: "Three phenomena [namely, greed, hate, and delusion], great king, when they arise (*uppajjamānā*) subjectively for someone, arise (*uppajjanti*) for his harm, suffering, and discomfort."[14] To give another example, a conversation between the wanderer Poṭṭhapāda and the Buddha is recorded as follows:

> "Lord, does perception arise (*uppajjati*) first and knowledge after, or does knowledge arise first and perception after, or do perception and knowledge arise (*uppajjanti*) simultaneously?"
>
> "Poṭṭhapāda, perception arises first and knowledge after; and from the arising of perception there is the arising of knowledge. In this way one knows that in fact my knowledge has arisen (*udapādi*) from that as its causal basis."[15]

---

10. PED 387, in relation to the occurrence of *pajjati* at AN IV 362 (in both PTS and Be); the PTS text lists variant readings of *paccati*, *pabbati*, and *gacchati*, suggesting uncertainty about the correct reading. DOP III 61 has "probably wrong" for *pajjati* here. According to Bryan Levman (personal communication) there is also a variant reading in a Sinhalese manuscript of *pacchati*, which would represent the regular prakritic phonological development of *prāpsyati*, future tense of *prāpnoti*; cf. Geiger 1994, §150f. This reading seems also to be implied by the commentary on AN IV 362 at AN-a IV 168, which glosses *pajjati* as *pāpuṇissati*, "will obtain" < *pāpuṇāti*, "obtains," equivalent to Sanskrit *prāpsyati* < *prāpnoti*.

11. PED 387; MW 582; cf. *Saddanīti* 480, 32: *pada gatiyaṃ: pajjati.*

12. CPD II 383; DOP I 416.

13. CPD II 515; DOP I 491; just like Sanskrit *utpadyate* MW 180.

14. SN 3: 2, PTS I 70: *tayo kho, mahārāja, purisassa dhammā ajjhattaṃ uppajjamānā uppajjanti ahitāya dukkhāya aphāsuvihārāya.*

15. DN 9, PTS I 185: *saññā nu kho bhante paṭhamaṃ uppajjati pacchā ñāṇaṃ udāhu ñāṇaṃ paṭhamaṃ uppajjati pacchā saññā udāhu saññā ca ñāṇañ ca apubbaṃ acarimaṃ uppajjantī'ti. saññā kho poṭṭhapāda paṭhamaṃ uppajjati pacchā ñāṇaṃ saññuppādā ca pana ñāṇuppādo hoti. so evaṃ pajānāti idappaccayā kira me ñāṇaṃ udapādī'ti.*

Many more examples could be cited in which *upajjati* is used in this way with the meaning of "arises." It should be noted, however, that in all such cases the verb *uppajjati* is used metaphorically, since, in the examples given, subjective mental states such as greed, hate, and delusion, or perception and knowledge, do not move vertically upward, but, rather, they "come into existence." The English "arises" is used metaphorically in exactly the same way. That is to say, the verb *uppajjati*, like "arises," involves a "conceptual metaphor"—a topic to which I will return.

But the verb *uppajjati* can also mean "appears." In a teaching to the monks about how to thrive in the spiritual life, the Buddha is reported to have shared this simile: "It is as if there were a great sal tree grove near a village or town,[16] overgrown with castor oil plants.[17] Some person might appear (*uppajjeyya*) wishing for its good, wishing for its welfare, wishing for its safety."[18] Such a person is not "arising" or "starting to exist" but rather "appearing" in the sense of "emerging into visibility." This suggests that Pāli *uppajjati* is used metaphorically to mean "appear" (in Pāli, *pātubhavati*) in a way that English "arise" is not so used.[19] This reminds us how words as apparently synonymous as *uppajjati* and "arises" are nevertheless not semantically identical. The verb *uppajjati* is also used to mean "is born": a verse in the *Dhammapada* reads, "Some are born (*uppajjanti*) in a womb,"[20] while the English "arises" is not used quite in this way.

Connected to a finite verb, an action noun denotes the abstract action of the verb;[21] hence, *uppāda* means "arising," "coming into existence," "origination," "appearance," and so on.[22] But the word we are analyzing is *sam-uppāda*. The prefix *sam-* means "with," "together" (like the Latin prefix con-), though it sometimes adds merely an intensive force to the

16. The sal tree (*Shorea robusta*) is common in the Indian subcontinent and valued for its timber.

17. The castor oil plant (*Ricinus communis*) can be an invasive shrub.

18. MN 21, PTS I 124: *seyyathāpi bhikkhave, gāmassa vā nigamassa vā avidūre mahantaṃ sālavanaṃ. tañcassa eḷaṇḍehi sañchannaṃ. tassa kocideva puriso uppajjeyya atthakāmo hitakāmo yogakkhemakāmo.*

19. Cf. the commentarial gloss Ud-a. 44, *pātubhavantī'ti uppajjanti* on Ud. 1.1.

20. Dhp. 126: *gabbhaṃ eke uppajjanti.*

21. See, for instance, Whitney 1889, §1145, 421.

22. CPD II 525, DOP I 496. While the English "arising" is a gerund, a verbal noun comparable to a Pāli action noun, English "origination" is a noun.

main verb, and indeed sometimes seems not add any additional meaning at all.[23] Hence, the PED gives *samuppāda* the same meaning as *uppāda*,[24] which suggests we should translate it "arising" and so on.

Some translators, however, render *samuppāda* in the context of *paṭicca-samuppāda* as "co-arising," "co-origination," "co-production," attributing the sense "with" to the prefix *saṃ-*.[25] Peter Harvey justifies this translation by citing the fifth-century CE Theravādin commentator Buddhaghosa, who, in his *Visuddhimagga*, explains the expression *paṭicca-samuppāda* as follows: "Moreover, 'it arises together with' (*saha uppajjati*), so it is a co-arising (*sam-uppāda*). Depending on, without rejecting any of, an assembly of conditions, it is a co-arising (*sam-uppāda*) dependent in this way; hence it is "dependent co-arising" (*paṭicca-samuppāda*)."[26] However, it is unjustified to explain the meaning of *samuppāda* in the Pāli canon from a commentarial text of many centuries later. In the background of Buddhaghosa's exegesis of the expression *paṭicca-samuppāda* is a metaphysical interpretation of the twelve *nidāna*s as a tightly interlocked set of mutually arising factors, an interpretation that developed long after the canonical discourses.[27] Moreover, it is likely that the Theravādin commentators were aware that their exegesis of the expression *paṭicca-samuppāda* was an edifying interpretation rather than a historically reliable guide to the meaning of the compound, since a slightly different exegesis of *samuppāda* in the

23. PED 655: *saṃ* is very often merely pleonastic, especially in combination with other prefixes.

24. PED 688; cf. MW 1162 *samutpāda* "rise, origin, production."

25. Recently by Harvey (2013); and, in an influential work, by Macy (1991, 34).

26. Vism 521. Harvey merely cites this passage: "Something can only arise when its conditions are gathered together (Vism 521). Something arises together with its conditions" (Harvey 2013, 48). Discussed in note 57 in this chapter. Buddhaghosa is not arguing for the idea that reality is an interdependent co-arising, only that any arising phenomenon depends on an assembly of conditions. But there is no evidence that *sam-* has this significance in the Pāli canon itself.

27. This point is also discussed in Schmithausen (1997, 57), in relation to Macy (1991, 34), who also cites Buddhaghosa in support of the translation of *samuppāda* as "co-arising." Schmithausen also refers to Candrakīrti, who explains *samutpāda* merely as *prādurbhāva*, "arising." Vasubandhu does likewise (Sangpo and de la Vallée Poussin 2012, 996), emphasizing that the interpretation of *samuppāda* as "co-arising" was not even the consensus among later Indian Buddhist exegetes.

commentary on the *Udāna* states:[28] "It is a right-arising (*sam-uppādo*) because it gives rise either rightly (*sammā*) or just by itself (*sayaṃ*)." This exegesis, taking the meaning of *sam-* not to be "with" (*saha*) but "rightly" (*sammā*) or "by itself" (*sayaṃ*), enriches the commentarial interpretation of *paṭicca-samuppāda*, based on the different meanings that can be drawn out of the prefix *sam-*.

In fact, examining the occurrence of the word *samuppāda* in the Pāli canon, it is not possible to identify any specific additional meaning implied by *sam-* to distinguish *samuppāda* from *uppāda*. A couple of citations show this point clearly. First, although the word *samuppāda* does occur in the Pāli canon as an independent word, it is mainly found in compound expressions, where the addition of the prefix *sam-* appears simply to allow ease of pronunciation. It is easier, for instance, to say *paṭicca-samuppāda* than *paṭicc'uppāda* (or, in Sanskrit, *pratītyotpāda*).[29] Second, in one discourse we find the verb *uppajjati* followed by *samuppajjati* with exactly the same meaning. The Buddha describes how, just as there are various kinds of wind, "so, in this body, various feelings arise (*uppajjanti*): pleasant feelings arise, painful feelings arise, and neither-pleasant-nor-painful feelings arise." Then there follows some verses restating the point, including:

> Just so, in this body, feelings arise (*samuppajjanti*),
> Which arising (*samuppatti*) is pleasant, painful, and neither
> painful-nor-pleasant.[30]

As can readily be seen, the verb *samuppajjanti* here (and its cognate *samuppatti*) is used synonymously with *uppajjanti*. The prefix *sam-* proves useful in that the word *samuppajjanti* fits the constraints of the *śloka* meter better than *uppajjanti*.

When translating the expression *paṭicca-samuppāda* in the Pāli canon, it therefore seems inappropriate to use words like "co-arising" or "co-production," with their connotations of a meaning beyond that

28. Ud-a. 37: *sammā sayameva vā uppādetīti samuppādo.*

29. A point indirectly confirmed by the occurrence of the expression *paṭicc'uppāda* in a *gāthā* at Netti 4, shortened from *paṭiccasamuppāda*, evidently for the sake of fitting into the *ārya* meter.

30. SN 36: 12, PTS IV 218: *kho . . . imasmiṃ kāyasmiṃ vividhā vedanā uppajjanti, sukhāpi vedanā uppajjati, dukkhāpi vedanā uppajjati, adukkhamasukhāpi vedanā uppajjatī . . . tathev'imasmiṃ kāyasmiṃ | samuppajjanti vedanā | sukhadukkhasamuppatti | adukkhamasukhā ca yā ||*

of "arising," as the prefix *sam-* appears in this context not to have the additional force implied by "co-." Rather, *sam-* appears to be pleonastic, easing pronunciation of the technical compound expression, and *samuppāda* is synonymous with *uppāda*. The concept of *samuppāda* as "co-arising" is specific to the context of later *Abhidhamma*. This point shows the importance of a context-sensitive translation of the concepts implied by Buddhist terms like *paṭicca-samuppāda*.

The Meaning of the Word *Paṭicca*

The word *paṭicca* is an absolutive from the verb *pacceti*, which is derived from the verbal root *i*, meaning "go" or "come," with the prefix *paṭi*, meaning "back" or "against."[31] The etymologically exact meaning of *pacceti* as "comes back to" is employed in the following example of a *Dhammapada* stanza:

> One who does wrong to a blameless man, to one who is
> pure and spotless,
> the harm comes back to (*pacceti*) that fool, like fine dust
> thrown against the wind.[32]

While the literal sense of *pacceti* as a verb of movement meaning "comes back to" is evident in this verse, *pacceti* is mainly used in the Pāli canon in a figurative way to mean "depends on," "relies on," "believes in," or "trusts in." We read for instance of a certain brahman, with superstitious beliefs familiar enough even today: "Now at the time a brahman named Saṅgārava lived in Sāvatthī, one who purifies himself with water, who 'comes back to' (*pacceti*) purification with water, and who dwells devoted to the practice of immersing himself in water morning and evening."[33] We could nicely trans-

31. In Sanskrit, the absolutive *pratītya* is derived from *pratyeti*, the root *i* with the prefix *prati*.

32. Dhp. 125: *yo appaduṭṭhassa narassa dussati | suddhassa posassa anaṅgaṇassa | tameva bālaṃ pacceti pāpaṃ | sukhumo rajo paṭivātaṃva khitto* || Also at SN 1: 22, PTS I 13; SN 7: 4, PTS I 164; *Sutta-nipāta* V 662; Ja 367, PTS III 203.

33. SN 7: 21, PTS I 182: *tena kho pana samayena saṅgāravo nāma brāhmaṇo sāvatthīyaṃ paṭivasati udakasuddhiko, udakena parisuddhiṃ pacceti, sāyaṃ pātaṃ udakorohanānuyogamanuyutto viharati*. The Pāli uses the present tense for narrative, where English would more naturally use the imperfect. The verses at *Sutta-nipāta* 788 also use *pacceti* in relation to religious purification.

late *pacceti* in this context using the English phrasal verb "falls back on,"[34] meaning that Saṅgārava "has recourse to," "relies on," or "depends on" purification with water.[35] To say that Saṅgārava "falls back on" purification with water is to say that he trusts in or believes in the efficacy of that practice. In another example, the Buddha describes the five qualities of a lay-follower who is like an outcaste (*caṇḍāla*), who is impure, like a leper; that person's third quality is that "he is superstitious and 'falls back on' (*pacceti*) fortune (*maṅgala*) and not action (*kamma*)."[36] This is to say that the poor-quality lay-follower "depends on," "relies on," or "trusts in" omens, luck, and fortune for his happiness rather than in doing good and avoiding evil.

We might say that the word *pacceti* is used of people whose reasoning is based on, or "falls back on," some inappropriate view or belief, such as the purificatory efficacy of water, rather than being based on appropriate views and beliefs. Likewise, the verb *pacceti* is also used for those whose reasoning is based on speculative views rather than on what they know for themselves. In some verses from the *Sutta-nipāta* the wise ascetic is said not to believe in speculative views:

> Letting go of what has been obtained, not grasping,
> one does not place dependence on (*nissaya*) even knowledge.
> Not siding with one party when among disputants,
> one does not "fall back on" (*pacceti*) any view at all.[37]

Once more these verses show how *pacceti* means "believes in," in the sense of "relies on," "depends on," though here in the context of views rather than practices.

34. OED s.v. "to fall back on": "2. *fig.* To have recourse to (something) when other things fail."

35. In fact, the verbs "rely" and "depend" also originally held meanings connected with verbs of physical movement, though these senses are now obsolete or literary: OED s.v. "rely": "5.a. *intr.* To rest *on* or *upon* a support (*lit.* and *fig.*). *Obs.*"; OED s.v. "depend" "1.a. *intr.* To hang down, be suspended. (Now chiefly in literary use.)"

36. AN 5: 175, PTS III 206: *kotūhalamaṅgaliko hoti, maṅgalaṃ pacceti no kammaṃ.*

37. *Sutta-nipāta* 800: *attaṃ pahāya anupādiyāno | ñāṇe pi so nissayaṃ no karoti | sā ve viyattesu na vaggasārī | diṭṭhim pi so na pacceti kiñci.* Norman (2001, 107) likewise translates, "He does not fall back on any view at all," citing (339) both Nidd I 108 and Pj II 530: *no pacceti no paccāgacchati*, "He does not fall back on means he does not come back toward," where *paccāgacchati* is also a verb of motion, from the root *gam*, "go."

The word *paṭicca* is the absolutive derived from *pacceti*, and in terms of its etymology it ought to express the idea of "having come back to" or "coming back to."[38] In practice, however, we do not find in the Pāli canon any examples of *paṭicca* used as the absolutive of a verb expressing movement. Instead, it appears as the absolutive of the figurative sense of *pacceti* as "depends on," and can be translated as "falling back on" in the sense of "dependent on." For instance, in the well-known story of Brahmā's request to the Buddha to teach, the Buddha is reported to have said: "And then, monks, knowing Brahmā's request, I surveyed the world with Buddha-vision 'falling back on' (*paṭicca*) compassion for beings."[39] This means that compassion for beings was the reason or explanation for the Buddha's surveying the world. In this sense, we can often translate *paṭicca* simply as "because of."[40] This is especially apt in the case of a common mode of expression, following some statement: "And because of (*paṭicca*) what was that said?" When the answer has been given, the correlative expression follows, "Because of (*paṭicca*) this was that said."[41] While a translation using "dependent on" would be perfectly intelligible in English here (such as, "Dependent on what was that said?"), it seems somewhat foreign, when what is being said is, "What is the reason that was said?"

38. The absolutive is here formed with the suffix *-ya*: the form *paṭicca* is from *paṭi+i+(t)ya*, via the phonological changes to consonant clusters typical of Prakrits, while the Sanskrit *pratītya* is more obviously identifiable as an absolutive in *-ya*. The absolutive in Pāli grammar, as in Sanskrit, is an indeclinable verbal derivative used to indicate an action prior to the action of the main verb of the sentence, though absolutive and main verbs have the same agent. The absolutive is extremely common. In the formulaic language of the Pāli discourses, when someone comes to visit the Buddha it is said that *bhagavantaṃ abhivadetvā ekam antaṃ nisīdi*: "Having greeted the Blessed One, he sat down to one side." "Having greeted" (*abhivadetvā*) is an absolutive, controlling a subclause ("having greeted the Blessed One"), expressing an action ("having greeted") prior to the action of the main verb ("sat down") and with the same agent as it ("he"). It would equally be possible to translate *abhivadetvā* simply as "greeting," which is a present participle in English: "Greeting the Blessed One, he sat to one side." Likewise, since we do not have absolutives in English, we can translate the Pāli absolutive *paṭicca* either as an English present participle, "coming back to," or as a perfect participle clause, "having come back to."

39. From the episode of Brahmā's request at, for example, MN 26, PTS II167: *atha kho ahaṃ bhikkhave brahmuno ca ajjhesanaṃ viditvā sattesu ca kāruññataṃ paṭicca buddhacakkhunā lokaṃ volokesiṃ*.

40. OED s.v. "because (of)" *adverb*: "2.a. By reason *of*, on account *of*."

41. *kiñ c'etaṃ paṭicca vuttaṃ? . . . idam etaṃ paṭicca vuttaṃ*.

These examples of *paṭicca* in the sense of "dependent on" imply a person as agent of the main action of the sentence. It is the Buddha who surveyed the world because of (*paṭicca*) compassion. It is some speaker of whom it is asked, "Because of (*paṭicca*) what was that said?" But *paṭicca* is also used in constructions that designate the impersonal dependence of something on something else. These impersonal constructions show the word *paṭicca* used as a philosophical term to designate the concept of the causal dependence of one phenomenon upon another. A paradigmatic example for our purposes is: "Dependent on (*paṭicca*) the eye and visible forms, eye-consciousness arises (*uppajjati*)." This is repeated for ear and sounds, and for the other senses including the mind and its ideas (*dhammas*).[42] While it is still possible to preserve the sense of a verb of motion by translating *paṭicca* here as "falling back on," the context shows that *paṭicca* is being used figuratively to mean "dependent on." It does not appear that the Sanskrit *pratītya* was used to express causal dependence in this way (except of course by Buddhists),[43] so perhaps we should consider the use of the word *paṭicca* in the Pāli canon (to mean "causally dependent on") as a term referring to a specifically Buddhist concept of causation.

The Meaning of the Compound *Paṭicca-samuppāda*

The compound expression *paṭicca-samuppāda* is a term referring to a specific concept. Its component words are likewise used with relation to one among their several meanings, *samuppāda* specifically in the sense of "arising" ("coming into existence") and *paṭicca* specifically in the sense of "dependent on." These two words are compounded in such a way as to create a philosophical term whose concept is said to be deep and profound. It is important, therefore, to understand the peculiarities of this compound. It might be noted at the outset that English expressions like "dependent arising" or "conditioned co-production" involve an adjective qualifying a noun. Yet *paṭicca* is not an adjective but an absolutive that does not qualify *samuppāda*. Such English expressions as "dependent arising" are more like attempts to render a construction that, in Pāli, has a peculiarly idiomatic flavor, which we might provisionally represent as

42. MN 18, PTS I 111: *cakkhuñcāvuso, paṭicca rūpe ca uppajjati cakkhuviññāṇaṃ.*

43. MW 673 s.v. *pratītya*; Apte 743.

"arising dependent on . . ." The idiomatic nature of the expression can be better understood by analyzing it as what has been called a "syntactical compound," which essentially allows a sentence concerning abstract causal dependence to be compressed into one compound expression. I will suggest that this compound is best understood as meaning "arising dependent on a causal basis," though "dependent arising" remains a convenient two-word rendering.

Compounds in Pāli, as in Sanskrit, comprise individual words put together in grammatical relationships that would otherwise be expressed by inflections. For instance, the Buddha is described as *vijjā-caraṇa-sampanno*,[44] literally, "wisdom-conduct-endowed," that is, "endowed with wisdom and conduct."[45] Compounds such as *paṭicca-samuppāda*, comprising an absolutive and a noun, have been described by Western scholars as "syntactical compounds,"[46] since they contain words compounded together that can only be understood in terms of some implied syntactical relationship, meaning that they can be unpacked to form a sentence. They are not unusual in Pāli but are nonetheless strange and have been described as "irregular" and "anomalous."[47] If in fact *paṭicca-samuppāda* is a strange, irregular syntactical compound, the convenient English rendering "dependent arising" may be misleading. To understand the meaning of the expression *paṭicca-samuppāda*, some grammatical analysis is required.

Hans Hendriksen has explained that we should understand compounds like *paṭicca-samuppāda* as having developed from a combination of

44. From the common formula of praise (*vandanā*) of the Buddha, found, for example, at DN 2, PTS I 49, and *passim*. The hyphens merely indicate for convenience the individual words of the compound.

45. As the commentaries put it, *vijjācaraṇasampannoti vijjāhi ca caraṇena ca sammanāgato*, "'wisdom-conduct-endowed' means endowed with the wisdoms and with conduct": the compound as a whole is a *tatpuruṣa* (determinative) containing a *dvandva* (coordinative). The various kinds of Pāli compounds are discussed in Collins (2006, 129ff.).

46. Discussed by Norman (1993); Norman also discusses other kinds of syntactical compounds besides those containing an absolutive and a noun, such as *ehipassiko*: this compound contains two verbs in the imperative tense (*ehi*, "come!" and *passa*, "see!") plus a suffix (*-ika*) expressing connection: the *dhamma* is "suitable to come and see" (DOP I 553).

47. By both Wackernagel and Whitney, cited in Norman (1993, 218).

a verb and an absolutive in a grammatical relationship with it.[48] Hendriksen takes as his example the syntactical compound *viceyya-dāna*, "giving with forethought,"[49] consisting of an absolutive *viceyya*, "discriminating," "having considered,"[50] and a noun *dāna*, "giving," and he explains that we should understand this compound as having been derived from a sentence such as *viceyya dadāti*, "discriminating, he gives," "he gives with forethought." Norman gives a complementary explanation, deriving the syntax of *viceyya-dāna* from a sentence such as *viceyya dānaṃ dadāti*, "having considered, he gives a gift."[51]

Likewise, we should understand *paṭicca-samuppāda* as deriving from a sentence whose form would be *paccayaṃ paṭicca uppajjati dhammaṃ*, "dependent on a causal basis a phenomenon arises." We can in fact easily find representative examples of such sentences in Pāli texts, where both causal bases and arisings are specified, for instance:

1. *cakkhuñ ca paṭicca rūpe ca uppajjati cakkhu-viññāṇaṃ*, "dependent on the eye and forms arises eye-consciousness";[52]
2. *phassanānattaṃ paṭicca uppajjati vedanānānattaṃ*, "dependent on a diversity of contacts arises a diversity of feelings";[53]
3. *ime pañca kāmaguṇe paṭicca uppajjati sukhaṃ somanassaṃ*, "dependent on these five kinds of sense-pleasure arise pleasure and happiness."[54]

In each of these cases, the absolutive *paṭicca*, "dependent on," takes a grammatical object or objects (in the accusative case), such as "the eye and forms," "a diversity of contacts," and "these five strands of sense-pleasure";

48. Hendriksen (1944, 157); also discussed in Norman (1993, 219).

49. For example, at SN 1: 33, PTS I 21: *viceyya-dānaṃ sugatappasatthaṃ*, "Giving with forethought is praised by the Perfect One."

50. See PED 616 s.v. *vicinati*. See also Collins (2006, 137): "a gift (given) after consideration."

51. Norman 1993, 219.

52. For instance, at MN 18, PTS I 111.

53. For instance, at SN 14: 4, PTS II 141.

54. For instance, at MN 13, PTS M I 85.

these are causal bases (*paccayas*). In each of these sentences, the absolutive *paṭicca* has the same agent or grammatical subject (in the nominative case) as that of the main verb of the sentence, *uppajjati*: hence, it is eye-consciousness that arises and is dependent on the eye and forms; it is the diversity of feelings that arises and is dependent on the diversity of contacts; it is pleasure and happiness that arise dependent on these five strands of sense-pleasure. Hence, eye-consciousness, the diversity of feelings and these five strands of sense-pleasure are examples of arising (*samuppāda*).

In short, *paṭicca-samuppāda* compresses into a syntactical compound the syntax of a sentence, such that we should understand it to mean "arising (something arises) dependent on (something that is a causal basis)."[55] It is difficult to know how exactly to render this expression in English, which has neither absolutives nor syntactical compounds. The expression "dependent arising" is useful for its brevity, but "arising dependent on a causal basis" conveys more exactly what *paṭicca-samuppāda* means.

This is of course not a new discovery. It is implied in an etymological analysis of *pratītya-samutpāda* found commonly in Indian Buddhist texts, for instance, by Vasubandhu:

> So, what is the meaning of the word *pratītyasamutpāda*? *Prati* means "meeting with" (*prāpti*), *i* means "go" (*gati*). *Pratītya*

55. Further examples of syntactical compounds with absolutives as their first members are *avecca-pasāda*, and *uddissa-kata*. The word *avecca*, the first member of *avecca-pasāda*, is an absolutive meaning "having gone into," that is, "understanding," taking an object in the locative case, while the second member is a noun, *pasāda*, meaning "confidence," from the verb *pasīdati*. This quality is a characteristic of the stream-entrant, who is said to be "a noble disciple who, having "gone into the Buddha, is endowed with confidence" (*ariyasāvako buddhe aveccappasādena samannāgato hoti*, at e.g., SN 12: 41, PTS II 70; the noble disciple also has perfect faith in the *dhamma* and *saṅgha*). This syntactical compound is usually translated "perfect confidence." The word *uddissa*, the first part of the compound *uddissa-kata*, is an absolutive from *uddisati*, "points to," "assigns," and so on; the second part, *kata*, is the past participle of *karoti*, "make," "do"; hence, *uddissa-kata* means "what has been made (*kata*) having been assigned (*uddissa*) (to someone)." The person to whom the food has been assigned (in the genitive case) is implied by the absolutive. This syntactical compound is usually translated "specially prepared" (in reference to food); for instance, in the *Vinaya*, the Buddha makes the rule: "monks, you should not knowingly eat meat that has been specially prepared" (*na bhikkhave jānaṃ uddissa-kataṃ maṃsaṃ paribhuñjitabbaṃ*, Mv 6.31.14 PTS Vin I 237; AN 8: 12 PTS IV 187).

> means "having met with" (*prāpya*) because of a change of the meaning of the verbal root [i.e., *i*, "go"] by the force of the prefix [i.e., *prati*]. *Pad* means "existence" (*sattā*); preceded by the prefixes *sam* and *ud*, *samutpāda* means "appearance" (*prādurbhāva*). Therefore *pratītyasamutpāda* means "origination" (*samudbhava*) "having met with its causal basis" (*pratyaya*).[56]

We see that Vasubandhu explains the compound as a whole by unpacking the syntactical relationship of the absolutive *pratītya* as "having met with (its causal basis)" to the action noun *samutpāda*, "arising."[57]

Likewise, Buddhaghosa unpacks the grammar of *paṭicca-samuppāda* to emphasize how it is a meaningful expression only if the agent of the absolutive *paṭicca* is the same as the agent of the action noun *samuppāda*:

> the word "dependent on . . ." (*paṭicca*) is grammatically meaningful when it is used in reference to an agent shared [with a verb] and in reference to its occurring at a time prior [to the verbal action]. For example, "Dependent on the eye and visual forms, eye-consciousness arises."[58]

Buddhaghosa appeals here implicitly to the Sanskrit grammarian Pāṇini,[59] but it seems reasonable to suppose that the early Buddhists likewise

---

56. *Bhāṣya* on ADK 3.28, Prahlad Pradhan 1975, 138: *atha pratītyasamutpāda iti kaḥ padārthaḥ | pratiḥ prāptyartha eti gatyarthaḥ | upasargavaśena dhātvarthapariṇāmāt prāpyeti yo 'rthaḥ so 'rthaḥ pratītyeti | padiḥ sattārthaṃ samutpūrvaḥ prādurbhāvārthaḥ | tena prātyayaṃ prāpya samudbhavaḥ pratītyasamutpādaḥ*. Similar analyses are found in Nāgārjuna, Candrakīrti, and so on: discussed in Hopkins (1983, 165); MacDonald (2015, 18–20); cf. Kardas (2015).

57. Although I am not thereby suggesting that we should etymologize the Pāli *paṭicca* as *pappuyya*, from *pāpuṇāti*. Rather, Ud-a. 37 glosses *paṭicca* as *paṭigantvā* ("moving back on"), and likewise at Vism 521 Buddhaghosa glosses *paṭicco* as *paṭimukhamito* ("gone against"): the Pāli tradition prefers to gloss *paṭicca* with verbs of movement.

58. Vism 519–520: *paṭiccasaddo ca panāyaṃ samāne kattari pubbakāle payujjamāno atthasiddhikaro hoti. seyyathidaṃ, cakkhuñca paṭicca rūpe ca uppajjati cakkhuviññāṇan ti* [SN 12: 43]; Buddhaghosa goes on to argue that for this reason *samuppāda* cannot mean an abstract "mere arising" (*uppāda-mattaṃ*), since such an abstract term would not have a grammatical agent.

59. Explained in Pind (1989, 50).

understood the grammar of the syntactical compound *paṭicca-samuppāda* to imply that that which "arises" is the same as that which is "dependent on" some causal basis. This implies that *samuppāda* must be understood to mean "arising (of a phenomenon)," so that *paṭicca-samuppāda* should be understood as implying "(a phenomenon's) arising dependent on (a causal basis)."

We can now appreciate how the authors of PED managed a nice literal translation of *paṭicca-samuppāda* with "arising on the grounds of (a preceding cause)." Even more exactly, we should translate *paṭicca-samuppāda* as "(a phenomenon's) arising dependent on (a causal basis)." This is hardly an elegant translation, while "dependent arising" is quite neat.

The Term *Paṭicca-samuppāda* and the Concept of Causation

The investigation of how to translate *paṭicca-samuppāda* in the Pāli canon could end at this point, with some clarity about the grammar of its construction and hence how to translate it as a term referring to a particular concept. My conclusion is that *paṭicca-samuppāda* means "dependent arising" and that it refers to a specific concept of causation. However, this raises the question of whether this concept of causation is adequately communicated simply by rendering *paṭicca-samuppāda* as "dependent arising." Even if one were to gloss "dependent arising" as "(a phenomenon's) arising dependent on (a causal basis)," it is not self-evident what concept of causation is implied. The concept to which the term *paṭicca-samuppāda* refers is not necessarily identical to our modern concepts of causation, which have developed in the course of centuries of Western philosophical and scientific endeavor and reflect quite different concerns to those of early Buddhism.

Causation, far from being a simple fact about the world as we encounter it, belongs rather to the range of culturally inherited concepts we habitually employ to make sense of facts. A comparison could be made with the concept of time. The presupposition of time as involving a cyclical structure, on both cosmic and individual levels, is a concept by which ancient Buddhists understood events in their experience.[60] By contrast, the concept of time as linear dominates in Western culture. It might be said that it is only by applying the concept of cyclical time to experience does

60. Discussed, for example, in Bronkhorst (2007, 69–71).

the Buddhist doctrine of rebirth become properly intelligible. Likewise, the term *paṭicca-samuppāda* refers to a concept of causation by which the early Buddhists could make intelligible how experience works, a concept that differs from modern Western concepts of causation, specifically that of causation as linear and mechanical, exemplified by one billiard ball causing another to move.

While the full exposition of this specifically Buddhist conception of causation would go beyond a discussion of translation issues, nevertheless I want to argue that the very term *paṭicca-samuppāda* gives expression to the basic concept of causation to which it refers. It does so by expressing in metaphorical terms the concept of a phenomenon coming into existence only when another phenomenon necessary for its coming into existence is present. This is what is meant by "arising dependent on a causal basis," and the expression *paṭicca-samuppāda* evokes specific metaphors to communicate this particular concept of causation.

Conceptual Metaphor in Early Buddhist Doctrine

Hence I now propose to explore how *paṭicca-samuppāda* implies a "conceptual metaphor" in which verbs of movement stand for the concept of causation. To speak of "metaphor" here is not merely to identify a figure of speech designed to transfer one kind of meaning to another context for the sake of literary color or imaginative insight; rather, it is to identify what Lakoff and Johnson describe as "conceptual metaphors" by which our ordinary ways of understanding and communicating involve the unconscious but analyzable transfer of meaning from one conceptual domain to another.[61] For instance, the English word "arise" is quite normally used in its literal sense to mean "get up" but also metaphorically to mean "come into existence."[62] When we say, for instance, that the Buddha's teaching "arose" in a particular intellectual context, we mean that it started to exist under the causal influence of its situation, not that it moved upward. The word "arose" expresses a natural process of causation through the metaphor

61. Lakoff and Johnson (1980). Jurewicz 2004 and 2008 are pioneering studies of conceptual metaphor in the Vedas.

62. OED s.v. "arise" *v.*: "I. To get up from sitting, lying, repose . . . III. To spring up, come above ground, into the world, into existence."

of upward motion. Following Lakoff and Johnson's lead, I will denote this conceptual metaphor, through the use of small capitals, as NATURAL CAUSATION IS UPWARD MOVEMENT.[63] Actually, such a metaphor is an ordinary, unconscious way in which we express ourselves in English, so that it is completely implicit in the way that we think and speak—so much so that it may not be immediately obvious that a metaphor is involved. Thus, inviting the reader to turn toward the hidden conceptual metaphors of language, I will argue that *paṭicca-samuppāda* presents the concept of natural causation through a metaphor of movement.

The Pāli language is most likely an artificial literary language developed to preserve the Buddha's teachings,[64] and for this reason it does not record the conceptual metaphors used in the ordinary speech of the Buddha's time. However, early Buddhist teachings themselves furnish examples of more deliberate conceptual metaphor; for example:

1. *Nibbāṇa*, referring to the *summum bonum* of the Buddhist spiritual life, means the "going out" of a fire, and is used as a metaphor for the ending of all psychological afflictions.[65]
2. *Taṇhā* means "thirst," used as a metaphor for "desire."[66] The psychological experience of desire is conceived of by comparison with the physiological experience of thirst.

To call *taṇhā* and *nibbāna* "conceptual metaphors" is to identify the origins of abstract ideas, such as "quenching psychological afflictions" or "psychological desire for personal satisfaction," through familiar experiences such as "the going out of a fire" or "thirst." A characteristic of these familiar examples is that both *nibbāna* and *taṇhā* evidently soon became technical terms in Buddhist doctrine, used without reference to their metaphorical origins. For instance, the Buddha is reported to have said, "I have removed

63. Explored in Lakoff and Johnson (1999, 213).

64. See Hinüber (1983); Norman (1983); cf. Gombrich, "Introduction: What Is Pāli," in Geiger (1994).

65. Discussed more fully in Gombrich (1996, 65f.); and s.v. *nibbāna* in Levman (2016).

66. DOP II 276 s.v. *taṇhā* "1. thirst, craving (for food or drink); 2. (a general) craving; strong desire." "Thirst" for "desire" is, strictly speaking, metonymy rather than metaphor, since "thirst," being a kind of desire, shares the same conceptual domain.

the arrow of *taṇhā*,"[67] which is a badly mixed metaphor if *taṇhā* is understood literally as "thirst," but makes more sense if *taṇhā* is understood to means "psychological desire."[68] Indeed, an awareness of the conceptual metaphors implied in technical terms helps us to understand their original significance, making their use as terms more intelligible. Likewise, I will show that *paṭicca-samuppāda* implies a conceptual metaphor, and that this metaphor illustrates the concept to which the term refers.

Conceptual Metaphor in the Expression *Paṭicca-samuppāda*

We saw earlier that *uppāda* is used in regard to the "arising" of mental states such as greed, hate, or delusion, even though mental states do not actually move. Likewise, in the statement "Seeing the arising (*uppāda*) of the sense spheres the mind is rightly liberated,"[69] we do not suppose that anyone sees the sense spheres moving upward but rather that they see how they start to exist. In such examples, "arising" is a *metaphor* for "starting to exist." It is a *conceptual metaphor* in both English and in Indic languages such as Pāli and Sanskrit, in that "arising" seems to be a way in which human beings think about and express the concept of "starting to exist."[70]

Given that "arising" is a conceptual metaphor for "starting to exist," it might seem that we could just as well translate *uppāda* as "origination," which also means "starting to exist." However, if we were to translate *uppāda* in this way, we would translate only the *conceptual domain* (that of EXISTENCE) of the meaning of *uppāda*, and not the *source domain* (that of MOVEMENT) of the conceptual metaphor STARTING-TO-EXIST IS ARISING. By translating *uppāda* as "origination," we would thereby bypass the metaphor through which the concept "starting to exist" is given a more accessible and less conceptual expression in the metaphor of "arising."

The early Buddhists were at least implicitly aware that *uppāda* was a metaphor, as is evident in the following passage in which *uppāda* is set alongside other words expressing the concept of existence through various metaphors:

---

67. MN 105, PTS II 105: *taṃ me taṇhā-sallaṃ pahīnaṃ*.

68. Gombrich 2009, 222 n.1.

69. AN 6: 55, PTS III 378: *disvā āyatanuppādaṃ, sammā cittaṃ vimuccati*.

70. OED s.v. arising "1.b.: springing up, origination."

> Monks, the arising (*uppāda*), standing (*ṭhiti*), production (*abhinibbatti*), and appearance (*pātubhāva*) of material form [and feeling, perception, formations, and consciousness]—this is the arising of suffering, the standing of illnesses, the appearance of aging and death.[71]

In this passage, which is repeated elsewhere for the four material elements,[72] the concept of "existence" is illustrated by means of four related but distinct metaphors:

1. *uppāda*, "arising," a metaphor for "starting to exist";
2. *ṭhiti*,[73] "standing," a metaphor for "continuing to exist";
3. *abhinibbatti*,[74] "production," a metaphor for "being brought into existence"; and
4. *pātubhāva*,[75] "appearance," a metaphor for "manifesting in existence."

Here we see that *uppāda* expresses the concept of existence through a metaphor of arising, alongside other words that express nearly the same concept through metaphors of standing, producing, and appearing, in this way making more accessible and vivid the point that the constituents of experience are unreliable because they do not exist unconditionally.[76]

With this passage in mind, it becomes understandable how *samuppāda* in *paṭicca-samuppāda* has been translated as "production" and "orig-

---

71. SN 22: 30, PTS III 31–32: *yo, bhikkhave, rūpassa [vedanāya, saññāya, saṅkhārānaṃ, viññāṇassa] uppādo ṭhiti abhinibbatti pātubhāvo, dukkhasseso uppādo rogānaṃ ṭhiti jarāmaraṇassa pātubhāvo. dukkhasseso uppādo rogānaṃ ṭhiti jarāmaraṇassa pātubhāvo.*

72. SN 14: 36, PTS II 175: *yo, bhikkhave, pathavīdhātuyā uppādo ṭhiti abhinibbatti pātubhāvo, dukkhasseso uppādo rogānaṃ ṭhiti jarāmaraṇassa pātubhāvo.*

73. From the verb *tiṭṭhati*, "stands," "remains."

74. From the verb *vattati*, "turns," with the prefixes *abhi*, "toward," and *nir*, "out."

75. From the verb *bhavati*, "becomes," with the prefix *pātu*, "open."

76. The same passage describes the "stopping" (*nirodha*), "pacifying" (*vūpasama*) and "setting" (*atthaṅgama*) of the constituents of experience as the cessation of suffering, the pacifying of illnesses and the setting of aging and death; three action nouns as metaphors for "ceasing to exist."

ination" as well as "arising." The word "production" expresses the concept of "starting to exist" through the metaphor of "bringing forth,"[77] while the word "origination," as shown earlier, expresses the concept of "starting to exist" in a nonmetaphorical way.[78] Yet, since the Pāli *uppāda* is clearly differentiated from words that express the concept "starting to exist" through other metaphors, it is more appropriate to translate *samuppāda* as "arising" in preference to "origination" or "production," as preserving the conceptual metaphor that may have been implied. In addition, I discussed earlier how the Pāli *uppāda* is used in the senses of "appearing" and of "birth." This suggests that we should also consider *samuppāda* to imply some secondary conceptual metaphors. My discussion of *samuppāda* can be summarized as follows:

> ***samuppāda*** = *sam* ("together," but here pleonastic) + *ud* ("up," "out") + *pad* ("go") = *uppāda* ("arising") from *uppajjati* ("arises") implies a conceptual metaphor in terms of:

STARTING-TO-EXIST IS	MOVEMENT-UP
origination	**arising**
	MOVEMENT-INTO-VISIBILITY:
	appearing
	BEING-BORN: birth, genesis[79]

Lakoff and Johnson point out, however, that when we speak in English of something arising, this implies that this existence-as-upward-motion is a natural effect—the *effect* of a *cause*.[80] We might say, for instance, "joy

77. OED s.v. "production": "1a.: The action or an act of producing, making, or causing anything; generation or creation *of* something."

78. OED s.v. "origination": "1a.: coming into existence, commencement, beginning (in reference to cause or source); rise, origin."

79. Hence the PED translation of *paṭicca-samuppāda* as "causal genesis"; cf. OED s.v. "birth": "2. *fig.* Of things: Origin, origination, commencement of existence, beginning." OED s.v. "genesis": "4. The origin or mode of formation of something."

80. We might speculate at this point on the pervasiveness of causality, or the principle of causation—that every effect has a cause—in human thinking. This principle certainly appears to be assumed in the early Buddhist discourses, and *paṭicca-samuppāda* would

arises"; the cause of this joy may not be made explicit, in which case the causal source of the arising may be taken to be its situation; for instance, meditation. Likewise in the Pāli discourses, we often find the statement: "A Realized One arises (*uppajjati*) in the world, a worthy one, a perfectly and completely awakened one . . ."[81] The implied causal source of this arising of Buddhas is the situation of humanity in the world, together with the aspiration and resolution of bodhisattas (Buddhas-to-be), since Buddhas do not spring into existence without a cause.

Now, in the expression *paṭicca-samuppāda*, a phenomenon's "arising" is explicitly related to its cause by the word *paṭicca*, another verb of motion expressing the idea of "falling back on" or, very literally, "moving against." Let us consider our paradigmatic Pāli sentence: " 'moving against" (*paṭicca*) the eye and visual forms, eye-consciousness arises (*uppajjati*)." To say that eye-consciousness "arises" is to imply a causal situation in which it comes into existence as an effect, and this situation is made explicit through *paṭicca*, expressing a relationship to a cause as a source against which consciousness moves upward or arises, namely, the eye and visual forms.

The full conceptual metaphor involved is laid bare by considering the causal source implied by *paṭicca*, expressed by the word *paccaya*. This is an action noun from *pacceti*, hence etymologically a "moving-against." But, as in Sanskrit, action nouns in Pāli are also used to designate concretely the thing in which the verbal action appears,[82] hence a *paccaya* is something moved against, that is, a "support" or "basis."[83] Outside philosophical discourse concerned with causation, the word *paccaya* is used to mean "support" as in "requisite": the *paccaya*s for a monastic are robes, bowl, lodgings, and medicines, according to the metaphor of a physical support for a necessity.[84] But within philosophical discourse, a *paccaya* is a "cause" or "condition" expressed in terms of the metaphor of a basis or source

be unintelligible without it. Moreover, at SN 22: 62 and elsewhere, the Buddha is reported to severely censure those *samaṇa*s who deny causality, though this censure generally concerns the denial of the efficacy of *kamma*.

81. For example, DN 2 PTS I 37: *tathāgato loke uppajjati arahaṃ sammāsambuddho*.

82. Whitney 1889, §1145, 422.

83. PED 384.

84. For example, Mil. 339: *paccaya-sannissita-sīlaṃ*, "virtuous conduct dependent on the [monastic] supports." In the Pāli canon itself the word used is *parikkhāra*, "requisites."

of movement.[85] Hence we find: "Moving against (*paṭicca*) whatever basis (*paccaya*) it arises (*uppajjati*), consciousness is reckoned accordingly."[86] This example illustrates nicely the full metaphor of NATURAL CAUSATION IS UPWARD MOVEMENT, consisting of various elements:[87]

upward motion (arising, *uppāda*) → natural causation
upward moving phenomenon
(e.g., consciousness) → a natural effect
original location (basis, *paccaya*) → situation taken as a natural cause

To say that consciousness arises from a basis or source is to say metaphorically that a certain situation is the cause of consciousness. In this case, the general philosophical claim is that consciousness is caused by the senses together with their objects.

This leaves the question of how exactly to understand the conceptual metaphor implied by *paṭicca* in the expression *paṭicca-samuppāda*. As we have seen, *pacceti* is a verb of motion, which can sometimes be translated "falls back on," in a nonmetaphorical way. But we have also seen that the word *paṭicca* is used in the sense of "because of," as when it is said that the Buddha surveyed the world "because of" (*paṭicca*) compassion. This usage conveys the conceptual metaphor REASONS ARE MOVEMENTS, which is also intelligible in English, in that we might say, "the Buddha's teaching goes back to his compassion" to express the idea that "the Buddha's teaching exists because of his compassion," or we might say "calm comes from meditation" to express the idea that "calm exists because of meditation." In this connection, the Pāli *paṭicca* is often glossed in the commentaries by *āgamma*,[88] the absolutive from *āgacchati*, "comes."[89]

85. I have generally previously translated *paccaya* as "causal basis" rather than "condition," first because "causal basis" preserves a connection with the conceptual metaphor implied by the Pāli *paccaya*, and second because the word "condition" in English is itself a metaphor for cause drawn from the language of agreements (from Latin *condicio*).

86. MN 38 PTS I 259: *yaññadeva paccayaṃ paṭicca uppajjati viññāṇaṃ tena teneva saṅkhaṃ gacchati*.

87. Adapted from Lakoff and Johnson (1999, 213).

88. For instance, in Ud-a. 429, on Ud. 8: 8: *paṭicca nissāya āgamma paccayaṃ katvā*: " 'Dependent on' means 'relying on,' 'owing to,' 'placing on a basis.' " I discuss *nissāya* later.

89. DOP I 280 s.v. *āgacchati*.

The verb *pacceti* is also used to express belief or trust, as in the Brahman who *pacceti*, "goes back to," "believes in," purification through water. In this case, the English phrase "falls back on" gives similar expression to a belief or trust, embodying the metaphor BELIEFS ARE MOVEMENTS.[90] *Paṭicca* is also glossed in the commentaries by *nissāya*, the absolutive from *nissayati*, which means "leans on," from the root *si* "lean," "lie" (Sanskrit *śri*), with the prefix *ni-*, "down," "back."[91] The connection between *pacceti* and the verb *nissayati* is evident in a verse from the *Sutta-nipāta*:

> So a monk should really not "lean on" (*nissayeyya*) the seen,
> the heard or the thought, or on virtue and vows.[92]

To say that the monk should not "lean on" experience is to say that he should not place his trust in how things appear, according to the metaphor of BELIEFS ARE MOVEMENTS.

There does not seem to be a particularly exact English equivalent to these Pāli words expressing reasons and beliefs in terms of movement. Instead, the absolutive *nissāya* tends to be translated "dependent on," "relying on,"[93] phrases expressing an attitude of trust; while the absolutive *āgamma* is translated "owing to," "in reference to,"[94] phrases that convey a reason or explanation. Turning now to our paradigmatic sentence, "dependent on (*paṭicca*) the eye and visual forms arises eye-consciousness," it is apparent that the relation of eye-consciousness (*cakkhu-viññāna*) to eye (*cakkhu*) and visual forms (*rūpā*) is impersonal; *paṭicca* expresses the idea neither of a reason nor of a belief, since the eye and visual forms do not constitute a person, but only constituents of experience. Rather, *paṭicca*

90. It is interesting to note that Sanskrit *pratyaya* also takes the meaning "belief," "trust" (MW 673), according to a conceptual metaphor of BELIEFS ARE MOVEMENTS; PED 384 gives the same meaning for *paccaya* but does not cite canonical sources.

91. DOP II 626 s.v. *nissayati*.

92. SN 798: *tasmā hi diṭṭhaṃ va sutaṃ mutaṃ vā | sīlabbataṃ bhikkhu na nissayeyya ||* (*nissayeyya* is the optative of *nissayati*). In the verses from the *Sutta-nipāta* cited earlier, note 37 in this chapter, the action noun *nissaya*, that is, "leaning on" (with *karoti*, "makes," "places"), is used in exactly the same way as *pacceti*.

93. DOP II 627 s.v. *nissayati*: "1.(i) depending on, relying on; using as one's support." *Nissāya* is also used in the sense of "(ii) because of, for the sake of," which, like *paṭicca*, expresses the concept of a reason.

94. DOP I 281 s.v. *āgacchati*.

cooperates in the expression of impersonal, natural causation within the philosophical discourse of early Buddhist doctrine. It is striking in this regard that the word *nissāya*, for all that it is similar in both etymology and usage to *paṭicca*, is not used impersonally in Pāli and did not become a technical term in philosophical discourse.[95]

Just as there does not appear to be an exact equivalent in English for Pāli words like *nissāya* and *āgamma*, expressing beliefs and reasons in terms of movement, so there is no exact equivalent for *paṭicca*, expressing causal relatedness as movement.[96] We saw, however, that we can use the English phrase "dependent on" to express the sense of "trusting in" implied by *paṭicca* and *nissāya*, and likewise we can use the phrase "dependent on" to express the sense of causal relatedness in *paṭicca*. The English phrase "dependent on" is in fact used very often to express the relation of an effect with a cause in the impersonal language of natural causation: we might say "consciousness is dependent on the sense and their objects" to express how the senses and their objects as cause relate to consciousness as effect. The adjective "dependent" means "hanging down,"[97] which is not quite a "moving-against," but it is used metaphorically to express the concept of something's "having its existence conditioned by something else."[98] Hence the English phrase "dependent on" offers a close analogy to *paṭicca*, even though the idea of an arising which is dependent on something else is a mixed metaphor, since something "moving up" cannot at the same time be "hanging down."

95. Instead it became a term in monastic *saṅgha* discourse to describe the relationship of a junior monk to a senior: DOP II 628 s.v. *nissāya*: "2. in (formal) dependence . . . having as mentor."

96. It would seem that the Chinese translators of the early Buddhism faced a similar problem when they came to render *paṭicca-samuppāda*. The standard translation is 緣起 (*yuánqǐ*), 緣 (*yuán*) meaning cause or reason, and 起 (*qǐ*) rise or start. Hence the Chinese translation of *samuppāda* as *qǐ* was able to preserve the metaphor of upward movement, while that of *paṭicca* as *yuán* rendered the concept rather than the metaphor.

97. From the French *dépendre*, "to hang down."

98. OED s.v. dependent: "1. Hanging down . . . 2.a. That depends *on* something else; having its existence contingent on, or conditioned by, the existence of something else."

In this section I have tried to indicate the importance of conceptual metaphor for an understanding of the expression *paṭicca-samuppāda*. I have suggested that "arising" is the most suitable translation of *samuppāda*, preserving the conceptual metaphor of NATURAL CAUSATION IS UPWARD MOVEMENT evident in the Pāli. Likewise I suggest that "dependent on" is the most suitable translation of *paṭicca*, even though it is not exact. However, it does preserve some sense of metaphor, unlike an alternative translation of *paṭicca* as "conditioned," which attempts to render the concept of causal relatedness without recourse to metaphors of movement.[99]

Conclusion: Causation and Organic Growth

I would like to finish this chapter on translating *paṭicca-samuppāda* with a consideration of the need for a translation that is down-to-earth. One can imagine the Buddha, having gained awakening, wondering how to express his newfound insights, so subtle and rare, in the language of his day. While certain concepts and metaphors were available in his religious and philosophical culture, his awakening was, so it is believed, something new and original in the experience of humankind, demanding new formulations as well as reformulations of the old. Such a scenario might explain the novel concept of *paṭicca-samuppāda*, apparently not otherwise found in the language of ancient India. Of course, ancient Indians, like human beings all over the world, had observed and described causation in the world around them, but the concept of dependent arising was an invitation into the systematic description and investigation of how experience works, how *dukkha* arises, and how it can be brought to an end. The natural and impersonal working of causation in experience is the conceptual key to the Buddha's teaching.

And yet this concept is formulated in language that is intimately related to ordinary human experience. To say that a phenomenon arises dependent on some causal basis allows the concept of causation to be easily imagined, even though the impersonal causation of human experience

99. And cf. note 85 in this chapter.

is in practice difficult to understand. One way in which this concept of causation can be imagined is in terms of a simple visual representation of the meaning of *paṭicca-samuppāda*, taking into account the implied conceptual metaphor UPWARD MOVEMENT IS NATURAL CAUSATION:

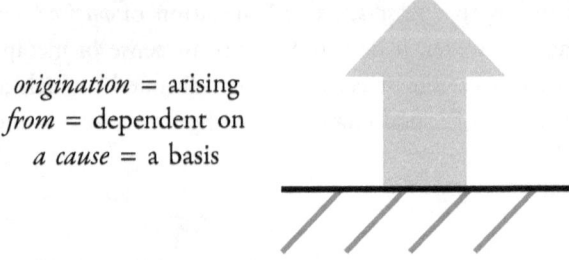

origination = arising
from = dependent on
a cause = a basis

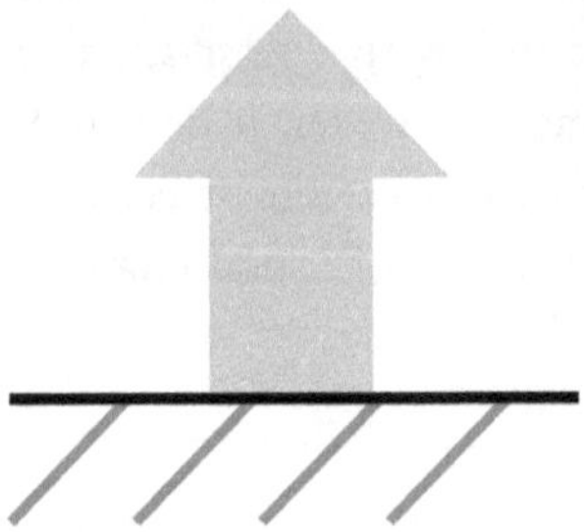

Figure 9.1. *paṭicca-samuppāda* as conceptual metaphor.

I am not suggesting that such a visual representation is anywhere implied in early Buddhist accounts of *paṭicca-samuppāda*; only that someone with a visual imagination, hearing the conceptual metaphor implied by the Pāli expression, might easily think of it in such a form.

However, although no such visual representation of *paṭicca-samuppāda* is found in early Buddhist accounts, it is in fact implied by illustrations of the working of dependent arising in terms of organic growth. These illustrations were evidently supposed to help early Buddhists to imagine what was meant by dependent arising. Some stanzas attributed to the *bhikkhunī* Selā do this most clearly. Replying to Māra, who has asked her if she knows anything about where her body has come from, its fate, and purpose, she says:

> This body was not made by myself, this pain[100] was not made by another.
> It has come to be dependent on (*paṭicca*) a cause, and ceases from the cause's breakup.

100. *agha*, "evil, sin, pain, distress" (DOP I 16), but probably figuratively the body: "This body (*kāya*) should be viewed as impermanent, as suffering, as a disease, as a boil, as an arrow, as a pain (*agha*), as an illness, as other, as decaying, as empty, as without self" (MN 74 PTS I 500).

> As a particular seed grows when sown in a field,
> Owing to (*āgamma*) both good earth as well as to moisture,
> So the constituents, elements, and six sense-realms
> Have come to be dependent on a cause and cease from the cause's breakup.[101]

Here, dependent arising is illustrated by the growth of a seed when the causes and conditions for that growth are present. In another example of an agricultural comparison for the workings of dependent arising, consciousness itself is compared to a seed, which grows in the presence of certain causal conditions: "Karma is the field, consciousness is the seed, craving is the moisture. For beings obstructed by ignorance and fettered by craving, consciousness is established in an inferior realm. In this way there is future production of renewed existence."[102] This comparison of consciousness to a seed is further developed in another discourse:

> The four continuities of consciousness should be seen as being like the element of earth. Passion and delight should be seen as being like the element of water. Consciousness should be seen as being like the five kinds of seeds. Consciousness, while it continues to exist, might continue to exist while being involved with form; having form as a basis and a ground and sprinkled with delight, it might come to increase, growth, and expansion.[103]

101. SN 5: 9 PTS I 134: *nayidaṃ attakataṃ bimbaṃ | nayidaṃ parakataṃ aghaṃ | hetuṃ paṭicca sambhūtaṃ | hetubhaṅgā nirujjhati || yathā aññataraṃ bījaṃ | khette vuttaṃ virūhati | pathavīrasañcāgamma | sinehañca tadūbhayaṃ || evaṃ khandhā ca dhātuyo | cha ca āyatanā ime | hetuṃ paṭicca sambhūtā | hetubhaṅgā nirujjhare ||*

102. AN 3: 76 PTS I 223: *kammaṃ khettaṃ viññāṇaṃ bījaṃ taṇhā sneho. avijjānīvaraṇānaṃ sattānaṃ taṇhāsaṃyojanānaṃ hīnāya dhātuyā viññāṇaṃ patiṭṭhitaṃ evaṃ āyatiṃ punabbhavābhinibbatti hoti.* This is repeated for rebirth in a "middle" (*majjhima*) realm and a "superior" (*panīta*) realm. Cf. AN 3: 77.

103. SN 22: 54 PTS III 54–55: *seyyathāpi bhikkhave pathavīdhātu evaṃ catasso viññāṇaṭṭhitiyo daṭṭhabbā. seyyathāpi bhikkhave āpodhātu evaṃ nandirāgo daṭṭhabbo. seyyathāpi bhikkhave pañca bījajātāni evaṃ viññāṇaṃ sāhāraṃ daṭṭhabbaṃ. rūp'upayaṃ bhikkhave viññāṇaṃ tiṭṭhamānaṃ tiṭṭheyya rūpārammaṇaṃ rūpappatiṭṭhaṃ nandūpasecanaṃ vuddhiṃ virūḷhiṃ vepullaṃ āpajjeyya.* This passage is repeated with form (*rūpa*) replaced by feeling (*vedanā*), perception (*saññā*), and formations (*saṅkhārā*).

The comparison of the workings of experience to the natural growth and development of plants, as would have been familiar to ancient Indian agriculturalists, is given fullest expression not in the Pāli discourses but in the Rice-Stalk Discourse (*Śālistamba Sūtra*), which is usually regarded as an early Mahāyāna scripture. Here, objective (*bahya*) dependent arising is explained in terms of the causes and conditions for the growth of stalk and fruit from a seed, while subjective (*ādhyātmika*) dependent arising is explained in terms of the twelve *nidāna*s from ignorance to aging-and-death and of the six elements.[104] That is to say, the same concept of dependent arising applies objectively to plants and subjectively to experience.

We see then that the language used by early Buddhists to explain how experience works is not a form of discourse that is remote from ordinary life but is rather drawn from the familiar workings of nature. The following visual representation is designed to suggest this familiarity while clearly communicating exactly the same concept as the more abstract visual representation suggested earlier:

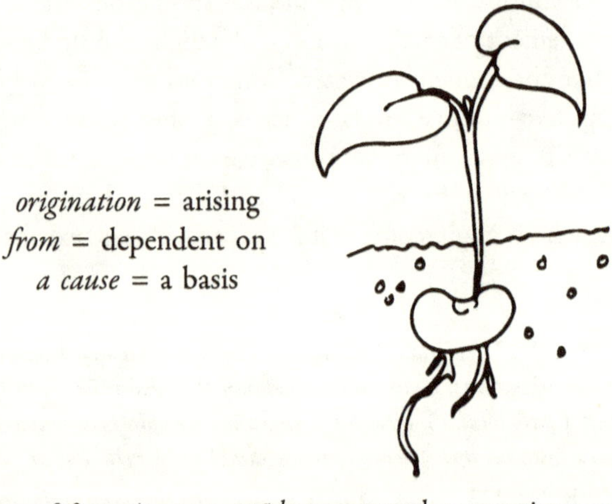

Figure 9.2. *paṭicca-samuppāda* represented as organic growth.

If it is indeed true that the language of *paṭicca-samuppāda* would have been accessible to its first listeners, and that the concept of causation that it expresses was constructed out of familiar metaphors, then our translation into English ought likewise to be at home in ordinary language. Hence, I contend, we should prefer the translation "dependent arising" over such

104. See Reat (1993, esp. 34ff.).

translations such as "dependent origination" or "conditioned co-production," which belong to the jargon of Buddhism rather than to the soil of life.[105] The translation "dependent arising" best suggests the naturalistic concept of causation to which the term *paṭicca-samuppāda* refers, in its own cultural context, as is illustrated through comparisons to organic growth.

References

Anālayo, Bhikkhu. 2011. *A Comparative Study of the Majjhima-nikāya*. Taipei: Dharma Drum.

Bingenheimer, Marcus, Bhikkhu Anālayo, and Roderick Bucknell, trans. 2013. *The Madhyama Āgama (Middle-Length Discourses) Volume 1 (Taishō Volume 1, Number 26)*. Moraga, CA: BDK America.

Bronkhorst, Johannes. 2007. *Greater Magadha: Studies in the Culture of Early India*. Leiden: Brill.

Buswell, Robert E., and Donald S. Lopez. 2013. *The Princeton Dictionary of Buddhism*. Princeton, NJ: Princeton University Press.

Collins, Steven. 2006. *A Pali Grammar for Students*. Chiang Mai: Silkworm.

Conze, Edward. 1953. *Buddhism: Its Essence and Development*. 2nd ed. Oxford: Bruno Cassirer.

———. 1956. *Buddhist Meditation*. London: George Allen & Unwin.

———. 1962. *Buddhist Thought in India: Three Phases of Buddhist Philosophy*. London: Allen & Unwin.

Geiger, Wilhelm. 1994. *A Pāli Grammar*. Edited by K. R. Norman. Translated by Batakrishna Ghosh. Oxford: Pali Text Society.

Gombrich, Richard. 1996. *How Buddhism Began: The Conditioned Genesis of the Early Teachings*. London: Athlone.

———. 2009. *What the Buddha Thought*. London: Equinox.

Griffiths, Paul J. 1981. "Buddhist Hybrid English: Some Notes on Philology and Hermeneutics for Buddhologists." *Journal of the International Association of Buddhist Studies* 4, no. 2: 17–32.

Harvey, Peter. 2013. "The Conditioned Co-arising of Mental and Bodily Processes within Life and Between Lives." In *A Companion to Buddhist Philosophy*, edited by Steven M. Emmanuel, 46–68. Chichester: Wiley-Blackwell.

Hendriksen, Hans. 1944. *Syntax of the Infinite Verb-Forms of Pāli*. Copenhagen: Einar Munksgaard.

105. Indeed, "dependent origination" and especially "conditioned co-production" are rather good examples of what Paul Griffiths (1981) has called "Buddhist Hybrid English."

Hinüber, Oskar von. 1983. "The Oldest Literary Language of Buddhism." *Saeculum* 34: 1–9.

Hopkins, Jeffrey. 1983. *Meditation on Emptiness*. London: Wisdom.

Jurewicz, Joanna. 2004. "The Rigveda, the Cognitive Linguistics and the Oral Poetry." *European Review* 12, no. 4: 605–613.

———. 2008. "Anger and Cognition: Conceptual Metaphor in the Ṛgveda." *Rocznik Orientalisticzny* 16, no. 1: 7–19.

Kardas, Goran. 2015. "From Etymology to Ontology: Vasubandhu and Candrakīrti on Various Interpretations of Pratītyasamutpāda." *Asian Philosophy* 25, no. 3: 293–317.

Lakoff, George, and Mark Johnson. 1980. *Metaphors We Live By*. Chicago: University of Chicago Press.

———. 1999. *Philosophy in the Flesh: The Embodied Mind and Its Challenge to Western Thought*. New York: Basic Books.

Lamotte, Étienne. 1980. "Conditioned Co-production and Supreme Enlightenment." In *Buddhist Studies in Honour of Walpola Rahula*, edited by S. Balasooriya et al., 118–132. London: Gordon Fraser.

Levman, Bryan. n.d. "Nibbāna." In *Pāli Dictionary*. http://palidictionary.com.

MacDonald, Anne. 2015. *In Clear Words: The Prasannapadā, Chapter One. Volume II: Annotated Translation, Tibetan Text*. Vol. 2. 2 vols. Vienna: Österreichische Akademie der Wissenschaft.

Macy, Joanna. 1991. *Mutual Causality in Buddhism and General Systems Theory*. Albany: State University of New York Press.

Norman, K. R. 1983. *Pāli Literature*. Vol. 7, fasc. 2. A History of Indian Literature. Wiesbaden: Otto Harrassowitz.

———. 1993. "Syntactical Compounds in Middle Indo-Aryan." In *Collected Papers* 4: 218–225. Oxford: Pali Text Society.

———, trans. 2001. *The Group of Discourses (Sutta-Nipāta)*. 2nd ed. Oxford: Pali Text Society.

Pind, Ole Holten. 1989. "Studies in the Pāli Grammarians I." *Journal of the Pali Text Society* 13: 33–82.

Prahlad Pradhan, K. P., ed. 1975. *Abhidharmakośa-Bhāṣyaṃ (of Vasubandhu)*. Rev. 2nd ed. Patna: Jayaswal Research Institute, TSWS.

Reat, N. Ross. 1993. *The Śālistamba Sūtra*. Delhi: Motilal Banarsidass.

Sangpo, Gelong Lodrö, and Louis de la Vallée Poussin, trans. 2012. *Abhidharmakośa-Bhāṣya of Vasubandhu: The Treasury of the Abhidharma and Its (Auto) Commentary*. Delhi: Motilal Banarsidass.

Schmithausen, Lambert. 1997. "The Early Buddhist Tradition and Ecological Ethics." *Journal of Buddhist Ethics* 4: 1–74.

Whitney, William Dwight. 1889. *Sanskrit Grammar*. 2nd ed. Cambridge: Harvard University Press.

Chapter 10

Why Is Literal Meaning Insufficient?

A Study of *Desanāsīsa* Explanations in the Pāli Commentaries

Aruna Gamage

Preamble

In this chapter, I study the meaning of *desanāsīsa* (hereafter DS), a special hermeneutic principle employed by Pāli commentators. The way DS is used in the commentaries alludes to the fact that the vicissitudes of DS are richer than and different from how they appear on the surface. In the last few decades, there has been an upsurge in Pāli commentarial studies; yet, none of them have been concerned with the exegeses related to DS, which are worth exploring. Accordingly, in this study, I attempt to fill that lacuna. As DS is primarily a commentarial compound, many Pāli dictionaries do not list it. Tin translates it as "heading of discourse,"[1] "principle term in the teaching,"[2] and "chief in the discourse"[3] in three places of his *Atthasālinī* translation (i.e., *The Expositor*). Bodhi and Nyānaponika also render this term with strikingly similar terms. Bodhi translates it as "heading of the teaching" (2000, 1952), for example, and Nyānaponika as "das Stich wort

1. Tin 1920, 1: 90.

2. Tin 1920, 1: 151.

3. Tin 1921, 2: 520.

der Darlegung" (2005, 145 and 211) or "das Leit wort der Erklärung" (2005, 602). These translations are apt to communicate the multivalent meaning of DS in some instances of its usage but not in others. DS does not ipso facto always stand for a "headword" but has multiple applications. Because of the extensiveness of the sources, the present study will be limited to the commentaries ascribed to Buddhaghosa by "tradition."[4] Unless otherwise stated, translations from Pāli in this chapter are my own.

Functions of DS

Buddhaghosa labels some lemmas[5] quoted from the canon as DSs[6] and provides brief interpretations for them. It is worth noting here that none of the lemmas that are labeled as DS are abstruse.[7] The purpose of labeling a canonical lemma as a DS is to signal to the reader that the literal meaning of the particular lemma is either incomplete or inappropriate in the canonical context.[8] Literally, DS can be translated as a "heading in the

4. See Minayeff 1886, 59. See also Ñāṇamoli 1956, xxxiii; Gunasekara 2008, 13–14.

5. Lemmas here refer to the words and phrases that are glossed in the commentaries: "a glossed word or phrase," WCD 483. Kieffer-Pülz uses *pratīka* for lemmas. See Kieffer-Pülz 2016, 12. See also DLP, s.v. lemma.

6. Some commentarial contexts replace *desanāmatta* for *desanāsīsa* that has approximately the same connotation (e.g., MN-a. III 351; Ud-a. 111). Because of the extensiveness of the scope of this chapter, I do not deal with those accounts here; they will be dealt with in a forthcoming article.

7. One of the major functions of Pāli commentaries is to elucidate the obscure terms in the canon. Buddhaghosa in particular uses the term *anuttānapadavaṇṇanā* (explanation for unclear terms) to qualify his exegeses. See DN-a. I 81; DN-a II 481; MN-a I 137, 207; SN-a. I 289. See also von Hinüber 1996, 116.

8. The commentarial literature heavily stresses that there are many pitfalls to grasping at literal meaning. Vism-ṭ. II 207^{Be}: *yathārutavasena pāḷiyā atthe gayhamāne bahudosā āpajjanti ti*. See also MN. II 240: *appamattakaṃ kho panetaṃ yad idaṃ byañjanaṃ. mā āyasmanto appamattake vivādaṃ āpajjitthā ti*. "But the phrasing is a mere trifle. Let the venerable ones not fall into a dispute over a mere trifle" (Ñāṇamoli and Bodhi 1995, 849). The commentaries pay greater regard to the meaning than the letters. See MN-a. II 351, SN-a. III 95: *attho hi paṭisaraṇaṃ na byañjanaṃ*. "Indeed, the meaning is refuge and not the letter." See also: AN-a. I 73. Pṭsm-a. II 508: *byañjane ādaraṃ akatvā adhippetam eva dassento*. "Showing the intended meaning without respecting the letters." See also V-a. II 437; V-a. III 519, 551. See for scholarly research: Lamotte 1993, 11–27; Pieris 2004, 184–185.

teaching." Numerous attestations of this term that occur in a variety of commentarial contexts, however, reveal the fact that it has several connotations. Subcommentaries, as well as recent scholarship, have defined this term in different ways, as will be explored near the end of this chapter. A close examination of divergent occurrences of DSs in Buddhaghosa's commentaries, together with their corresponding canonical contexts, enables us to identify its two major functions: 1) Extension: when the commentator feels that a term in the canon expresses only a part of its whole meaning, he labels it as a DS and offers an interpretation in order to extend the whole meaning of that part up to its totality. This totality is, however, merely conceptual. 2) Substitution: sometimes, Buddhaghosa substitutes a DS with a new meaning when he presumes that the literal meaning of it contradicts Theravāda theories of *Abhidhamma*. These two functions of DS, therefore, lead the reader to conclude that the denotative meanings of those lemmas do not exhaustively express their connotations. As I will point out in the following passages, DS behaves as a synecdoche, merismus, and as a metonymy in Buddhaghosa's commentaries.

DS as Synecdoche

According to the commentator, some terms appearing in the canon as single elements actually stand for two components that are mutually associated. For instance, we can look at the first verse of the *Sukajātaka* that runs as follows:

> As long as that bird knows the measure in eating,
> Then [it] would return, and nourish also [its] mother.[9]

As this stanza relates, a certain bird, who was aware of the measure in eating, supported its mother. However, the commentary states that "also [its] mother" of this verse is a DS, and thus, it is interpreted as the following: " 'Also [its] mother' is a DS. [This] means [it] also supported mother and father."[10] It is clear that the preceding verse does not mention

9. J. II 293: *yāvaṃ so mattam aññāsi bhojanasmiṃ vihaṅgamo, tāva addhānam āpādi mātarañ ca aposayi.* "What time the bird without excess did eat. He found the way, and brought his mother meat" (Rouse 1895, 204).

10. J-a. II 293: *mātarañ cā ti desanāsīsam etaṃ, mātāpitaro ca aposayī ti attho.*

that the bird supported its father. The main purpose of the *Sukajātaka*, which consists of three verses, is apparently to give an admonition to those who overeat and encourage them to be moderate in eating. Hence, the final two verses of this *Jātaka* also have no reference to the bird's father, so we find it only in the commentary. As this interpretation obviously shows, *mātaraṃ*, which is a single element, stands in the canon for two elements. The commentator seems to take *ca* (in *mātarañ ca*) as an elliptical particle[11] that represents both mother and father in order to suit the narrative that he offers in the commentary. It should be taken into account here that the commentator's perspective sounds plausible when considered in light of linguistic surveys on ellipsis.[12] Aelbrecht's research leads us to think that there is a mismatch between what is written and its meaning, and as a result, the interpretation of an elliptical utterance becomes richer than it was initially intended.[13] This DS interpretation moreover is reminiscent of *ekaśeṣadvandva* that can be attested in both Sanskrit[14] and Pāli literatures.[15] I have noted another three instances that fall under this category in Buddhaghosa's commentaries. Interestingly, two of these occur in the commentary of the *Jātaka*.[16] At times, DS appears

11. The particle *ca*, as the commentators realize, sometimes occurs in the canon just for completion of the line due to *metri causa* (see Ud-a. 254: *casaddo nipātamattaṃ* on the Ud. 43: *pātimokkhe ca saṃvaro*). See also DOP II 89–90. At times, they consider this particle redundant in some canonical passages (see Itv-a. I 178: *casaddo vyatireke* on the Itv. 43: *cakkhumanto ca passanti*).

12. "Syntactic ellipsis is the non-expression of a word or phrase that is, nevertheless, expected to occupy a place in the syntactic structure of a sentence" (McShane 2005, 3).

13. "Ellipsis, however, is the omission of elements that are inferable from the context and thus constitutes a mismatch between sound and meaning. When one utters an elliptical sentence, its interpretation is richer than what is actually pronounced" (Aelbrecht 2010, 1).

14. Cf. *jagataḥ pitarau vande* (Kale 1922, 1.1:2).

15. See M I 206: *kacci vo Anuruddhā*. MN-aṭ II 182[Be]: *Anuruddhā ti vā ekasesanayena vuttaṃ*.

16. See i. Bad destinations for both good and bad destinations (AN. I 136: *vijjaṃ uppādayaṃ bhikkhu sabbā duggatiyo jahe*; AN-a. II 224: *desanāsīsam evetaṃ. sugatiyo pi pana so khīṇāsavo jahati yeva*). ii. Mother for mother and father (J. III 274: *tadāhaṃ sukhito mutto mātaraṃ daṭṭhum āgato*; J-a. III 274: *desanāsīsam etaṃ . . . mātāpitaro daṭṭhuṃ āgatosmī ti attho*). iii. Cause to drink for cause to bathe and drink (J. I 185: *aññam aññehi titthehi assaṃ pāyehi sārathi*; J-a. I 185: *pāyehī ti desanāsīsam etam. nahāpehi ca pāyehi cāti attho*).

in the canon as a single term to denote many components that have a remarkable correlation with each other. A great deal of examples of this type of usage can be attested in the commentaries.[17] However, for the sake of convenient reference, I pay attention only to two of those instances.

The *Dhammaddhajajātaka* portrays the exact nature of deceptive people while encouraging one to live in accordance with the *dhamma*. The third line of the first verse of this *Jātaka* runs thus: "He who practices the doctrine sleeps happily."[18] Buddhaghosa notices the peculiarity of "sleeps" (lit., *seti*) in this line. I am not quite certain whether he has prudently foreseen a possibility of a slapdash reader taking this line as "one who

17. It should be noted here that some accounts use *desanāsīsamatta* tantamount to *desanāsīsa*. See i. Sleeps happily for be happy in all postures (J. I 141; J-a. I 142). ii. Should sit at ease for should be at ease in four postures (J. V 222; J-a. V 226), iii. Should sit together for should associate all postures (SN I 18; S-a. I 55). iv. Food for four requisites (DN I 5; DN-a. I 81). v. Barley for all kinds of grains (J. II 174; J-a. III 174, but, see: MW 847). vi. Free from a cloud to denote the release from fivefold hindrances that begin with cloud (MN II 104; MN-a. III 340). vii. Swans for all birds (Dhp. 26; Dhp-a. II 170). viii. *Vetaraṇi* for thirty-one hells (SN I 21; SN-a. I 61). ix. *Vetaraṇī* for twenty-four hells (J. III 472; J-a. III 473). x. Not for own sake for "not for own sake, another's sake, for fame, for wealth, and for benefit (J. V 146; J-a. V 147). xi. Garland of *Sereyyaka* (*Barleria cristata*) for any kind of flowers without fragrance but color (J. III 253; J-a. III 253). xii. Faith in Buddha's enlightenment for the faith in the threefold Gems (DN III 237; DN-a. III 1029; MN II 95; MN-a. III 326; AN. III 65; AN-a. III 257). xiii. Those who abstained from divisive words for those who abstained from falsehood, divisive words, harsh words, and those who speak wisely (DN III 196; DN-a III 963). xiv. Should not steal (*nāvahare*) and "should not tell lies" (*na musā bhaṇe*) to denote the abstinence from ten paths of unwholesome deeds (J. III 88; J-a. III 88). xv. Stream-enterer's claim (*sotāpannohamasmī ti*) for four noble individuals' claim (DN II 93; DN-a. II 544). xvi. A consciousness has arisen (*cittaṃ uppannaṃ hoti*) also for the emergence over fifty wholesome thoughts (Dhs. 9; Dhs-a. 67). The case of the exegesis on the *Kurudhammajātaka* is a bit different. It initially equates "color" (*vaṇṇa*) with "gold" (*suvaṇṇa*) and, thereafter, expands it for manifold wealth that begins with coined gold, uncoined gold. See J. II 369: *tava saddhañ ca sīlañ ca viditvāna janādhipa, vaṇṇaṃ añjanavaṇṇena Kāliṅgasmiṃ nimimhase* (Rouse 1895, 2: 253). J-a. II 369: *vaṇṇan ti tadā tasmiṃ dese suvaṇṇaṃ vuccati. desanāsīsam eva cetaṃ. iminā pana padena sabbam pi suvaṇṇahiraññādidhanadhaññaṃ saṅgahitaṃ*. However, taking *vaṇṇa* and *suvaṇṇa* as synonymous can be justifiable. See MW, s.v. *varṇa*: "gold, property (applied to person and things)."

18. J. III 268: *dhammacārī sukham seti*. Cf. Dhp. 22: *dhammapīti sukhaṃ seti*. But the commentary uses *desanāmattaṃ* to qualify *seti* in the Dhp-a. II 127.

practices the doctrine is happy only in sleeping and he is not happy in other postures." In the following interpretation, he extends the literal meaning of "sleeps" by employing this hermeneutical device: " 'Sleeps happily' is a DS. He who practices the doctrine stands, walks, sits, and sleeps happily. [This] illustrates that he is happy in all postures."[19] This interpretation first extends the meaning of "sleeps" to encompass its conceptual totality, that is, the four postures.[20] Subsequently it goes on to apply this term to "all" the postures (*sabbiriyāpathesu*), perhaps on the grounds that there are some postures that cannot be directly included in these four.[21] If we understand the verse line of the *Dhammaddhajajātaka* quoted earlier in accordance with this interpretation, he who practices doctrine obviously lives happily in all postures. In fact, "sleeps happily" (*sukhaṃ seti*) and "sleep happily" (*sukhaṃ senti*) are idioms that are typically used in the canon to denote one's happiness prevailing in all manners of one's behavior.[22] It is now manifest that this DS explanation is helpful to understand "sleeps" more pragmatically.[23] In this way, this DS exegesis usually guides the reader to see the forest for the trees. These kinds of exegeses are equally supportive to the general reader who is unfamiliar with canonical idioms[24] to understand the original meaning of the text. The characteristics of the canonical lemmas qualified as DS that have been discussed so far bring

19. J-a. III 268: *sukhaṃ setī ti desanāsīsam etaṃ, dhammacārī pana sukhaṃ tiṭṭhati gacchati nisīdati sayati, sabbiriyāpathesu sukhito hotī ti dīpeti.*

20. It is generally accepted that there are four basic postures of human beings. This motif is not foreign even to the Pāli canon. See SN 78: *pāṇā cattāro iriyāpathe kappenti kālena gamanaṃ kālena ṭhānaṃ kālena nisajjaṃ kālena seyyaṃ*; Pṭsm. II 19: *catusu iriyāpathesu*. See also DN-a. II 386, MN-a. I 301. Nevertheless, this is not constant in the canon. For instance, MN I 92–93 refers to "walking, standing, asleep, and awake" (*carato ca me tiṭṭhato ca suttassa ca jāgarassa ca*) and here "sitting" is not mentioned.

21. For instance, Ānanda attained final liberation "remaining in a position outside the four postures" (Jayawickrama 1962, 10). See *catu-iriyāpathavirahitaṃ* V-a. I 12. See also Vin. II 286.

22. Especially to convey the idea of "living at ease," these two expressions occur in the Pāli canon. See SN I 41, A. I 138, Dhp. 22, Th. 62, J. I 14.

23. Pragmatics offers an "analysis of what people mean by their utterances [rather] than what the words or phrases in those utterances might mean themselves. Pragmatics is the study of speaker meaning" (Yule 1996, 3).

24. The Pāli canon contains a bulk of idioms. Some of those are fairly inscrutable by examining their morphemes. For example, *lomaṃ pāteti* (MN I 443, Vin. III 183) literally means "to let one's hair drop" (see PED, s.v. *loma*:), yet this is an idiom,

to mind *lakkhaṇāhāra*, one of the hermeneutic principles described in the *Nettippakaraṇa*.[25] Ñāṇamoli translates this term as a "mode of conveying characteristics."[26] As this principle relates, "when one phenomenon is stated out of many phenomena that have common features, the rest of those [that are unstated] are considered to have been stated." These DS exegeses, moreover, resemble synecdoche, a hermeneutic device.[27] Synecdoche functions also as a figure of speech that constitutes in metonymy,[28] as will be indicated shortly. According to Bullinger, synecdoche is one of the prominent rhetorical devices occurring in the Bible.[29] It usually refers to "a figure of speech by which a part is put for the whole."[30] For instance, the Bible uses bow for all kinds of weapons.[31] Furthermore, in Hamlet, we read

---

which denotes one's subduedness or modesty (PED, s.v. *loma*:). As Horner states, "This phrase is almost certainly meant to be taken metaphorically" (1938–1966, 384n1). She renders *na lomaṃ pāteti* as "is not subdued" (Horner 2002, 114), while Ñāṇamoli and Bodhi translate it as "he does not comply" (Ñāṇamoli and Bodhi 1995, 547). See also MN-a. III 153, V-a. III 625.

25. Nett. 30: *ye dhammā ekalakkhaṇā, tesaṃ dhammānaṃ ekasmiṃ dhamme vutte avasiṭṭhā dhammā vuttā bhavanti*. See also Nett. 3: *vuttamhi ekadhamme ye dhammā ekalakkaṇā keci, vuttā bhavanti sabbe so hāro lakkhaṇo nāma*. "When one idea is mentioned, all ideas of like characteristic are mentioned too: this constitutes The Mode Conveying Characteristics" (Ñāṇamoli 1977, 8). It is, however, of worth noting here that the commentators do not juxtapose this hermeneutical strategy in relation to *desanāsīsa* explanations.

26. Ñāṇamoli 1977, 51.

27. McEvoy and Dunne 2002, 71.

28. Synecdoche "is sometimes used as a traditional term for part-and-whole metonymy" (Knowles and Moon 2006, 48); "It is important understand that every metonymy is a synecdoche, but not every synecdoche is a metonymy" (Garcez 1996, 9). See also for metonymy: Littlemore 2005, 193.

29. Bullinger 1898, 625.

30. WCD 894. See also "a figure of speech by which a part is put for the whole . . . the whole for a part" (Whitsitt 2013, 7); "act of taking together" (Enos 2009, 712); "Synecdoche is a trope which heightens the meaning by substituting genus for species, species for genus, part for whole, whole for part" (Joseph 2005, 112; see also Westhelle 2016, 74).

31. KJV 426, Psalm 44: 6: "For I will not trust in my bow, neither shall my sword save me." See also Bullinger 1898, 625. It is interesting to note here that a strikingly similar account appears in the commentary of the *Saṃyuttanikāya* wherein a dagger denotes many weapons with sharpen blades (see S. I 13: *sattiyā viya omaṭṭho*; S-a. I 48: *sattiyā ti desanāsīsam etaṃ. ekatodhārādinā satthenā ti attho*).

brain "for the whole person."[32] According to modern critics, Shakespeare employs this literary device in his works "to achieve verbal economy."[33] It is also justifiable to presume that the commentator's metrical license in versification might have been one of the reasons for the inclusion of a single element to embrace many components in some *gāthās*.

The commentator sometimes employs this hermeneutic device to harmonize some intertextual dichotomies existing in the canon. For example, a number of canonical references demonstrate that the consciousness and mental concomitants (*cetasikas*) are always co-nascent,[34] whereas, as we read in some references in the *sutta* collection[35] and the *Dhammasaṅgaṇī*, a consciousness (*citta*) can also arise alone.[36] Since the Theravāda sources categorically affirm the inseparability and co-nascence of the consciousness and mental concomitants,[37] the *Atthasālinī*, the commentary of the latter text, uses DS interpretation in order to eliminate this discrepancy. Following is one of those references in the *Dhammasaṅgaṇī* (i.) in tandem with its exegesis (ii.):

1. When a wholesome consciousness belonging to the sphere of sensual experience has arisen . . .[38]

2. "Consciousness has arisen" is the heading of this discourse. But consciousness does not arise singly. Just as in saying, "The king has arrived," it is clear that he does not come

32. Vigors 1813, 512. See "The very place puts toys of desperation, / Without more motive, into every brain, / That looks so many fathoms to the sea, / And hears it roar beneath" (*Hamlet*, act 1, scene 4). See Dowden 1899, 41. Shakespeare here uses "brain" for the whole person.

33. Garcez 1996, 9–10.

34. See DS as metonymy later in this chapter.

35. See AN IV 189: *cittaṃ uppādeti*; MN I 79, S V 351: *cittaṃ uppādetā*; MN I 43, 97: *cittaṃ uppādetabbaṃ*.

36. See Dhs. 9 and 234. In addition, some canonical attestations relate that the consciousness arises before mental concomitants. AN I 11: *dhammā akusalā akusalabhāgiyā . . . kusalā kusalabhāgiyā sabbe te manopubbaṅgamā. mano tesaṃ dhammānaṃ paṭhamaṃ uppajjati*; Dhp. 1: *manopubbaṅgamā dhammā*.

37. Karunadasa 2010, 71.

38. Dhs. 9: *yasmiṃ samaye kāmāvacaraṃ kusalaṃ cittaṃ uppannaṃ hoti* (Rhys Davids 1997, 1).

alone without his attendants but comes attended by his retinue, so this consciousness should be understood to have arisen with more than fifty moral (mental) phenomena.[39]

The purpose of this interpretation is obviously to insist the co-nascence as well as the inseparability of mind and mental factors. In the *Kathāvatthu*, we read that a certain Buddhist school attempted to refute the existence of mental concomitants, but, the Theravādins, by adducing two canonical attestations, were able to prove the baselessness of their argument.[40] As the commentary of this text identifies, the Rājagirikas and Siddhatthikas[41] who appear to be subgroups of the Mahāsāṅghika School[42] upheld this view. The present DS exegesis, which is reminiscent of this scholastic debate, can therefore be recognized as a commentator's response to these opponents. Furthermore, this DS interpretation compels the reader to determine that what the canon says is not always equal to what the canon means.

DS as Merismus

As some commentarial exegeses reveal, a pair from a selective list is expressed in the canon to represent the whole list. We can easily identify this feature in the first verse of the *Garahitajātaka*[43] and its commentary as follows:

39. Tin 1920, 1: 90; Dhs-a. 67: *cittaṃ uppannaṃ hotī ti cetaṃ desanāsīsam eva. na pana cittaṃ ekakam eva uppajjati. tasmā yathā rājā āgato ti vutte na parisaṃ pahāya ekako va āgato, rājā parisāya pana saddhiṃ yeva āgato ti paññāyati, evam idam pi paropaṇṇāsakusaladhammehi saddhiṃ yeva uppannan ti veditabbaṃ.*

40. Kv. 338–339: *natthi cetasiko dhammo*. See Aung and Rhys Davids 1915, 197–198; Nyānaponika 2005, 145; Law 1940, 116–117.

41. Kv-a. 95: *seyyathāpi RājagirikaSiddhatthikānaṃ.*

42. Kv-a. 52: *Andhakā nāma Pubbaseliyā Aparaseliyā Rājagiriyā Siddhatthikā ti ime pacchā uppannanikāyā*. See also Law 1940, 62. The *Pañcappakaraṇa-anuṭīkā*, accepting this opinion, further mentions that these four subgroups mostly belong to the Mahāsāṅghika family. Ppk-anṭ. 132[Be]: *Andhakā ti Pubbaseliya-AparaseliyaRājagirikaSiddhatthikā pi yebhuyyena Mahāsaṅghikā evā ti*. See also Bareau 2013, 130 and 134.

43. J. II 185: *hiraññaṃ me suvaṇṇaṃ me esā rattiṃdivā kathā, dummedhānaṃ manussānaṃ ariyadhammaṃ apassataṃ*. "The gold is mine, the precious gold!" so cry they, night and day: These foolish folk cast never a look upon the holy way (Rouse 1895, 2: 130).

> "I have coined gold; I have uncoined gold" this is the
> day-and-night-talk of ignorant people
> who do not see the noble doctrine.

As the commentarial exegesis shows, the coined gold (*hiraññaṃ*) and uncoined gold (*suvaṇṇaṃ*)[44] of this verse represent the whole property (of foolish people).

> "I [have] coined gold; I have uncoined gold" is a mere DS. With these two terms, [he] expressed the entire property, such as ten kinds of gems, grains and curries, fields and land, the biped and the quadruped.[45]

It is obvious that this is a pragmatic interpretation of coined gold and uncoined gold that guides the reader toward a more vivid picture of the message conveyed in the preceding verse, without being confined to its literal meaning. The fact that it alludes to one's manifold possessions and wealth is expressed with these two all-inclusive terms for either the convenience of expression, verbal economy, or *metri causa*. It is also worth considering here that the present verse is octosyllabic. This meter often militates against the poet, expressing his or her ideas in detail. Conversely,

---

44. I follow Norman's rendering of *hirañña* and *suvaṇṇa*. Due to the perplexity of clearly differentiating for these two terms, scholars have attempted to understand them in various ways. See *hiraññasuvaṇṇa* (M. II 70); "gold coins and bullion" (Ñāṇamoli and Bodhi 1995, 688, S I 102[Be]); "bullion and gold" (Bodhi 2000, 193, Vin. I 150); "I will give you gold or I will give you gold ornaments" (Horner 1938–1966, 1602), but Horner differs from this interpretation in Ibid. 106. See also Ibid. 1974 long note, PED, s.v. *hirañña*: "gold & money." Thi. 157: *na hiraññasuvaṇṇena parikkhīyanti āsavā*. "The *āsavas* do not diminish because of gold, coined or uncoined" (Norman 1995, 35). Pruitt, who "relied heavily on" (1999, ix) Norman's translation, gives the same rendering (see Pruitt 1995, 303). See also Vaidya 1958, 302: *dhanadhānyahiraṇyasuvarṇatathaiva ca vastraśubhā*.

45. J-a. II 185: *hiraññaṃ me suvaṇṇaṃ me ti desanāsīsamattam etaṃ. iminā padadvayena dasavidham pi ratanaṃ sabbaṃ pubbaṇṇaparaṇṇaṃ khettavatthuṃ dvipadaṃ catuppadañ ca sabbaṃ . . . āha*. See for *pubbaṇṇa* and *aparaṇṇa* Nidd. II 175: *pubbaṇṇaṃ nāma sāli vīhi yavo godhumo kaṅgu varako kudrūsako. aparaṇṇaṃ nāma sūpeyyaṃ*. Nevertheless, this interpretation is somewhat different in the V-a. II 340. PED, s.v. *sūpeyya*: "belonging to soup, broth, soup."

it urges the poet to write in a more condensed manner.[46] This exegesis demonstrates that the meanings of some canonical terms are richer than they first appear. It further enables the reader to apprehend the ethical admonition in the aforementioned verse in a broader sense, by leading the poet to realize that boasting of his or her own financial prosperity and social status is an ignoble trait. According to theologians, the Bible also contains some expressions that behave in the same manner. At times, the text of the Bible enumerates only two aspects of a phenomenon that consists of many elements in order to encompass the whole. As the rhetoricians point out, this is a literary device named merismus.[47] According to Wasserman, in this figure of speech "a conceptual totality is expressed, *concretum pro abstracto*, by the use of two antipodal terms."[48] Nevertheless, the use of two polar word pairs, as Watson remarks, is not an indispensable feature of this literary device. He further observes, "*Selective listing* is another convenient form of merismus."[49] On this ground, it seems fair to think that any pair from a phenomenon that is endowed with many components can be represented in this figure of speech. Unlike the synecdoche that indicates only "one component for the whole," the present rhetorical device refers to "two elements for the whole." Thus, if the present commentator were writing today, he might very well have argued that this verse from the *Garahitajātaka* carries a merismus. Apart from this instance, this figure of speech is used in several places in the commentarial literature. In a few cases, it is apparent that the commentator implements his proficiency in parallel discourses in the canon when commenting on some terms. He typically does this for the purpose of heightening the doctrinal significance of the exegesis. We

46. In this meter, some ideas are expressed in abbreviated forms in the canon. For instance, Th. 22: *cattāro satipaṭṭhāne satta aṭṭha ca bhāvayaṃ*. According to the commentary, *satta* and *aṭṭha* in this octosyllabic verse line are condensed forms of "seven awakening factors" and "eightfold limbs of the path," respectively (see Th-a. II 42: *sattāti satta bojjhaṅge. aṭṭhāti aṭṭha maggaṅgāni*). See also Norman 1995, 21.

47. This rherorical device also can be recognized as another metonymic term.

48. Wasserman 2003, 61; Klein 2004, 302.

49. Watson 1984, 321. "Merismus belongs to metonymy (the part for the whole) and is a form of ellipsis, akin to hendiadys. . . . It is the total concept that is important; the components are not significant in isolation. Merismus, then, is an abbreviated way of expressing a totality" (Watson 1984, 321).

find the following statement in the *Ādittasutta* of the *Saṃyuttanikāya*: "The world is ablaze with aging and death."[50] As the introduction of this discourses reveals, an anonymous deity made this utterance. It insists that both aging and death are highly immutable factors that govern in the world. The deity uses the metaphorical term *ādīpito* (lit., is ablaze) to vividly illustrate the inevitable influence of these two forces upon all living beings. The interpretation of this utterance given as follows makes obvious that aging and death here play the role of a merismus: "This, 'with aging and death' is a DS. Indeed, the world is ablaze with eleven kinds of fires that begins with lust."[51] With the help of information given in commentarial literature,[52] we are able to ascertain that the (extended) *Ādittasutta* in the *Saṃyuttanikāya*[53] as well as Uruvelakassapa's account in the *Mahāvagga*[54] were in the commentator's mind when he offered this DS interpretation. Everything is ablaze, as these two canonical accounts demonstrate, with eleven factors, namely, i. lust, ii. hatred, iii. delusion, iv. birth, v. aging, vi. death, vii. sorrow, viii. lamentation, ix. pain, x. displeasure, and xi. despair. This exegesis is reasonably plausible since it is supported by reliable textual affirmations.[55]

50. Bodhi 2000, 120; S. I 31: *ādīpito loko jarāya maraṇena ca.*

51. S-a. I 82: *jarāya maraṇena cā ti desanāsīsam etaṃ. rāgādīhi pana ekādasahi aggīhi loko āditto va.* See also J. III 471; J-a. III 471.

52. The motif of eleven kinds of fire beginning with lust is common in the commentarial literature (see for *rāgādīhi ekādasahi aggīhi* Dhp-a. III 103, Ud-a. 356, Th-a. I 98. See also S-a. II 279, Vism-ṭ. II 448[Be]: *ekādasahi aggīhi*). According to the subcommentary of the *Saṃyuttanikāya* (6th c. CE?), these eleven kinds of fire begin with lust and end with despair (see SN-aṭ. 227[Be]: *ekādasahī ti rāgādīhi upāyāsapariyosānehi ekādasahi santāpanaṭṭhena aggīhi*). The *Sāratthadīpanī*, subcommentary of the *Vinaya* (12th c. CE) goes further, enumerating eleven components of metaphorical fire (Sd-ṭ. II 89[Be]: *ekādasahi aggīhī ti rāgadosamohajātijarāmaraṇasokaparidevadukkhadomanassupāyāsasaṅkhātehi*).

53. SN IV 19–20.

54. Vin. I 24–35.

55. SN IV 20, Vin. I 34: *sabbaṃ bhikkhave ādittaṃ . . . kena ādittaṃ? rāgagginā dosagginā mohagginā ādittaṃ, jātiyā jarāya maraṇena sokehi paridevehi dukkhehi domanassehi upāyāsehi ādittan ti vadāmi.* See also Bodhi 2000, 1143; Horner 1938–1966, 1433. The deity's utterance quoted previously states that the world (*loko*) is ablaze whereas, in line with these two attestations, the whole (*sabbaṃ*) is aflame. Since the "world" constitutes a "whole" (SN IV 39–40, 52), this appears no contradiction. Furthermore, these two canonical references do not recognize all eleven factors as fires but the

DS as Metonymy

At times, DS behaves as a "substitution, which resembles metonymy,[56] which is "one of the most common figures of speech in the Bible."[57] As linguists show, this literary device deals with a "vehicle" and "target" relationship. Kövecses explains its nature thus: "There is an entity, or element, that "stands for" another entity, or element. The element that stands for another element is the vehicle and the element for which it stands is the target."[58] For instance, we can consider the sentence: "The dam has dried up." Here, "the dam" refers to the water in it.[59] Shakespeare substitutes steel for sword in *Macbeth*.[60] The commentators substitute new (ahistorical) meanings to lemmas when they consider that the literal meaning of those convey controversial or inappropriate notions. The most significant reason for Buddhaghosa to provide new interpretations of a number of canonical lemmas in a number of accounts is most probably his preference to be in tune with Mahāvihāra *Abhidhamma* theories. The following statement that appears in the *Dīghanikāya* is particularly interesting with regard to this tendency: "There are, O monks, certain gods called nonpercipient beings."[61] As the literal meaning of this statement suggests, there are certain deities who do not have perception (*saññā*), thus they are qualified as nonpercipients (*asaññasattā*). Whereas Buddhaghosa's exegesis on this statement establishes a totally different opinion: " 'Non-percipient beings' is a DS. [This] means the beings who bear mere material bodies in whom

first three. Yet, "is ablaze" (*ādittaṃ*) is commonly used to qualify all eleven features. Perhaps, because of this reason, the commentarial interpretation identifies all the components as fires (*ekādasahi aggīhi*).

56. "A Metonymy is the substituting of one word for another" (Zuck 1991, 150).

57. Phillips 1987, 45.

58. Kövecses 2006, 98. See also Dancygier and Sweetser 2014, 5.

59. Seto 1999, 103.

60. See "Disdaining fortune, with his brandish'd steel, / Which smoked with bloody execution" (Chambers 1907, 30). See also, "The material cause may also be substituted for the object which is formed of it" (Vigors 1813, 506). In addition, Shakespeare, in *The Merchant of Venice*, uses "the wry-neck'd fife" for a fife-player: "when you hear the drum And the vile squealing of the wry-neck'd fife" (act 2, scene 5; see Withers 1916, 31).

61. DN I 28: *santi bhikkhave Asaññasattā nāma devā*.

consciousness does not arise."[62] Nonpercipient gods do not have, as this DS interpretation shows, a consciousness; thus they merely possess physical bodies. We are able to notice that this explanation cleverly equates consciousness with perception. That is to say, as Buddhaghosa tells us, *asañña* (lit., nonpercipient) is tantamount to *acitta* (lit., nonconscious) in this context. In accordance with the linguistic viewpoint previously mentioned, here *saññā* is the vehicle and *citta* is the target. I believe that several canonical attestations have prompted Buddhaghosa to make this metonymic interpretation. First, the *Vibhaṅga* mentions that the nonpercipient gods come into being without contact, feeling, perception, and consciousness.[63] Second, as the *Kathāvatthu* depicts, a certain non-Theravāda school maintained a view that perception is extant in nonpercipient beings.[64] As we see in the latter text, the Theravāda fraternity who stands in opposition to this idea attempts to defeat the opponents by posing an array of cross-questions.[65] The commentary of this text relates that Andhakas also held this view.[66] This DS interpretation obviously attacks the opponent's perspective on the existence of nonpercipient beings. Third, in addition to the references mentioned here, some other canonical, para-canonical, and commentarial accounts further affirm the inseparability of the mind and perception. As the *Cūlavedallasutta* and *Kāmabhūsutta* emphasize, perception is bound up with consciousness,[67] while the *Milindapañha* insists that seven mental concomitants, including perception (*saññā*), co-arise (*taṃsahajātā*) with consciousness (*viññāṇaṃ*).[68] The *Visuddhimagga* also confirms this opinion, stressing the co-nascence (*cittehi sahajāto*) of these same mental concomitants.[69] Besides, as the chapter titled "Cetasikakathā" of the *Kathāvatthu*

62. DN-a. I 118: *Asaññasattā ti desanāsīsam etaṃ, acittuppādarūpamattaka-attabhāvā ti attho.*

63. Vibh. 419: *Asaññasattā devā . . . aphassakā avedanakā asaññakā acetanakā acittakā pātubhavanti.*

64. Kv. 260: *Asaññasattesu saññā atthī ti? āmantā.*

65. Kv. 260–263.

66. Kv-a. 72.

67. M. I 301, S. IV 293: *saññā . . . citta-paṭibaddhā.*

68. Mil. 56.

69. Vism. 589.

demonstrates, thirteen mental concomitants, including perception, are concomitant, co-nascent, con-yoked, conjoined with consciousness. These mental concomitants have simultaneous arising and simultaneous cessation, with consciousness. Furthermore, they share the same physical base and apprehend the same object as consciousness.[70] All of these accounts clearly portray the fact that consciousness and perception are inseparable. On these grounds, it is justifiable to presume that the former does not exist without the latter. On the other hand, in line with the Theravāda *Abhidhamma* treatises, perception is one of the seven universal concomitants, and it always occurs with the other six *cetasika*s such as "contact" and "feeling."[71] However, it should be stressed here that unlike the canonical *Abhidhamma* texts and treatises, the term nonpercipient abode (*asaññasatta*) does not occur in an explicit or a demarcated sense in the discourses. As far as I can tell, the term "nonpercipient" cannot be found in the books of the Discipline (*vinaya*), while few references to it can be attested in the *sutta* collection.[72] I shall return to the entire sentence[73] of the *Brahmajālasutta* reference that is partly mentioned earlier, since it gives a clearer picture of the perception of nonpercipient deities: "There are *bhikkhus*, certain gods called 'nonpercipient beings.' When perception arises in them, those gods pass away from that plane."[74] As this statement explicitly states, these gods named "nonpercipients" pass away from that abode as a consequence of the emergence of perception (*saññuppādā*), and it further points out

70. Kv. 338–339: *cittena sahagatā sahajātā saṃsaṭṭhā sampayuttā ekuppādā ekanirodhā ekavatthukā ekārammaṇā*. See also Kv-a. 95. Law 1940, 116–117; Karunadasa 2010, 71–72.

71. See Bodhi 1999, 77–78. The Sarvāstivāda *Abhidharma* also maintains that mental concomitants including perception occur in every consciousness. "What corresponds to *sabbacittasādharaṇa* in the Sarvastivada *Abhidharma* is the category called the Mahabhūmika-dharma" (Y. Karunadasa email correspondence on May 18, 2016); Gokhale 1947, 79: *vedanā cetanā saṃjñā chandaḥ sparśo matiḥ smṛtiḥ manaskāro'dhimokṣaś ca samādhiḥ sarvacetasi;* AKB 54 (Pradhan 1975): *ime kile daśa dharmāḥ sarvatra cittakṣaṇe samagrā bhavanti*; AKB 189 (Pruden 1988–1990).

72. DN III 33, A. IV 401, Nidd. 280. DN II 69–70: *asaññasattāyatanaṃ*.

73. DN I 28: *santi bhikkhave Asaññasattā nāma devā, saññuppādā ca pana te deva tamhā kāyā cavanti.*

74. Bodhi 2007, 27.

that they are able to survive in that abode "as long as" the perception does not arise in them.[75] This reference suggests that perception might suddenly be activated in them, which perhaps had previously been deactivated. The opponent that we saw earlier in the *Kathāvatthu* insists that although perception is extant in nonpercipient beings, it does not perform its function.[76] He further stresses that those deities possess perception only in the moments of decease and rebirth, but not in the moment of existing.[77] By contrast, as previously noted, the *Vibhaṅga* categorically states that consciousness arises in them only when they come into being. It is worth noting here that the Theravādins do not reject the existence of consciousness in this controversy, even though they fervently attempt to refute the presence of perception in the abode of nonpercipients. As we already know, both canonical as well as commentarial affirmations support the view that perception always occurs with consciousness (*citta*), and existentially depends upon it. On these grounds, one cannot reject the existence of only perception in the nonpercipient abode because it clearly contravenes those Theravāda scriptural authorities. Accordingly, to be in agreement with the Theravāda perspective on perception, one has to refute the existence of consciousness in the nonpercipient abode as Buddhaghosa does in the present DS interpretation. Obviously, when consciousness is rejected, the mental factors are also automatically to be rejected. It is interesting to note here that Dhammapāla (6th c. CE) and Upasena (9th c. CE) apparently did not share this view while also disagreeing with each other. The former accepted the existence of immaterial phenomena (i.e., mental concomitants including perception) in the nonpercipient abode.[78]

---

75. Some renderings support this view. See: "As soon as an idea occurs to them they fall from that state" (Rhys Davids 1900, 1: 41); "those devas decease from that group as soon as consciousness arises in them" (Law 1940, 88).

76. See Kv. 262 *Asaññasattesu saññā atthi na ca tāya saññāya saññākaraṇīyaṃ karotī ti? āmantā.*

77. See Kv. 263: *saññā . . . cutikāle ca uppattikāle ca atthi, ṭhitikāle natthi.* See also Aung and Rhys Davids 1915, 153.

78. DN-aṭ. I 217: *saññaṃ dhuraṃ katvā Bhagavatā ayaṃ desanā katā. na pana tattha aññesaṃ arūpadhammānaṃ abhāvato.* "This preaching is made by the Buddha having taken perception as its main factor, but it is not due to the absence of other immaterial phenomena in that [abode]." But, both *Chaṭṭhasaṅgīti* and Sinhalese (SHB) editions read this as *atthibhāvato* instead of *abhāvato* (Be [Burmese edition] I 166 and Se [Sinhalese edition] 117). *Dhuraṃ katvā*, subcommentaries define, is "taking [it] as

Whereas according to the latter, only perception disappears there.[79] This shows a lack of uniformity regarding some doctrinal theories within the Mahāvihāra fraternity. Apart from this account, Buddhaghosa employs several metonymic DS interpretations in his commentaries. For instance, he substitutes wisdom (*paññā*) and feeling (*vedanā*) for perception (*saññā*) and attention (*mansasikāra*), respectively. Notably, all these substitutions are employed to suit *Abhidhamma* analyses.[80]

Inconsistencies

Some DS exegeses are debatable, and a few of those contradict the canon. It would suffice to pay our attention to one such references appearing in *Sumaṅgalavilāsinī*, the commentary of the *Dīghanikāya*. As the *Saṅgīti-sutta* of the latter canonical text states, the monk whose taints are fully abandoned (*khīṇāsavo*) never[81] 1) kills a living creature, 2) steals, 3) engages in sexual intercourse, 4) speaks falsehood, and 5) does not hoard

---

forerunner or main factor." See Nett-ṭ. 147[Be]: *dhuraṃ katvā ti jeṭṭhakaṃ pubbaṅgamaṃ katvā*; Vjb. 171[Be]: *dhuraṃ katvā ti purimaṃ katvā*. The *Satyasiddhiśāstra* also mirrors a controversy regarding the cessation of consciousness in the nonpercipient sphere. See Sastri 1978, 400. Many dictionaries silently accept Buddhaghosa's interpretation of nonpercipient beings. See BHSD, s.v. *asaṃjñisattva*: "having a nature that is free from consciousness"; CPD, s.v. *asaññasatta*: "the Unconscious Beings."

79. Nidd-a. II 357: *Asaññasattā ti sabbena sabbaṃ saññ'ābhāvena Asaññabhave nibbattā.*

80. Furthermore, he substitutes feeling (*vedanā*) for both rapture (*pīti*) and mental formation (*cittasaṅkhāra*). See MN-a. IV 140 (on MN III 84) and SN-a. V 271(on the SN V 324): *desanāsīsaṃ panetaṃ. yath'eva hi 'aniccasaññābhāvanānuyogamanuyuttā ti ettha saññānāmena paññā vuttā, evam idhāpi manasikāranāmena vedanā vuttā ti veditabbā. ekasmiṃ hi catukke paṭhamapade pītisīsena vedanā vuttā, dutiyapade sukhan ti sarūpeneva vuttā. cittasaṅkhārapadadvaye 'saññā ca vedanā ca cetasikā ete dhammā cittapaṭibaddhā cittasaṅkhārā'[1] ti vacanato'vitakkavicāre ṭhapetvā sabbe pi cittasampayuttakā dhammā cittasaṅkhāre saṅgahitā'[2] ti vacanato cittasaṅkhāranāmena vedanā vuttā. taṃ sabbaṃ manasikāranāmena saṅgahetvā idha sādhukaṃ manasikāran ti āha*. See also Ñāṇamoli and Bodhi 1995, 1331n1123; Bodhi 2000, 1952n309. The underlined first citation is from the *Paṭisambhidāmagga* (Pṭsm. I 188). Although the second citation is apparently taken from the *Yamaka* (Ymk. I 229), the last part of it is slightly changed.

81. This discourse reads *abhabbo* (lit., "is incapable of").

possessions.[82] Buddhaghosa remarks that the term *khīṇāsava* is a DS in this context. This term, therefore, refers not only to one who is fully liberated[83] but also to three other types of individuals who are in lower stages of realization, namely, 1) Stream-enterer, 2) Once-returner, and 3) Nonreturner.[84] It is obvious that *khīṇāsava* here functions as a synecdoche when considered from a rhetorical perspective. We should bear in mind that *khīṇāsava* and *arahant* are synonymous;[85] they thus refer to fully liberated ones. The canon typically uses several specific appellations that illustrate *khīṇāsava*'s profundity, such as "he who utterly destroyed the fetters of existence," "completely liberated through final knowledge," and so forth.[86] By contrast, in the canon, this kind of superlative designation is not used in relation to individuals who have attained one of the other three stages of realization because they have not yet attained full enlightenment.[87] The application of the aforementioned five qualities to these three individuals is, therefore, very problematic. On the other hand, some textual attestations militate against Buddhaghosa's claim. For instance, as the third of these five qualities, *khīṇāsava* does not engage

82. DN III 235: *abhabbo āvuso khīṇāsavo bhikkhu sañcicca pāṇaṃ jīvitā voropetuṃ . . . adinnaṃ theyyasaṅkhātaṃ ādiyituṃ . . . methunaṃ dhammaṃ paṭisevituṃ . . . sampajānamusā bhāsituṃ . . . sannidhikārakaṃ kāme paribhuñjituṃ seyyathāpi pubbe āgārikabhūto*. The Elder Sāriputta preached this discourse and the Buddha attested it. See DN III 271.

83. *Khīṇāsava* is a popular epithet in the canon for the *arahant*, that is, he who attained fully liberation.

84. DN-a. III 1027: *desanāsīsam eva. sotāpannādayo pi pana abhabbā*. "This is indeed a *desanāsīsa*. [Other three individuals that] begin with the stream-enterer are incapable of [doing these five things]."

85. See DN III 83: *bhikkhu arahaṃ khīṇāsavo*. See also DN III 97, Ud. 46.

86. DN III 83, MN I 4, SN III 161, AN III 359: *parikkhīṇabhavasaṃyojano sammadaññāvimutto*. See Bodhi 2012, 921.

87. The canon, by using different idioms to qualify these three individuals, clearly demarcates them from the *arahant*. The *Mahālisutta* is one of the best examples to ascertain this difference. See DN I 156: (i.) *sotāpanno hoti avinipātadhammo niyato sambodhiparāyaṇo* . . . (ii.) *rāgadosamohānaṃ tanuttā sakadāgāmī hoti, sakid eva imaṃ lokaṃ āgantvā dukkhassantaṃ karoti* . . . (iii.) *pañcannaṃ orambhāgiyānaṃ saṃyojanānaṃ parikkhayā opapātiko hoti, tattha parinibbāyī, anāvattidhammo tasmā lokā*. These divergent phraseologies well depict their spiritual status, and explain how they are distinguishable from *arahant*.

in sexual intercourse. On the contrary, this is not true with regard to the cases of the stream-enterer and once-returner since they can have family lives. Dhammadinna and his five hundred followers, for example, who have evidently attained stream-entry, had sexual relationships with their wives,[88] as did Isidatta, who was a once-returner.[89]

DS and Multiple Connotations

As previously noted, to translate the word DS as "heading for a discourse," or render it in similar ways, does not always do justice to the multivalence of the term. Any translation of the word needs to incorporate the range of ways it is employed to highlight different aspects of canonical expression of meaning. One further example can be used to demonstrate this. The following stanza occurs in the *Āṭānāṭiyasutta*, and its commentary: " 'Those who have been quenched in this world, had insight in accordance with reality';[90] such persons who abstained from [speaking] divisive words are great and free from diffidence."[91] This verse shows that those who see reality abstain from speaking divisive words (*apisuṇā*). It is obvious that *apisuṇā* is one of the components of fourfold virtuous verbal conduct.[92] Accordingly, Buddhaghosa extends this term to those four factors in the *Sumaṅgalavilāsinī* as follows: "This, *apisuṇā*, is a mere DS. This means [they] abstain from speaking falsehoods, divisive words, and harsh words; and [they] speak wisely."[93] According to this interpretation, *apisuṇā*, being

88. See SN V 407. This account relates *puttasambādhasayanaṃ ajjhāvasantehi*. As the literal meaning of this statement says, they are "dwelling in a home crowded with children" (Bodhi 2000, 1834). This is obviously a euphemistic expression that often occurs in the Pāli canon to symbolize one's sexual relationship.

89. AN III 348: *Isidatto abrahmacārī ahosi sadārasantuṭṭho*; Bodhi 2012, 911; Hare 1973, 246.

90. Anālayo 2012, 48.

91. DN III 196: *ye cāpi nibbutā loke yathābhūtaṃ vipassisuṃ, te janā apisuṇā mahantā vītasāradā*; Walshe 1995, 472; Rhys Davids and Rhys Davids 1921, 3: 190.

92. See DN II 312: *musāvādā veramaṇī pisuṇāya vācāya veramaṇī pharusāya vācāya veramaṇī samphappalāpā veramaṇī ayaṃ vuccati bhikkhave sammāvācā*. See also MN III 74, SN V 9.

93. DN-a. III 963: *apisuṇā ti desanāsīsamattam etaṃ, amusā apisuṇā apharusā mantabhāṇino ti attho.*

a synecdoche, represents those who refrain from fourfold verbal misconduct. I don't know of any canonical proof to establish the view that the "abstinence from [speaking] divisive words" has special prominence among the fourfold virtuous verbal conduct. The discourses typically list these four as equally important factors under right speech. Alternatively, the canon supports the view that abstinence from falsehood is the most prominent of verbal misdeeds, since telling lies is a serious offense.[94] These facts show that Buddhaghosa's label, that is, DS, does not stand for the "headword" in this context. It instead denotes the sense of "part of the whole." To put this differently, *apisuṇā* here plays the role of *lakkhaṇāhāra* or synecdoche. Cone renders DS as "indication of a category."[95] This evokes two subcommentarial interpretations offered for this term:

1. A part of the [main] teaching[96]
2. A mere example or a sign of the whole by means of a single component[97]

In addition to these two, the explanation appearing in the subcommentary of the *Saṃyuttanikāya* shows the possibility of DS occurring in the sense of substitution, that is, metonymy.[98]

Conclusion

DS is widespread in Buddhaghosa's commentaries. It is utilized for special modes of interpretation that exhort the reader to transcend the literal meaning of some canonical statements. The ways in which it is employed, to indicate that more than the literal meaning is inferred, is primarily

94. Itv. 18: *ekadhammaṃ atītassa bhikkhave purisapuggalassa nāhaṃ tassa kiñci papakammaṃ akaraṇīyan ti vadāmi. katamaṃ ekadhammaṃ? yathayidaṃ bhikkhave sampajānamusāvādo*. See also Dhp. 50.

95. See DOP, s.v. *desanāsīsa*.

96. DN-aṭ. III 320: *desanāpadeso*.

97. DN-aṭ. III 196: *nidassanamattaṃ . . . avayavena vā samudāyupalakkhaṇam*.

98. SN-aṭ. II 522[Be]: *sarūpato aññāpadesato apadisati*.

threefold, notwithstanding some inconsistencies, as synecdoche, merismus, and metonymy. In general, the three ways in which DS is employed are instances of substitution, either of a part for a whole, or based on some aspect of equivalence. The range of uses are highly nuanced and reveal more than one single exegetical word should; that is, even *abhidhamma* rivalries come into view when we attempt to analyze its meaning. Given all of this, it is difficult to imagine a translation of the term that does full justice to the vicissitudes of meaning of DS. Perhaps Cone comes closest, especially if conjoined with the subcommentarial explanatory notes.

References

Aelbrecht, Lobke. 2010. *The Syntactic Licensing of Ellipsis*. Amsterdam: John Benjamins.

Anālayo, Bhikkhu. 2012. "The Dynamics of Theravāda Insight Meditation." In *Buddhist Meditation Traditions: An International Symposium*. Taiwan: Dharma Drum.

Aung, Shwe Zan, and C. A. F. Rhys Davids, trans. 1915. *Points of Controversy or Subjects of Discourse, Being a Translation of the Kathā-vatthu from the Abhidhamma-piṭaka*. Oxford: Pali Text Society.

Bareau, André. 2013. *The Buddhist Schools of the Small Vehicle*. Honolulu: University of Hawai'i Press.

Bodhi, Bhikkhu, ed. 1999. *A Comprehensive Manual of Abhidhamma: The Abhidhammattha Sangaha of Ācariya Anuruddha*. Onalaska, WA: Pariyatti.

———, trans. 2000. *The Connected Discourses of the Buddha*. Boston: Wisdom.

———, trans. 2007. *The Discourse on the All-Embracing Net of Views: The Brahmajāla Sutta and Its Commentaries*. Kandy: Buddhist Publication Society.

———, trans. 2012. *Numerical Discourses of the Buddha*. Boston: Wisdom.

Bullinger, E. W. 1898. *Figures of Speech Used in the Bible*. London: Messrs. Eyre & Spottiswoode, Great New Street, E. C.

Chambers, E. K. 1907. *The Tragedy of Macbeth*. Toronto: Morang Educational.

Dancygier, Barbara, and Eve Sweetser. 2014. *Figurative Language*. Cambridge: Cambridge University Press.

Dowden, Edward. 1899. *The Works of Shakespeare: The Tragedy of Hamlet*. London: Methuen and Co.

Enos, Theresa. 2009. *Encyclopedia of Rhetoric and Composition*. New York: Routledge, Taylor & Francis Group.

Garcez, Christopher M. 1996. *William Shakespeare's "The Taming of the Shrew."* N.p.: Research and Education Association.

Gunasekara, L. R. 2008. *Buddhist Commentarial Literature*. Kandy: Buddhist Publication Society.
Hare, E. M., trans. 1973. *Book of the Gradual Sayings*. Vol. 3. London: Pali Text Society.
Hinüber, Oskar von. 1996. *A Handbook of Pāli Literature*. Berlin: Walter de Gruyter.
Horner, I. B., trans. 1938–1966. *The Book of the Discipline*. London: Pali Text Society.
———, trans. 2002. *The Collection of the Middle Length Sayings*. Vol. 2. Oxford: Pali Text Society.
Jayawickrama, N. A. 1962. *Inception of Discipline and Vinaya Nidāna*. London: Pali Text Society.
Joseph, Sister Miriam. 2005. *Shakespeare's Use of the Art of the Language*. Philadelphia: Paul Dry Books.
Kale, M. R. 1922. *Raghuvaṃśa of Kālidāsa*. Bombay: Gopal Narayen & Co.
Karunadasa, Y. 2010. *Theravāda Abhidhamma*. Hong Kong: Centre of Buddhist Studies.
Kieffer-Pülz, Petra. 2016. "Reuse of Text in Pāli Legal Commentaries." *Buddhist Studies Review* 33, nos. 1–2: 9–46.
Klein, William W. 2004. *Introduction to Biblical Interpretation: Revised and Explained*. Nashville: Thomas Nelson.
Knowles, Murray, and Rosamund Moon. 2006. *Introducing Metaphor*. Oxon: Routledge.
Kövecses, Zoltán. 2006. *Language, Mind, and Culture: A Practical Introduction*. New York: Oxford University Press.
Lamotte, Étienne. 1993. "The Assessment of Textual Interpretation in Buddhism." In *Buddhist Hermeneutics*, edited by Donald S. Lopez, 11–27. Delhi: Motilal Banarsidass.
Law, B. C. 1940. *Debates Commentary*. London: Oxford University Press.
Littlemore, Jeannette. 2005. *Metonymy: Hidden Shortcuts in Language, Thought and Communication*. Cambridge: Cambridge University Press.
McEvoy, J. J., and Michael Dunne, eds. 2002. *History and Eschatology in John Scottus Eriugena and His Time*. Leuven: University Press.
McShane, Marjorie J. 2005. *A Theory of Ellipsis*. New York: Oxford University Press.
Minayeff, J., ed. 1886. "The Gandha-vaṃsa." *Journal of the Pali Text Society* 12: 54–81.
Ñāṇamoli, Bhikkhu, trans. 1956. *The Path of Purification*. Kandy: Buddhist Publication Society.
———, trans. 1977. *The Guide (Netti-ppakaraṇaṃ)*. London: Pali Text Society.
Ñāṇamoli, Bhikkhu, and Bhikkhu Bodhi, trans. 1995. *The Middle Length Discourses of the Buddha*. Kandy: Buddhist Publication Society.

Norman, K. R., trans. 1995. *The Elders' Verses*. Vol. 2. Oxford: Pali Text Society.
Nyānaponika, Bhikkhu, trans. 2005. *Darlegung Der Bedeutung* (*Atthasālinī*). Oxford: Pali Text Society.
Phillips, John. 1987. *Bible Explorer's Guide: How to Understand and Interpret the Bible*. Grand Rapids: Kregel.
Pieris, Aloysius. 2004. *Studies in the Philosophy and Literature of Pāli Ābhidhammika Buddhism*. Colombo: Ecumenical Institute for Study and Dialogue.
Pradhan, P., ed. 1975. *Abhidharmakośabhāṣyam of Vasubandhu*. Patna: Jayaswal Research Institute
Pruden, Leo, M., ed. 1988–1990. *Abhidharma Kosa Bhasyam of Vashubandhu*. Berkeley: Asian Humanities Press.
Pruitt, William, trans. 1999. *The Commentary on the Verses of the Therīs*. Oxford: Pali Text Society.
Rhys Davids, C. A. F., trans. 1900. *A Buddhist Manual of Psychological Ethics of the Fourth-Century CE (Dhammasangiṇi)*. London: Royal Asiatic Society.
Rhys Davids, T. W., and C. A. F. Rhys Davids, trans. 1910–1921. *Dialogues of the Buddha*. 3 vols. London: Oxford University Press.
Rouse, W. H. D., trans. 1895. *Jātaka or Stories of the Buddha's Former Births*. Vol. 2. Cambridge: Cambridge University Press.
Sastri, N. Aiyaswami. 1978. *Satyasiddhiśāstra of Harivarman*. Vol. 2. Baroda: Oriental Institute.
Seto, Ken-ichi. 1999. "Distinguishing Metonymy from Synecdoche." In *Metonymy in Language and Thought*, edited by Klaus-Uwe Panther and Günter Radden, 91–120. Amsterdam: John Benjamins.
Tin, Maung, trans. 1920–1921. *The Expositor (Atthasālinī)*. 2 Vols. London: Pali Text Society.
Vaidya, P. L., ed. 1958. *Lalitavistara*. Buddhist Sanskrit Text. No. 1. Dabhanga: Mithila Institute of Post-Graduate Studies.
Vigors, N. A. 1813. *An Inquiry into the Nature and Extent of Poetick License*. London: T. Bensley Printer.
Walshe, Maurice, trans. 1995. *Long Discourses of the Buddha*. Boston: Wisdom.
Wasserman, Nathan. 2003. *Style and Form in Old-Babylonian Literary Texts*. Boston: Brill.
Watson, Wilfred G. E. 1984. *Classical Hebrew Poetry: A Guide to Its Techniques*. Sheffield: JSOT Press.
Westhelle, Vitor. 2016. *Transfiguring Luther: The Planetary Promise of Luther's Theology*. Eugene, OR: Cascade Books.
Whitsitt, Samuel Porter. 2013. *Metonymy, Synecdoche, and the Disorders of Contiguity*. N.p.: libreriauniversitaria.it edizioni.
Withers, H. L. 1916. *The Merchant of Venice*. London: D. C. Heath and Company.

Yule, George. 1996. *Pragmatics*. Oxford: Oxford University Press.
Zuck, Roy B. 1991. *Basic Bible Interpretation: A Practical Guide to Discovering Biblical Truth*. N.p.: Victor Books.

Contributors

Alice Collett is a specialist in ancient Indian religion, especially Buddhism, and most of her work to date concentrates on women in the ancient world. She has published over twenty journal articles and book chapters on the topic, as well as several full-length volumes. Her first edited volume is entitled *Women in Early Indian Buddhism: Comparative Textual Studies* (2013) and her first monograph, *Lives of Early Buddhist Nuns: Biographies as History* (2016). She is currently working on two monographs, the first entitled *Women in Early Historic India: The Changing Political Landscape* and a second book on women in Buddhism aimed at the general reader. She is currently Director of the South Asia History Project, United Kingdom.

Collett Cox is Professor Emerita of Sanskrit and Buddhist Studies at the University of Washington. Her main area of research is early Indian Buddhist Abhidharma, specifically, Abhidharma doctrinal controversies and Sarvāstivāda textual history. She is also Assistant Director of the Early Buddhist Manuscripts Project at the University of Washington and is completing a translation and study of a Gāndhārī manuscript containing an early exegetical or Abhidharma text.

Aruna Gamage is Senior Lecturer at the Department of Pali and Buddhist Studies, University of Kelaniya, Sri Lanka. He received undergraduate and postgraduate training in Pāli and Buddhist Studies at Kelaniya University. After completing his PhD at SOAS, University of London, he carried out research at IIAS, Leiden University, as a Research Fellow.

Natalie Gummer, who received her PhD from Harvard University in 2000, is Professor of Religious Studies at Beloit College in Beloit, Wisconsin. Her research examines textual practices in premodern South Asian Mahāyāna Buddhist literary cultures, especially ritual uses of texts and oral performance, as well as the translation practices through which those cultures are transmitted and transformed. She is coeditor of *Defining Buddhism(s): A Reader*, the author of several articles on Buddhist ritual and literary culture, and is currently completing a monograph entitled *Performing the Buddha's Body: Mahāyāna Sūtras as Ritual Speech Acts.*

Elizabeth Harris is currently an Honorary Senior Research Fellow within the Edward Cadbury Centre for the Public Understanding of Religion at the University of Birmingham, United Kingdom. Previous to this, before her retirement, she was Associate Professor in Religious Studies at Liverpool Hope University, United Kingdom. Her specialist research areas include Theravada Buddhism, Buddhism and conflict, the encounter between Buddhism and the West under imperialism, and Buddhist-Christian studies. Her publications include: *Theravada Buddhism and the British Encounter: Religious, Missionary and Colonial Experience in Nineteenth Century Sri Lanka* (2006); *Religion, Space and Conflict in Sri Lanka: Colonial and Postcolonial Contexts* (2018); and, coedited with John O'Grady, *Meditation in Buddhist-Christian Encounter: A Critical Analysis* (2019).

Oskar von Hinüber is Professor Emeritus for Indologie of the Albert–Ludwigs Universität, Freiburg. After acting as professor in Mainz (1974–1981) he took up the professorship for Indology at the Albert Ludwigs–Universität, Freiburg (1981–2006). He is ordinary member of the Akademie der Wissenschaften und der Literatur, Mainz; associé étranger (Membre de l'Institut) of the Académie des Inscriptions et Belles-Lettres, Paris; and corresponding member of the Österreichische Akademie der Wissenschaften, Vienna. In 2001 he received the Friedrich Weller Award, Sächsische Akademie der Wissenschaften, Leipzig, and in 2002 honorary memberships in the American Oriental Society, the Deutsche Morgenländische Gesellschaft, and in 2014 the International Association of Buddhist Studies. He was and is member of the board (sometimes chair) of various organizations in the field of humanities and held visiting professorships in Vienna, Oxford, Paris, and Tokyo, conducting field research in India, Thailand, and North Pakistan. His publications concentrate mainly on the linguistic history of Buddhism, epigraphy, and cultural history.

C. V. Jones is Affiliated Lecturer at the Faculty of Divinity and Bye-Fellow of Selwyn College, University of Cambridge. He completed doctoral research on the Indian *tathāgatagarbha* tradition and postdoctoral research concerned with Indian Buddhist attitudes to their religious interlocutors at the University of Oxford. His first monograph, *The Buddhist Self: On* Tathāgatagarbha *and* Ātman, was published in 2020.

Dhivan Thomas Jones lectures in Buddhism and Religious Studies at the University of Chester in the United Kingdom. He is a member of the Triratna Buddhist Order and is the author of *This Being, That Becomes: The Buddha's Teaching on Conditionality* (2011).

Amy Paris Langenberg is a specialist in Indian Buddhism with a focus on gender, sexuality, the body, and monastic law. She also conducts research on contemporary Buddhist feminism and female Buddhist monasticism. Her monograph, *Birth in Buddhism: The Suffering Fetus and Female Freedom*, was published in 2017. In addition, she has published articles in the *Journal of the American Academy of Religion*, *History of Religions*, *Religions*, *Religion Compass*, and the *Oxford Handbook of Buddhist Ethics*. Her current project is a collaborative book on generative responses to sexual abuse in American Buddhism, to be cowritten with Ann Gleig (University of Central Florida). She is Associate Professor of Religious Studies at Eckerd College, where she also teaches in the Women's and Gender Studies, Animal Studies, and Environmental Studies programs.

Ligeia Lugli holds a PhD in Study of Religion from SOAS and is currently Research Fellow at King's College London (UK) and head of lexicography at the Mangalam Research Center in Berkeley (CA). Her research lies at the intersection between Buddhist studies, Sanskrit lexicology, and digital humanities. She has also contributed to the development of a number of electronic dictionaries in a variety of languages.

Index

abhidharma / *abhidhamma*, 8, 32, 35, 36, 37, 111, 113, 114, 132, 150, 159, 160, 162, 165, 167, 195, 229, 235, 261, 271, 273, 275; *Abhidharmakośabhāṣya*, 24, 36–38, 162, 163, 165, 166, 204
ācārya / *ācariya*, 12, 176–79, 90, 178, 179, 182, 183
Aggañña-sutta, 132
Ājīvikas, 200, 214
alms and almsgiving, 80, 82, 132
Amarāvatī, 183, 187
Ānanda, 213, 217, 227, 228, 264
Andhra Pradesh, 181, 183
Aṅguttaranikāya, 115, 119, 132, 200, 218, 228, 231, 236, 241, 246, 255, 260, 262, 263, 266, 276, 277; *Aṅguttaranikāya-aṭṭhakathā*, 115, 119
ānīcolaka / *āṇicolaka*, 93–98
antevāsin / *antevāsinī*, 4, 12, 100, 175–94; *antevāsībhikkhunī*, 185
Āpastamba Dharmasūtra, 90–92
arhat / *arahant*, 60, 61, 188, 189, 276
Arthaśāstra, 161, 209
ascetics, 69, 70, 71, 81, 86, 91–96, 100, 138, 199, 200, 203, 206, 211, 212, 236
Aśokāvadana, 161
Aṣṭasāhasrikāprajñāpāramitā, 39, 161, 163, 207
Aśvaghosa, 161, 217
Atthasālinī, 259, 266
avadāna, 29, 161

Bactrian, 111
Bajaur collection, 88
Bamiyan manuscripts, 29
Baudhāyana Dharmasūtra, 90
Bhārhut, 181, 182
bhikṣu / *bhikkhu*, 12, 62, 112, 120, 133, 139, 176, 180, 181, 182, 232, 241, 251, 255, 262, 270–73, 276
bhikṣuṇī / *bhikkhunī*, 69–105, 177, 181, 182 185, 186, 187, 254; *bhikṣuṇī-vinaya*, 69–105
Blackburn, Anne, 84–87, 129, 133
Bodhi, Bhikkhu, 139, 214, 259–60, 265, 268, 270, 272, 274, 275, 277
Bodhicaryāvatāra, 36, 37
Bodhisattva / *bodhisatta*, 49, 51–53, 58, 64, 66, 138, 188, 205, 208–12, 217, 249
Bodhisattvabhūmi, 161
Bodhisattvacaryāvatāra, 36, 37

Bodhisattvagocaropāyaviṣayavikurvāṇanirdeśasūtra, 208–12
Brahmajālasutta, 132, 273
brahman, 90, 94–96, 139, 235
brāhmaṇas, 179, 200–18
Brahmanism, 51–53, 76, 91, 92, 96, 176, 179, 200–18
Buddhaghosa, 8, 9, 14, 15, 78, 109–26, 204, 214, 233, 242, 259–82
Buddhamitrā, 187, 188
Buddhas / buddhahood, 6, 22, 49–68, 73, 81, 92, 136, 139, 140, 183, 228, 230, 237, 244, 245, 249, 250, 253, 263; biography of the Buddha, 139–41; characteristics of disciples, 195–226
Burma, 85, 86, 274

Cabré, Maria Teresa, 150, 153, 154, 163
Caraka-saṃhitā, 98, 132
Cariyāpiṭaka, 132
caste, 90, 91, 96
causation, 14, 227–58
Cerquiglini, Bernard, 27, 33, 41
Chinese language, 5, 21, 22–24, 28, 33, 36, 37, 39, 70, 73, 76, 98, 122, 196, 202, 205, 206, 208, 210, 217, 252
Christianity, 127–48
Clarke, Shayne, 69–71, 81, 82, 88
Clough, Benjamin, 10, 127–48
Collins, Steven, 51, 84, 239, 240
Colombo, 129, 130, 133, 142
colonialism, 4, 9, 15, 127–48
commentaries, 1, 8, 9, 14, 15, 28, 31, 32, 36, 37, 72, 73, 76, 78, 80, 85, 91, 93, 94, 109–26, 133, 185, 186, 191, 204, 205, 207, 214, 232–34, 239, 250, 251, 259–82
commentators, 5, 9, 13, 25, 40, 98, 109–26, 204, 233, 259–82
conceptual metaphor, 5, 14, 231–53, 254
Cūḷakammavibhaṅga, 10, 132, 139
Cullavagga, 93, 94, 177, 185, 213

Daśabhūmikasūtra, 161
Deleanu, Florin, 157–59
Deorkothar, 115, 182
desanāsīsa, 5, 14, 15, 259–82
Dhammapada / *Dharmapada*, 23, 44, 132, 141, 181, 232, 235; *Dhammapada-aṭṭhakathā*, 263, 270
Dhammapāla, 119, 274
Dhammasaṅgaṇī, 35, 263, 266; *Dhammasaṅgaṇī-aṭṭhakathā*, 113, 263, 267
dharmabhāṇaka, 7, 50, 53, 59, 60, 62, 65–66
dharmakāya, 50, 53–56, 205
dharmaśāstras, 8, 72, 79, 89–92, 96, 216
dharmasūtras, 90–92, 216
Dīghanikāya, 98, 114, 115, 117, 132, 211, 212, 213, 215, 228, 231, 239, 249, 260, 263, 264, 271, 272, 273, 274, 275, 276, 277, 278; *Dīghanikāya-aṭṭhakathā*, 260, 263, 264, 272, 275–77; *Dīghanikāya-aṭṭhakathā-ṭīkā*, 274, 278

Edgerton, Franklin, 79, 199–201, 203, 211, 212
Eltschinger, Vincent, 202, 204, 205, 219
Emmerick, Ronald D., 50, 57, 58, 111

Faber-Benítez, Pamela, 150, 152–54, 156

Finnegan, Diana Damchö, 7, 77, 78, 81, 83, 85, 96
Frauwallner, Erich, 75, 76, 115, 178

Gandhāra, 36
Gāndhārī, 5, 6, 20, 24, 28–30, 34, 35, 37, 39
Gartodara's mother, 69–71, 82, 96
Gautama-dharmasūtra, 90
Gogerly, Daniel John, 10, 127–29, 131–35, 139, 141–46
gurudharmas, 72, 73, 89–93
Gyatso, Janet, 157–59

Haberman, David J., 2, 3
Hallisey, Charles, 7, 78, 83, 85, 129
Harrison, Paul, 36–37
Hendriksen, Hans, 239, 240
hermeneutics, feminist, 69–105
Hinüber, Oskar von, 175, 182, 183, 186, 187, 245, 260
Hirakawa, Akira, 73, 76, 81, 98
historiography, 69–105
Horner, I. B., 93, 94, 116, 139, 178, 179, 185, 189, 190, 199, 265, 268, 270
Hüsken, Ute, 72, 73, 86–88, 93–95

inscriptions, 28, 115, 120–22, 175–94
Itivuttaka, 181, 262, 278; *Itivuttaka-aṭṭhakathā*, 262

Jain literature / Jainism, 112, 179, 200, 206, 209, 213, 214, 219
Jamison, Stephanie, 71, 99–100
Jātakas, 122, 132, 133, 138, 208, 217, 261–64
Jātakamalā, 161
Johnson, Mark, 244, 245, 248, 250
Johnston, E. H., 165, 205–7

Kandy, 128, 133, 135
Kane, P. V., 216
Kathāvatthu, 37, 38, 267, 272, 273, 274; *Kathāvatthu-aṭṭhakathā*, 267, 273
khīṇāsava, 262, 275, 276
Kieffer-Pülz, Petra, 76, 86–88, 112, 260
kilesa / *kleśa*, 51, 63, 116, 117, 137
Konow, Sten, 180
Kumārajīva, 23, 24, 208, 209

Lakoff, George, 244, 245, 248, 250
Lammerts, Christian, 85, 86
Lamotte, Étienne, 75, 201, 229, 260
lemmas, 260, 261, 264, 271
León-Araúz, Pilar, 153, 154, 15
lexical gap, 11, 157, 167–70
Lokakṣema, 39
Lubin, Timothy, 89, 96

Magadha, 110, 111, 115, 213, 217
Mahābhārata, 91, 161, 166, 216
Mahāsāṅghika-Lokottaravāda tradition, 69–108
Mahāvastu, 109, 110, 199, 200, 211, 212
Mahāvihāra tradition, 9, 109, 113, 119, 121, 271, 275
Mahāyāna tradition, 3, 6, 13, 30, 49–68, 161, 195–226, 256
Mahāyānasūtrālaṃkāra, 161
Majjhimanikāya, 98, 99, 109, 121, 132, 139, 201, 209, 215, 219, 227, 232, 237, 238, 240, 246, 250, 254, 255, 260, 263, 264, 266, 275, 276, 278; *Majjhimanikāya-aṭṭhakathā*, 260, 263–65, 275; *Majjhimanikāya-aṭṭhakathā-ṭīkā*, 262
Mangalam Research Centre, 3, 10, 149

Māra, 64, 207–208, 254
Marino, Joseph, 182, 183
McGann, Jerome, 25–27, 32
meditation, 79, 138, 189, 211, 249, 250
metonymy, 15, 245, 261, 265, 266, 269, 271–75, 278–81
Milindapañha, 132, 133, 272
Mūlamadhyamakakārikā, 161
Mūlasarvāstivāda tradition, 73, 76, 83, 85, 87, 178, 181

Nagārjunakoṅḍa, 9, 120
Nakanishi, Maiko, 121, 186, 187
Ñāṇamoli, Bhikkhu, 139, 146, 156, 260, 265, 268, 275
Nattier, Jan, 2, 3, 52, 81, 82, 83, 111
nirvāṇa / *nibbāna*, 51, 109, 130, 138, 196, 203, 205, 206, 211, 245
nirgranthas, 206, 209, 210
Nobel, J., 50, 54, 57, 60, 63
Norman, K. R., 1, 79, 117, 156, 236, 239, 240, 245, 268, 269
novices, 12, 19, 176, 179, 183, 185
Nyānaponika, Bhikkhu, 259, 267
Nyāyasūtrabhāṣya, 161

Oghataraṇasutta, 214
orientalism, 9, 10, 127–48, 198

Pañcaskandhaka, 161, 166
Pañcatantra, 161
pārājika, 70, 97–99, 190, 191
pratītya-samutpāda / *paṭicca-samuppāda*, 5, 13, 14, 181, 227–58
Prakrit, 9, 70, 114, 175–94, 227, 231
prātimokṣa / *pāṭimokkha*, 72, 88, 94, 132, 185, 189, 262
Pravrajyāvastu / *Mahākkhandaka*, 177, 189, 190
preceptor, 12, 176, 177, 179, 183, 186–88

Rāmāyaṇa, 161
Rāṣṭrapālaparipṛcchāsūtra, 67, 161
Ratnagotravibhāgavyākyyā, 161, 205–207
rebirth, 61, 65, 139, 196, 201, 211, 215, 216, 218, 228, 244, 255, 274
relics, 54, 66, 121, 139, 181
Rhys Davids, Caroline, 198, 266, 277
Rhys Davids, Thomas W., 10, 141, 143, 198, 199, 212, 230, 268, 274, 277
Roth, Gustav, 70, 72, 73, 79–81, 86, 89–92, 94, 95, 97, 99

Saddharmapuṇḍarīkasūtra, 165, 200, 201, 206, 208
saddhivihārin / *saddhivihārinī*, 176, 177, 179, 185, 186; *saddhivihārika* / *saddhivihārikā*, 12, 176
Salomon, Richard, 28, 29, 41, 181, 182, 183
saṃjñā / *saññā*, 10, 11, 157–66, 167, 168, 169, 170, 231, 247, 255, 271, 272–75
Saṃyuttanikāya, 115, 122, 132, 180, 181, 214, 265, 270, 278; *Saṃyuttanikāya-aṭṭhakathā*, 260, 263, 275; *Saṃyuttanikāya-aṭṭhakathā-ṭīkā*, 270, 278
saṅghātiśeṣa /*saṅghādisesa*, 86, 116, 191
Śāntideva, 13, 36, 37
Sarvāstivāda tradition, 38, 39, 88, 120, 273
Sāvatthī, 180, 185, 235
Schopen, Gregory, 71, 73, 74, 76–78, 80, 83, 86, 88, 100, 181, 188
Schøyen collection, 29

Seyfort Ruegg, David, 30, 46, 111, 157–60, 167, 168
Śikṣāsamuccaya, 36, 37, 208
Sinhala, 8, 9, 10, 110, 114, 116, 118, 122, 127–31, 133, 134, 136–38, 140, 141, 231, 274
Skilling, Peter, 115, 120, 157–60, 167, 181–83
Skjaervø, P.O., 50, 54, 57, 60, 63
Spence Hardy, Robert, 10, 127–29, 131–33, 135, 136, 139–46
Sthūlanandā / Thullanandā, 76, 79–82, 86, 90, 94–96, 185
Sutta-nipāta, 213, 214, 235, 236, 251
Suvarṇabhāsottamasūtra, 6, 49–68
Suvarṇavarṇāvadāna, 161

terminology, 149–72; Buddhist, 156, 170, 214; classical model of, 10, 11, 15, 152, 154, 156, 157, 158, 163, 184, 191; technical /technical terms, 3, 4, 11, 12, 16, 150, 174–94, 245, 246
textual criticism, 25–34; Genetic Criticism 27, 28; historically sensitive approach, 36–40; New Historicism / New Historicists, 27, 28; New Philology/New Philologists, 26–28, 32; Reader-Response model, 27, 28
Theravāda tradition, 9, 78, 84, 85, 88, 109–26, 127–48, 233, 259–83; Theriya 9, 120, 121, 122
Tibetan language, 2, 39, 85, 86, 87, 111, 121, 190, 202, 203, 205, 206, 209, 210
tīrthika, 5, 12, 13, 195–226; *anyatīrthika*, 200, 201, 206, 207, 214; *tīrtha* / *tittha*, 196, 200, 201, 203, 209, 211, 213–20; *tīrthaṅkara*, 203, 213, 214, 219; *titthiya*, 196, 199, 200, 212, 213, 215

Vajracchedikā, 161
Vasubandhu, 36, 204, 233, 241, 242
Vedas, 51–53, 89, 91, 99, 179, 200, 203, 209, 213, 215–17, 244
Vimalakīrtinirdeśasūtra, 23, 53, 161, 206, 209
vinaya, 7–9, 12, 69–105, 93, 132, 175–77, 181, 183–91, 199, 200, 215, 241, 264, 268, 270, 273; Mahāsāṅghika, 73, 81; Mahāsāṅghika-Lokkottaravāda, 69–105; Mūlasarvāstivāda, 76–78, 81, 86, 94; Theravāda / Pāli, 73, 78, 86, 93, 94, 97; Pāli *vinaya-aṭṭhakathā*, 111, 112, 113, 118, 119, 204, 260, 264, 265, 268; *vinaya-piṭaka*, 84, 114, 116, 117, 177, 178, 179, 183, 185, 186, 191, 200, 241, 264, 268, 270
vinayadhāra, 83, 181, 187–90
Visuddhimagga, 133, 233, 272; *Visuddhimagga-ṭīkā*, 260, 270

Wesleyan Methodist mission, 127, 129, 131, 132, 137, 142
Witkowski, Nicholas, 81, 83, 84
women, 4, 12, 69–105, 131, 175–94, 213

Xuanzang, 23, 24

Zeller, Hans, 25, 27, 31, 33

www.ingramcontent.com/pod-product-compliance
Lightning Source LLC
Chambersburg PA
CBHW032050230426
43672CB00009B/1549
* 9 7 8 1 4 3 8 4 8 2 9 4 1 *